WITH
HONOURABLE
INTENT

WITH HONOURABLE INTENT

A NATURAL HISTORY OF FAUNA & FLORA INTERNATIONAL

Tim Knight & Mark Rose

WILLIAM
COLLINS

William Collins
An imprint of HarperCollins*Publishers*
1 London Bridge Street
London SE1 9GF
WilliamCollinsBooks.com

First published by William Collins in 2017

Text © Fauna & Flora International 2017
Photographs © individual copyright holders
Designed by TwoSheds Design
With design assistance by
Gareth Butterworth

10 9 8 7 6 5 4 3 2 1

Fauna & Flora International assert their moral right to be identified as
the authors of this work

A catalogue record for this book is available from the British Library

Trade ISBN 978 0 00 827645 4
Special edition ISBN 978 0 00 796733 9

p.2: illustration of a pygmy hippopotamus by Denys Ovenden

Printed and bound by Latvia

Gone but not forgotten

Fauna & Flora International (FFI) owes its continued success to the bravery, generosity, selflessness and unwavering commitment of an ever-growing cast of characters. This book is dedicated in particular to all those members of the wider FFI family who – as a result of cruel illness, armed conflict, natural catastrophe and tragic accident – have been taken from us too soon.

Sugarbush flowers painted by FFI vice-president Professor
Jonathan Kingdon, who has helped draw attention to South
Africa's unique flora.

Foreword

I have been a member of Fauna & Flora International (FFI) for more than 60 years and am proud to be associated with what I regard as the doyen of all conservation societies. When I joined the organisation in the 1950s, global conservation was still a relatively unknown concept, and it certainly wasn't on the agenda of the distinguished naturalists who set up the original society way back in 1903. At that time, they were solely concerned with addressing the drastic decline in African and Indian game species. Nevertheless, these far-sighted individuals laid the foundations for the modern conservation movement that today plays such a vital role in safeguarding the natural world and the entire spectrum of species within it. I would even go as far as to say that FFI invented modern-day conservation. More than a century later, FFI continues to reflect the pioneering spirit of its founders. Resourceful, innovative and unencumbered by red tape, it remains at the forefront of enlightened conservation practices, continually developing new techniques, forging bold new partnerships and adapting to changing circumstances. Many activities that are now considered mainstream – incorporating biodiversity conservation measures into business strategy, international protected area management, captive breeding of species on the verge of extinction – first saw the light of day as groundbreaking

FFI initiatives. Iconic species such as the Arabian oryx and the mountain gorilla, and unique landscapes such as the precious floral kingdom at the southernmost tip of Africa, the forested wilderness of Cambodia's Cardamom Mountains and Romania's biologically rich mosaic of traditional farmland and forest – one of the last refuges for Europe's large carnivores – owe their survival to timely and imaginative interventions by FFI and its partners. Throughout its history, FFI has succeeded in establishing links with prominent, influential people who have helped to champion the conservation cause. Drawing on a rich archive of historical documents and photographs, this book provides a fascinating insight into some of the seminal moments in the organisation's evolution and reveals many of the colourful characters and unsung heroes with whom FFI has been associated from its inception at the start of the last century right through to the present day.

Sir David Attenborough
FFI Vice-President

CHAPTER 1

FOUNDATION

'We, the undersigned, are deeply interested in the preservation of the larger animals, some of which are so rapidly disappearing in parts of Africa under British control. We regard this disappearance or diminution as something to be deplored and, if possible, to be arrested.'

Memorial to Lord Cromer and the Governor-General of the Sudan, 1903

On 17 December 1903, on a windswept beach at Kitty Hawk in North Carolina, on the east coast of the USA, history was made. Orville Wright piloted the first ever flight in a powered, controlled aeroplane, remaining airborne for 12 seconds and covering a distance of 120 feet. It was one short flight for a man, one giant leap for aviation. Earlier that same week, several thousand miles away on the other side of the Atlantic, at the Natural History Museum in London, history of a very different kind was also being made. Six days before Orville Wright took to the skies, a fledgling international wildlife conservation organisation, another world first, was spreading its wings and taking its first few tentative flaps, ready to embark on a maiden flight of its own.

Although greeted with very little fanfare at the time, this event was, in its own way, just as significant for the future of wildlife conservation as the Wright brothers' breakthrough would prove to be for the world of aviation. That first powered flight ushered in a series of previously unimaginable technological developments that enabled humans to fly faster than the speed of sound, put a man on the Moon and carry 850 passengers halfway around the world overnight in the belly of an aircraft weighing 650 tonnes – achievements that we now take for granted. Similarly, the pioneering founders of the organisation now known as Fauna & Flora International (FFI) unwittingly paved the way for today's sophisticated and multifaceted

global conservation network, and for its less-welcome by-product, a plethora of largely impenetrable acronyms.

The flying analogy is apposite for another reason. One of the enduring strengths of FFI, no less relevant today than it was in 1903, has been its ability to garner support from friends in high places. As we shall see, this manifests itself not only in a metaphorical sense – in royal patronage, aristocratic beneficence, philanthropy, the generosity of famous artists, political clout and commercial backing from captains of industry – but also literally, in the case of the Royal Air Force and larger-than-life characters such as the renowned aviator Captain Charles Lindbergh.

Paradoxically, it was big-game hunters who kick-started the international wildlife conservation movement, after they realised that they were in danger of running out of things to shoot. Edward North Buxton set the wheels in motion when, in early 1903, he organised a petition to dissuade the colonial authorities in the Sudan from opening up the vast, recently established White Nile Reserve to hunting.

Buxton had recently written a book entitled *Two African Trips*, in which he had been openly critical of the administration's apparent disregard for the sanctity of its so-called protected areas. His recent visits to East Africa and the Sudan had given him a personal insight into the potential problems confronting the would-be conservationist. In his view, the dramatic decline in the populations of antelope and other large animals that we might broadly categorise as charismatic megafauna – big cats, elephant, rhinoceros and hippopotamus – was the direct consequence of an unethical and gung-ho approach to hunting that, in the long run, was

Opposite The society's earliest meetings at the Natural History Museum pre-date the arrival in 1904 of 'Dippy', the gargantuan diplodocus skeleton that would continue to tower over visitors for more than a century, including the guests at FFI's centenary celebrations, who dined beneath its replica bones in 2003.

simply unsustainable. He lamented the poor sportsmanship and lack of foresight exhibited by the perpetrators and warned of the very real possibility of destroying an irreplaceable natural heritage, citing the example of South Africa, where whole swathes of wildlife had been 'irretrievably lost through the carelessness and wastefulness of white men'.

One of the main catalysts for Buxton's crusade against the despoilers of Africa's wildlife heritage was the International Conference held in London in 1900. Attended by representatives from all the European colonial powers that had interests in Africa, this conference spawned the 1900 Convention for the Preservation of Animals, Birds and Fish in Africa, which aimed to introduce consistent and effective game protection legislation throughout colonial Africa. Signatories were committed to drawing up a list of threatened species that warranted urgent protection from hunting, adhering to a lower weight limit below which elephant tusks could not be traded, and establishing protected areas that could be guaranteed free from encroachment.

The aftermath of the 1900 conference was the backdrop against which Buxton and his band of merry men operated, and his petition was designed to bring pressure to bear at the highest level. The list of eminent signatories flexing their considerable aristocratic muscle included the Duke and Duchess of Bedford, whose personal commitment to wildlife conservation was already evident in their efforts to rescue Père David's deer from oblivion (see Herbrand Russell, overleaf). Swayed by the strength of their argument and, no doubt, by the collective weight of their nobility, the then Governor-General of the Sudan, Lord Cromer, relented. Emboldened by their success, Buxton and his distinguished cohort of fellow naturalists saw the potential benefits of a more formal collaboration and, later that same year, on 11 December, the snappily named Society for the Preservation of the Wild Fauna of the Empire was born.

The very name is redolent of a bygone era: a colonial name for colonial times. Heavyweight friends of the co-founders were quickly recruited as honorary members – among them Lord Kitchener and US President Theodore Roosevelt, an ardent conservationist whose love of nature did not preclude him from mounting an African hunting expedition in 1909–10 during which over 11,000 animals were trapped or killed in the name of science. Other prominent members of the newly formed society included the brewing magnate Samuel Whitbread, whose name features prominently in the early records, and the renowned hunter Frederick Selous, who accompanied Roosevelt intermittently on that same expedition.

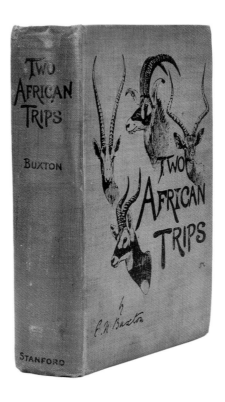

First edition of Edward North Buxton's account of his travels in then British East Africa and the Sudan, published in 1902 by Edward Stanford, and containing 'Notes and Suggestions on Big Game Preservation in Africa'.

The society's main preoccupation at this stage was to halt the decline in the numbers of game animals of the African savannah, which many of its founders took pleasure in shooting for sport. With no hint of irony, the organisation adopted the motto 'Live and let live' as a kind of unofficial mission statement to reflect the principles on which it had been founded. Though the intentions of the co-founders were perfectly honourable, newspapers inevitably seized on their apparent hypocrisy and wasted no time in branding them 'The Penitent Butchers'. That derogatory label, dreamed up by the society's detractors, would quickly prove to be spectacularly wide of the mark. Some 75 years later, the very same phrase was chosen as the ironic title of a book published by the then Fauna Preservation Society to commemorate three-quarters of a century of conservation success. By then, the society occupied a pre-eminent position within what had become a worldwide conservation movement and enjoyed an enviable reputation for championing endangered species and their habitats, not only in Africa, but across the globe.

From the very outset, the number one priority of the society's star-studded cast was to establish sanctuaries for beleaguered wildlife. Game reserves in the African colonies

Preservation of Big Game Society.

The Memorial to Lord Cromer and Sir Reginald Wingate relating to the Game Reserve in the Soudan has, we are happy to say, been entirely successful. The intention of abandoning that Reserve has been given up, and it has been determined to retain it, and above all to constitute it for the first time a genuine sanctuary. This is a good instance of the value of bringing the public opinion of persons at home who are interested in the preservation of the African fauna to the notice of the officials on the spot. It seems desirable that those who have taken an interest in the matter should continue to act together.

It has been suggested that a small association should be formed for the purpose of disseminating among its members information which is to be found scattered in a great number of official reports, and in other sources, dealing with game reserves, game laws, the amount of game killed, the gradual disappearance of species, etc., throughout Africa.

The great object of the association is to further the formation of game Reserves or Sanctuaries, the selection of the most suitable places, and the enforcing of suitable game laws and regulations. At the present time the principal officials in the several departments in charge of the various sections of British Africa are impressed with the importance of immediate steps being taken for the preservation of African game, and have shown a readiness to receive suggestions from private individuals which encourages us to think that a society formed of persons interested in the subject, and, in many cases, possessing a knowledge of the districts, might render useful service.

Where a contrary spirit prevails it may be desirable to take joint action.

A subscription of 10s. per annum would cover the cost of printing. This is the only expense the society would have.

It is proposed to hold a meeting at the Natural History Museum on December 11th, at 4 p.m., to discuss the matter.

Knowing that you take an interest in this subject we trust that you will become a member of the Society and be able to attend the meeting.

EDWARD NORTH BUXTON.

December 4th, 1903.

RHYS WILLIAMS, *Hon. Sec.,*
2, TEMPLE GARDENS.

Above Original invitation to attend the inaugural meeting of the Society for the Preservation of the Wild Fauna of the Empire on 11 December 1903.

Right The first entry in the society's original handwritten minutes book.

were few and far between at that time, and those that did exist were scarcely fit for purpose, being inappropriately located, badly managed and frequently treated as personal hunting concessions by the very people assigned to police them. The uncomfortable reality was that white officials in Sudan were able to hunt indiscriminately and were slaughtering the local wildlife with virtual impunity. As Buxton noted wryly: 'A sanctuary where people are allowed to shoot is a contradiction in terms.'

The society embarked on a concerted campaign to win over hearts and minds among the wider public, but particularly in political circles. It set about the task with great gusto, badgering and cajoling the British government into sending out numerous missives to African protectorates and self-governing colonies, impressing upon them the importance of preserving the local wildlife and habitats.

The tactics of Buxton and his willing accomplices were clear: if the new society was to maximise its effectiveness as a pressure group, it needed firstly to establish its credibility as an independent source of expert advice and secondly to give itself the best chance of persuading the decision makers

FRIENDS IN HIGH PLACES

Portraits of some of the eminent signatories to the original petition that led to the formation of the Society for the Preservation of the Wild Fauna of the Empire, including an insight into their day jobs:

Herbrand Russell, 11th Duke of Bedford, served in the Grenadier Guards, rose to the rank of Colonel and saw active combat during the First World War, being mentioned in dispatches. Among many prestigious appointments he was president of the Zoological Society and military aide-de-camp to King Edward VII and King George V. Russell's credentials as a conservationist were also pretty unimpeachable, in that he was instrumental in saving Père David's deer from extinction. By 1900 this species was already extinct in the wild in its native China, and the last survivors of the only remaining captive herd belonging to the Emperor had been shot and eaten by troops during the Boxer Rebellion. Russell took great pains to track down the few remaining deer held captive in European zoos, released them within the protective walls of his Woburn Abbey estate, and almost single-handedly engineered the species' recovery. The entire world population of this deer, which is now widely distributed among zoos throughout the globe and has been successfully reintroduced into reserves within China, is directly descended from that original rescued herd at Woburn.

Sir Edwin Ray Lankester, eminent zoologist and evolutionary biologist, was an Oxford graduate who later studied under Thomas Huxley and became a hugely influential teacher in his own right. He was an enthusiastic advocate of establishing nature reserves in his native Britain. As Director of the Natural History Museum, his efforts to emancipate science from the clutches of the traditionalists brought him into direct conflict with several powerful individuals, but he was held in high regard by prominent public figures including the Archbishop of Canterbury, and was a close friend of Karl Marx. A colourful character with a forceful personality, Lankester was the inspiration for several fictional incarnations in novels written by, among others, H.G. Wells, who had been one of his students.

The intriguing Père David's deer, photographed in the grounds of Woburn Abbey at the turn of the century, owes its survival to the dedication of Herbrand and Mary Russell, Duke and Duchess of Bedford, pictured here on their estate.

Above left Caricature of Sir Ray Lankester by Leslie Ward (pseudonym 'Spy'), published in *Vanity Fair* on 12 January 1905.

Above right Signed photograph of Frederick Selous in a classic pose with one of the many rifles built specially for him.

Left Illustration of an okapi by Sir Harry Johnston, originally painted for a 1901 edition of the *Proceedings of the Zoological Society* in London.

Sir Henry 'Harry' Hamilton Johnston, explorer, naturalist, author and colonial administrator, was one of the key players in the unedifying 'scramble for Africa' by the European colonial powers, and once had a Dr Livingstone-style encounter with Sir Henry Morton Stanley in the Congo. It was rumoured that Johnston provided the real-life inspiration for the fictional Dickens aficionado in Evelyn Waugh's *A Handful of Dust*. Johnston was instrumental in bringing the okapi to the attention of science, an achievement that led to the species being named *Okapia johnstoni* in his honour.

John Lubbock, 1st Baron Avebury, was a banker, politician, philanthropist and scientist. Among his various claims to fame, he helped to establish archaeology as a scientific discipline and influenced several nineteenth-century debates on evolutionary theory. In his youth he was a frequent visitor to the house of Charles Darwin, who became a major influence and long-term correspondent; such was Lubbock's rapport with Darwin that he was a pallbearer at the great man's funeral. Lubbock was the first recipient of the Prestwich Medal, awarded for the advancement of geology. His name is inextricably linked with the Bank Holidays Act 1871, which established the first bank holidays in the UK, and the Ancient Monuments Protection Act 1882, which protected national heritage sites such as Stonehenge, as well as other stone circles and tumuli. The uncharitable could be forgiven for suggesting that the latter act might well have benefited some of the society's own members, given their average age. Lubbock spoke in support of Thomas Huxley at the 1860 Oxford evolution debate, published the most influential archaeological textbook of the nineteenth century, and is responsible for inventing the terms palaeolithic and neolithic.

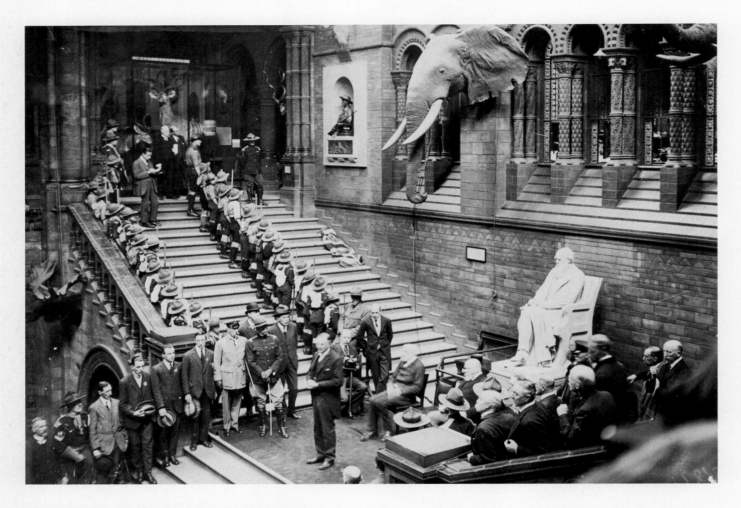

Unveiling of the bronze bust of Frederick Selous at London's Natural History Museum in 1920.

Sir Edward Grey was a Liberal politician who, as Foreign Secretary at the outbreak of WWI, is credited with uttering the immortal lines: 'The lamps are going out all over Europe; we shall not see them lit again in our lifetime.' Grey became Foreign Secretary in 1905 on the formation of the Liberal government, a post he retained for over a decade. In a 2014 profile of Grey published online by *The Telegraph* to commemorate the centenary of the outbreak of the First World War, Sir Hew Strachan, Fellow of All Souls College, Oxford, observed that the then Foreign Secretary was originally a somewhat reluctant politician who 'seemed happier as a country gentleman, enjoying his enthusiasms of fishing and ornithology'.

Frederick Courteney Selous was the archetypal great white hunter and explorer, whose marksmanship and personal magnetism have become the stuff of legend. His life story reads like a cocktail of Indiana Jones screenplays, and it was he who provided the main inspiration for H. Rider Haggard's fictional hero, Allan Quatermain. Wealthy and well-connected, Selous came from aristocratic stock but was drawn to Africa by tales of intrepid explorers whose exploits fired his own youthful imagination. An avid natural history enthusiast from an early age, he gravitated from collecting butterflies at Rugby School to shooting elephants for a living in South Africa. In the words of his close friend Theodore Roosevelt, 'he led a singularly adventurous and

fascinating life, with just the right alternations between the wilderness and civilization'. With his establishment roots, Selous retained a foot in both camps, but ultimately the call of the wild proved irresistible. He spent his formative years trophy hunting and collecting specimens in previously unexplored corners of the globe for, among others, London's Natural History Museum, in gratitude for which it unveiled a bust in his honour in 1920. Killed in action during the latter stages of the First World War, he was buried in what is now Selous Game Reserve in modern-day Tanzania, his memory fittingly preserved in the name of one of the world's largest protected areas, since designated a World Heritage site. ■

*'If species were to become lost [...] this generation would be
held responsible by those who come after us.'*

Edward North Buxton, 1905

to heed that advice. Within a year of its formation, the
society had recruited 70 ordinary and 30 honorary members.
These included 'the ablest and most long-sighted' of the
administrators and political figures from the British colonies
and dependencies throughout Africa and further afield. By
virtue of the fact that the then British Empire covered about
a quarter of the Earth's surface at the time, the society
became the world's first de facto international conservation
organisation. But the membership roll of honour wasn't
confined to British interests; it also included distinguished
figures from other parts of the world, such as Prince Henry
Liechtenstein in Vienna, the Duke of Grazioli-Lante in Rome
and various other foreign luminaries. The personal contacts
of influential members ensured that the society was able to
move in the appropriate circles and gain access to the men
in power. (And yes, they were all men; hence the urgent
need for the campaign that was being simultaneously
waged by Emmeline Pankhurst and her fellow suffragettes.)
At the same time, it could tap into the expertise and local
knowledge of those working at the coalface of conservation,
which gave the society a hard core of scientific
respectability beneath the aristocratic veneer that helped it
secure an audience with those in authority.

As the minutes of the earliest meetings reveal, even at that
embryonic phase in the society's history many of the
preoccupations that feature on the conservation agenda to
this day were already evident. Whilst the need for protected
areas took centre stage, a society deputation sent to engage with
the Secretary to the Colonies in 1905 was already highlighting
issues that were, in many ways, ahead of their time. The
delegation expressed concerns about the phenomenon, known
in modern conservation parlance as 'paper parks', whereby
conservation areas exist solely on paper due to inadequate
enforcement of the laws designed to protect them: 'Some
reserves [...] which have a very fine appearance on the map, but
which are really only laid out on the map.' Anticipating the
need for a treaty such as the Convention on the International
Trade in Endangered Species of Wild Fauna and Flora (CITES)
by some six decades, they drew attention to the unsustainable
trade in wildlife products, including 'the sale of horns and
of hides ... their export or their sale on a large scale'. There
was also recognition of the need to recruit well-trained and
adequately remunerated park rangers capable of policing
protected areas: 'In many of these territories there is an

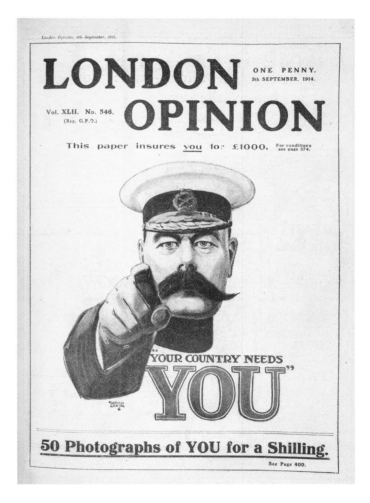

Your planet needs you! Lord Kitchener was also a poster boy for the society's own
recruitment campaign.

excellent game officer, and there ought to be such an officer
in all of them.' Ideas that we now take for granted would, at
the time, have been considered quite radical and far-sighted.

The 1905 meeting with the Secretary to the Colonies was
the first of several productive face-to-face dialogues, all of
which resulted in conservation gains. There was no
exponential leap forward, no sudden epiphany on the part
of the authorities; rather than trying to browbeat the
government into policy U-turns, the society kept up a
constant drip-drip pressure through its high-level networking,
achieving incremental improvements that, cumulatively,
amounted to significant progress.

A JOURNAL IS BORN

The society published the first issue of its *Journal* in 1904, the year following its formation. The *Journal of the Society for the Preservation of the Wild Fauna of the Empire*, as it was imaginatively named, originated as little more than an in-house logbook in which the society recorded its members' conservation concerns, aspirations and activities, as well as the minutes of meetings. But it quickly evolved into a more comprehensive publication that incorporated contributions not only from its own members, but also from others with an interest in wildlife conservation. As news spread that the society was a force to be reckoned with in the lobbying department, the flow of correspondence grew from a trickle to a minor tsunami of letters containing petitions, cries for help, tall stories, progress reports and polite suggestions from interested parties throughout the then British Empire. Well over a century later, *Oryx – The International Journal of Conservation*, as it is now known, is an acclaimed quarterly, peer-reviewed publication, widely regarded as the conservationist's vade mecum and a leading authority on all things faunal and floristic.

Even in its earliest guise, the *Journal* was eliciting positive feedback from many of the influential figures on the distribution list. In 1908, nearing the end of his second term in office, and presumably with more time to catch up on some light reading, President Theodore Roosevelt sent an uplifting message of encouragement to the society, an extract from which was proudly displayed in the fourth volume: 'I was particularly pleased to receive the journal. It is most interesting. I congratulate you upon the admirable work you are doing, and I wish you would extend to your colleagues my hearty sympathy with all that is being accomplished by the Society for the Preservation of the Wild Fauna of the Empire.'

Roosevelt proved to be a staunch ally and an astute choice as an honorary member. He had been the first US president to express views on conservation. 'When I hear of the destruction of a species I feel just as if all the work of some great writer had perished; as if we had lost all instead of part of Polybius or Livy.' He backed up those erudite words with action, significantly expanding his country's network of national parks and national forests. More than 60 wildlife refuges were founded in the United States during his presidency. ∎

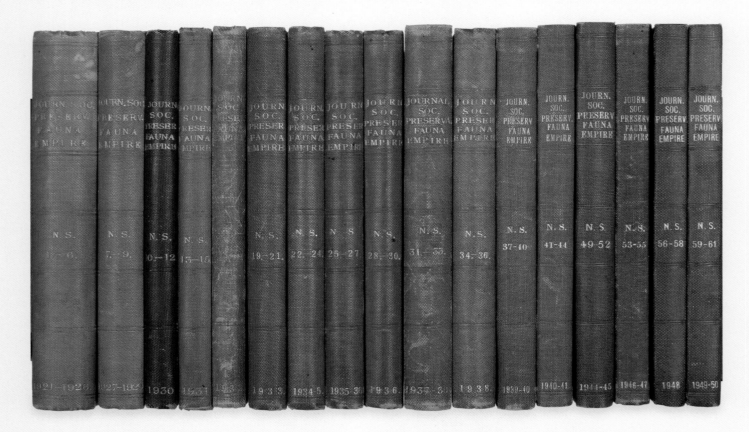

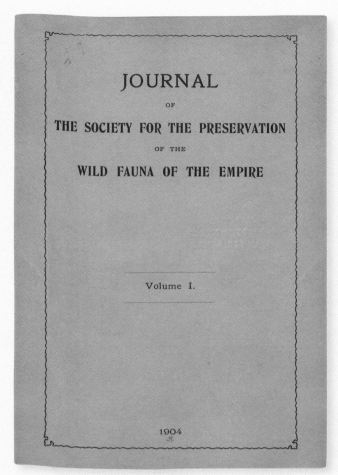

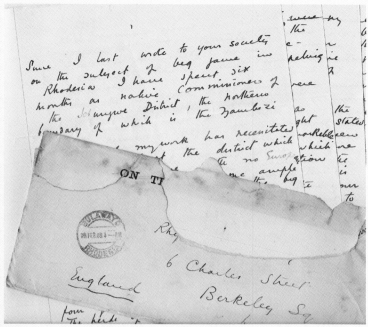

Above Front cover of the first ever edition of the society's *Journal*, issued in 1904.

Top right An early example of the correspondence received by the society from various colonial outposts within and beyond Africa.

Right Correspondence from Edward Stanford, founder of the specialist map and travel bookshop that is synonymous with exploration and adventure.

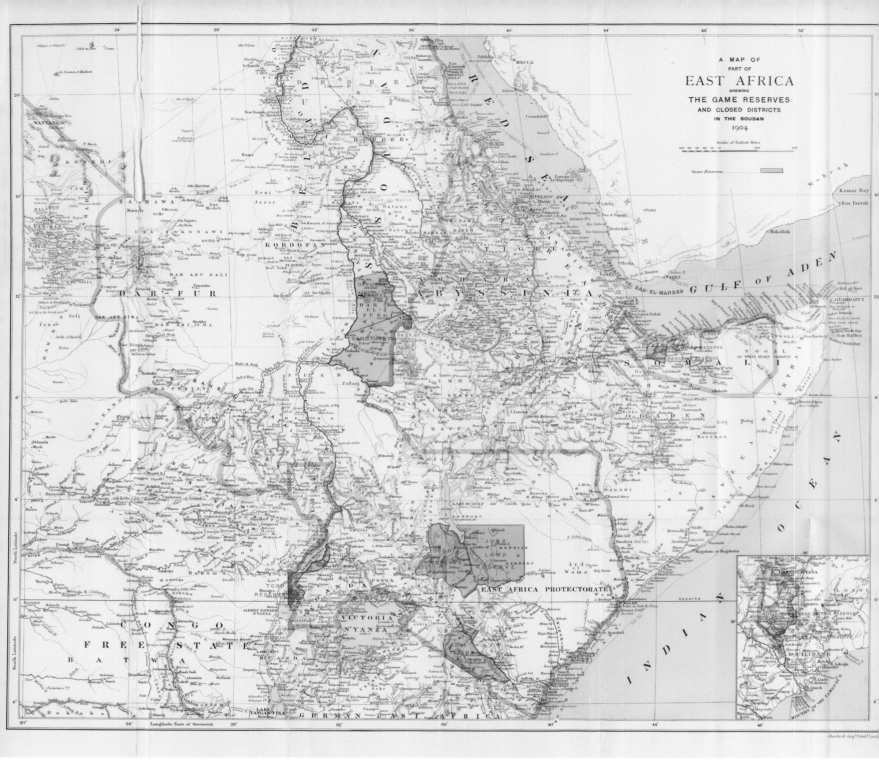

A MAP OF
PART OF
EAST AFRICA
SHEWING
THE GAME RESERVES
AND CLOSED DISTRICTS
IN THE SOUDAN
1904

Scale of English Miles

Game Reserves

Colonial complexity

Although it was never ratified, the so-called African Convention of 1900 presaged the start of a new era of international co-operation in the pursuit of wildlife conservation goals. Where British territories were concerned, it also stimulated the drafting of various ordinances and proclamations relating to the preservation of wild animals in Africa, as well as whole forests of paper correspondence between 1906–13, which were compiled into volumes referred to collectively as 'Blue Books'.

The society's main concerns – securing protected areas for Africa's threatened game and ensuring that the other agreed goals of the convention were achieved – soon proved to be difficult to address in isolation. The sheer complexity of the colonial landscape in Africa demanded a more holistic approach, but the very urgency of the problems it was facing precluded the society from taking the time to stand back and view the bigger picture. The conflicting demands of wildlife, indigenous groups and settlers were not easy to reconcile. Poaching and the illegal trade in wildlife products were threatening to reach epidemic

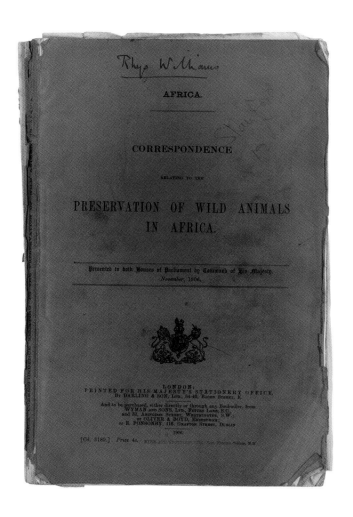

GENERAL RECOMMENDATIONS.

We venture to make the following general recommendations :—

(1.) That the returns of all game animals killed should continue to be included in the Annual Reports of each Protectorate or Colony. To them should be added statements, showing the receipts from all sources connected with the preservation of game, such as licenses, fines, etc.

(2.) That a map should be prepared showing the present game reserves in Africa.

(3.) That the sale of hides, horns, etc., of game animals in the British Dominions in Africa and at Aden, should be prohibited.

(4.) That the sale of elephant tusks weighing less than 25 lbs. should be prohibited and the tusks confiscated.

(5.) That no shooting whatsoever, except for administrative reasons, should be permitted in a reserve.

(6.) That a strict return of all game killed should be made annually by every license holder.

Left Personalised copy of the November 1906 'Blue Book' containing correspondence relating to the preservation of wild animals in Africa, from the archive of Sir Rhys Rhys-Williams, the society's first honorary secretary.

Above List of recommendations drawn up in preparation for a meeting with Lord Elgin, Secretary of State for the Colonies, who had agreed to receive a deputation of the society at the Colonial Office on 15 June 1906.

Opposite This 1904 map of colonial East Africa – with game reserves delineated in green – was included in the very first volume of the *Journal*.

proportions. Elephant protection measures introduced in Uganda at the turn of the century had proved so successful that the expanding herds were forced to forage further afield and had developed a taste for crop-raiding. Meanwhile, a rash of ill-informed press reports about the role that big game played as a natural reservoir for African trypanosomiasis – carried by the tsetse fly – had caused virtual hysteria among the white settlers, who were demanding nothing less than the wholesale slaughter of wild animals in order to protect their families and livestock from the menace of sleeping sickness.

And that was just in Africa's big game heartlands. Elsewhere in the world, wildlife was in equally urgent need of protection. Among the species jostling for attention were Egypt's egrets and herons, threatened by the fashion for hats decorated with their feathers; irate New Zealanders wrote to complain that deforestation to make way for

settlement was causing 'an alarming decrease of edible native birds'; grizzly bears and other big game were reported to be in increasingly short supply in the Canadian Rockies, as their habitat was being destroyed by mining and logging interests.

Undaunted by the magnitude of their stated mission, Buxton and his team demonstrated a special talent for multitasking and made significant breakthroughs on several fronts. Colonial Secretary Alfred Lyttelton was charmed into putting his official seal on a number of items from the society's long wish-list, including the idea that well-patrolled and professionally managed game reserves should be set up throughout British colonies in Africa. Despite initial protestations that there was no money available to fund additional and better-paid game staff, the relevant budget for the then East African Protectorate was increased almost eightfold in 1908.

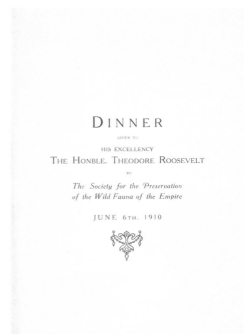

DINNER

GIVEN TO

HIS EXCELLENCY
THE HONBLE. THEODORE ROOSEVELT

BY

*The Society for the Preservation
of the Wild Fauna of the Empire*

JUNE. 6TH. 1910

WINES	MENU
Pale Dry Sherry	Melon Cantaloup Glace
Berncastler Dr.	
Chât. Palmer Margeaux	Consommé Julienne aux Perles
Pol Roger 1900	Creme Portugaise
G. Goulet 1900	
Dow's Port 1890	Saumon Braise au Champagne
Courvoisier's Fine	Pommes Nature
Champagne 1865	Salade de Concombres
Liqueurs	
Minerals	Selle d'Agneau a la Broche
	Haricots Verts Maitre d'Hotel
	Pommes Macaire
	Mousse de Jambon Westphalien Froide
	Poularde en Casserole
	Salade de Saison
	Asperges d'Argenteuil Sauce Mousseline
	Bombe Americaine
	Friandises
	Cafe

Above In 1910 the society held a dinner in honour of President Theodore Roosevelt, who was breaking his journey in London en route to the United States after his prolonged shooting spree in Africa.

Left Frederick Selous and President Theodore Roosevelt, fully paid-up members of the mutual admiration society, seated side by side on the cowcatcher that they rode from Mombasa to Nairobi at the start of the latter's 1909–10 African safari.

MAN-EATERS AND LADYKILLERS

The inspiration for a trio of Hollywood films about his lion-killing heroics, J.H. Patterson was a founder member of the society and attended its inaugural meeting.

Man-eating lions were by no means the only wild beasts to find themselves on the wrong end of Patterson's marksmanship. During a later hunting trip to Tsavo, he bagged what turned out to be a new subspecies of eland, subsequently named *Taurotragus oryx pattersonianus* in his honour. Its mounted head took pride of place on his trophy wall back home, a privilege that the unfortunate animal was unable to appreciate fully.

His role as game warden in East Africa became mired in controversy when one of his high-society safari guests died from a gunshot wound – whether self-inflicted or otherwise remained a mystery – and Patterson took the decision to bury the body in the wilderness and carry on regardless before accompanying the victim's widow back to England, amid much muttering and raising of eyebrows.

In later life Patterson devoted more of his time to shooting wildlife through a camera lens. The minutes from a 1930 meeting of the society refer to his screening of a wildlife film. Most of the footage had been secured during a visit to the Serengeti under the guidance of another close associate of the society, the dashing and debonair Denys Finch Hatton, himself no stranger to romantic entanglements in Africa.

It was Finch Hatton who, shortly before his fateful final flight in his beloved *Gypsy Moth*, hosted two visits by the then Prince of Wales – featured in the Channel 4 documentary *Edward VIII: The Lion King* – during which the future king was first acquainted with a more enlightened, camera-based version of the safari experience that persuaded him to embrace the concept of conservation. In 1928, he became the society's first royal patron. ∎

One of the members of that first 1905 deputation to the Colonial Office was appointed Chief Game Warden with responsibility for overseeing all new staff across the territory. He was none other than Lieutenant-Colonel John Henry Patterson, the renowned tiger and lion hunter who recorded his deeds of derring-do in *The Man-Eaters of Tsavo and other East African Adventures*, published in 1907 and rapturously reviewed by, among others, Theodore Roosevelt and Frederick Selous.

The ivory trade and its potentially devastating effects on elephant populations was a problem that required international co-operation. The society pressed continually for an increase in the minimum permissible weight of any tusk intended for sale, remarking that it would be 'a disgrace to our age to allow such a fine and noble animal as the African elephant to perish off the face of the Earth'. But the authorities correctly pointed out that the trade would simply move to other territories not governed by such legislation.

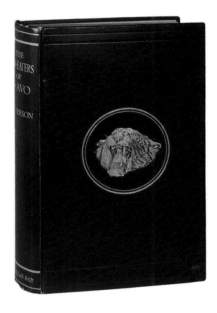

Right Original 1907 edition of *The Man-Eaters of Tsavo* by John Henry Patterson, a founder member of the society.

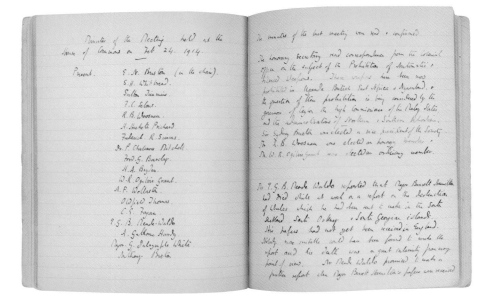
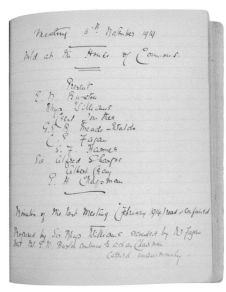

Above A five-year lacuna between successive entries in the society's minutes book provides silent testimony to the fact that the world has stood still for five years.

Below View of the Parrot House within the grounds of London Zoo, site of the society's first permanent office.

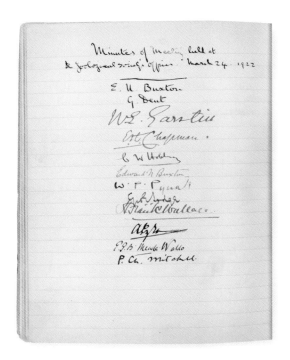

Bigger battles

An international conference on this issue had been organised in 1914, with a view to achieving blanket protection for elephants and rhinoceros, but by then the world had other priorities. Time was running out for Buxton and his boys. While they were busy spinning plates in Africa, the tectonic plates of world affairs were shifting ominously. The society was overtaken by events beyond its control that would have a seismic impact on the twentieth century and put conservation on the back burner for the better part of a decade.

Before the shadow of the Great War fell over the world, the society had been rapidly extending its remit. Concern about the decline in numbers of the game animals pursued by sportsmen had given way to the realisation that conservation measures were urgently needed for all forms of wildlife throughout the then British Empire. With this in mind, the society had endeavoured to establish stronger links with overseas individuals and institutions, in order to facilitate better international co-operation. Four years of conflict, bloodshed and sacrifice robbed the society of its forward momentum and brought its activities to a virtual standstill. Nevertheless, after peace was signed in 1919 the society was quick to resume its work, and took two important steps to strengthen its position; firstly by securing office space and meeting rooms in Regent's Park,

Extract from the minutes book showing the signatures of those attending the first meeting at the society's new home, in March 1922.

courtesy of the Zoological Society of London, and secondly by appointing a permanent secretary to ensure greater continuity for its previously sporadic operations.

There was, inevitably, a discernible whiff of post-war malaise in some of the comments recorded by the society in the years immediately after the armistice. One early editorial bemoaned the general lack of enthusiasm for wildlife preservation and ended with a very gloomy prognosis: 'All the signs point to a very early disappearance of the larger wild fauna of the Dark Continent.'

The society's *Journal* did not actually reappear until 1921, seven years after the last issue, but it took up where it had left off, focusing largely on the need to protect the African elephant. It was also notable for highlighting the plight of even larger mammals. A report on whaling in the Falkland Islands emphasised the potentially disastrous effects of over-exploitation on whale stocks and the need for greater regulation. This is virtually the first mention of cetaceans in the *Journal*, but from that point forward concerned reports on the plight of the world's great whales are an almost good Dr Hornaday could be found fulfilling his prestigious role as the first director of the New York Zoological Park, known today as the Bronx Zoo. It was in this influential capacity that he was able to help press the South African government for greater protection for the white rhinoceros. By then already an honorary member of the society, Hornaday was subsequently elected as one of its vice-presidents and played a prominent role in its affairs until long after his retirement.

Dr William Hornaday (left) inspecting a caged American bison awaiting shipment to Wichita, Kansas.

Warnings from history

By the time the Society for the Preservation of the Wild Fauna of the Empire was formed in 1903, the indiscriminate slaughter of wildlife in Africa and other parts of the world colonised by men with too many guns and too much time on their hands had long since taken a heavy toll on wildlife. The efforts of Buxton and his allies came too late to save the quagga, which resembled a half-finished painting of a zebra abandoned by a child artist who had quickly grown bored with adding all the stripes. By 1878, the quagga was already extinct in the wild, and it was irretrievably lost to the world when the last remaining captive specimen died in Amsterdam, 20 years before the society was even conceived.

permanent fixture in its pages. Tirades concerning the intransigence and blind selfishness of the whaling industry run like a leitmotiv through the *Journal* for the next 50 years, reflecting the evident frustration of a succession of society officials.

Although the outbreak of war had scuppered hopes of ratifying the international convention restricting the sale of ivory and rhino horn, there was renewed determination within the society not to let this issue rest. Whilst Uganda's elephants were thriving to the point where they were coming into conflict with people, other populations were facing severe pressure from poaching, and urgent intervention was needed. Rhinoceros numbers were also declining alarmingly throughout their range, and the imminent extinction of one specific population was a particular cause for concern: 'Something should be done to try to save the few remaining white rhinoceros in Zululand.' To this end, the society enlisted the support of a certain William T. Hornaday, a somewhat counter-intuitive choice, you might think, given his ominous surname and his formidable reputation as a big game hunter in his native North America. Nevertheless, he turned out to be the perfect candidate. When not out bagging trophies, the

The March 1921 edition of the *Journal* ran the first in a series of what could be described as warnings from history, comprising a full-page black-and-white photograph and potted biography of an extinct species. The first defunct specimen to be showcased in this monochromatic mausoleum was the blaubok. The dubious claim to fame of this South African antelope is that it was the first large African mammal to disappear since records began. The last survivors were shot around 1800. As the opening line had it: 'The blauuwbok (*sic*) heads the sad procession of exterminated and threatened fauna.' Further species profiles were to follow in subsequent issues, including the quagga, the Réunion starling and the enticingly named Labrador duck, which – disappointingly – turns out to have been a doomed species of North American wildfowl, rather than an extreme and ill-fated early prototype for the cross-bred designer pets that have recently become de rigueur among dog lovers. Some 80 years later, when the redesigned FFI members' magazine was published, it incorporated a more uplifting variation on this theme. The *Species Profile* feature is now a permanent fixture in *Fauna & Flora*. These days, gratifyingly, it focuses on endangered species that are benefiting from FFI's timely intervention, rather than lamenting the extinction of species that are 'beyond salvation'.

PIGEON HOLLANDAIS
(Alectroenas Nitidissima)
From the Specimen in the Museum of Science and Art, Edinburgh.

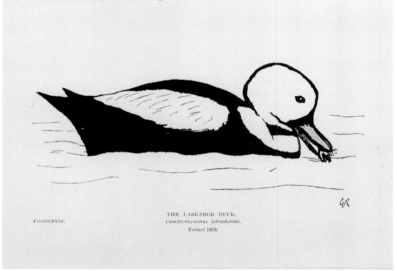

Frontispiece.

THE LABRADOR DUCK.
Camptorhynchus labradorius.
Extinct 1878.

Clockwise from top left Among the extinct species profiled in the post-war pages of the *Journal* were the Mauritius blue pigeon, which outlasted its distant cousin the dodo but ultimately suffered the same fate; the Réunion starling, confined to the island of that name; the blaubok, blasted into oblivion by 1800; the Labrador duck, complete with this artist's impression by Dr Graham Renshaw; and the quagga, pictured here languishing in London Zoo.

By January 1924, a shade over 20 years after the society was formed, its founding father, first president and later chairman was dead. Edward North Buxton's final, symbolic act, which epitomised his devotion to conservation, was to purchase Hatfield Forest from his deathbed and donate it to the National Trust. A lengthy obituary paying tribute to his contribution appears in the *Journal*: 'It is true to say that the great African game reserves owe as much to the appeals of Mr Buxton through the Fauna Society as to any other man.' Whilst undeniably an establishment figure and fully paid-up member of that old school of colonial hunters characterised by their utilitarian view of wildlife, Buxton was ahead of his time in many ways. He was sufficiently enlightened to admit that the traditional local native hunters were not the problem, observing that 'from time immemorial the destruction caused by the indigenous inhabitants has not appreciably diminished the stock',

Charcoal sketch of Edward North Buxton, founding father and early driving force behind the society, who died in 1924.

and he made the far-sighted suggestion that the Masai might make good game guards. His influence rubbed off on others. Addressing the Kenya and Uganda Natural History Society shortly after Buxton's death, one of the co-founders remarks, 'The game does not belong to the Game Department, but to the people of the country.' A century later, what was, to some, a radical idea has now become accepted conservation practice. Buxton's tacit acknowledgement that the fate of wildlife should ultimately be entrusted to local communities reveals an intuitive understanding of how conservation might work in the future and prefigures the approach that continues to make FFI so successful to this day.

Perennial problems

Even a cursory examination of the first two decades of the society's *Journal* unearths page after page where we find Buxton and his contemporaries waxing lyrical about many of the very same species and conservation issues that preoccupy FFI and its partners in the twenty-first century. In a 1924 address to members of the Museums Association, the society asks for restraint in the acquisition of specimens of the rarer species, using the mountain gorilla as a prime example of unnecessary slaughter: 'There exists in Central Africa a remarkable species of gorilla, and its habitat is partly in the Belgian Congo and partly in Uganda; it is a rare beast and limited in its range. Probably fifty of these unique creatures have been shot since the war, and if strict preservation is not instituted they will soon disappear.' Over 50 years before the launch of the renowned Mountain Gorilla Project that FFI was instrumental in establishing, the seeds of that acclaimed partnership were already being sown.

That same year, an editorial highlights the need to raise environmental awareness: 'A wider interest in the future of the wild fauna must be promoted.' To this end, the potential benefits of what we now call ecotourism are discussed: 'The more people who see the game in their natural setting, the more it will be realised that here is a national possession worth maintaining for all time. If such a marvellous wealth of wild life is allowed to disappear, generations yet unborn will anathematise our short-sightedness and apathy.'

Concern at the destructive trade in rhino horn elicited a letter from a correspondent in Asia, to the effect that the Malayan one-horned rhinoceros (today known as the Javan rhino, *Rhinoceros sondaicus*) was at considerable risk from the burgeoning market in exotic ingredients for traditional Chinese medicine. African rhinos were suffering a similar fate. In 1929, news that just 20 southern white rhinoceros survive in the wild led to calls for drastic action, including a suggestion that the remaining population should be rounded up and moved to safety. Anyone who has registered the logistical difficulties that FFI and its partners were required to overcome as recently as 2009, when translocating the world's last four known breeding northern white rhinos from Dvůr Králové Zoo in the Czech Republic to Kenya's Ol Pejeta Conservancy, will appreciate how ambitious this concept would have seemed some 80 years earlier.

In 1927, several decades before the publication of the now legendary Red Data Books on threatened species (which will feature prominently in a later chapter), the society's *Journal* included a list of animals that were either already extinct or 'in grave danger of early extermination through human agency'. This coincided with the publication of a leaflet featuring vanishing species and intended for general distribution and was followed by a pamphlet, *The Passing of Wild Life*, issued the following year.

Even then, there was already recognition of the importance of long-term sustainability when attempting to devise solutions to conservation problems. The 1929 annual report from the Kenya Game Department concluded that 'all consideration – action also – must be based on the needs of the future; and the future must not mean ten, twenty, fifty years hence. We must look just as far as the possibilities of imagination and prescience will allow us.'

Kruger man

Notwithstanding the breadth of conservation topics covered by the *Journal*, the lion's share of every issue was devoted to the national park agenda. And in this regard no one was more prominent than Major James Stevenson-Hamilton, who contributed articles to the society's *Journal* for almost 50 years, from its inception until 1952. His name appears on the earliest list of members alongside Kitchener and Roosevelt, and he would later enjoy two brief spells as honorary secretary of the society.

In 1902 Stevenson-Hamilton was appointed as the first warden of Sabi Game Reserve in South Africa's eastern Transvaal. His early tenure at Sabi was characterised by a single-minded determination to ensure that the reserve was a genuinely protected area. He imposed a strict 'no shooting' rule, enforced it ruthlessly, and made it clear that no one would be above the law by arresting several senior policemen who were caught poaching. He also used his powers of persuasion to secure additional land, achieving the remarkable feat of increasing the original size of the reserve more than tenfold to 36,000 square kilometres. He proposed that Sabi should be opened to visitors in order to secure widespread approval for the idea of transforming the reserve into a national park. Although these plans were interrupted by the onset of the Great War, Stevenson-Hamilton eventually achieved his aim. Sabi was renamed Kruger National Park in 1926, in honour of the state president who had first advocated setting aside protected areas in South Africa, and opened to the public the following year. At first the park received very few visitors, but by 1935 numbers had reached 26,000. Today around a million visitors pass through its gates annually.

Major influence

Stevenson-Hamilton's influence extended well beyond the boundaries of Kruger. In the 1920s he was responsible for drafting Sudanese game protection legislation that endured for decades, and he was instrumental in the establishment of a network of five game reserves in that country. He was a vocal critic of the prevailing attitudes to wildlife of the colonists in East Africa and was horrified to discover during a visit to Kenya that the authorities wanted game laws suspended and unbridled trade in hide and horn permitted.

He condemned officials who had violated an elephant sanctuary by hunting there, and even found time to question the hunting ethics of a young Winston Churchill, whom he had witnessed blasting away indiscriminately at the local wildlife. An obsessive recorder and observer of nature in all its forms, Stevenson-Hamilton gained an enviable reputation as a naturalist in his own right. He was a prolific author and a stalwart contributor to the *Journal* under the 'Sabi' pseudonym.

A tribute from the acting chair at the society's 1931 annual meeting, held at the Zoological Society of London's offices, reveals the high regard in which Stevenson-Hamilton was held: 'The Kruger National Park is intimately associated with one of our Members, because if any one man is entitled to the credit for founding that Park it is Major Stevenson-Hamilton, our former Secretary.'

Above Portrait of James Stevenson-Hamilton, who – but for a brief interlude during the First World War when he was posted to Sudan – was a permanent fixture at Kruger National Park until 1946, just before his eightieth birthday.

Opposite One of Kruger's impressive tuskers - dubbed the 'Magnificent Seven' - Shingwedzi was estimated to be around 56 years old when he died in January 1981, meaning that this legend among elephants was probably already on the scene in 1926 when his birthplace was declared South Africa's first national park.

In 1930 a deputation from the society sought a meeting with the Secretary of State for the Colonies at which it advocated that a joint conference of game wardens of the East African dependencies be convened to discuss conservation policy. Stevenson-Hamilton was proposed as the society's representative. Among the subjects under discussion would be permanent sanctuaries and national parks, hunting legislation and more effective game preservation measures outside the reserves. The idea was to ensure that the protected areas throughout the African dependencies were stabilised and made permanent by legislation, in order to safeguard wildlife in perpetuity. There was broad recognition of the enormous economic potential of such parks for tourist purposes.

Stevenson-Hamilton was dispatched to East Africa with a brief to assess the best way forward. He returned convinced that a network of national parks was essential to replace the existing game reserves, and they should be created along the lines of those found in the United States, Canada, Australia and South Africa.

The society's advocacy of the introduction of a national park system was not confined to Africa. Acting Secretary Charles (C.W.) Hobley suggests in the *Journal* that it would be 'a commendable step if some wild tract in the British Isles could be proclaimed a National Park where the indigenous fauna could be allowed to survive in its state of natural balance'. The society had helped to spearhead the establishment of, and was represented on, the Government Committee on National Parks, which drew up a comprehensive list of biologically rich UK sites where the designation of national parks or other forms of protected area was warranted.

In October 1928, a future vice-president of the society, Syed Waris Ameer Ali, was first elected as a member of the Executive Committee. From that date he was present at virtually every society meeting, until the point when poor health precluded further attendance. He was a very early champion of India's fauna at a time when the focus was almost exclusively on Africa. His first recorded activity for the society was an address to the East Indian Association in which he lamented the unwitting neglect of Indian wildlife. A devoted fan of the tiger, Ali was keen to explode the myth that this animal was a ferocious enemy of humans. Between the wars, he became a strong advocate for national parks in India, showing more foresight than the rest of the committee, who claimed that parks were unnecessary as animal numbers were increasing in forest areas and the forest department could be relied on to create natural sanctuaries.

Royal society

Around this time, as the breadth of the society's activities continued to expand, the magnitude of its task began to hit home. On the one hand, the signs were encouraging. Its sphere of influence was growing. In Lord Onslow, it had a new president with a well-known name. The work of the society was also being well received in the corridors of power – 'A sympathetic hearing is given by great officials with immense responsibilities on their shoulders.' It continued to benefit from the patronage of high-ranking members of society, as witnessed in the slightly smug report of the Executive Committee to the General Meeting in February 1928: 'We have great pleasure in inviting the attention of members to the fact that certain persons of the highest eminence in the public life of this country have kindly consented to become Vice-Presidents of the Society.' For a status-conscious group that set such great store by its aristocratic links, the news that HRH the Prince of Wales (the future Edward VIII) had consented to become the society's first royal patron, announced with appropriate ceremony in 1928, must have elevated them to a state of sheer rapture.

For all its connections and privileged access, however, the society was labouring under a number of constraints, the most obvious of which was financial. Any further extension of its activities would be contingent on raising more money. In 1926 an appeal for increased funds had appeared as an insert in the *Journal*. The most obvious means of generating additional funds was to recruit new members, a fact tacitly acknowledged in the appointment of a sinister-sounding Propaganda Secretary, whose brief was specifically to increase membership of the society. Membership rose quickly in the wake of a recruitment drive in *The Times* to coincide with the distribution of the pamphlet, prompting the society to readjust its sights above the initial target of 500 members and aim for a more ambitious total of 1,000. By 1929, it had 541 people on board, but there seemed to be little prospect of doubling that figure in the near future.

In November 1929 Charles Hobley visited the United States with the aim of interesting American conservationists in the work of the society and, one imagines, an unspoken agenda that revolved around fundraising. Among those he encountered was John C. Phillips, an independently wealthy wildlife enthusiast and philanthropist. In 1930 a special committee, with Phillips as its first chairman, was formed under the aegis of the Boone and Crockett Club for the specific purpose of furthering the society's aims. The committee was proposed and organised by Dr Harold J. Coolidge, then Curator of the Harvard University Museum of Comparative Zoology. Coolidge had participated in scientific expeditions in Africa and

OBJECTS OF THE SOCIETY.

The main object of the Society is to ensure that no more species of wild animals shall be exterminated within the British Empire.

It considers that this can be best effected by creating a sound public opinion on the subject at home and abroad, by furthering the formation of National Parks, and by enforcing suitable game laws and Regulations. It believes that practical measures can be found by which every species of wild life can be preserved without hampering in the slightest the economic development and civilization of our territories.

It is no part of the aim of the Society to preserve animal life at the expense of human industry or natural development; nor does it offer any opposition to the fair and legitimate pursuits of the sportsman.

The Society cannot attain its object without a large and influential membership. It therefore invites the co-operation and assistance of all persons throughout the Empire who are interested in the preservation of wild life.

The society's revised mission statement, published in the *Journal*, demonstrates the extent to which its remit had already begun to broaden by 1930.

South East Asia, and was a passionate supporter of international conservation. The American Committee for International Wild Life Protection, as it was known, would prove to be an invaluable source of financial and moral support. This assistance was not without strings, however. The society came under increasing pressure to secure a similar level of funding at home in order to ensure that it would begin to make a bigger splash on its own side of the pond.

The latest fundraising initiatives coincided with a changing perception about the overall rationale for conservation: 'In the past the preservation of game has been almost entirely for the purposes of sport, but now a new conception is abroad.' The novelty of conservation for its own sake was just starting to poke its head above the parapet. It was perhaps this realisation that explained the society's evident reluctance, in 1925, to sanction closer co-operation with the Shikar Club, a sports shooting club formed in 1909 by Eton and Rugby alumni. The latter was keen to join forces for the purposes of big

game preservation, but it was felt by the Executive Committee that the respective societies now had differing priorities.

In 1929, the society formalised this new way of thinking with an official announcement in the *Journal*: 'We must extend the sphere of our activities; the character of our endeavour during the next ten years will do much to decide the fate of the wild life of the world.'

These words would prove to be prophetic. Less than three years later, the society was to play a pivotal role in securing an international agreement that was described by American environmental historian Roderick Nash, in his seminal *Wilderness and the American Mind*, as 'the high point of institutionalised global nature protection before the Second World War'.

CHAPTER 2
PROTECTION

'This was the greatest event, to date, in the history of the society, marking, as it did, a great extension of its aims beyond the original purpose of its foundation, and providing evidence of its powers of achievement.'

Sir Peter Chalmers Mitchell, 1944

In 1933 a conference was called in London with the objective of establishing a treaty for the conservation of wildlife in Africa. From our twenty-first-century vantage point it is difficult to appreciate the enormous significance of something as apparently mundane as an international conference.

We are inclined to view such things through jaundiced eyes as a result of having witnessed too many climate change summits, wildlife trade conventions and sustainable development pow-wows that promise little and deliver even less. For the shakers and movers within the Society for the Preservation of the Wild Fauna of the Empire who had dedicated themselves to the task of corresponding, lobbying and fighting their conservation corner, this was the culmination of a collective effort that had begun 30 years earlier and, therefore, a moment to savour: 'It is a matter of great satisfaction that an aim for which we have been working for some years past should be in sight.'

In the preceding decades, proposals had been put forward and meetings had been convened, but all the good intentions had failed to produce tangible results. However, the 1933 International Conference for the Protection of the Fauna and Flora of Africa was the first such initiative to gain any traction.

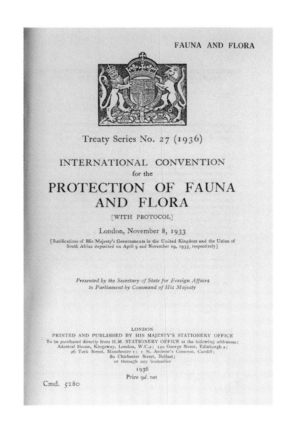

Above right The London Convention of 1933 provided a blueprint for future wildlife conservation agreements throughout the world.

Opposite The weird and wonderful Welwitschia, found only in the Namib Desert, produces just two strap-like leaves, which become twisted and frayed throughout a lifespan that may exceed 1,500 years. It was the first named plant species to be granted international protection.

The mother of conventions

As we have seen, the European powers with territorial interests in Africa had already come together in 1900 to sign the London Convention, which aimed to protect wild animals, birds and fish in those overseas dependencies, but the outbreak of hostilities in 1914 had torpedoed hopes that it could be ratified. Viewed against this historical backdrop of failure, the 1933 proceedings assumed even greater significance; they not only gave conservation an international platform, but also ensured that it remained centre stage. By agreeing a protocol that committed the parties to additional conferences at predetermined future dates, the event succeeded in establishing conservation as a permanent fixture on the agenda of all the governments concerned.

Lord Onslow, president of the society since 1926 and a man of great influence, chaired the conference. In this capacity he was ably assisted by the very same John C. Phillips who, as Chairman of the American Committee for International Wild Life Protection, had helped to generate valuable transatlantic support for the work of the society. The United States had been invited to send an official observer to the conference and Phillips was the obvious choice. Working closely with a select group of conservation leaders, Onslow and Phillips combined forces to draw up a convention that would form the bedrock of a protected area network and supporting legislative framework throughout much of Africa.

A blueprint for global conservation

The Convention Relative to the Preservation of Fauna and Flora in the Natural State, which has mercifully come to be known as the London Convention of 1933, was a momentous agreement. Dubbed 'the Magna Carta of wildlife conservation' by Robert Boardman in a 1981 book, *International Organization and the Conservation of Nature*, it broke new ground in several respects. As the first of its kind, the convention provided a blueprint for future wildlife conservation agreements not only in Africa, but also throughout the rest of the world. Notably, it was the first such agreement to grant protection to a specific species of plant, in this case the intriguing Welwitschia, which is endemic to the Namib Desert.

The first signatories were the United Kingdom and its dependencies, other European colonial powers in the shape of France, Belgium and Italy, and several African nations, namely Egypt, the Sudan and South Africa. By 1935 the agreement had been ratified by virtually all these nations, with other countries signing up at a later date, including Portugal and Tanganyika. The 1933 Convention was to remain in force for 35 years until superseded by the 1968 African Convention on the Conservation of Nature and Natural Resources.

This 1968 makeover was intended to take account of the political reconstruction of Africa in the wake of the Second World War. The newly independent African states recognised the fundamental importance of wildlife and natural resources for their economy and future. Consequently, the articles of the new convention were characterised by a positive attitude to conservation based on broad ecological principles encompassing preservation, management, sustainable use of natural resources – defined as soil, water, vegetation and fauna – as well as research, education, legislation and administration. After a similar 35-year interval, the 1968 version was itself subject to further revision. Signed in Maputo in 2003, this veritable palimpsest of a document reflects how conservation priorities changed throughout the twentieth century.

As far as the 1933 version is concerned, its most noteworthy achievement was to nail down the principle that creating national parks or strict nature reserves was the most effective way to protect wildlife. The London Conference was responsible for the evolution of a universally accepted definition of the term 'national park', and also secured protection for particular species that were in urgent need of conservation action. Signatories were committed to setting up parks and reserves in which human settlement would be restricted and carefully monitored, ensuring that 'unsportsmanlike' and unnecessarily destructive methods of hunting were prohibited, and controlling the trade in animal trophies.

On the origin of species protection

The list of species granted special protection was divided into categories according to the perceived level of threat to their long-term survival. This primitive but logical triage approach to wildlife protection anticipated the more sophisticated attempts by modern-day conservationists to classify species according to their relative proximity to extinction, as with the International Union for Conservation of Nature (IUCN) Red List of Threatened Species, or to provide a level of protection commensurate with their relative vulnerability to overexploitation through international trade, as with the Appendices of CITES. Not to be confused with one of the twelve labours of Hercules, the latter may sound like the stuff of Greek mythology but are, in fact, lists containing the names of plant and animal species protected to a greater or lesser extent from the ravages of the wildlife trade. As we shall see, the society was to play a pivotal role in the establishment of both IUCN and CITES.

The human factor

It is apparent from reports in the *Journal* that the society's president, Lord Onslow, needed to draw on all his powers of persuasion and diplomatic skills in the drafting and redrafting of the most sensitive sections of the agreement, in order to remove all potential obstacles to ratification.

The end product was seen by the society as a vindication of the president's attention to detail, and of the years of hard graft leading up to the meeting itself. 'The conference of 1933 embodies the principles and methods of conservation consistently advocated by the Society [...] so that wildlife may be preserved, not only without detriment to human progress, but to the benefit of the local inhabitants and the perpetual gain of civilised man.' What is also evident is the fact that the society has already begun to see the bigger picture at this point. The open acknowledgement of the importance of the human dimension is one of the earliest references in FFI's history to its now-familiar mantra of choosing conservation solutions that 'take account of human needs'.

In this context, the society was conscious of the need to demonstrate the broader social and economic benefits, as well as narrow conservation gains, that protected areas could offer. In February 1934 it noted with evident satisfaction that the presence of Kruger National Park had done much to stimulate local industries, with new shops and hotels springing up to cater for a growing stream of tourists visiting the park.

There is also early evidence of the emphasis on locally managed solutions, which has more recently become one of the distinctive hallmarks of the society's modus operandi. Referring to the recent increase in wildlife numbers within an Australian park, following its designation as a National Reservation, a 1933 editorial in the *Journal* notes: 'Perhaps one of the most important features of the change is that people living in the district have begun to take a pride and an interest in this unique portion of the globe.' What the writer fails to acknowledge, of course, is that the indigenous Australians had been taking a pride and interest in their

Lord Onslow served as president of the society from 1926 to 1942. He represented the British government at the International Congress for the Protection of Nature, which met in Paris in 1931, and was appointed president of the Convention Relative to the Preservation of Fauna and Flora in the Natural State in 1933.

natural heritage for an estimated 50,000 years before white settlers arrived, but that's another story.

Back in the UK, there was frustration that the British government did not actually ratify the African convention until early 1935, because many other would-be signatories were waiting for it to take the lead. Ratification was obviously just the starting point, but when the convention finally came into force on 14 January 1936, the society hailed it as 'the first and very important stage in preserving the fauna and flora of the continent of Africa'.

Despite the society reaffirming its commitment to the cause and expressing its determination to 'influence public and official opinion with unflagging persistence', there was unease in certain quarters that the contents of its *Journal* implied a narrow focus on Africa. The accusation was

CLASS ACTION

The London Convention of 1933 'Class A' list comprised 17 mammals, three birds and a solitary plant species, which were considered to merit absolute protection from anything other than licensed hunting or collection for the purposes of scientific research. It included every subspecies of gorilla, Madagascar's lemurs and fossa, aardwolf, okapi, pygmy hippopotamus, mountain zebra, white rhinoceros, elephants with tusks weighing under five kilos, several antelope species and an apparently arbitrary avian trio comprising shoebill, northern bald ibis and white-breasted guinea fowl.

Interestingly, black rhinoceros, chimpanzee, giraffe and ostrich were among those species deemed to require a less stringent form of protection and, accordingly, were relegated to the 'Class B' list, meaning they could be shot without scientific justification provided a special permit had been secured. ∎

rebuffed by pointing out that this was merely a reflection of where the news came from. As far as the society was concerned, Africa was simply the launch pad for a suite of broader conservation activities.

There was a firm belief that, quite apart from helping to safeguard Africa's threatened wildlife, the 1933 Convention would bring far wider benefits by serving as a model for similar conventions that would gradually spread a protective blanket over the greater part of the world. Sure enough, the Africa blueprint would eventually be replicated first in India, then in Malaysia, and ultimately across the whole of Asia.

In 1935 the Viceroy of India, Freeman Freeman-Thomas, 1st Marquess of Willingdon (whose son, Inigo, would later serve as president of the society from 1951 to 1974) convened a wildlife conference in Delhi, at which the society was represented and its advice actively sought. Gratified that the all-India conference had followed so closely on the heels of the Africa convention, the society expressed the view that 'the doctrine of preservation is now spreading'.

Preaching to the unconverted

There was no denying the validity of this claim, and no denying that word was also spreading about the work of the society itself. The worldwide publicity afforded to the international conference by widespread media coverage was focusing public attention on the need for such an organisation. Despite this, there were concerns that a higher public profile was having little discernible impact on membership recruitment. In May 1935, the Belgian ambassador expressed surprise that 'in a great nation like this [...] there are only about 1,000 willing to support a society like this, which is doing such important work'. A *Journal* editorial from the same period bemoaned the difficulty of persuading the great British public to embrace the global conservation cause and overcome its apathy towards 'wildlife in distant lands'. This grouse was accompanied by a sideswipe at the swelling ranks of the animal welfare brigade that was evidently helping the RSPCA to make huge inroads in its work with domestic animals: 'Those rejoicing in their success should give thought to the creatures of the wild, which are facing annihilation rather than [mere] exposure to cruelty.'

Aware that it needed to explore innovative ways to turn the tide of opinion in its favour, the society identified the Film Institute as a potential – and virtually untapped – source of

visual instruction about the importance of wildlife protection. Given the seismic impact on public opinion of wildlife documentaries such as *Life on Earth* in later years, this was clearly an astute move.

Some two years later, the society announced a further initiative that it hoped would generate additional public interest. A deal was struck with the BBC to hold a series of five talks under the umbrella title *Saving the Animals*, 'in order to stimulate interest in fauna preservation and to inform a wider public of the destruction of wild life, and of the desirability as well as the practicability of the preservation of species'. The first lecture, in October 1937, was delivered by Dr Julian Huxley, grandson of Thomas Henry Huxley, whose fierce public support for the theory of evolution earned him the unedifying nickname 'Darwin's bulldog'. A member of the society since 1931, the younger Huxley would go on to play a prominent role in its future direction, not least in his capacity as the first director-general of UNESCO.

The message in that first lecture was a stark one, as the excerpts from his talk reproduced in the *Journal* reveal: 'We maintain museums for dead specimens while we kill off the specimens in the museum of life. We blame our ancestors for thoughtlessly exterminating the dodo and the quagga; there will be less excuse for us if we leave our descendants a world further denuded of life's abundance and life's variety.' The fifth and final lecture took the form of a debate about whether wildlife conservation was ultimately incompatible with human interests. Agreement was reached that it was a question of give and take, and that, shock horror, national parks offered the most effective means of preventing the extinction of valuable, interesting and beautiful species.

Troubled times

If the British public appeared reluctant to engage with the global conservation debate during this period, its reticence could reasonably be put down to the fact that other, more pressing concerns were vying for its attention. In Europe, the rise to power in Germany of Adolf Hitler and the Nazi Party was becoming more than a mild distraction. At home, the death of King George V in 1936 was the signal for a period of mourning and introspection. The relief felt by the society when Edward VIII agreed to continue his royal patronage after acceding to the throne was short-lived. Within less than a year, the newly crowned king had abdicated amid the constitutional crisis caused by his

The future King George VI and Queen Elizabeth avoiding the heat of the day in Uganda's Semliki Valley during their extended African safari in 1926.

proposed marriage to the American socialite, Wallis Simpson. Happily, the society was only briefly denied the kudos afforded by having a monarch as patron. King George VI graciously consented to assume that mantle in February 1937, shortly after ascending the throne. In May that same year, the society included a photograph of the royal couple, taken a decade earlier while they were on a hunting safari in Africa, as the frontispiece of the *Journal*, pointing out to members that their royal patron 'is not only King of England, but a sportsman who appreciates wildlife'. Where some other members of the royal family were concerned, this appreciation tended to manifest itself in mysterious ways. During a ten-day hunting trip in India in 1911, his father, King George V is reported to have shot 21 tigers, eight rhinos and a bear.

Letters from Malaya

While British citizens at home in the UK were preoccupied with the threat to world peace posed by Hitler and mesmerised by the game of royal musical chairs being played out in public, the relative normality of life in the colonies was enabling those in the far-flung corners of the British Empire to spend time contemplating more mundane matters. The conservation-minded were especially exercised

by the woeful lack of protection for the local wildlife, with South East Asia, in particular, a cause for concern.

No one was more vociferous in this regard than Theodore Rathbone Hubback, a self-appointed conservationist in what was then Malaya. Hubback had left England as a young man to join his elder brother, Arthur, a renowned architect who designed the iconic main railway station in Kuala Lumpur. Later in life, as a plantation owner, Hubback gained a reputation as a hunter of big game but, like the 'Penitent Butchers' of the society before him, ended up dedicating himself to its preservation. Among other feathers in his cap, he is credited with discovering the seladang, a Malaysian subspecies of the gaur, which bears his name.

A compulsive letter writer, Hubback was engaged in a virtually unbroken correspondence course with the society throughout the 1920s. His opening gambit in 1920 related to the plight of the lesser one-horned rhino in Lower Burma, for which he was soliciting society support. At the following year's AGM, a proposal to allow Hubback to form a branch of the society in Malaya was approved. In 1923 he wrote to the society to express the hope that 'in this part of the world sufficient interest will be taken [...] to ensure the preservation and protection of the big and small game of Malaya will be placed on such a sound basis that those responsible for the measures taken now will be able [...] to

Left These two examples of Theodore Hubback's literary output, published in 1905 and 1929 respectively, bear witness to a quarter of a century of big game hunting and also reveal the geographical reach of his rifle.

Below The Malaysian subspecies of the gaur, *Bos gaurus hubbacki*, is named after the reformed hunter who devoted his later years to wildlife conservation and became the society's ears and eyes in what was then Malaya.

Hubback poses with his latest trophies, including several seladang skulls and the severed feet of an elephant.

look back on their work with some small feeling of satisfaction'. The following year, he observed that a shortage of game wardens was a serious barrier to effective conservation: 'The reason is not far to seek: the Government will not spend sufficient money to make it possible to enforce the law in an efficient manner.' Hubback also urged the society to press the relevant authorities in Malaya, Burma and Siam [Thailand] regarding what measures they were taking to protect their wildlife, and proposed that a joint conference be organised to expedite the process. In 1926, frustrated at the evident lack of progress, Hubback reiterated this suggestion and emphasised the urgent need for a bespoke organisation to protect Malay fauna. By the end of the decade, his letters to the society were openly accusing the authorities of sloth, indifference and penny-pinching.

On a mission

In 1937 the society sent a mission to both Malaya and Ceylon, as Sri Lanka was then known, in the hope of stimulating greater local interest in conservation. The subsequent report was by no means discouraging, but it did highlight the importance of focusing on local community priorities in order to win hearts and minds: 'The belief is prevalent that the rights of animals are given more consideration than the rights of man.' Interestingly, the society's secretary, Henry Maurice,

alluded to a similar issue the following year, this time in an African context, when reviewing the recently published memoir of Baroness Karen von Blixen-Finecke, *Out of Africa*, which inspired the 1985 film of the same name: 'We, who are intent on the preservation in natural conditions of the fauna of our colonies, are all too apt to forget that the human native is as much a part of the native fauna.'

Thanks largely to the relentless pressure exerted by Hubback and, at his behest, by the society back home, the wheels of progress were grinding imperceptibly forward. Later in 1937, a stop-press announcement appeared in the *Journal* to the effect that Kenya's highly experienced Chief Game Warden, Captain Ritchie, was being seconded to Malaya. His brief was to organise a game department in preparation for the gazetting of the country's first national park, scheduled for the following year. King George VI National Park, later renamed Taman Negara following independence in 1957, was the ultimate reward for years of campaigning by conservationists. It was Hubback himself, in his capacity as the first Wildlife Commissioner of Malaya and, subsequently, as an unpaid game warden for the Department of Wildlife and National Parks, who had successfully lobbied the local sultans for land to be set aside for forest conservation. The society was quick to acknowledge the part played by Hubback 'who for the last twenty years or so has laboured in season and out of season for better measures of wildlife preservation in Malaya. The monumental report of the Wildlife

Commission in Malaya, for which he was responsible, will for long remain an encyclopaedia on the question, and the steps now announced can be safely stated to be an outcome of the pertinacity of his efforts.' This glowing, if somewhat flowery, tribute was an acknowledgement of Hubback's single-minded pursuit of his conservation goal. He went on to guard the national park on a voluntary basis, continuing even after war broke out, until he was forced to take refuge from the invading Japanese army in the nearby Krau Wildlife Reserve, where he was subsequently found dead.

No peace in our time

A mere 31 years after the armistice brought an end to the 'war to end all wars', the world was plunged back into the abyss. In the face of so much abject human misery, it seems insensitive to focus on the consequences for wildlife preservation, but from a narrow conservation perspective the Second World War could not have come at a more inopportune moment. The movement was gathering momentum and appeared to be on the brink of breaking through on a global scale.

Above left Theodore Hubback, an inveterate correspondent, continually bombarded the society with letters.

Above right Between the First and Second World Wars Hubback underwent a Damascene conversion from hunter to self-appointed protector of Sumatran rhinos and other Malayan wildlife.

In early 1939, in an address to the society extolling the virtues of Kruger National Park, Colonel Stevenson-Hamilton expresses the view that its popularity heralds a new era: 'There has been an astonishing change in public sentiment towards wild life during recent years. Today we see everywhere the camera replacing the rifle more and more.'

A second London Conference on the Preservation of African Fauna, again chaired by the society's president, had been held in May 1938, and a third international conference devoted specifically to wildlife conservation in Australasia and Asia was inked into the conservationists' diary for the following year. The renewal of hostilities dashed all hopes of holding an Asiatic conference in the foreseeable future, and it was postponed indefinitely.

In an open letter to members in December 1939, president Lord Onslow urged them to maintain their support and emphasised the need for the society not to take its eye off the conservation ball: 'The present war has come at so critical a stage of our work that it is a matter of fundamental importance to keep our organisation alive.' Moreover, he permitted himself the luxury of looking further ahead to a time when conferences might bring together Asian, African, European, Australasian and Pacific representatives as a collaborative force for wildlife conservation.

Keep the fauna flag flying

The society expressed its determination 'to make the voice of wildlife conservation heard above so hideous a din of war' and, displaying the intrepid attitude that characterises FFI's modern-day commitment to working in post-conflict zones, declared itself 'ready to seize the first opportunity presented on the cessation of hostilities to press for the immediate initiation of the fullest possible programme of active measures of preservation'.

Anticipating that wildlife conservation might not be high on the list of government priorities after the war, Lord

Onslow proposed an initiative, to be debated at the forthcoming Scientific Congress, aimed at ensuring that this issue would be incorporated into post-war reconstruction plans. Neglect of fauna preservation would, he insisted, 'display a lamentable lack of judgement on the part of those responsible for the great task of scientific, economic and [...] cultural reclamation after the present orgy of destruction'.

The attitude of its president during these dark times sent out a very positive message to members and was undoubtedly a critical success factor in the society's survival. The following excerpt from a letter dated 15 January 1940, from Willard G. Van Name, curator of invertebrate zoology at the American Museum of Natural History and an ardent supporter of the society, typifies the favourable reaction in many quarters at the time to Lord Onslow's steely resolve: 'As an evidence of my confidence that the conservation work of your organisation will keep on, I am enclosing a P.O. money order for $200 as a contribution.'

Five years later, the society was still on its feet, describing itself as 'a modest beacon standing for the conservation of worthwhile things in a world engulfed in the gloom of devastation'.

This well-worn tome, containing the collected wisdom from the second international conference in 1938, was rescued from a skip during a 2015 office move. The original 1933 London Convention papers were reproduced and cunningly concealed within the pages of the 1938 volume.

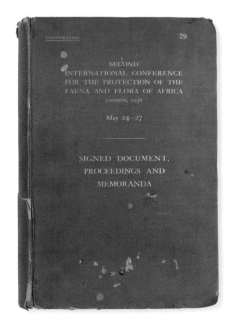
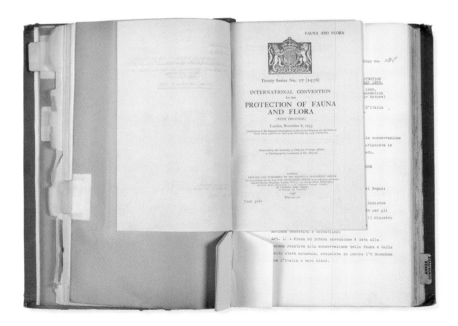

Short-eared owl family photographed by Eric Hosking just a few years after he was partially blinded by a tawny owl in similar circumstances. To paraphrase Oscar Wilde, to lose one eye while photographing an owl at its nest may be regarded as a misfortune; to lose the other would have looked like carelessness.

In a symbolic gesture of defiance, the society continued to publish its *Journal* throughout the 1939–45 conflict. These editions were noticeably pared down, but they still managed to convey the impression that conservation activity had not ground to a complete halt because of the war. They also provided a showcase for the pioneering photographic work of Eric Hosking, arguably the doyen of modern bird photography. Famously blinded in one eye in 1937 by a tawny owl defending its nest, Hosking continued to take pictures for a further 50 years.

From a twenty-first-century standpoint, where cameras are ubiquitous to the point of intrusiveness and technological advances enable even the most technically incompetent to take a decent snapshot of a blue tit on a bird feeder, it is hard to appreciate the degree of difficulty involved in photographing birds at that time. Before the advent of through-the-lens viewing, the photographer had to anticipate where a bird would land and pre-focus the camera on that spot. Unless the bird was at its nest, this was no mean feat. Film had to be reloaded, in total darkness, between every single exposure. The black-and-white bird photographs that first appeared in the *Journal* in 1943 were a revelation at the time.

Medal of honour

While war was still raging, and perhaps inspired by the flow of reports about awards bestowed for valiant deeds in the heat of battle, the society hit upon the idea of commissioning its own medal to honour 'persons who have done valuable service in support of the preservation of wild life'.

The silver medal was designed by John Skeaping, first husband of Barbara Hepworth and a renowned sculptor in his own right, who had been awarded the prestigious British Prix de Rome in 1924. The costs of design and production were met by Alfred Ezra, a self-effacing but generous supporter of the society, famous for the magnificent collection of rare birds at his Surrey home, and posthumously acknowledged as the most generous benefactor the London Zoological Society had ever known.

The first recipients of the society's silver medal were two former secretaries: Colonel Stevenson-Hamilton, of Kruger National Park fame, and Charles Hobley, of whom it was said that he had 'greatly enhanced the reputation of the Society' and 'made valuable contacts all over the world'. Hobley was particularly lauded for his visit to the United States, where he had enlisted considerable sympathy – and financial support – for the society's aims.

Designed by sculptor John Skeaping, the society's silver medal depicts a secretary bird subduing a snake on the obverse. The reverse features a generic antelope figure that bears a passing resemblance to an impala.

Among the seemingly endless casualties of war, the society suffered numerous losses of its own, although the highest-profile of these were not directly related to the conflict. Herbrand Russell, 11th Duke of Bedford, saviour of Père David's deer and a long-standing vice-president of the society, died in August 1940, just four years after being elected honorary president for life. An obituary in the *Journal* paid tribute to his contribution to the development of the society: 'During his Presidency the Society advanced to great prosperity, much of which it owed to his generosity, but far more to his shrewd judgment and wise counsel.'

Done too soon

Lord Onslow withdrew from the affairs of the society in December 1942 due to ill health. The loss of such a towering figure, and with it the political clout that he brought to bear, was a heavy blow: 'He used to the limit [...] positions which gave him great opportunities to press the cause of Conservation on Ministers of the Crown.' Regret that his unforeseen departure from the scene had left the society with unfinished business was tempered by the knowledge that he had raised the bar and, in doing so, set the standard for his successors. 'To him, more than to any other, we and the world in general owe the African Convention of 1933. His ambition for the cause of Fauna Preservation aimed higher and wider [...] for nothing less than a World Convention would have satisfied him.'

In November 1944, the 'irreplaceable' Lord Onslow was awarded the society's first Gold Medal. Making the presentation, Sir Peter Chalmers Mitchell, vice-chairman of the Executive Committee and himself a former president of the society, argued that the outgoing president's biggest contribution was in enlisting the support of other countries for the aims of the society. 'Through his many diplomatic and political contacts he had been able to secure the sympathy not only of numerous foreign embassies, but also of the then Prime Minister, Ramsay MacDonald, and to bring about the conference in London which led up to the signature, in 1933, of the International Convention for the Preservation of Wild Life in Africa. This was the greatest event, to date, in the history of the society, marking, as it did, a great extension of its aims beyond the original purpose of its foundation, and providing evidence of its powers of achievement.'

Lord Onslow made a short but visionary acceptance speech in which he speculated on the possible future shape of conservation. He advocated worldwide collaboration and

the establishment of what he called a 'Central Bureau of Wild Life Preservation', which he hoped might be set up in London, although he insisted that location was of less importance than its worldwide recognition and authority. His remarks would prove remarkably prescient.

The medal presentation and warm tributes came not a moment too soon. Lord Onslow died just a few months later, in June 1945, in the period of limbo between the German and Japanese surrender that marked the official end of the Second World War. His enduring legacy is that he, perhaps more than any other individual, elevated Britain to pride of place as leader of the movement for 'practical, international co-operation in the rational conservation of nature', and turned the society itself into a force to be reckoned with.

Lord Onslow's successor the 10th Duke of Devonshire wasted no time in letting everyone know where he felt the organisation's priorities should lie: 'The strength of a propaganda society is to be measured chiefly in terms of numbers.' The familiar refrain about the need to increase membership was back to haunt the new regime: 'Our own experience is that there are very many persons who are keenly interested in wild life, but have never heard of the Fauna Society, and would have joined long ago had they known of its existence.' If this was intended as a post-war call to arms, it was also tantamount to a rebuke.

Just as the hangover from the horrors of the Great War had dampened enthusiasm for something as trivial as wildlife conservation, a similar pall of indifference appears to have afflicted the nation in the aftermath of the Second World War. In 1947 the society published a very downbeat editorial in which it lamented the low membership and even the general apathy among existing members, going as far as to suggest that most did not even bother reading the *Journal*. 'We need not only funds, but active members. But what can 800 do in a world set on destruction?'

If the society was concerned about the continuing shortage of members, it appears to have derived some consolation from the knowledge that it could still count on aristocratic support. At a meeting immediately prior to the war, it had received warm words of encouragement from the Duke of Gloucester, its guest speaker on the night: 'Your society rightly believes that modern progress and the conservation of wild life in all its variety are not incompatible [...] your efforts to educate public opinion on questions of animal conservation are of the greatest possible value.' In 1946, Princesses Elizabeth and Margaret attended the society's annual general meeting in order to watch a film about Kruger National Park, which they were scheduled to visit the following year. The safari theme was to feature even more prominently in the life of the then Princess Elizabeth less than six years later, as it was while on honeymoon at the Treetops game-viewing lodge in Kenya that she heard of the death of her father King George VI, waking to find herself elevated to the throne at the age of 25. As well as receiving the crown, she also agreed to inherit her father's mantle as patron of the society, a position that she still holds well over 60 years later.

Start of the union

Less than four years after Lord Onslow's exhortations for the world to unite behind conservation, his vision became a reality. At the joint invitation of the French government and the United Nations Educational, Scientific and Cultural Organization (UNESCO), an international conference assembled at Fontainebleau on 30 September 1948 to consider the establishment of an International Union for the Protection of Nature. The impetus for this historic event came from efforts during the 1930s to establish an international conservation body, which were put on hold during the Second World War but resurrected at a conference held in 1947 at the behest of the Swiss League for the Protection of Nature, to which the

This plaque – as it helpfully tells us – was installed in November 1969 to commemorate the formation of the organisation now known as the International Union for the Conservation of Nature and Natural Resources (IUCN) during the Fontainebleau conference held in the autumn of 1948.

society had sent an observer. Comments in the *Journal* hint at a certain initial scepticism on the part of some of the society, and indeed the British government, regarding its prospects of long-term success, but the involvement of UNESCO, and Sir Julian Huxley in particular, was a significant factor in the subsequent change of heart.

As Chairman of the Wild Life Conservation Special Committee (subsequently dubbed the Huxley Committee), which was set up by the British government to assess nature conservation needs in England and Wales and led ultimately to the formation of the Nature Conservancy, Huxley had arranged for a delegation to visit the Swiss National Park. This proved to be a major catalyst for the idea of organising an international wildlife conference. Since Huxley was also, at this time, director-general of UNESCO, he became the unifying figure who helped to pull together the various strands of this bold initiative.

Once Huxley's UNESCO had indicated its willingness to help organise the 1948 conference, the society's Executive Committee appears to have embraced the idea enthusiastically. The conference was attended by representatives from 33 countries, including a British delegation led by the secretary of the society, Henry Maurice, who was appointed as one of three vice-presidents on the first executive board of the newly formed international union. The final text agreed at Fontainebleau was arrived at following revisions undertaken by a small drafting committee chaired by Dr Herbert Smith, a member of the society's council since 1938 and himself a future vice-president of the union. A total of 18 governments, seven international institutions and 107 national non-governmental

IN THE FOOTSTEPS OF GIANTS

A Fellow of the Royal Society, evolutionary biologist and leading proponent of natural selection, Sir Julian Huxley also had a lifelong interest in the wildlife of Africa and was to play an increasingly influential role in what became the Fauna Preservation Society, culminating in his election as a vice-president in 1962. He helped to set up and took charge of the UK's Nature Conservancy in 1948, and co-founded the World Wildlife Fund in 1961 with Sir Peter Scott and other luminaries. Among his other notable conservation achievements, he was instrumental in launching the Charles Darwin Foundation for the Galápagos Islands, through which a research station was established to watch over one of the most precious ecosystems known to world science. Over the following 20 years the society made a number of grants to the Charles Darwin Research Station, particularly for its *in situ* breeding programme to save giant tortoise subspecies such as the vanishingly rare Española tortoise. But Huxley's greatest contribution was arguably to help nurture the embryonic International Union for the Protection of Nature and bring it kicking and screaming into this world in his capacity as head of UNESCO in the late 1940s. When Huxley died in 1975, his obituary in the society's *Journal* referred to him as 'the doyen of British conservationists'. ■

Sir Julian Huxley, vice-president of the society from 1962 until the time of his death in February 1975, demonstrates his fascination for wildlife.

organisations put pen to paper to approve the wording of the constitution. Predictably, there was plenty of squabbling about the choice of location for the seat of the union, and the nationality of its first president, but when the dust finally settled, it was decided that all roads would lead to Brussels, while the Swiss had the consolation of knowing that their man would be the big cheese.

Location aside, the advent of the International Union for the Protection of Nature – more familiar today as the International Union for Conservation of Nature and Natural Resources (IUCN) – would have been music to the ears of the late Lord Onslow. The organisation's overall purpose chimed with his own views, elucidated shortly before his death, about the importance of a worldwide agreement aimed at conserving the natural environment. Whilst the society cannot claim credit for the Fontainebleau conference itself, or indeed the preceding Swiss initiative, there is little doubt that the earlier London conferences, and the vision of Lord Onslow, were instrumental in persuading governments and other decision makers that nature conservation warranted inclusion on their agenda. In particular, these conversations paved the way for the establishment of a global network of national parks and other protected areas, for broader endangered species protection measures, and for a wider public awareness programme advocating careful use of the valuable, but finite, natural resources on which we all depend.

The society described the establishment of the union as 'an act of faith'. It was patently obvious to all concerned that achievement of its wide-ranging objectives would be contingent on securing the appropriate level of financial support. Unless all parties were willing and able to commit themselves to a meaningful contribution, the new union was destined to remain, in the words of the society, 'an engine without fuel'. In due course this ongoing cashflow crisis would prove to be a key factor in the decision to set up a separate, bespoke fundraising entity.

One of the first official resolutions of the union, agreed at a technical conference in 1949, was to set up a so-called Survival Service Commission. Familiar today as the more appositely renamed Species Survival Commission (SSC), this science-based network has grown to include over 10,000 volunteer experts from virtually every corner of the globe, collaborating to realise IUCN's grand vision: 'A just world that values and conserves nature through positive action to reduce the loss of diversity of life on Earth.'

Portrait of Henry Gascoyne Maurice, whose death in 1950 'robbed the Fauna Society not only of its Secretary, but also one of the most active supporters the Society has yet had'.

Engine of survival

The commission's original aims were extremely ambitious, if expressed slightly more prosaically at the time. The first step was to collect all available information on threatened species; historically, the relevant data had been in short supply, largely because researchers preferred to work with abundant species, and information relating to less-common species tended to come from enthusiastic amateur observers. Step two was to verify the accuracy of the available data using tools such as questionnaires to establish past and current range and numbers, reasons for a species' decline and possible measures to mitigate threats to its survival.

The third step was to disseminate this information more widely via existing media. Data on mammals, for example, were made available through a supplement in US publications on *Extinct and Vanishing Mammals*. The fourth and final step was to work closely with governments in order to persuade them to take tangible measures to conserve these species. The society itself would become increasingly closely associated with the SSC, particularly after the sixth general assembly in 1958, at which its secretary was appointed chairman of the commission. From that date forward, much of the SSC work was done from the society's premises, on the basis that there was complete harmony of purpose. This necessitated opening an additional office, ostensibly to cope with the increased commission workload, but also no doubt to accommodate the growing mountains of paperwork that the society itself was accumulating.

Less than two years after the formation of the IUCN, the society was deprived of the services of two of its highest officials within the space of just a few months. The first of these was Henry Maurice, who had been secretary for the previous 15 years. The tributes to Maurice included some interesting factual nuggets about the man who edited the *Journal* for 14 years, including the revelation that he was primarily responsible for establishing a herd of white-tailed gnu – also known as black wildebeest – at Whipsnade Zoo. This herd contributed to the rescue of the species after the wild population in southern Africa was effectively exterminated by white settlers, who viewed the gnus as pests. Today's 'wild' white-tailed gnus are, apparently, all descended from captive individuals.

Then in November 1950, Edward Cavendish, 11th Duke of Devonshire and president of the society for the previous five years, died suddenly after a suspected heart attack, at the age of 55. His experience of public affairs and influence in official circles had served the society well, albeit for such a brief period.

The untimely death of these two senior figures paved the way for a changing of the guard, and not just in personnel terms. A retired British army officer was elected as the new secretary in June 1950, and his arrival heralded a new dawn for the society.

Above Lieutenant-Colonel Charles Leofric Boyle (seated, right) in his army days, with a Polish contingent being repatriated after the Second World War.

Below left Colonel Boyle in 1940, showing Winston Churchill the so-called 'Boche-Buster', an improvised set of heavy-duty guns.

Below right Colonel Boyle's involvement with the society pre-dates his appointment as secretary. During the latter years of his military career, he submitted numerous images of birds photographed at their nests during his time in India, several of which – including this paradise-flycatcher – were printed in the August 1942 edition of the *Journal*.

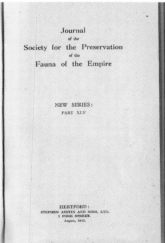

CHAPTER 3

MUTATION

'The society has lost the Empire from its name, and the empire itself is long gone, but it is in the forefront of the battle to preserve the fauna and flora of the whole world.'

Oryx, 1950

The appointment of Lieutenant-Colonel Charles Leofric Boyle as secretary of the society proved to be the catalyst for a series of momentous reforms. It was Boyle who instigated the society's first significant rebranding exercise. The organisation had already lost the word 'Wild' from its original name shortly after the end of the First World War, or perhaps temporarily mislaid it, given the lack of fanfare to accompany its almost imperceptible morphing into the infinitely more succinct Society for the Preservation of the Fauna of the Empire. This time, however, the changes amounted to a far more radical overhaul and conscious break with the past, and they were ushered in with appropriate ceremony.

Above The Empire struck off: the society's new stationery reflects the end of an era and a new phase in its evolution.

Opposite Furcifer chameleons are among the many species to have benefited from FFI support for conservation in Madagascar.

End of empire

There was unanimous approval of the proposal to change the society's name to the Fauna Preservation Society (FPS) in order to reflect its broader geographical remit and, equally importantly, though only tacitly acknowledged, to dispense with a moniker that was starting to feel uncomfortably archaic. Someone at the decisive meeting was moved to observe, 'The society has lost the Empire from its name, and the empire itself is long gone, but it is in the forefront of the battle to preserve the fauna and flora of the whole world.'

Not content with a name change for the society itself, the committee also sought approval to treat its journal to a similar makeover. Somewhat prophetically, its name was changed to *Oryx*, an animal with which the society's own name would come to be inextricably linked in the not-too-distant future.

With the benefit of hindsight, we can safely say that the Arabian oryx would have been a far more apposite emblem for the society than the beisa oryx favoured at the time by Boyle, but he could not possibly have anticipated the confusion that his infelicitous choice of species would later cause.

The cover of the rebranded journal was designed by Barbara Prescott, an artist whose illustrations would feature regularly in the early issues of *Oryx*. The intention was clear: 'We hope that the design [...] and the use of a convenient and attractive name will help to popularise our Journal and so forward the cause of wild life preservation.' In anticipation of a broader readership, it was decided to introduce a correspondence page featuring 'Letters to the Editor'. The first volume of *Oryx* appeared in 1950.

EVOLUTION OF A CONSERVATION JOURNAL

In its various incarnations, from the original *Journal of the Society for the Preservation of the Wild Fauna of the Empire*, to its more enlightened moniker of today, *Oryx – The International Journal of Conservation* has provided the bedrock on which the society has built a reputation for scientifically sound conservation.

The longest-running journal of conservation science, it supports the publication and communication aspirations of conservation practitioners and researchers worldwide.

Oryx editors past and present have all contributed to the journal's longevity and helped to cement its status as the go-to publication for authoritative conservation research, news and opinion.

1903–1913
Sir Rhys Rhys-Williams
Honorary Secretary
The first editor of the *Journal*, Rhys-Williams was one of the founding fathers of the society and had attended its inaugural meeting. His literary, administrative and research contributions provided an important practical element in the running of the organisation its first decade.

1913–1921
Major Anthony Buxton
Honorary Secretary
Son of Edward North Buxton, who called the meeting that led to the formation of the society, Major Buxton was a well-travelled field naturalist whose trips were often recorded in the *Journal*. His particular interest in deer was no doubt inspired by growing up within an arrow's arc of Epping Forest.

1921–1923
Geoffrey Dent
Honorary Secretary
Although his sojourn as editor was brief, Geoffrey Dent made a wider contribution to the society, not only as Honorary Secretary but also as Honorary Treasurer, from 1925 to 1950, and he remained a member of the Council until 1958. He also served on the Executive Committee, and by 1974 was reputedly the oldest surviving FFI member, having been elected in 1919. Dent also enjoyed a long stint (not to be confused with the more familiar little stint) as an officer and council member of the Royal Society for the Protection of Birds.

1923–1936
Charles William Hobley
Honorary Secretary
A geologist by training, Charles Hobley was Commissioner of Mines in Kenya for many years, where he developed a profound interest in both Africa and natural science. Appointed Companion of the Order of St Michael and St George in 1904, he retired to England after the First World War, where he occupied a seat on the council of the Royal Geographical Society and several other notable scientific institutions. Hobley travelled abroad in his capacity as secretary of the society and made valuable contacts, particularly in the USA, where his lectures – according to his obituary in the *Journal* – 'not only roused very real interest in the preservation of fauna but also prompted considerable donations to our funds'. He was elected vice-president of the society in 1938 and was awarded its prestigious silver medal in 1940. In retirement Hobley remained a contributor to the *Journal* and sat on the Executive Committee.

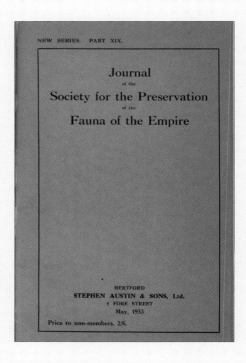

As this early example of the society's *Journal* demonstrates, the original cover was long on title, but short on visual appeal, traits that Colonel Boyle sought to rectify in 1950.

1936–1950
Henry Gascoyne Maurice
Honorary Secretary
A lawyer by profession, Henry Maurice held a succession of government roles, during which time he was created Companion of the Order of the Bath. Evidently inspired by this aquatic honour, he went on to become Fisheries Secretary at the Ministry of Agriculture and Fisheries, and served concurrently as president of the International Council for the Exploration of the Sea, reflecting his deep interest in whaling and marine conservation. In retirement, he devoted a great deal of his time to the affairs of the society, developing a broader focus for its work, which included greater emphasis on the marine issues where his expertise lay.

1950–1963
Lt. Colonel Charles Leofric Boyle
Secretary
An officer in the army for 30 years before he embarked on a second career in conservation, Colonel Boyle had always been fascinated by wildlife, particularly birds, an interest inspired by journeys undertaken in his military days. Given a new lease of life as a born-again civilian, Boyle took to his role with characteristic efficiency and energy, throwing himself into a succession of initiatives that left an indelible mark on the society and its journal (changing the name to *Oryx* was his idea). He reinforced the society's reputation for developing cutting-edge solutions and, more widely, helped to push the boundaries of accepted conservation practice. He was awarded an OBE (Order of the British Empire) in 1963 for services to conservation, not least his contribution to a parliamentary bill restricting the importation of endangered species.

One of the early volumes of the rebranded journal, complete with the new oryx logo designed by wildlife artist Barbara Prescott.

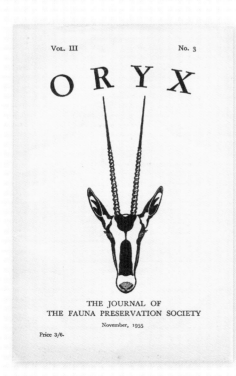

VOL. III   No. 3

O R Y X

THE JOURNAL OF
THE FAUNA PRESERVATION SOCIETY
November, 1955

Price 3/6.

1963–1982
Alice Mary Stewart (Maisie) Fitter
As editor of *Oryx*, Maisie Fitter immediately began honing its reputation as a primary source of conservation news and opinion, and in doing so built a worldwide network of conservation contacts that were of great benefit both to the society and to the journal itself. She also created and maintained the Species Survival Commission's newsletter *Species*, and was a keen member of the County Naturalists Trust movement and a founder member of the Berkshire, Buckinghamshire and Oxfordshire Naturalists Trust. Her contributions to conservation were formally recognised when she was admitted to the Species Survival Commission's Roll of Honour and decorated with the Order of the Golden Ark. As if to demonstrate how much Maisie's editing skills were missed, her 1996 obituary in *Oryx* noted that 'to win conservation battles you need accurate, succint (sic) data'.

1982–2000
Dr Jacqui Morris
Jacqui Morris initiated and presided over a number of significant changes during her 18 years as editor of *Oryx*, including major transitions in both content and design. She appointed the journal's first editorial board, oversaw three redesigns of the journal, introduced peer reviewing for submitted papers, increased its frequency of publication to a quarterly schedule and negotiated a publishing agreement with Blackwell Scientific Publications. She also introduced a separate members' newsletter, *Fauna & Flora News*, in order to differentiate society-related information from the academic content of the journal.

2000–2001
Camilla Erskine
During her brief tenure Camilla Erskine oversaw – in consultation with senior editors – the development of the

Code of Conduct for contributors to the journal and made arrangements for *Oryx* to be published by Cambridge University Press. She also increased the coverage of plant conservation, and of the social context within which conservation operates.

2001–present
Dr Martin Fisher
Martin Fisher has edited the journal since February 2001. During this time he has overseen the transition to Cambridge University Press, a redesign of the journal's cover and format, a doubling of the number of articles in each issue, publication of the centenary issue and the centenary archive for 1903–2003, the development of freely available, online-only appendices on the journal's website, the initiation of Writing for Conservation workshops, and the publication of the *Graphics for Conservation* and *Writing for Conservation* manuals. In 2011 he was awarded the Silver Medal of the Zoological Society of London for contributions to the understanding and appreciation of zoology. ■

A cross section of *Oryx* covers spanning 50 years, several rebrands and a multitude of conservation topics.

Journal of the
Fauna Preservation
Society
August 1965

Britain and the Beasts of Prey

Catching White Rhino

Conservation in Hong Kong

Plight of the Whales

A Future for Borneo's Wildlife?

Journal of the
Fauna Preservation
Society
October 1975

Whales: a Dance of Death

Elephant Rescue

Turtles of the Indian Ocean

Guanaco in Peru

The Grass Snake in Britain

Fauna and Flora
Preservation Society
February 1982

What Hope for the Right Whales?

Giant Golden Mole

Logging on Slopes Kills

Otters in Greece

How Many Elephants Killed for Ivory?

Volume XVII   July 1983

Fauna & Flora
Preservation Society **Oryx**

Volume 25 October 1991

Volume 27   Number 4   October 1993

1903–1993
Ninety years of
conservation

Oryx

Volume 33 Number 2 | April 1997

The International Journal of Conservation

Oryx

www.oryxthejournal.org

Published for
Fauna & Flora International   January 2016 · Volume 50 · Number 1

Fall, resurrection & uncertainty
An Arabian tale

Conservation of & beyond the oceans
Enforcement & compliance
Reassessment of protection targets
Seahorse trade & CITES

Hunting, poaching & bushmeat
Effect of ammunition price
Vulnerable white-lipped peccary
People & predators share wild meat
Hunting pressure on large birds
Can bushmeat trade be regulated?
Elephant poaching in Mozambique

Continuing mortality of vultures
Illegal use of veterinary medicines

Irruption interrupted
Eradication of wild turkeys

Newly discovered wildlife migration
Burchell's zebra in Botswana

The International Journal of Conservation

Oryx

www.oryxthejournal.org

Published for
Fauna & Flora International   April 2017 · Volume 51 · Number 2

Positive shifting baselines
The importance of optimism

Hippopotamus conservation
Good news from north-central Africa
Preventing crop raiding in Guinea-Bissau
Endangered pygmy hippopotamus

Influence of protected areas
Fish in a large tropical river

A stand against illegal wildlife trade
Pangolin conservation in Zimbabwe

Endangered Chacoan peccary
Broader distribution than formerly known

Multiple methods increase mammal detection
Working with volunteers

Above left December 1950 marked the appearance of the society's first official Christmas card, which featured a scimitar-horned oryx painted by wildlife artist Barbara Prescott specifically for FPS.

Above right Photograph of Woburn Park published in *The Times* in 1951, advertising the fact that, courtesy of the Duke of Bedford, the grounds were open to the public and had been made available to promote the work of the society.

The use of other printed materials to promote conservation in general, and FPS in particular, also became more prevalent during this period. A marketing pamphlet entitled *Going, Going, Gone* was redesigned and reissued. In one of the earliest examples of the society's forays into the world of merchandising, it began selling packs of 12 postcards depicting wildlife protected by national parks. The cards bore a small oryx head alongside the FPS name.

In the following year, the society pulled off a far more significant promotional coup. The 1951 Festival of Britain was organised by the government to move the country beyond post-war introspection and celebrate Britain's contribution to scientific, technological, architectural and artistic progress. As part of this national exhibition, the 12th Duke of Bedford announced that he would open his estate, Woburn Abbey, to the public for a week in conjunction with FPS.

Fans across the water

In addition to raising its profile on the home front, the society's work was also arousing interest well beyond its own shores. In 1951, Walt Disney himself wrote to FPS to express his

empathy with, and support for, the work of the society. Half a century later, that moral support would turn into tangible support, in the shape of vital funding from the Disney Foundation (now the Disney Conservation Fund) which provided financial assistance to the Antiguan racer project in 1999–2000 and, in the following year, helped to fund FFI's efforts to safeguard the recently discovered population of Siamese crocodiles in Cambodia's Cardamom Mountains.

Disney was not the only American who admired FPS from across the water. One of its most generous benefactors in the 1950s was Willard Van Name, who had already demonstrated his confidence in the society's activities with a wartime donation. Considered a maverick figure at the American museum where he worked, Van Name was a controversial figure on his own side of the pond. At one stage, adamant that gun companies were controlling the Audubon Association, the putative bird conservation society that counted him as a member, Van Name made himself extremely unpopular after he determined to reform it from within. He certainly doesn't receive a particularly sympathetic hearing from Stephen R. Fox, author of *The American Conservation Movement: John Muir and His Legacy*, in which he is described as someone whom conservationists 'regarded as a quixotic, truculent curiosity', and is depicted as 'a monastic bachelor whose love for wild creatures compensated for his distrust of human beings'. That distrust wasn't universal, evidently. Van Name had sufficient faith in FPS to bestow substantial gifts on the society, beginning with $1,200 and $2,000 in 1952 and 1953 respectively, and culminating in what was, in 1955, an eye-wateringly large donation of $10,000. This says as much about the real impact that FPS was perceived to be having on wildlife conservation as it does about Van Name's own generosity. Indeed, one of the letters accompanying these donations reveals that his continued support was due 'to my interest in African fauna and to my realisation that the Fauna Preservation Society is actually accomplishing important work in saving it'. This statement alone undermines the book's claim that 'he spent most of his income on militant conservation projects initiated – and usually conducted – solely by himself'. Still, America's loss was the society's gain.

At the same time as it was receiving welcome contributions to its own coffers courtesy of wealthy donors like Van Name, FPS was itself providing vital support to other societies, organisations and individuals. In 1950, correspondence between the society's president and the governor of then Nyasaland led to the establishment of a protected area at Mijeti Hill, in modern-day southern Malawi. FPS provided an annual grant to the Nyasaland Fauna Preservation Society, formed in 1947, which enabled it to pay the wages of a ranger recruited to enforce the hunting ban at Mijeti. The success of this initiative led to the area being declared an official game reserve. FPS continued to support local efforts to preserve the integrity of a sanctuary that had been established specifically to protect the threatened nyala antelope, but which was in danger of being undermined by a proposal to run a road through the heart of the reserve. This work was just one part of a fruitful ongoing collaboration with a certain G.D. Hayes, a member of the society since 1945 and the eventual chairman of the Nyasaland Fauna Preservation Society. Numerous non-shooting areas were created through the joint efforts of the two societies, and the link between them remains strong to this day, in their current incarnations as FFI and the Wildlife and Environmental Society of Malawi.

During this period there were also several reports in *Oryx* relating to FPS support for the Wild Life Protection Society of Rhodesia, including a donation that enabled it to purchase land for the purpose of establishing a sanctuary to protect the declining population of red lechwe in Northern Rhodesia, as it was then known. As we shall see, this part of Africa was also destined to provide the backdrop for a timely FPS intervention following a local cry for help.

Subcontinent support

The influence of FPS continued to extend well beyond its African roots, however. There is a record of the society providing financial support in the early 1950s for an

individual's efforts to establish a National Trust for Ceylon. Later in that decade, Salim Ali, world-famous ornithologist and then editor of the Bombay Natural History Society's journal, paid tribute to the key role played by FPS member Lieutenant-Colonel R.W. Burton, whose 'missionary zeal for conservation [and] ceaseless demand for action' were evidently instrumental in persuading the Indian government to constitute the Indian Board for Wild Life.

The board's first chairman was no less a figure than Colonel His Highness Maharaja Sri Sir Jayachamarajendra Wadiyar Bahadur, Maharaja of Mysore, GCB, GCSI. Usually referred to by his shorter title in the interests of good timekeeping at board meetings, the (25th and last) Maharaja of Mysore was also a close associate of the society. His subsequent election as an FPS vice-president further strengthened the bonds between the society and its wildlife ambassadors in India, and no doubt precipitated a frenzied scramble to order new headed notepaper that would be wide enough to accommodate his official title when the relevant minutes were published.

Partnership and international co-operation were all the rage, as the president's report of his visit to Canada and the USA in the summer of 1952 was at pains to emphasise: 'I believe these personal contacts are invaluable and help to smooth the way for the innumerable international problems which are bound to crop up in endeavouring to further the aims of our society and the preservation and conservation of nature as a whole.'

Parks central

Personal contacts notwithstanding, the new era of collaboration to tackle global conservation issues signalled by the launch of IUCN presented its own set of challenges. Among the inevitable teething problems was the difficulty in reconciling the respective agendas, priorities and viewpoints of all the parties that had signed up to the constitution. As far as FPS was concerned, however, protected areas had to be the cornerstone of any coherent conservation policy, and the national park concept remained very much at the forefront of its thinking.

The society's single-minded pursuit of this goal was vindicated when Serengeti National Park was established in 1951 in what is now Tanzania. This wildlife-rich landscape had been among the areas recommended for full national park status in the wake of Colonel Stevenson-Hamilton's mission to East Africa between the wars to assess the need

In 1952, FPS was among the influential backers of a concerted effort to save the Caribbean flamingo, national bird of the Bahamas, from local extinction. This culminated in the formation of the delightfully named Society for the Protection of the Flamingo, with retired antiques dealer, amateur naturalist and FPS member Arthur Vernay at the helm. The now-thriving population of flamingos in the Bahamas numbers over 50,000 birds and is the largest colony in the entire Caribbean. To this day, it continues to be protected by wardens from that same society, and has featured on numerous environmental awareness materials, including this colourful poster produced to instil increased respect for the wider biodiversity of the islands.

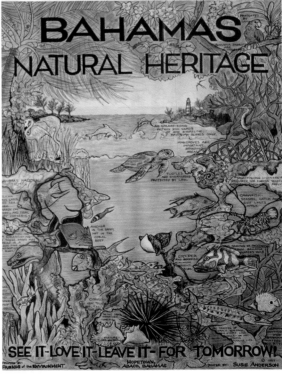

for protected areas in that corner of the then empire. Unfortunately, the Serengeti's hard-won status as a protected area did not prevent it coming under constant pressure throughout the first decade of its existence, and the society was very much in the vanguard of the fight to combat the threats to the national park's integrity during this crucial period.

To paraphrase the cliché about London buses, you wait decades for one national park, then three come along at once. Hot on the heels of the glad tidings from the Serengeti in 1951 came the news that the Ugandan authorities had seen fit to establish Murchison Falls National Park and Kazinga National Park (renamed Queen Elizabeth National Park two years later, following a royal visit). The British administration in Uganda had been under pressure, not least from society officials, to fulfil its share of the wildlife conservation obligations agreed at the London Conference in 1933, but had been largely preoccupied with protecting colonial cattle from the scourge of rinderpest, a devastating disease which wild ungulates were helping to spread.

In 1952, with public opinion more favourable to wildlife, the necessary legislative machinery was set in motion in the shape of the National Parks Act of Uganda, which was the first step on the path to establishing a national park system. This was subsequently described in the society's journal as 'the outstanding event of 1952', although it is safe to assume that the death of King George VI, the society's patron, had a more cataclysmic impact on the rest of the world.

Many of the vast tracts of African savannah that still exist today owe their survival to the foresight of the early conservationists who fought to protect the Serengeti and other vital havens for some of the continent's most charismatic wildlife.

Safeguarding the Serengeti

The value of international co-operation was perfectly illustrated in 1956 when FPS joined forces with a handful of influential US conservation organisations and took concerted action to save Serengeti National Park from being partitioned. IUCN's first staff ecologist, Lee Talbot, visited Tanganyika, where he obtained a *sub rosa* copy of the White Paper detailing the government's plans to dismantle the park. He also conducted a brief survey of the entire park. After Talbot had organised a petition, signed by the majority of US conservation organisations, this joint lobby petitioned the Colonial Secretary and urged the authorities to delay any decision until experts could assess the full ecological ramifications. The IUCN Survival Committee tabled a resolution at its Edinburgh conference requesting the Tanganyikan government to appoint a Serengeti Committee, supported by a qualified ecologist and scientific team provided by FPS 'having in mind the disastrous effects in many parts of the world of adopting land-use policies without sufficient consideration of ecological factors'. A comprehensive ecological survey was proposed, commissioned and financed by the society. One of the first examples of the rigorous biodiversity assessments for which FFI and its partners have become renowned, the 1956 survey spawned a groundbreaking report on the ecosystem of the Serengeti Plains. The man who conducted that survey was W.H. Pearsall, a vice-president of the society. His report, which was approved by FPS before submission to the Serengeti Committee, is widely credited with having ensured that this jewel in the crown of modern-day Tanzania's protected areas survived intact.

Responding to the threats to the integrity of the Serengeti, the society's secretary, Colonel Boyle, was moved to publish a lengthy diatribe in *Oryx*, entitled 'What of the Serengeti?', in which he condemned the myopia of the authors of the relevant White Paper who were proposing the break-up of this flagship national park. The article reflects changing times and attitudes, asserting that the traditional view of Homo sapiens as the subjugator of nature had already been superseded by a deeper awareness of our dependence on the natural world: 'Man is a part of nature and is the only animal which can significantly modify its environment. If he destroys it, he himself has no future.'

In this same article, in a classic example of the enlightened, forward-thinking approach that has characterised FFI since its formation, Boyle revealed himself to be a man ahead of his time. Speculating about possible solutions to the overgrazing caused by the presence of inordinate numbers of domestic livestock well beyond the number required to

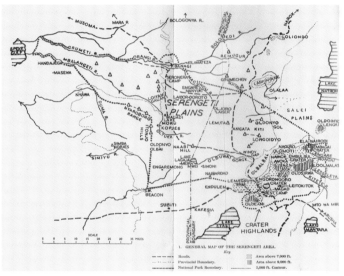

Lee Talbot, pictured here with his wife, Martha, enjoys a close encounter with a wildebeest during a 1960 survey to map the wildlife of the Serengeti.

fulfil the Masai's economic needs, he wondered whether they might somehow be persuaded to reduce livestock numbers. 'Is this suggestion too visionary? Could not the men of the Masai be appointed "Guardians of the Game" throughout Masailand and be allowed a considerable share of whatever gain came to the country through the world-wide interest in African animals?' In fairness to Edward North Buxton, this was not an entirely original idea. The founding father of FFI had already alluded to the possibility of using the Masai as guards in his 1902 book. But Boyle's suggestion is part of a more coherent overall vision, and demonstrates that he is already seeing the bigger, post-colonial picture. 'Is there a chance now to direct change into ways useful to the conservation of nature, for the benefit not only of the Masai but of the whole of mankind?'

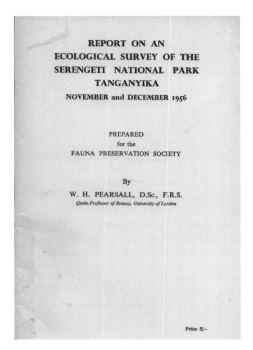

REPORT ON AN
ECOLOGICAL SURVEY OF THE
SERENGETI NATIONAL PARK
TANGANYIKA
NOVEMBER and DECEMBER 1956

PREPARED
for the
FAUNA PRESERVATION SOCIETY

By

W. H. PEARSALL, D.Sc., F.R.S.
Quain Professor of Botany, University of London

Price 5/-

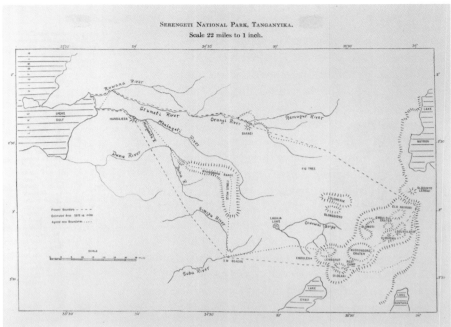

This groundbreaking report by William (W.H.) Pearsall, commissioned and financed by FPS, led directly to the creation of the Serengeti National Park and the Ngorongoro Conservation Area.

The pressure applied to the Tanganyikan authorities by FPS and its US counterparts ultimately paid off. The Serengeti Committee's recommendations, finally published in November 1957, bore a remarkable resemblance to those in Pearsall's original report. The overall protected area was expanded, resulting in a net gain for the national park. The only drawback was the fact that the redrawn boundaries excluded Ngorongoro. This glaring omission was later rectified through the creation of a separate Ngorongoro Conservation Area, but not without a great deal of wrangling.

Whilst the need for national parks dominated the global conservation agenda, the early IUCN meetings were already characterised by the breadth of issues under discussion. The sole UK representative at the 1952 gathering in Venezuela was a close friend of the society, Miss P. Barclay-Smith, whose name sounds as though it has been plucked straight from the pages of a John Betjeman anthology. The choice of venue may have deterred the society from sending its own representative, but it certainly had the desired effect of heightening interest in conservation on the South American continent.

Many of the resolutions passed at this conference related to themes that would later become central planks of the society's work. Approval of the principle of *ex situ* conservation – whereby captive breeding of endangered species outside their natural habitat could contribute to their long-term survival – prefigured the now-celebrated FPS initiative to save the Arabian oryx from extinction.

Recommended measures to protect the flora and fauna confined to small islands, particularly in the Caribbean, set the stage for FFI's more recent programmes on behalf of critically endangered endemic species such as the Antiguan racer. One key resolution, anticipating the later convention that would address the need to introduce more effective measures against the illegal wildlife trade, proposed that the importation of animals illegally taken in their country of origin should be prohibited in all other countries.

Home affairs

The spirit of co-operation inherent in the IUCN concept was also evident back home. FPS held a joint meeting with the Royal Society for the Protection of Birds (RSPB) in 1953 to commemorate the society's fiftieth anniversary. This eagerness to rub shoulders with the RSPB was one manifestation of the society's determination to become more active on the domestic front, in order to plug some of the perceived gaps in British wildlife conservation. Prior to the 1950s, the existence of the Society for the Promotion of Nature Reserves (SPNR) had, at

least in theory, precluded the need for FPS to dip its toes into the murky waters of UK conservation. In truth, SPNR could be euphemistically described as a low-profile organisation, despite its being on the receiving end of a chunky £50,000 donation from Lord Rothschild. A less charitable view might be that it appeared to behave like an elite dining club whose interest in British wildlife was restricted to the species that its few members consumed at high table. This society only stirred into action after a number of English counties, frustrated at the lack of progress, independently set up their own wildlife trusts, which SPNR then deigned to oversee.

At the suggestion of the society's newly elected vice-president, Richard Fitter, a man who would become a pivotal figure in the long-term evolution of FPS, it was agreed that all future issues of *Oryx* would include a new section dedicated specifically to native mammals. As Fitter eloquently puts it in his introductory note to the new feature: 'The study of mammals in Great Britain has been greatly handicapped by the lack of a specialist journal. This deficiency it is now hoped to remedy by publishing in *Oryx* a regular section devoted to the natural history and conservation of British mammals.' This initiative coincided with the formation, independently, of the Mammal Society, which ultimately prospered and began publishing its own bulletin, enabling FPS to discontinue the special section in *Oryx*.

Mammals were not the only beneficiaries of the society's increasing involvement in UK conservation. Consultations

Above left Advertisements for the FPS tie, emblazoned with its iconic oryx design, became a regular feature in the pages of the society's journal.

Above right An original example of the highly coveted gold oryx brooch, which has since been reproduced by FFI and today serves as a token of thanks to its most generous benefactors.

with the British Herpetological Society led FPS to consider the need to protect native species including the common frog, natterjack toad, smooth snake and sand lizard. It is interesting to note the absence, at this stage, of any reference to the other native snakes, or newt species, but this early concern for British reptiles and amphibians anticipates the later, more concerted, action that the society was to take on their behalf.

One of the motivating factors behind the society's attempts to increase its profile at home in the UK was its growing recognition of the need to raise awareness among the wider British public and mobilise more support for its global conservation efforts. The education theme runs like a continuous thread through the *Oryx* journals during this period, and it is clear that FPS viewed environmental education as a key plank in its long-term conservation strategy. Towards the end of the decade the society recruited the well-known travel writer John Hillaby as a part-time public relations officer. By then, Hillaby had already written an article for *The Guardian* entitled 'Life in the shadow of the dodo', which coincided with the release of the society's own propaganda pamphlet, authored by the same journalist.

Pulling power

Several years earlier, in 1955, FPS vice-president Mervyn Cowie, founder and first director of the Royal National Parks of Kenya, had embarked on a highly productive UK-wide lecture tour – which included the Royal Festival Hall, filled to capacity – in order to promote the cause of wildlife conservation in Africa and elsewhere. The success of this venture, arguably the first of its kind, was a tribute to Cowie's staying power, as well as his gifts of oratory, but it also owed something to the involvement of a certain Peter Scott, another titanic figure in the story of conservation and whose presence would loom larger in FPS affairs in the coming years. It was Scott, in his capacity as the presenter of the natural history series *Look*, who introduced two half-hour BBC television broadcasts by Cowie and, by association, was seen to endorse the society's message. After completion of the tour, courtesy of Scott's pulling power, Cowie was granted an audience with the Secretary of State for the Colonies and was able to convey his message, and that of the society, face to face. In his analysis of the UK tour's impact, Cowie generously acknowledged the broadcaster's role: 'The fame and popularity of Peter Scott himself [...] was in itself a factor of the greatest importance.' This would prove to be the start of one of the most productive associations in the society's history.

Gratifying though it was to discover that audiences were receptive to the conservation message that FPS and others were keen to promulgate, it was equally clear that wholehearted approval was merely the starting point. Given the sheer scale of the task that the global conservation community had set itself, footing the bill was proving more problematic than winning over hearts and minds. IUCN was recognised as the main international link in all matters concerned with nature conservation, but its workload continued to outweigh its financial resources. As the new decade began, it was obvious that a shortage of money was severely hampering the union's development.

Stolan idea

The World Wildlife Fund was founded specifically as a fundraising vehicle to tackle this very problem head on. Although the idea is widely credited to a triumvirate of conservation heavyweights, its origins can be traced back to a piece of correspondence sparked by a series of newspaper articles on the conservation crisis in Africa, written by Julian Huxley. The first of these appeared in *The Observer* in November 1960. The measured language used to describe the parlous state of Africa's wildlife incurred the wrath of one reader, a Czech refugee, who wrote to Huxley lamenting this typically English use of elegant understatement. What they needed, according to an animated Victor Stolan, was a little less conversation and a little more action. Specifically, he proposed setting up a funding mechanism aimed at 'accumulating some millions of pounds without mobilising commissions, committees etc. as there is no time for Victorian procedure'. Stolan's letter struck a chord with Huxley, who introduced him to the 'omnipresent and indefatigably vigorous' Max Nicholson, environmentalist, ornithologist and director-general of Britain's Nature Conservancy. Nicholson met Stolan, incorporated some of his inspired ideas into a draft paper entitled *How to Save the World's Wildlife*, invited Huxley and Peter Scott on board to help refine this document, and then appears to have gradually shut out the unsung Czech hero of the piece, dismissing him as 'too much the naive enthusiast'.

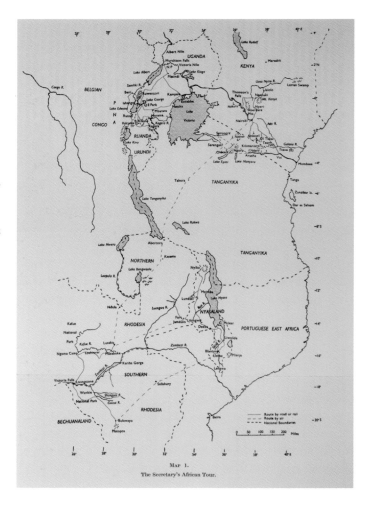

MAP 1.
The Secretary's African Tour.

Map of Colonel Boyle's 1959 Africa tour, which brought home to the society the magnitude of their task and the urgent need to raise additional funds.

HUXLEY IN AFRICA

Millions of wild animals have already disappeared from Africa in this century. Does the wild life of the continent now face extinction—threatened by increases in population and the growth of industry in the emergent nations? What, if anything, can be done to safeguard it?

Sir Julian Huxley has spent several months in Africa investigating the problem for Unesco. In this series of articles, reprinted from The Observer and illustrated with his own photographs, he reports on his findings.

PUBLISHED by THE OBSERVER
and sent to you by the Fauna Preservation Society, c/o Zoological Society of London, Regents Park, N.W.1.

502.3 (6)
HUX

3

WILD LIFE AS A WORLD ASSET

This series of articles by Sir Julian Huxley, published in *The Observer*, provided the catalyst for the establishment of the fundraising vehicle that has since metamorphosed into the Worldwide Fund for Nature.

Affectionately referred to by Scott as 'the community chest' for international wildlife conservation in general and IUCN in particular, the World Wildlife Fund was officially launched in late 1961, with Scott as its first chairman and Prince Bernhard of the Netherlands as president. FPS collaborated with the fund from its very inception. The British National Appeal, which later morphed into WWF UK, was the first such fund to be established, and a substantial proportion of its early trustees were FPS officers and council members. WWF has since grown into one of the world's largest non-governmental charities and is now a household name with five million members globally.

The problem of funding was also uppermost in the minds of officials within FPS itself. An African tour undertaken in 1959 by the secretary, Colonel Boyle, had rammed home the point. It wasn't enough to persuade people that wildlife needs and human interests were compatible. With so many urgent and equally worthy causes competing for the society's attention, lack of finance was potentially the biggest stumbling block: 'We wish we could do these things but can't afford them.' Fortunately, there will always be conservation causes that capture the public imagination and elicit generous support. One of these was the heroic FPS rescue mission that helped to avert ecological disaster on the Zambezi River.

Here comes the flood

Although it is now well over half a century since its creation, Lake Kariba remains the world's largest artificial lake and reservoir, four times larger in volume than the controversial Three Gorges Dam. It was filled over a five-year period, beginning in late 1958, following completion of the hydroelectric dam, which was constructed in order to generate additional electricity for Zambia and Zimbabwe (in those days, Northern and Southern Rhodesia respectively). The vast Kariba Gorge through which the Zambezi River flowed was completely flooded, displacing some 50,000 Tonga tribesmen and threatening the survival of the area's wildlife. The closing of the two ports through which the whole volume of the Zambezi was then flowing signalled the beginning of what an *Oryx* article described as 'the greatest environmental upset ever to befall a population of animals and birds within the African continent, in the memory of man'.

Increasingly frustrated by the inertia of its own government, and concerned about the apparent lack of any meaningful rescue plan for the threatened wildlife, the Northern Rhodesian Game Preservation and Hunting Association decided to enlist the help of FPS. On 19 March 1959 the society launched a public appeal to raise £10,000

The good ship *Erica*, which acted as a kind of floating mission control for Operation Noah but doubled as a mid-lake holding pen for wildlife that couldn't be shipped to shore immediately.

in order to save the animals marooned on islands of varied but ever-decreasing size amid the rising waters at Kariba. The fund was intended to provide and operate rescue units, including boats capable of translocating large volumes of wildlife, until such time as the new lake had reached its full extent – projected to be some 5,500 square kilometres, an area almost the size of the Indonesian island of Bali.

Ark angels

The London press conference generated a huge amount of publicity both at home and abroad, with national and local newspapers highlighting the plight of the stranded animals. The story evidently touched a nerve among the general public; donations soon began – appropriately enough – to flood in, enabling the purchase of boats, outboard motors, camping equipment and medical supplies essential to the long-term success of the rescue operation. Operation Noah, as it was inevitably dubbed, was quickly afloat and the serious rescue work began in earnest in April 1959. Within just five months the £10,000 target figure was

reached, and the advertisement withdrawn, but in true Sorceror's Apprentice fashion the money continued to flow in. These donations enabled FPS to fund construction of a rescue ship, *Erica*. Her chief function was to act as the parent ship from which other, smaller boats could operate, but she also had a large space aboard that could serve as temporary quarters for rescued animals.

By all accounts the rescue work was laborious, chaotic and hazardous, with teams exposed to injuries inflicted by captured animals as well as the dangers presented by opportunistic crocodiles in the water and an unprecedented concentration of venomous snakes on the dwindling landmasses. Looking back from our privileged viewpoint here in the twenty-first century, with its sophisticated gadgetry and conservation know-how, it is easy to underestimate the technical difficulties and potential pitfalls that the rescuers would have had to overcome. The fictional, Booker Prize-winning *Life of Pi* – in which a shipwrecked youth finds himself sharing a lifeboat with a 450-pound Bengal tiger and other seriously traumatised wild animals – no longer seems like such a remarkable feat of the imagination once you know the gory details of Operation Noah.

LADY OF THE LAKE

The Operation Noah rescue ship was named in honour of Erica Critchley, the fearlessly outspoken and indefatigable champion of wildlife conservation whose cry for help FPS had answered. Erica and her husband Ron were co-founders in 1953 of the then fledgling association that survives to this day as the Wildlife and Environmental Conservation Society of Zambia. It was her forthright criticism of government apathy towards the plight of its wildlife that rocked the boat sufficiently to bring about urgently needed reforms. The Critchleys went on to establish Blue Lagoon National Park, which remains a vital haven for black lechwe and other Zambian wildlife in the Kafue Flats. Her most enduring legacy, however, was in the shape of school camps and the renowned children's clubs, formed in 1972 and still thriving over 40 years later. The so-called Chongololo Clubs were instrumental in instilling in the younger generation an appreciation of their country's natural heritage, a contribution acknowledged by President Kaunda, who declared, 'Let what she stood for not be forgotten by Zambia – especially its youth.' ∎

Undeterred by the magnitude of their task, the teams rose to this seemingly insurmountable logistical challenge, learning by trial and error and devising novel techniques that included capturing leaping impala in game nets and extricating stranded hyraxes from their treetop refuges with the aid of gravity and a landing net. Where possible, larger mammals were driven into the water and induced to swim towards the mainland. Smaller animals were captured and transported by boat. In the interests of self-preservation, the rescuers took the sensible decision to let big cats and buffalo fend for themselves. Where elephants were concerned, direct intervention was a last resort, sanctioned only when these accomplished swimmers were reluctant to abandon the shrinking islands.

The black rhino population presented a different problem entirely. In stark contrast to their Asian cousins, African rhinos are not noted for their aquatic prowess. Early attempts to capture or drive them into the water proved utterly ineffectual, and succeeded merely in putting man and beast in an equally foul temper. Irascible and immoveable, the terrestrial heavyweights clung stubbornly to their doomed postage stamps of land. Evidently, a novel approach was needed.

Black rhino rafting

The difficulty of capturing and handling wild animals had long been acknowledged as a major headache for wildlife conservation, but it had arguably never manifested itself in such stark terms before the flooding of Kariba Gorge. Serendipitously, FPS had recently been funding research into new immobilisation techniques involving the use of more sophisticated tranquilliser guns. Dutch-born Dr Toni Harthoorn, who had studied veterinary medicine in London before emigrating to Africa, was the man behind this revolutionary method of incapacitating large mammals. Since tests had been successfully conducted in Uganda on zebra and various large antelope species, it was a relatively small step, geographically and zoologically, to apply the same procedure to Kariba's stranded black rhinos, and this was duly done in May 1960. The preparations were meticulous and ingenious; a robust sledge was improvised, large enough to bear the weight of a rhino, as well as a giant raft that floated on eighteen 44-gallon petrol drums and was capable of withstanding the 12-mile journey to the mainland without breaking up. The tranquilliser darts, basically flying syringes, were due to be fired from a carbon-dioxide-powered gun, but in practice most of them

Opposite (Clockwise from top left) A sedated rhino is examined while its feet are being securely tethered; the tranquilliser dart is removed from the prostrate pachyderm; approximately two dozen grown men competing for first prize in the rhino-rolling contest.

Above The recumbent rhino on the makeshift raft used to transport it across the submerged savannah swallowed by the rising waters of Lake Kariba.

Fortunately, not all the animals in Kariba Gorge were as difficult to rescue as a one-tonne black rhinoceros.

ended up being propelled by a kind of makeshift crossbow. The first rhino to be captured and moved showed its gratitude in characteristically belligerent fashion as soon as the effects of the anaesthetic had worn off, reportedly chasing its rescuers up trees and into the water. Seven further rhinos were subsequently rescued using this drug-immobilisation method.

The entire episode was immortalised in a humorous parody of an epic poem, published in *Punch* magazine. 'How the rhino got the hump', by Richard Usborne, includes the memorable description of a tranquilliser shot as a 'subpachydermitous Mickey Finn'.

The Kariba rhino translocation exercise was a resounding success in its own right. Equally importantly, it demonstrated what could be achieved through a combination of careful planning and sophisticated equipment, and paved the way for the increasingly ambitious translocation initiatives that would be undertaken in future. As we shall see later, this reached its apogee in 2009, with FFI's improbable intercontinental airlift of the world's last-known breeding

population of northern white rhinos from a Czech zoo to the Kenyan grasslands.

Operation Noah unfolded like an enthralling soap opera, with its fair share of highs and lows, individual triumphs and tragedies and comedy moments. Lasting almost five years and covering around 500 islands, the campaign succeeded in rescuing over 6,000 animals, from aardvarks to zebras, though not necessarily in alphabetical order. Most of these were relocated into the area that would later become Matusadona National Park where, appositely, FFI is now poised to re-engage in landscape conservation work some six decades later. The Dunkirk spirit that characterised the rescue activities struck a chord with the British public and, indeed, the international community, a point not lost on FPS. 'The tragedy of Kariba may help in the future to focus public attention on the many other conservation problems which are waiting to be solved.'

Political pressure

Whilst it kept one eye on the local drama being played out at Kariba, the society was determined to remain focused on the broader African canvas. In May 1960, a deputation from FPS met the Secretary of State for the Colonies, Iain Macleod, to lobby for formal recognition of the importance of African wildlife conservation. The rationale was presented as a threefold justification. Firstly, there was a socio-cultural need to protect the land itself, given that people and wildlife depended on it in equal measure, 'In the set of ecological conditions presented in a large part of Africa, care of the animals and their habitat IS primarily care for the people.' Secondly, there was an economic argument for conserving wild animals, in that they offered a reliable and potentially sustainable source of food in areas where domestic animals simply could not survive. Thirdly, the burgeoning and highly lucrative tourist trade represented a valuable long-term source of income for the local communities.

The society petitioned the government to acknowledge the economic value of wildlife, to formulate scientific policy that took full account of nature conservation in African territories, and to commit financial support to anti-poaching and environmental education initiatives among the local communities. It also mooted the idea of organising a meeting with post-independence African leaders in order to achieve a declaration in principle on their part in support of wildlife conservation. Questions subsequently asked in parliament on behalf of FPS elicited a favourable response. 'I am glad of this opportunity to reaffirm Her Majesty's Government's concern for wildlife in Africa.'

At the same time as FPS was leaning on the British government to take conservation more seriously, it was working on a parallel initiative with IUCN. From its new home in Switzerland, the union was in the process of putting together the so-called Africa Special Project, an ambitious three-year programme intended to inform and influence public opinion regarding the importance of water, soil, vegetation and wildlife conservation for all African countries. The society decided to devote a significant chunk of its capital resources to the project, describing it as 'the most farsighted and hopeful recent step towards the conservation of the wild life of Africa'. The first stage, supported by a contribution from FPS, was a whistle-stop tour of West, East and Central Africa to discuss principles and practices with African movers and shakers in 16 countries. Stage two of the process was to gather the relevant people under one roof and hammer out some kind of formal agreement about the way forward. The final, implementation stage, scheduled to commence in late 1961, was to involve commissioning an ecologist and an expert in agriculture, livestock and forestry to work with governments in Africa, helping them to develop wildlife resources in ways consistent with the agreed recommendations. Here again, FPS footed the bill for an annual grant, payable for a maximum of five years, which cumulatively amounted to the equivalent of around £40,000 today.

The Arusha manifesto

The international wildlife conference was held in September 1961 at Arusha, in then Tanganyika. Officially entitled the Symposium of Conservation of Nature and Natural Resources in Modern African States, it is popularly referred to simply as the Arusha Conference, in the interests of saving time and paper. Widely regarded as the most important gathering of conservationists and ecologists ever held in Africa, and possibly anywhere else for that matter, the conference owed much of its success to the contribution, financial and otherwise, of FPS. In addition to a substantial grant towards the cost of the survey that preceded Arusha, the society also provided funds that enabled 12 African representatives to attend the conference and one of the post-conference tours. Among the great and the good who jetted in from the non-African nations with a vested interest in the continent were FPS president Lord Willingdon, director-general of the Nature Conservancy of Great Britain Max Nicholson, and UNESCO's Sir Julian Huxley, shortly to

become a vice-president of FPS. Other representatives of the society included long-time FPS council members Professor W.H. Pearsall, author of the original report confirming the urgent need for national parks, and Dr Frank Fraser Darling, vice-president of the Conservation Foundation of New York (which was absorbed into WWF in 1990). The Arusha manifesto, hailed as a 'landmark for Africa', was formally communicated by Julius Nyerere, the newly independent Tanganyika's first prime minister. 'The survival of our wildlife is a matter of grave concern to all of us in Africa. These wild creatures amid the wild places they inhabit are not only important as a source of wonder and inspiration, but are an integral part of our natural resources and of our future livelihood and well-being.'

Arusha came at a crucial juncture for African wildlife. The need for urgent action had been evident to all the conference delegates during their visits to reserves. Overgrazing, deforestation and other damaging forms of human intrusion pointed to a desperate need for more sustainable management of Africa's natural resources. In his closing remarks to the conference, the society's president, Lord Willingdon, revealed that FPS had really pushed the boat out, or as he euphemistically put it 'dipped somewhat extensively into its accumulated funds', on the basis that this initiative might be the last chance to avert disaster. The society's decision to commit so much time and money to Arusha and its aftermath proved to be an astute move. A later, 1965 report on the success of the protected area at Ngorongoro came to be seen as sufficient vindication in itself. Referring to the enlightened approach of the Tanzanian government and other stakeholders, which contributed to the success of Ngorongoro in particular and African wildlife conservation in general, it identified the conference as 'probably the greatest single factor in developing this attitude'.

Double-barrelled diplomacy

If FPS had been gratified to hear of its own government's firm commitment to the welfare of African fauna, the society must have groaned in disbelief when it emerged that a senior minister in that very same administration saw no inherent contradiction in gunning down an endangered species in a different geographical corner of the former empire. In February 1961, someone had the bright idea of commemorating a royal visit to Nepal with the shooting of a greater one-horned rhinoceros by, of all people, the then Foreign Secretary, Alec Douglas-Home. As soon as FPS learned of the proposal, which had been sanctioned by King

Whilst Africa inevitably remained the society's primary concern during this period, safeguarding the wildlife of the Indian subcontinent was still high on its list of priorities. No one was more active in keeping this corner of the former colonies in the spotlight than the Anglo-Indian tea-planter and amateur naturalist Edward Pritchard Gee – widely known as E.P. – not least because he succeeded in photographing many of its most charismatic species during the course of the surveys that he undertook on behalf of FPS. A member of the society from the year of India's independence in 1947 until his death 20 years later, he was a passionate protector of his adopted country's fauna. As an editorial in the 1952 edition of *Oryx* pointed out, 'Much of what is being done in Assam to preserve the rhinoceros and other animals is, without question, due to Mr Gee's tireless work.' Gee would go on to write the authoritative guide, *The Wild Life of India*, published by Collins in 1964. More significantly, his persistent advocacy for protected areas was to prove instrumental in ensuring national park status – shortly before his death – for his beloved Kaziranga, a crucial sanctuary for, among other species, the great Indian rhinoceros.

E.P. Gee (seated centre) took many of his most iconic wildlife photographs from the back of an elephant, which enabled him to approach these Bengal tigers more closely than would otherwise have been possible. The other endangered species featured opposite are (clockwise from top) the Asiatic lion, Himalayan black bear, greater one-horned rhinoceros and swamp deer – known locally as barasingha – all of which Gee was instrumental in conserving.

Mahendra, it sent an urgent cable to Her Majesty the Queen, pointing out the rhino's extreme rarity. The IUCN president sent a similar message to the Nepalese king. Unfortunately, the petition came too late to save the luckless female rhino, shot while suckling her young calf. FPS was apoplectic and a strongly worded condemnation, drafted by its secretary, Colonel Boyle, was published in *The Times*. 'The report of the shooting of a Great Indian Rhinoceros in Nepal by the Foreign Secretary will cause dismay among all those interested in the preservation of rare animals. [...] The loss of a single animal is very regrettable, but even more important is the question of example.' Professor J.G. Baer, president of IUCN, wrote subsequently to the King of Nepal deploring the killing and offering the expert assistance of technical consultants in conservation. Arguably, that particular horse had already bolted.

This incident served as a timely reminder that the increasing pressure on wildlife populations and their habitats was a worldwide phenomenon that required vigilance on a global scale. By this stage the society's journal was already providing ample evidence of its commitment to conservation beyond Africa, and the May 1960 issue of *Oryx* was no exception. It was almost exclusively devoted to the comprehensive report of the young IUCN staff ecologist, Lee Talbot, on threatened species of the Middle East and Southern Asia.

The hapless great Indian rhinoceros, whose dwindling population would shortly be further reduced by a trigger-happy future prime minister, was one of six species singled out for special attention by the author. The other five were the Sumatran and Javan rhinoceros, the Indian lion, Syrian wild ass and, most significantly for FPS, the Arabian oryx. By the time Talbot's report appeared in its journal, preparations were already underway for one of the society's most celebrated conservation coups.

CHAPTER 4

INNOVATION

'Very glad to hear of your remarkable success in capturing three Arabian oryx so that they may breed in captivity and thereby save the species from extinction. The cooperation of The Fauna Preservation Society and the World Wildlife Fund in this Noah's Ark operation is a splendid precedent for future efforts to save the world's endangered species. – Philip.'

HRH The Duke of Edinburgh, 1962

If its diamond jubilee celebrations in December 1963 were an opportunity for the Fauna Preservation Society to look back with satisfaction at 'achievements innumerable', they also marked the end of an era and the beginning of a new phase in the society's development. After 14 years of unstinting devotion to the cause, the stalwart Colonel Boyle used the occasion to announce that he was stepping down as secretary of FPS and as editor of *Oryx*. His colleagues were effusive in their praise: 'It is not overstating the case to claim that there are many species of wild animals now enjoying a better prospect of survival thanks to his zeal and unremitting efforts.'

bird protection in May 1952. In the following years he became an increasingly prominent figure. By the early 1960s, as the heir apparent to Colonel Boyle, he was already playing a pivotal role in the strategic direction of the society. Although modesty forbade Fitter from subsequently claiming personal credit for his part in saving the Arabian oryx from extinction, he was a leading protagonist, along with the good colonel, in the opening scenes of what was to become a conservation drama of epic proportions.

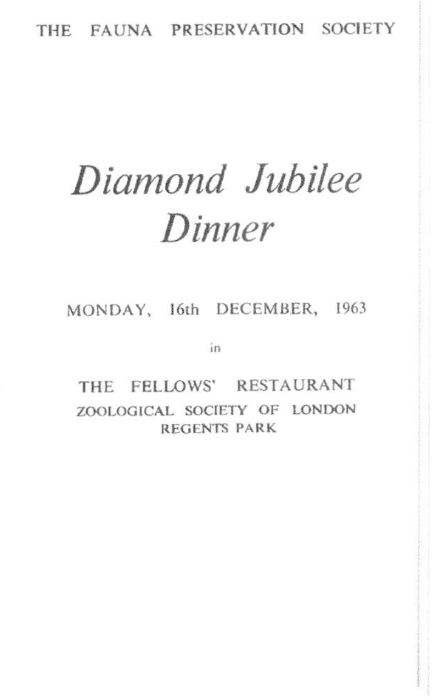

Fitter for purpose

Boyle's secretarial and editorial responsibilities were divided between the formidable husband and wife team of Richard and Maisie Fitter. As the new editor of *Oryx*, Maisie was quick to make her presence felt. Although superficially similar to previous editions, the April 1964 issue, her first, was notable for subtle but discernible changes that hinted at a more professional approach to layout and design.

Richard Fitter had first appeared on the FPS scene a decade earlier, when he was elected to the council shortly before representing the society at an international conference on

THE FAUNA PRESERVATION SOCIETY

Diamond Jubilee Dinner

MONDAY, 16th DECEMBER, 1963

in

THE FELLOWS' RESTAURANT
ZOOLOGICAL SOCIETY OF LONDON
REGENTS PARK

Opposite This painting of an Arabian oryx herd by FPS chairman Sir Peter Scott featured on the society's 1978 Christmas card.

Right Documentary evidence that the society's diamond jubilee year had provided ample food – and drink – for thought.

THE QUIET ENGLISHMAN

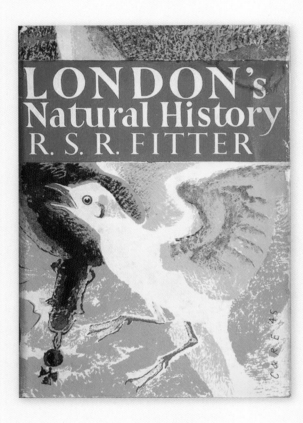

Richard Sidney Richmond Fitter, honorary secretary of the society from 1964 until 1981, was described in his 2006 *Oryx* obituary as 'a quiet man of great humility, one of the last of the great British naturalists'. In an era when conservation was dominated by larger-than-life personalities, Fitter was one of the self-effacing individuals who operated largely behind the scenes, but nevertheless succeeded in exerting considerable influence over the conservation infrastructure that we see today. One of the least clubbable but most capable figures to have taken the reins at the society, he had an enviable grasp of conservation politics and international issues.

Fitter never enjoyed being centre stage, and was undoubtedly more comfortable in the field than rubbing shoulders with the men in suits. He was evidently impatient of social chat, preferring to roll up his sleeves and get things done, and he was definitely no fan of committees. This did not preclude him from attending many key meetings in his capacity as honorary secretary of FPS, and he played an active role at such landmark events as the founding of the IUCN, the signing of the Convention on Migratory Species and the birth of CITES.

Richard Fitter's contributions to conservation extended well beyond his work with the society. He was also the editor of *Kingfisher*, a news service founded in 1965, which at that time was the only newsletter with a global remit devoted to news and views about wildlife and the problems inherent in conserving it. By 1969 *Kingfisher* was being read in over 40 countries. His other roles over the years included secretary of the Wildlife and Countryside Committee, which established the framework for UK national parks and nature reserves, assistant editor of *The Countryman*, director of the Council for Nature's intelligence unit, and 'open air correspondent' for *The Observer*. He also served on the councils of the RSPB and the British Trust for Ornithology, and helped found the Berkshire, Buckinghamshire and Oxfordshire Naturalists' Trust and the British Deer Society.

Fitter was a pioneer of the modern field guide and the author of iconic publications such as *Collins Pocket Guide to British Birds*, illustrated by R.A. Richardson, which first appeared in 1952. His earlier books included the widely admired *London's Birds* (1949) and *London's Natural History*, which was the third in the Collins New Naturalist series. He later co-authored numerous other Collins publications, including the popular *Pocket Guide to Wild Flowers* (1956) and *Birds of Britain and Europe, with Africa and the Middle East,* published in 1972. Some of Fitter's work, including *The Penguin Dictionary of Natural History* (1967), was produced with his wife Maisie, herself an accomplished editor, writer and naturalist (and editor of *Oryx* from 1964 until 1981). At the time of his death, aged 92, he was writing a book on the wild flowers of France.

Although Fitter earned numerous accolades and won many awards for

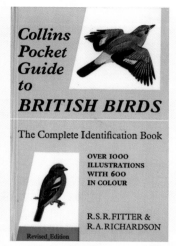

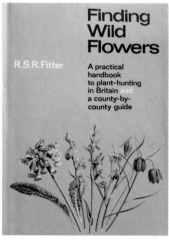
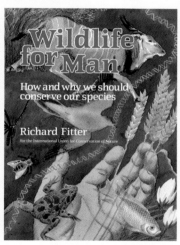
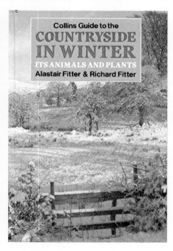
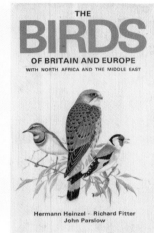

his work, he seems to have remained indifferent to this kind of official recognition of his achievements. His former colleagues remember the occasion when he received a letter informing him that he had been awarded the prestigious Order of the Golden Ark by Prince Bernhard of the Netherlands, in recognition of his outstanding contribution in the field of conservation. Fitter's reaction was to write back informing them that he had no plans to be in Amsterdam during the week of the award ceremony and would not, therefore, be attending. He may not have added that he would rather be birdwatching, but the thought probably crossed his mind. ∎

Above Fitter was a prolific author of natural history guides, including seminal works that helped to popularise birdwatching and increase public awareness of the natural world on their own doorsteps.

Opposite Published in 1945, *London's Natural History* helped set the gold standard for the long-running *New Naturalist* series, and provided a fascinating overview of the dynamic interaction between a growing metropolis and its wildlife.

Major Ian Grimwood, leader of Operation Oryx.

probable that the oryx is exterminated everywhere but in the extreme southern Rub-al-Khali [...] it is probably only a matter of a few years at most until the wild Arabian oryx is totally exterminated.'

Operation Oryx

Without urgent action, the Arabian oryx was undoubtedly doomed to follow in the hoofprints of the quagga and blaubok, but in Talbot's opinion there was a brief window of opportunity to save this particular ungulate. 'I believe the only way to assure survival of this interesting species is to transfer some specimens to a safer habitat. [...] This should be done as soon as possible, to be assured of finding enough animals.' Talbot's subsequent report to the IUCN General Assembly in Edinburgh, held in 1956, included a proposal for the Arabian oryx. This was accepted as an IUCN project, but only in principle. Not for the first time in that organisation's history, finding the money to pay for it was a problem.

To all intents and purposes, IUCN's coffers were empty. Since its inception in 1948, the organisation had consistently struggled to support *itself*, let alone finance ambitious and expensive conservation initiatives around the globe. According to Talbot, it might well have collapsed on numerous occasions without the intervention of its founding director, Hal Coolidge, who seems to have been almost single-handedly responsible for keeping IUCN afloat for the first three decades of its existence. During his occasional visits to London, Talbot continued to discuss the question of how to fund an Arabian oryx rescue mission with FPS officials including Colonel Boyle and Richard Fitter, sowing the seed of an idea that would burgeon into one of the most remarkable conservation success stories of the twentieth century.

In the late 1920s, the Duke of Bedford, one of the society's original founder members and the man famous for rescuing Père David's deer from oblivion, had written an article in the *Journal* advocating the captive breeding of other animals that were threatened with extinction in the wild. At that time, it had been widely acknowledged that this was outside the province of the society, but by the early 1960s its remit had broadened beyond all recognition. And drastic times called for drastic measures. Undeterred by the lack of precedents, FPS was about to embark on a rescue mission that would later be hailed by Fitter as 'the classic instance of successful captive breeding'.

The Arabian oryx was one of the six endangered animals 'threatened with extermination' and singled out for particular scrutiny during the 1955 field mission undertaken by Lee Talbot on behalf of IUCN. Until that point, this animal was a relatively obscure desert antelope, well on the way to becoming a footnote in the natural history books. At the time of Talbot's visit, the situation could not have been graver. His concluding remarks on its imperilled status were depressing in the extreme: 'It seems

Lack of finance was by no means the only obstacle to this plan. Even if sufficient funds could be raised, there was uncertainty over who might lead the rescue mission in the field. The breakthrough came in 1960 during one of Talbot's visits to Kenya and, more precisely, an evening spent in the company of his very good friend Major Ian Grimwood. Recently appointed Chief Game Warden of Kenya, Grimwood had a colourful history, which included surviving Japanese prisoner-of-war camps and eventually commanding the Frontier Force regiment of the Indian army, which he had joined in 1935. Appropriately enough for such a larger-than-life character, this man's home was, literally, a castle, though not a very comfortable one by all accounts. Talbot recollects that he and his wife Martha had

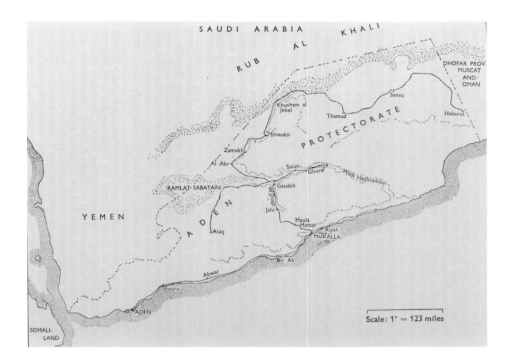

Map of the route taken by the expedition.

to cross a large moat in order to reach Grimwood's rather grand accommodation on the outskirts of Nairobi. As they sat in front of the necessarily large fireplace, drinking an unnecessarily large Scotch, Talbot suggested to his friend that he might like to consider leading an expedition into the immense expanse of the Arabian Desert in search of some vanishingly rare antelopes. How could he refuse?

As if to confirm the desperate plight of the Arabian oryx, news reached the FPS about an attack on what was believed to be the last remaining population in then Eastern Aden, by a motorised raiding party from Qatar. At least 28 oryx were slaughtered. Only one animal, a pregnant female, was found alive by investigators. This was the final spur to prick the sides of the society's intent, and discussions began in earnest about the planning of an expedition to capture some surviving oryx before it was too late.

From the outset, there was widespread acknowledgment that the capture and subsequent captive breeding of the Arabian oryx must not be an end in itself. The ultimate goal was reintroduction into the wild, and all parties were adamant that the next generation of these charismatic antelopes, guaranteed crowd-pullers though they might be, should not end up as permanent exhibits and status symbols in zoos at home and abroad. Initially, FPS considered the idea of establishing an oryx breeding facility

in Arabia itself, but the logistical difficulties involved in maintaining such a reserve made this unrealistic. It was therefore agreed that the only hope was to attempt captive breeding outside the species' natural range, with the aim of reintroducing the oryx into the wild at an appropriate future date. Isiolo in northern Kenya was initially earmarked for this purpose, and plans for the expedition were crystallised, but not before Qatari raiders had killed 16 more of the dwindling wild oryx population.

First, capture the imagination

The expedition aroused great interest around the world, with help ultimately elicited from six governments, five zoos, scores of societies and clubs, hundreds of individuals, several oil companies and even an electricity company in Kenya that donated its entire showroom of ovens in order to heat the temporary quarters of the captured oryx. A PR campaign masterminded by John Hillaby succeeded in securing financial help from the *Daily Mail*, and the World Wildlife Fund offered a grant to support the venture. Thirteen individual donors, one of them anonymous, chipped in with significant contributions of their own. In March 1962, expedition leader Ian Grimwood and an advance party flew from Kenya to Aden along with their

Piper Cruiser spotter plane, generously lent by the East African Wild Life Society, an organisation with which FFI still has a fruitful partnership today. The following month, once Grimwood had completed all the preliminary preparations, he was joined in Mukalla by the remaining volunteers and the party drove 500 miles north to Sanau, the starting point for a proposed six-week sojourn in the vast northern desert of what was then the Eastern Aden Protectorate.

The expedition was to suffer its fair share of setbacks in the shape of mechanical breakdowns, equipment delays, intransigent bureaucracy and physical injuries – including a set of broken ribs sustained by the expedition leader himself. Like the fictional heroes in a soon-to-be-published Willard Price *Adventure* classic, they cracked on regardless, overcame the odds and bagged their prize.

In his later report on the oryx rescue mission, Grimwood was at pains to stress that the venture owed its success to

Scanning the vast and virtually featureless sea of sand for signs of the elusive Arabian oryx. The expedition was heavily dependent on local knowledge to help locate the last surviving herds.

the collaborative efforts of a vast number of individuals and organisations. What is clear, however, is that a section of the Hadhrami Beduin Legion, under the command of Lieutenant-Colonel Quaid Gray, played a crucial role by shouldering the immense administrative and logistical burden that might otherwise have weighed down the expedition. Red tape and shattered gearboxes were apparently tackled with equal gusto.

Friends in sky-high places

The RAF was similarly enthusiastic; protocol dictated that personnel and equipment could not be seen to be hijacked for non-military purposes, particularly something as frivolous as rescuing a few antelopes. Nevertheless, the expedition flight schedule – and the eventual date of the oryx evacuation to Nairobi – somehow seemed to coincide with times when the RAF was already transporting cargo to and from Aden, and always when there was surplus room in the hold to accommodate such bulky items as a disassembled light aircraft, several large ungulate enclosures and copious

Above The almost supernatural tracking ability of Tomatum bin Harbi (pictured left) enabled the convoy to locate and capture a mature male oryx, later named in honour of the man who had picked up his trail.

Below Sharp practice: mastering the art of manhandling a trussed but well-armed oryx into a holding crate.

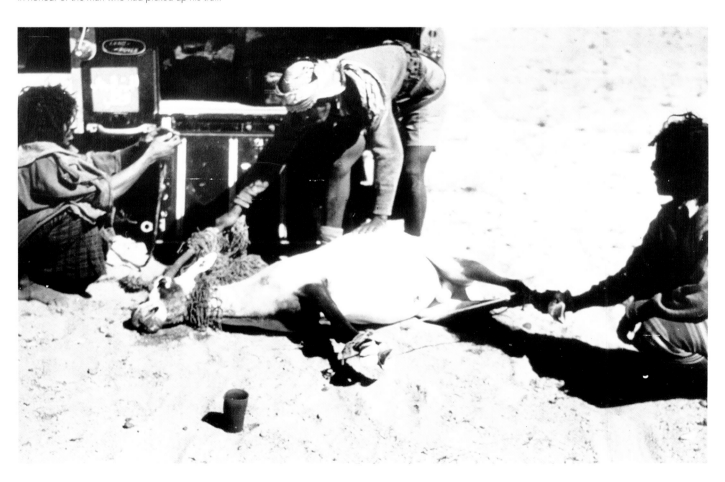

quantities of donated beer. Many officers took a keen personal interest in the mission and evidently pushed their decision-making authority to breaking point in their eagerness to help. Their efforts ensured that all members of the field party and their equipment, including the spotter plane, were transported in and out of Aden, while the captured oryx were flown to Nairobi.

Invaluable though they were, all the logistical legs-up and oiling of bureaucratic wheels would ultimately have been wasted effort if the expedition had returned empty-handed or, more accurately, with empty enclosures. By this time, the beleaguered Arabian oryx was heart-stoppingly close to being completely effaced from the map. Scouring 6,000 square miles of desert in search of a handful of antelopes was the zoological equivalent of looking for the proverbial needle in a haystack. Local knowledge and tracking ability would prove indispensable in locating what was potentially the last surviving wild herd on the planet. Two men, Mabkout bin Hassanah and Tomatum bin Harbi, excelled in this department, impressing everyone with their 'uncanny skill', which included an ability to follow faint and distant tracks completely indiscernible to others from a vehicle moving at 20 miles per hour.

In all, the rescue mission lasted an entire month, during which the expedition found tracks of just 11 oryx. The first specimen captured, a mature bull, was named 'Tomatum', in honour of the man who had tracked him down. Three males and one female were eventually caught, but one of the males collapsed and died shortly afterwards. A post mortem revealed that the chase alone was not responsible. They found a hunter's rifle bullet lodged deep in its thigh, which no doubt contributed to the animal's weak condition. The team was remorseful, but sanguine about the need to persevere, given the circumstances. As Grimwood said, 'when the species appeared doomed and the individual almost certain to fall victim to the raiders on their next visit, it seemed justifiable to continue while there was any hope of catching the oryx alive'.

Above right Facsimile of the congratulatory telegram from Prince Philip.

Opposite (clockwise from top left) Tomatum, the first Arabian oryx captured, comfortably ensconced in his temporary quarters in Isiolo, Kenya. The society used this iconic image on the FPS Christmas card in 1962.

Expedition vet, Michael Woodford, temporarily relinquishes his official duties and seizes the opportunity to film proceedings.

The sweet smell of success mingles with the smell of stale sweat as the Operation Oryx team drinks a toast to mission accomplished. From left to right: Tony Shepherd, Peter Whitehead, Michael Crouch, Mick Gracie and Donald Stewart, with a bashful Ian Grimwood concealed in the background.

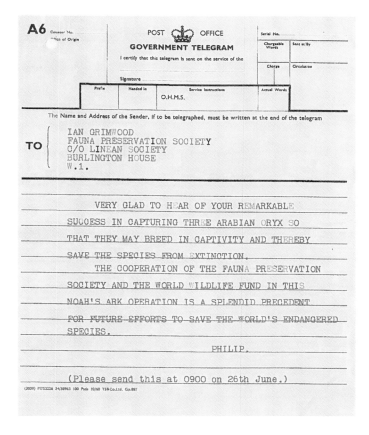

Precious cargo

The three captured oryx were airlifted to Nairobi in May, but an untimely outbreak of foot-and-mouth disease at Isiolo necessitated a hasty change of plan. The animals had to be held in temporary quarters in the Kenyan capital, where the prevailing cold and damp conditions posed a serious threat to their survival. Cue the resourceful deployment of improvised heaters in the form of electric ovens hung from the walls, which were later replaced with slightly more conventional heat lamps. The move to Isiolo was finally completed two months later, bringing the first stage of the rescue process to a satisfactory conclusion. On 26 June 1962, a press conference was held at the Linnean Society in London, prompting HRH Prince Philip to send Grimwood a congratulatory telegram.

As Grimwood was quick to concede, however, Operation Oryx had only partially succeeded. Four animals did not constitute a viable breeding nucleus. It was beginning to look like a case of too little, too late. 'The lesson to be learned is how terrifyingly quickly, and irrevocably, a locally favourable situation can be destroyed by thoughtless selfishness and how that destruction can imperil the very existence of a whole species.'

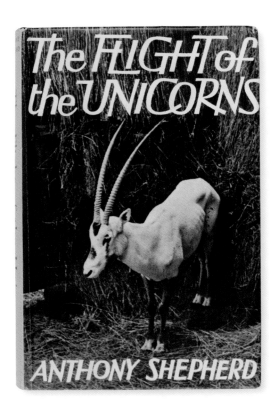

Recovery ward

The successful capture of three Arabian oryx was merely the starting point in a laborious recovery process. It was imperative to build up a larger, healthy captive population with a view to eventual reintroduction. They were effectively in a race against time to find enough animals to achieve a critical mass of breeding stock for the 'World Herd', as it became known. This realisation triggered a renewed bout of intensive searching and a spate of wild antelope chases – both literal and metaphorical. The occasional rumours of an Arabian oryx sighting proved to be greatly exaggerated. The beasts in question were invariably hybrids, or cases of mistaken identity in the shape of the superficially similar scimitar-horned oryx. Fortunately, that first groundbreaking expedition had captured the imagination of the wider world. In its aftermath, with the plight of the Arabian oryx now on everyone's radar, it gradually came to light that other specimens were already held in various zoos and private collections around the world. If these captive antelope could be pooled along with the three recently captured oryx, there was still a chance that FPS could realise its vision of establishing a functional breeding population as an insurance policy against the extermination of the species in the wild.

It was agreed that FPS would maintain the studbook for the species, with breeding conducted on scientific lines. A committee appointed by the FPS council to determine the best long-term destination for the captive herd recommended Arizona, not least because its desert climate would simulate Arabian conditions. The three oryx were airlifted out of Kenya in May 1963, just in time as it turned out; five days later a pitched battle between police and Somali secession protesters was raging in the precise area of the Isiolo holding pens. The oryx were flown via British Airways from Nairobi to London, where they were united with a second female that had been housed temporarily at London Zoo, before all continuing together to New York.

Above An account of Operation Oryx, entitled *The Flight of the Unicorns* and written by expedition member Tony Shepherd, was published in 1965. Half the royalties were donated to FPS.

Opposite The desert conditions encountered by the Arabian oryx on arrival in Phoenix, Arizona ensured that they could acclimatise quickly to their new home once they had been unloaded from the cargo plane and released from their crates. The arrivals were provided with a combination of extensive outdoor enclosures and custom-built indoor stalls.

After a brief period of quarantine in New Jersey they were finally shipped to their ultimate destination, Phoenix Maytag Zoo. In the meantime, courtesy of the private collection of Sheikh Jaber Ahmad al-Jaber al-Sabah, ruler of Kuwait, FPS had received an additional female oryx, which was already in calf after being mated with a beisa oryx.

HM King Saud of Saudi Arabia, doubtless not wishing to be outdone by his Kuwaiti neighbour in the benevolence stakes, generously offered to donate four Arabian oryx to WWF to supplement the World Herd. No doubt the visiting Ian Grimwood was suitably effusive in thanking the Saudi ruler for his beneficence, but you cannot help feeling that the man who braved cracked ribs and weeks of hardship to capture three Arabian oryx would have been more than a little miffed to discover no fewer than 13 of these elusive antelopes, all in pristine condition, ensconced in the spanking-new zoo at Riyadh. Two of the four animals earmarked for WWF were captive-bred. The wild-caught members of this zoo herd were believed to have been captured in the Rubʿ al-Khali area. The only reports of oryx surviving in the wild came from Bedouins travelling in Oman. It was thought possible that one or two hundred antelopes might still be out there somewhere, thanks to a protection order issued by the Sultan, but in reality this was no deterrent for encroachers from outside.

Until this point, investigations into the wider prevalence of captive, and indeed wild, Arabian oryx had yielded depressing results, with only two other individuals (at a zoo in Yemen) tracked down in the whole of Arabia. Nevertheless, it was encouraging that worldwide interest in the mission was generating widespread international co-operation and helping to unearth secret stashes of the species. It emerged that there was a 19-strong herd, founded in 1962, at the farm of HH Sheikh Qassim bin Hamad al Thani, Minister of Education in Qatar. The Sheikh went on to become a life member of FPS in 1966.

Sacred cow

Of course, the long-term survival prospects of the Arabian oryx were contingent on producing a new generation of animals, rather than simply adding more adults to the World Herd. The first captive-bred addition to the Phoenix herd was a male calf born on 26 October 1963. This exotic newcomer was given the touching, if slightly prosaic, name of Ian in honour of the intrepid leader of the Operation Oryx expedition. To everyone's increasing consternation, the next four calves born were also male. Normal service was finally resumed when, to general relief, the third of three more calves born in August 1966 proved to be female.

Not everyone had the best interests of the species at heart. The same edition of the society's journal that conveyed news of a fourth calf being born at Phoenix in May 1965 was also highly critical of a Dutch animal dealer who was offering two more captive oryx at extortionate prices, the fear being that the rumoured price tag might induce other unscrupulous people to attempt to capture whatever remained of the wild population. While some were openly profiteering, others were merely thoughtless. An undertone of barely disguised incredulity at the folly of man pervades one *Oryx* entry reporting on a private expedition mounted in Oman that captured a female calf for use as a regimental mascot.

Rise of the Phoenix herd

Despite these occasional setbacks, the overall population trend was upward. By 1971 there were 30 oryx at Phoenix Zoo, 11 of which 'belonged' to FPS. Rather than keep all the oryx in one Arizona basket, it was deemed sensible to move some of them elsewhere, in order to insure against the threat of disease obliterating the entire World Herd at a stroke. Accordingly, six animals were transferred to San Diego Zoo. Just five years later, Phoenix and San Diego between them held 82 Arabian oryx. In view of the growing surplus at Phoenix, two pairs were transferred to Brownsville Zoo, Texas, four pairs to San Diego, and two pairs to London Zoo. With one eye on the ultimate reintroduction prize, four males were offered to Jordan.

By 1980, the breeding of captive Arabian oryx had been so successful that there were believed to be over 300 of these magnificent antelopes in zoos and animal parks around the world. The official World Herd, consisting of 50 oryx in the United States and a further 15 in Europe,

Below left This newly born male calf – the first captive-bred addition to the Phoenix herd – was subsequently named 'Ian' in tribute to the original expedition leader, Major Grimwood.

Below right Every captive birth at Phoenix was a significant leap forward, but the arrival of the first female calf in 1966 elicited a huge collective sigh of relief.

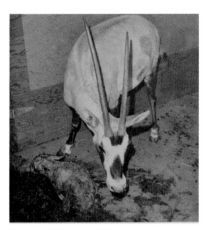

therefore comprised a relatively small proportion of the entire captive population.

With this in mind, FPS and the other trustees agreed to a radical proposal made by IUCN's recently established Captive Breeding Specialist Group, whereby ownership of all animals in the World Herd would be transferred to the zoos where they were currently held captive. In thanking all the various bodies whose co-operation had contributed to the success of this first phase of the rescue, Richard Fitter made a point of reminding them, presumably with posterity in mind, that it was FPS who had originated the idea of Operation Oryx.

There had always been general agreement at the SSC and on the FPS council that it was vital to establish four or five independent captive herds in different parts of the world before contemplating any attempt to restore the Arabian

oryx to the wild. It was widely believed that the last remaining wild Arabian oryx in Oman, and possibly in the world, had been captured or killed in late 1972, which was when a safari undertaken by one D.S. Henderson came upon three corpses and found irrefutable evidence that four more individuals had been taken away in vehicles. 'Even if a handful remain, what we found undoubtedly ranks as a major wildlife disaster.'

With the future of an entire species now almost certainly dependent on the fate of the captive population, it was even more imperative that the reintroduction should be carefully choreographed in order to prevent mishaps.

Arabian oryx at Los Angeles Zoo. In 1972, an exchange was arranged between Phoenix and Los Angeles in order to even up the male–female ratio at the respective zoos, which were both suffering from a gender bias.

Homeward bound

A prime candidate for the location of phase one of the reintroduction project was the Shaumari Wildlife Reserve, in Jordan. In the previous decade, a comprehensive but alarming report on the threats facing that country's biodiversity had led King Hussein of Jordan to decree the country's first national park in the Azraq desert, declaring that it would be 'not merely the world's newest national park, but [...] the only working example on Earth of the latest concepts and designs for a truly modern type of national park'. The aim was to integrate local education, foreign tourism and wildlife conservation within an overall framework that would serve, it was hoped, as a blueprint for other such parks elsewhere in the Middle East. From the very outset, this park had also been seen as a potential release site for captive-bred oryx. By the end of the 1960s, however, the harsh realities of war had put paid to these best-laid plans. Shaumari and the proposed Jordanian International Biological Station at the nearby Azraq oasis had to be mothballed until the end of hostilities.

In 1974, Jordan's Royal Society for the Conservation of Nature, which since its inception has received institutional support from FPS and then FFI, restarted the programme. The curator of mammals at Phoenix Zoo, where the nucleus of the World Herd was thriving, visited Shaumari and pronounced it to be an eminently suitable springboard for the first phase of the planned Arabian oryx reintroduction programme. This gave the green light for the trustees of the World Herd to present Jordan with four male oryx, the foundation of what they hoped would be the first herd in Arabia deriving from Operation Oryx. They arrived intact in February 1978 and formed the basis of what grew into a 31-strong captive herd that was eventually released into the Shaumari Reserve itself. Unfortunately, release into the open desert was not feasible, given the reserve's proximity to the Saudi border and the more populous areas of Jordan.

Running wild

Oman was a different story. Home of the last known wild Arabian oryx, the country had also expressed a desire to release oryx into the Jiddat-al-Harasis, a vast stony plateau relatively unaffected by modern developments, covering an area of some 50,000 square kilometres. Encouragingly, the local Harasis tribe, a small group of nomadic stock-breeders, viewed the totemic oryx as its rightful property and was therefore fully committed to protecting the reintroduced herd. By 1981, the final phase of Operation Oryx was

Still contriving to look dignified despite their improvised protective headgear, Aziz (top) and Amir (above) await their release into Jordan's Shaumari Wildlife Reserve.

underway, thanks largely to the involvement of the young Sultan Qaboos bin Said, who was keenly interested in conserving his country's wildlife. It was he who had decreed total protection for the oryx in 1976. The Sultan's conservation adviser, Ralph Daly, and his Omani colleagues, set about planning the reintroduction with the enthusiastic co-operation of the Harasis community. Ten oryx were flown in from San Diego Zoo and quickly settled into their new enclosure under the watchful gaze of 17 local tribesmen employed to guard them. After careful observation revealed they had developed a stable social structure and were behaving as a single, cohesive group, they were released into the open desert, but not before they had been fitted with radio collars to enable rangers to track their movements. This was a momentous occasion for all concerned, but above all for FPS, which had initiated the original rescue.

Above A newborn Arabian oryx calf in the Shaumari Reserve, one more step in the reintroduction process.

Right Isolated and relatively well-vegetated, Wadi Yalooni was identified as the most suitable site for the climactic release of the Arabian oryx into Oman's vast Jiddat-al-Harasis plateau.

'To witness the release of the group of white oryx into the wild desert of Oman was a very moving experience. It was made even more emotional when a member of the local Harasis tribe sang a blessing as they moved into their new home. This was the culmination of a major international and inter-organisational conservation project which had succeeded beyond all expectations.'

HRH The Duke of Edinburgh, 2015

Supplementary feeding was required initially because the area had been subjected to six years of virtual drought, but a visit by The Duke of Edinburgh coincided with a massive downpour that flooded their new desert home and stimulated the growth of lush new grass. Although heavily guarded and intensively studied, this herd became completely independent. By the time a second herd of oryx was released two years later, the first herd had already produced wild-born offspring. Data collected from the radio collars was used to produce a range map, and also revealed that the herd was capable of making a 120-kilometre round trip in just two nights.

Eternal vigilance

By 1996 there were more than 300 wild Arabian oryx roaming freely across the deserts of the Middle East. Predictably, however, this has turned into a never-ending story for conservationists. Poaching soon resumed and then intensified to such an extent that it was considered prudent to recapture some of the wild oryx as an insurance policy against history repeating itself. That would have been a doubly bitter pill to swallow. Hunting remains a threat even today, particularly in Oman. Ironically, one of the most serious problems is the illegal live capture of oryx to satisfy the demands of private collectors. Nevertheless, the current problems cannot detract from the magnitude of the original achievement: this was the first time an animal that had actually become extinct in the wild was successfully reintroduced into its original habitat.

There are now over 1,000 Arabian oryx running wild across the Middle East, with thousands more held in various degrees of captivity worldwide. By way of a footnote – or hoof note in this case – the Arabian oryx was downlisted in 2011 from Endangered to Vulnerable on the IUCN Red List, which is unprecedented for a species previously listed as Extinct In The Wild. This accomplishment is one of the society's enduring legacies.

The use of captive breeding to help save a species on the brink of extinction was nothing new to another society heavyweight, Peter Scott, who had been an FPS council

In 2003, the UK's best-selling pencil artist, Gary Hodges, generously donated a set of artist's proofs for his limited-edition Arabian oryx print to the society for fundraising purposes.

GREAT SCOTT

Sir Peter Markham Scott was the son of Antarctic explorer Robert Falcon Scott. A renowned wildlife artist, whose paintings were exhibited at the Royal Academy, Scott became a well-known broadcaster and was central to the development of the BBC Natural History Unit in Bristol.

Scott's long-term association with the society culminated in his appointment as president in 1982, and he played a fulcral role throughout his life in the conservation of the natural world. He took practical steps to prevent the extinction of species, most famously the

Hawaiian goose, and to protect natural areas, by raising public awareness through his writing, art and media activities. He worked tirelessly in a voluntary capacity for a string of international NGOs, some of which he was instrumental in creating, and was a ubiquitous presence in the conservation world for several decades, not least as chairman and then president of FPS.

Awarded a knighthood in 1973 in recognition of his outstanding services to wildlife conservation, Scott was showered with numerous other

Peter Scott (left) pictured with Richard and Maisie Fitter during a visit to Qatar in the aftermath of Operation Oryx.

conservation-related awards, including, in 1977, sharing with Jacques Cousteau the $50,000 Pahlavi Environment Prize, awarded by the government of Iran.

Richard Fitter, in *The Penitent Butchers*, refers to Scott's 'genius for public relations', and there is no doubt that he was second to none at winning hearts and minds. In his role at FPS he was described as 'a chairman who demands – and gets – action'. ∎

member since 1962. The wild population of the Hawaiian goose, or ne-ne, had fallen below 50 birds when Scott intervened in 1949, setting up a rescue operation at Slimbridge under the auspices of the Severn Wildfowl Trust (now the Wildfowl & Wetlands Trust), which he himself founded. Today the ne-ne population stands at 2,500, and the vast majority of these birds are descended from captive-bred geese that were later reintroduced into the wild in Hawaii.

Red alert

By the time he was elected chairman of FPS in 1965, Scott's conservation credentials were impeccable. He was already chairman of the World Wildlife Fund and its British National Appeal. Having joined the executive board of the IUCN in 1956, he was appointed chairman of its Survival Service Commission in 1963, in which capacity he devised and launched the renowned Red Data Books. The first of these was intended, rather optimistically, to be a complete record of the status of – and the threats facing – every rare and endangered plant and animal species.

Whilst the Red Data Book concept was undoubtedly the brainchild of Scott himself, part of the inspiration for an all-encompassing reference tool of this nature may arguably have come from the earlier pioneering work of a certain John C. Phillips, the very same US conservationist and philanthropist who had worked closely with the society during Lord Onslow's tenure and helped to develop the framework for the 1933 conference in London. By 1935, Phillips was becoming increasingly aware of the need for a comprehensive scientific review of existing knowledge of vanishing species in order to pinpoint those mammals and birds that might be saved from extinction. He and Harold Coolidge raised the funds and enlisted the services of Francis Harper and Glover M. Allen, who prepared the basic volumes on *Extinct and Vanishing Mammals of the Old and New World*, published in 1942 and 1945.

Colonel Boyle, who preceded Scott as chairman of the Survival Service Commission, had already introduced a simple card index system which served as a valuable reference source for FPS activities and, subsequently, in his work for the commission after his appointment in 1958. To all intents and purposes, this was the world's first database

A quick rummage through the card index system introduced by Colonel Boyle reveals that many of the species with which FFI is intimately associated today – such as black rhino, Iberian lynx, leatherback turtle, mountain gorilla and pygmy hippo – were already on the society's watch list half a century ago.

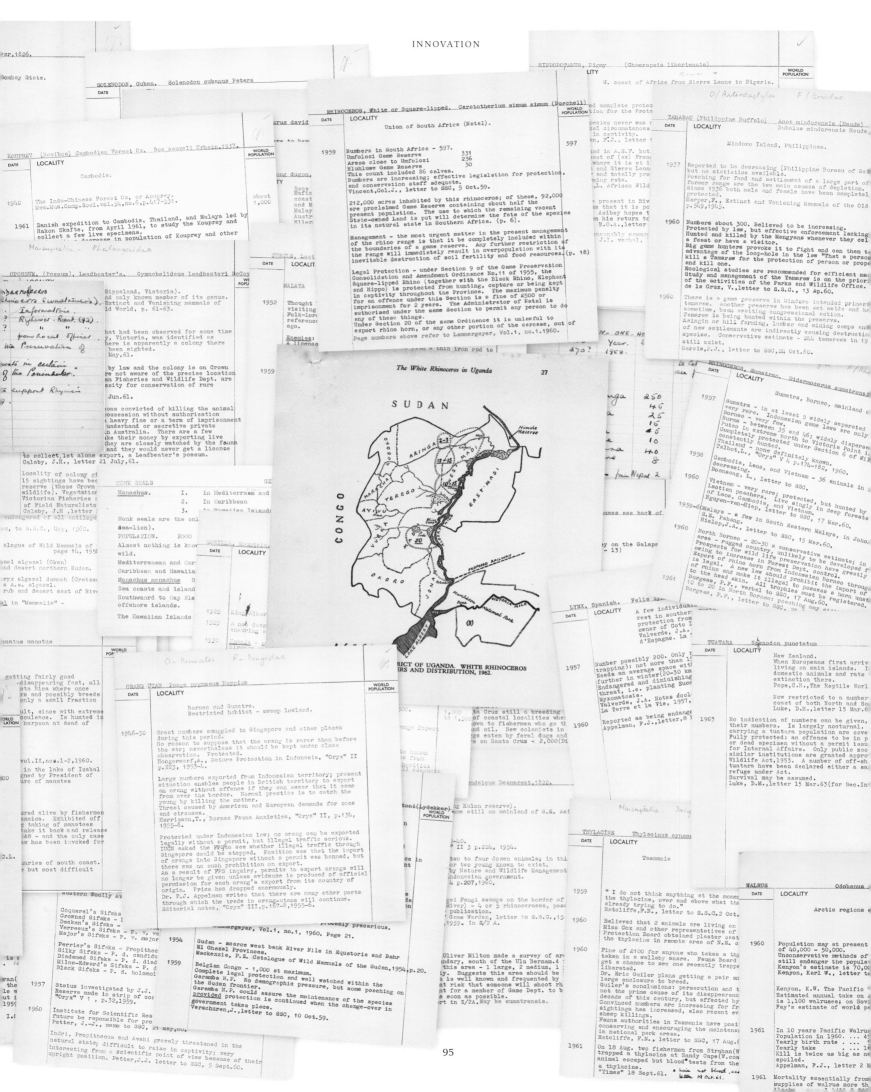

Early examples of the now-legendary series of Red Data Books, originally launched in 1966.

for threatened species of animals. It helped to lay the foundations for the Conservation Monitoring Centre, which was established by IUCN in 1979 and – as the World Conservation Monitoring Centre – has since been subsumed into the United Nations Environment Programme. Data from Boyle's card index system was used as a basis for discussions at the IUCN assembly in Warsaw in 1960. The proceedings included an appendix that listed and gave brief information on the status, distribution and survival prospects of 34 endangered species and 'certain other mammals' considered worthy of conservation attention. From an FFI perspective, it is interesting to note that the latter category included the Iberian (then Spanish) lynx, orang-utans in Borneo and Sumatra, black and white rhinoceroses, the Mediterranean monk seal, mountain gorilla, Asian elephant and pygmy hippopotamus, all of which the society continues to be instrumental in protecting to this day.

It was Scott who took the bare bones of this data-gathering idea and assembled them into a meaningful body of work that first took shape in 1963 as 'a register of threatened wildlife that includes definitions of degrees of threat'. Rather than compiling a single, unwieldy list of all endangered species, Scott hit upon the idea of splitting them into separate categories. The original definitions (Extinct, Endangered, Vulnerable, Rare, Indeterminate and Not Threatened) remained in use, with relatively few changes, for several decades. Issuing this information in a loose-leaf, ring-bound form ensured that each volume could be updated as required by removing obsolete sheets and inserting new or replacement text as the latest data became available and additional species were evaluated. Produced

with the aid of a large grant from the World Wildlife Fund, even in its incomplete state the Red Data Book was already, as early as 1964, being hailed as 'an invaluable tool for all who are trying to save the world's wildlife'.

The first two volumes in what was intended to be a whole series of Red Data Books saw the light of day in 1966. Published by the IUCN's Survival Service Commission, they covered 277 mammal and 321 bird species respectively and were designed, as the promotional literature put it, to provide 'in a conveniently classified form the most up-to-date and reliable data available on all species considered to be in danger of extinction'.

At this stage it was envisaged that companion volumes on reptiles and amphibians, insects, fish and plants would follow. These all materialised in due course, but not in the order originally anticipated. In the event, the insect volume did not take flight until 1983, by which time it had metamorphosed to encompass all invertebrates.

Rose-tinted spectacle

The loose-leaf format of these books, with each species allocated a single sheet that could be regularly updated, was generally well received. The pages were colour-coded according to the relative rarity of a species, which allowed readers to differentiate quickly between those in dire straits and other, lower, priorities. Pink paper was used for the pages describing species that were gravely endangered,

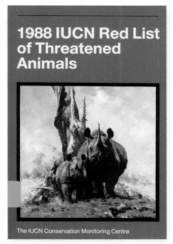

while green was used for those currently off the critical list. This simple design feature also provided a graphic illustration of the uphill task facing conservationists. As one reviewer remarked in *Oryx*, the pink-tinged edges of the closed book were a regrettable reminder of the precarious state in which much of the world's wildlife found itself.

It is difficult to overstate the importance of the information contained within the ring-bound pages of these first books. Providing the basis for all future plans and priority setting in the field of mammal and bird conservation, the sheets represented a vital weapon in the conservationists' armoury. To his credit, however, Scott saw clearly that his magnum opus was merely the first act of a two-stage process. Stage two, which he dubbed 'the action treatment', was to list the possible steps required to save a particular species from extinction, which might encompass everything from land purchase for the purpose of habitat protection, to detailed research, to the issuing of commemorative postage stamps to promote the plight of a species to the wider public.

Whilst it is broadly acknowledged today that Scott deserves the credit for the Red Data Book concept, there appears to have been a brief attempt to airbrush him out of the picture when the second edition of the series was published.

The first of these revised editions, a new volume on mammals published in 1974, contained no reference on the cover or title page to the existence of a previous version, nor did it mention the role of the then FPS chairman, instigator of the original series.

Action man

Apparently, the second edition, credited to 'the Secretariat of IUCN with the advice and guidance of the Survival Service Commission', was compiled in a way that did not meet with universal approval within the commission. A number of members clearly felt aggrieved that their advice and guidance had been largely ignored. You don't need to read between the lines of his comments in the February 1974 issue of *Oryx* to surmise what reviewer Dr Tom Harrisson, a member of the commission since 1963 and a significant and active conservationist within the society, thought of some of the inconsistencies, inaccuracies and sloppy editing in the new series. He was acerbic in his criticism of the contrast between the lengthy scientific preamble and the loose, unscientific terminology that followed in the actual text. He also remarked on IUCN's perceived attempt to use the second edition to rewrite history: 'The information about the FPS's *Operation Oryx* is quite wrong and was not checked with the FPS. It was FPS, aided by a WWF grant, who took the initiative, organised the operation and negotiated the founding of the World Herd in Arizona, not IUCN/WWF.'

Harrisson also derided the inclusion of, and misplaced concern for, a particular species of Bornean squirrel that featured in the revised mammal volume. 'Schedule a team for three years, with desirable helicopter support, and God bless my soul if they find six *Lariscus hosei*, let alone one of the factors that have made it specialised, remote, unthreatened, undisturbed today, as probably all through the Pleistocene.' Nor was he a fan of endless surveys as a primary means of stemming the extinction tide, branding it the conservation equivalent of fiddling while Rome burns.

His scathing attack on what he saw as the navel-gazing tendencies of the ivory tower bureaucrats at IUCN headquarters in Morges 'with its gently inland-lacustrine naivety', reads like a call to arms. 'It is high time, right now, that each and every one of us become more involved, more assured, more active, not less.' His diatribe hinted at a growing split between the more proactive conservationists with practical experience at the coalface – including the FPS overseas correspondents feeding back news from the front line, and the advocates of a top-down approach whose perceived obsession with data gathering and taxonomic niceties left them, in his view, out of touch with what was actually happening in the field.

Two years later, Harrisson was dead, killed along with his second wife in a car crash in Thailand. His untimely death deprived the conservation world of a buccaneering spirit who epitomised the values of the society. He demonstrated a practical, hands-on approach to conservation and knew that an understanding of local context was key to success. Turtles, orang-utans, dwarf buffalo and the world's largest eagle were among the many endangered species in South East Asia to benefit from his energetic input. A line from his obituary in *Oryx* hits the nail on the head: 'There was nobody like Tom Harrisson for blowing away cobwebs, sweeping away outworn rules, and penetrating behind bureaucratic verbiage and obstructions.'

Action plan

In the wake of Harrisson's diatribe, Richard Fitter adopted a more sanguine approach to compiling a list of endangered species, picking out the 25 most gravely threatened – excluding the 'hopeless cases' – among the 269 endangered mammals listed in the Red Data Books and outlining his own proposals for the action required to save them. In some cases, he argued, the society knew what needed to be done, but was precluded from doing it by financial, political, economic and cultural hurdles. In other words, the real reason why these animals were becoming extinct was that 'for the most part man does not care enough whether they do or not'. For years the wildlife conservation movement had been at the mercy of events. In Fitter's view, it was time to put long-term plans in place to avoid emergencies rather than firefighting when they arose. Although the most important need was for the creation of reserves to safeguard many of these species, Fitter also identified a number of

other urgently required measures, including status surveys, captive breeding, law enforcement, education, accordance of legal protection, ending persecution, clampdown on trade, help for local farmers and the promotion of tourism. He was subsequently commissioned by IUCN to revise the Red Data Books.

Whilst acknowledging the value of Harrisson's go-getter approach, Fitter was at pains not to denigrate the importance of fact gathering, without which, he believed, it was impossible to grapple with the practicalities of saving species. Leaving aside the philosophical disagreements for a moment, it is hard to dispute Fitter's assertion that the publication of the Red Data Books 'has probably done more to popularise and publicise the task of saving endangered species than almost any other single event'. Fifty years of evolution has seen the original concept develop from a series of lists and books into a painstakingly researched, comprehensive, online storehouse of information that is too vast to publish as a single book. This invaluable conservation database continues to be updated on an annual basis, as more species are added or the status of those already listed changes. To date, around 50,000 species have been assessed. Alarmingly, almost 40 per cent of these are threatened to a greater or lesser degree.

Frame of reference

The early influence of these books was widespread. Just two years after the first volume on mammals appeared, it was used as the primary reference source for the US Endangered Species Act. Five years later, the Red Data Books would

Professor Andrei Bannikov, a vice-president of the society from 1976 until his death in 1985, was one of the Soviet Union's most distinguished zoologists and an authority on Central Asian wildlife, including the saiga, currently one of FFI's focal species.

provide the framework for the preparation of the appendices to the 1973 Washington Convention, more familiar today as CITES (the Convention on the International Trade in Endangered Species of Wild Fauna and Flora), of which more later.

The first Red Data Books also inspired numerous countries to begin producing their own versions for national conservation purposes. Among them was a characteristically weighty, 460-page doorstopper published in 1979 by the then Soviet Union. Professor A.G. Bannikov, a vice-president of FPS and arguably the best-known Soviet conservationist in the West at that time, played a key role in its preparation.

The books were undoubtedly the most significant contribution made by the SSC, even if opinions were divided at the time about how effectively the commission used this resource. Some saw the Red Data Books as a list of urgent projects, while others appeared to regard them merely as an information source. Certainly, the creation of a network of specialist groups for single species, genera or families was a major step forward, and many of these made tangible progress. The SSC Rhinoceros Committee, for example, was set up at the suggestion of Peter Scott himself to address the plight of all five rhino species. He proposed a worldwide campaign, jointly sponsored by WWF and FPS, in co-operation with the IUCN-backed commission.

The relevant governments were urged to consider establishing additional national parks and reserves, and to introduce more effective measures to combat the trade in rhino horn. In the case of Nepal, E.P. Gee was commissioned to revisit the Chitwan Valley that he had first surveyed for FPS in 1959. His comprehensive list of proposed conservation measures included clearing illegal settlements from the existing wildlife sanctuary and extending its boundaries to incorporate important rhino habitat south of the Rapti River. Within just two years of these recommendations being implemented on the orders of King Mahendra, it was reported that rhinoceros numbers were increasing. In 1965 alone, 35 calves were seen. Chitwan was subsequently declared a national park, the first in Nepal.

Little red book

Equally importantly, the SSC under Scott's chairmanship played an influential role in the broader sense. Its very existence served to raise awareness of the threats facing endangered species and inspired people to *want* to save

them – and that included people outside conservation circles. Whilst the Red Data Books were not intended to be the exclusive preserve of the experts, their main target audience was never likely to be the enthusiastic amateur naturalist. If the hefty price tag had not been enough to deter that particular audience, forbidding gold-embossed titles like *Mammalia*, *Aves* and, later, *Angiospermae* probably did the trick. In a bid to make the information more accessible to the wider public, the commission published *The Red Book: Wildlife in Danger*.

Bafflingly, it had a black dust jacket. Years from now, an authority on anarchic humour in the twentieth century may hypothesise that it was this book, rather than the collected wisdom of Chairman Mao, that provided the inspiration for the wilfully misleading title of *Monty Python's Big Red Book*, published with a blue cover just two years later.

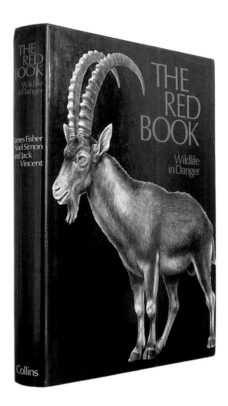

Never judge a book by its cover, particularly when it appears to contradict itself. *The Red Book: Wildlife in Danger* was an attempt to raise broader public awareness of conservation issues.

Above This painting, *Elephants in Thorn Scrub*, presented to the society by David Shepherd, formed the frontispiece to *Oryx* in August 1965 and reappeared later that same year as a Christmas card. The original was sold at the artist's autumn exhibition in London, with proceeds donated to FPS. Many of the wildlife paintings scattered throughout the pages of this book were created specifically to support the society's work.

Left This delightful painting of a puku by David Shepherd was reproduced as a Christmas card in 1966. Shepherd's distinctive portraits of other African wildlife, including impala, cheetah and zebras, were featured in later years.

Cover aside, this 1969 book was a no-nonsense guide to which species were in trouble, and why. Based as it was on the source documents used to compile the official Red Books, it inevitably focused on mammals and birds, reflecting the commission's own priorities. The descriptions remained authoritative and accurate, but the tone was less clinically scientific, and the text more emotive.

This increasing focus on the need to engage with a wider audience was one of the hallmarks of Peter Scott's tenure at SSC and FPS. The society continued to bang the drum for protected areas, but overall there was a discernible change in emphasis. In particular, the illegal trade in wildlife was demanding greater attention, at consumer as well as policy level. Following an IUCN conference in 1963, FPS launched twin campaigns to address the slaughter of spotted cats for the fur coat market and the unsustainable consumption of turtle soup. The society wrote to fashion editors to point out the barbarity and wastefulness of leopard-skin coats. Two decades before the iconic Dumb Animals campaign was launched by the anti-fur organisation Lynx, FPS was already on the case. Unfortunately, it didn't have at its disposal the artistic clout of photographer David Bailey or the creative might of the advertising industry, but it established the principle of undermining the fur trade by killing demand. Of course, there will always be some who miss the point.

A fur-clad American lady in Nairobi, asked whether she realised that leopards might soon become extinct because of people like her, confirmed that, yes, she assumed it would happen, which was why she was buying two coats now. If it felt like an uphill struggle to educate the person in the street, the task was no less arduous at government level. At a 1964 meeting with Sukarno, first President of Indonesia, Robert Kennedy, younger brother of the recently assassinated US president and already a prominent politician in his own right, was presented with a pair of Komodo dragons, listed by IUCN as 'threatened with extermination'. It was clear that public engagement needed to include those in powerful positions.

Emergency fund

One of the great advantages of the close working relationship enjoyed by FPS, IUCN and WWF, and personified by Peter Scott with his triple crown of chairmanships, was that the society had its finger permanently on the pulse and was made immediately aware of the latest, most pressing conservation problems as they came to light. The ability to act on this information,

however, was constrained by financial considerations. In 1965, aware of the need to accelerate the process of rescuing animals that were in imminent danger of extinction, FPS came up with the idea of a fund specifically earmarked to enable a rapid response to urgent conservation crises.

The FPS Revolving Fund was created in conjunction with WWF, with FPS contributing an initial grant to kick-start the initiative. The idea was for WWF to repay half of any funds expended, if and when it had a sufficient surplus of uncommitted project money. An appeal to private donors yielded additional support, including a hefty anonymous donation. Such an encouraging initial response from the public augured well for the long-term success of this embryonic funding mechanism. The first beneficiaries of the fund were Javan and Sumatran rhinos and the Persian fallow deer, all under the auspices of WWF projects. Paradoxically for an organisation set up as a fundraising vehicle that would enable IUCN conservation policy to be turned into action on the ground, by the late 1960s WWF seems to have metamorphosed into a project implementer in its own right, supported by the fundraising efforts of FPS. The doubts expressed at the time by Lee Talbot and other conservationists who were 'not wholly convinced that creating a potential competitor was a good idea' were turning out to be prophetic. Leaving aside the irony of supporting a support vehicle, the benefits for the wildlife itself were clear. Ian Malcolmson, honorary treasurer of FPS at the time, urged members to subscribe and persuade their friends to subscribe 'in the full knowledge that every penny given would go direct to the task of saving wildlife'. The precise wording of Malcolmson's exhortation to supporters reveals the Revolving Fund as the direct forerunner of the renowned 100% Fund, of which more later, which would be launched by FPS in 1971.

In its five years of operation, the Revolving Fund supported 36 projects in 22 countries. The most striking aspect of this initiative is not just the diversity of species involved – which included Asian elephant, aye-aye, Japanese crested ibis, dugong, Somali wild ass and tamaraw – but also the sheer breadth of the conservation activities and tools that it funded: game warden training in Ghana; reintroduction of Swinhoe's pheasant in Taiwan; a car sticker campaign to improve the public image of brown bears in Italy's Abruzzo National Park; anti-poaching equipment to protect Nile crocodiles in Uganda; a Madagascar wildlife conference; improvement of facilities at the Jordan International Biological Station; a fibreglass boat for the use of scientists and guards in a Javan rhino sanctuary; and even, wait for it, the purchase of six giant tortoises (£230) included in the asking price for Cousin Island in the Seychelles, which was

ART FOR WILDLIFE'S SAKE

Just as the spectacular images and film footage of wildlife photographers and camera crews play a vital role in focusing wider public attention on the natural world, wildlife artists often use their creative talents to highlight the plight of endangered species and promote their conservation. The society has benefited from this kind of collaboration throughout its history, and nowhere is this more evident than in its long sequence of Christmas cards featuring work reproduced with the kind permission of numerous artists. These perennial favourites helped to swell the society's coffers each festive season. In 1973, FPS sold a jaw-dropping 62,745 cards, a record unlikely to be surpassed. These cards – spanning a 50-year period from 1950 to 2000 – are merely a representative sample of the complete collection, which is too large to include here. ∎

being bought by the International Council for Bird Preservation (today known as BirdLife International), with a little help from the FPS members who had answered an appeal in *Oryx*.

Two of the six Aldabra giant tortoises that formed one of the Revolving Fund's most bizarre emergency purchases.

Guided tours

Another innovation that first saw the light of day in the late 1960s was the idea of offering organised overseas wildlife tours, dubbed Oryx Tours, to FPS members. The first, to East Africa, arranged by FPS in February 1966, was so heavily oversubscribed that a decision was made to double the spaces by running a second tour the following year, this time to Kenya and Uganda. They succeeded in filling both trips with ease. The feedback from the 50 members who joined the inaugural tour to Kenya and Tanzania was universally effusive. By all accounts, the tour party was treated to spectacular views of a quantity and variety of wildlife that, to the uninitiated, must have been nothing short of staggering. Many participants were instantly hooked and demanded more. In view of the success of this first venture, FPS resolved to make these tours a regular feature. Tours duly followed to Iceland and Greenland, to

India's flagship national parks and reserves, and to Kenya once more, all with equally encouraging results. At the request of members with shallower pockets, a cheaper European tour to Holland and the Swiss National Park was also arranged.

The society was not the first organisation to offer overseas wildlife tours, but it had the advantage of being able to call upon the expert knowledge of its extensive local contacts, many of them in far-flung locations. It was astute enough to differentiate itself from the competition by offering 'longer tours, off the beaten track'. This was no idle boast: later trips took some of the more intrepid (and doubtless deep-pocketed) members to Bhutan and Nepal, Mongolia and Siberia, Ecuador and the Galápagos, Madagascar, Mauritius and Réunion.

Participants even found themselves contributing to new discoveries. During a tour of India they were witness to the rediscovery of the pygmy hog in the Himalayan foothills of Assam on the Bhutan border. They obtained what turned out to be the first photographs ever taken of this diminutive

Above left Jeremy Mallinson, Director of Jersey Wildlife Preservation Trust, Sir Ghillean Prance, Director of Royal Botanic Gardens, Kew, and FFI trustee Robin Sharp putting pen to paper in July 1997 to put the official seal on a collaborative working relationship that had thrived informally for many years. The three organisations continue to collaborate on a variety of conservation projects to this day.

Above right The successful Pygmy Hog Conservation Programme, which has seen over one hundred of these diminutive pigs released into the wild since its formation in 1995, had its origins in the 1971 initiative that sprang out of discussions in Assam between FPS staff and Jeremy Mallinson, Gerald Durrell's erstwhile sidekick at Jersey Zoo.

Right A car sticker campaign, supported by the FPS Revolving Fund, formed an integral part of an awareness scheme to protect Italy's brown bears in Abruzzo National Park. Franco Zunino, the naturalist whose research FPS helped to fund, is now Secretary General of the Italian Wilderness Society, which he himself founded – another example of the many individuals who have gone on to make their mark in conservation after receiving early support from the society.

species, believed to be extinct by many people at the time – including, apparently, the tour leader. A few months earlier, hearing rumours of pygmy hog sightings in this area, the naturalist and author Gerald Durrell had sought approval from FPS, IUCN and the Indian authorities to mount an expedition on behalf of the then Jersey Wildlife Preservation Trust, in the hope of capturing several of the hogs and starting a captive breeding programme at his zoo.

Further enquiries elicited the news that around 14 pygmy hogs were already in captivity on a tea estate after being flushed from deep cover by a raging bush fire, and Durrell dispatched one of his team to advise on the most appropriate care for this critically endangered species.

This encounter with Durrell was one of the earliest recorded instances of co-operation between FPS and the Jersey-based trust, but it was a sign of things to come. The two organisations went on to establish a mutually beneficial collaborative relationship that has stood the test of time, as we shall discover.

Distant acquaintances

The success of the Oryx Tours had highlighted how invaluable the society's overseas connections were, and no doubt influenced its decision to formalise these relationships. In early 1967 FPS announced the formation of a global network of local contacts, all distinguished conservationists, who had agreed to appear on a list of 'overseas consultants', with a brief to keep the society informed about conservation activities, problems and progress in their respective corners of the world, from Australia to Zambia. By 1979, this panel of experts exceeded 120 consultants and correspondents, and FPS had fingers on the conservation pulse in 75 countries throughout the continents of Africa, Asia, Australasia, Europe and the Americas. Anyone doubting the effectiveness of this arrangement could do worse than organise a trip to the most famous national park in deepest, darkest Peru, home not only to the spectacled bear and real-life inspiration for the perennially popular Paddington character, but also to the richest diversity of life on Earth.

Given the breathtaking nature of the local wildlife, including spectacular sights such as this violet-breasted hummingbird and myriad bromeliads (above right), it is no surprise that Major Ian Grimwood felt compelled to extol the manifold virtues of Manú.

flora, 222 different mammals and well over 1,300 varieties of butterfly. The list goes on. The reserve is also a living, breathing example of the art of balancing conservation with sustainable use; tourism, hunting, logging and harvesting of non-timber forest products are all permitted in the protected areas that abut the national park proper.

From an FFI perspective, however, it is the park's origins, as much as its spectacular flora and fauna, that warrant closer scrutiny. According to Wikipedia, 'before becoming an area protected by the Peruvian government, the Manú National Park was conserved thanks to its inaccessibility'. Digging deeper, we are informed that Manú was designated as a protected area in 1973. Regrettably, this date is inaccurate. Entries in the May and December 1968 issues of *Oryx* place the Peruvian government's declaration of Manú Nature Reserve five years earlier. More regrettably, from an FFI viewpoint, no amount of digging on *Wikipedia* can unearth the fact that the society, through one of its overseas consultants, played a vital role in influencing this decision.

Manú National Park which was declared a World Heritage site by UNESCO in 1987, is the largest national park in Peru. Home to around 1,000 species of bird, it is a magnet for birdwatchers and wildlife photographers, who flock to witness iconic scenes such as myriad macaws gathering at riverside clay licks. This is just one of the reserve's many ecological claims to fame, and some of them bear repeating. Thanks to its varied topography, which includes lowland tropical rainforest, wet cloud forest and montane grassland, the park boasts one of the highest levels of biodiversity in the world. Manú harbours more than 20,000 species of

An Englishman in Peru

The overseas correspondent playing the part of our man in Manú was no less a figure than Major Ian Grimwood, of Operation Oryx fame. *Oryx* reports that this astonishingly rich area was 'discovered' by Grimwood while working in his capacity as wildlife adviser to the Peruvian government from 1965–67. 'Discovered' is clearly hyperbole, but there is no doubting Grimwood's influential role in focusing attention on the area, and in the decision-making process that followed. The recommendations in his report, extracts from which appeared in *Oryx*, were accepted by the Peruvian government in March 1968. Writing to FPS, he had described Manú as 'of such outstanding interest that, if set aside as a national park, it would provide an area of worldwide scientific importance which could also in the course of time become one of the major tourist attractions of the South American continent'. To Major Grimwood's many talents we can now add the art of prophecy. He had also warned that time was of the essence, because the area faced an imminent threat from professional hunters, logging interests and a new road that would pave the way, literally, for an influx of workmen and would-be colonists. Bearing in mind the urgency of the situation, the FPS council agreed to dip into the Revolving Fund and allocate emergency money towards the proposed national park at the precise moment when the Peruvian government was considering the area's status. The rest is history. Today's World Heritage site stands as a living monument to Grimwood's perspicacity and FPS foresight.

As if it wasn't enough to wrestle endangered antelopes in Arabia and help preserve a South American biodiversity hotspot for the world's future delight and delectation, Grimwood then turned his versatile hand to helping IUCN assess the urgent conservation needs of South East Asia's vast but diminishing natural heritage. An action plan for the entire region, from Burma in the north-west to Papua New Guinea in the south-east, included specific recommendations for the orang-utan, tiger, clouded leopard, kouprey and monkey-eating eagle, and proposed further surveys to assess how much tropical rainforest could and should be protected from logging and development. By 1977, with a string of valuable contributions to the cause under his belt, Grimwood was a fully-fledged member of the FPS nest, having been elected vice-president. His outstanding achievements in wildlife conservation within and beyond the society were also recognised with the award of that year's J. Paul Getty Prize.

Where there's a wool . . .

Manú National Park is by no means the only Peru success story with which the society's overseas correspondents are associated. Felipe Benavides, a Peruvian former diplomat and vice-president of FPS, was an ardent conservationist who dedicated much of his life to preserving his country's natural heritage. Described in an *Oryx* editorial as 'not so much a breath of fresh air as a whirlwind', he first exploded onto the Latin American conservation scene in the 1950s. He founded the Peruvian Zoological Society and several other ecological institutes. In particular, he was a vociferous

champion of the vicuña, a high-altitude cousin of the llama threatened with extinction due to the rocketing demand for its valuable wool. The vicuña formerly ranged across Argentina, Bolivia, Chile, Ecuador and Peru in the hundreds of thousands. Centuries earlier, the Incas had rounded up the herds to shear them and harvest their wool. Unfortunately, sustainability wasn't on the agenda of the poachers, who between 1950 and 1970 killed an estimated 400,000 of these animals, which by then were largely confined to Bolivia and Peru. Benavides badgered the respective governments of these two countries to prohibit the export of vicuña wool and to create reserves in order to protect the remaining populations. He also badgered his friends at FPS, who in turn pressed the British government to ban the importation of all vicuña products. After several years of determined lobbying by, among others, FPS council member and former British ambassador to Peru, Sir Berkeley Gage, the requested ban was eventually imposed in October 1970. The vicuña population recovered so well that in some reserves it expanded beyond the carrying capacity of the protected area. Benavides was awarded the J. Paul Getty Prize for outstanding achievement in conservation in 1975, and promptly donated the entire $50,000 towards the creation of a scientific station in an area of coastal desert envisaged as the site of a new national park.

The success of Benavides and FPS in lobbying the respective governments at each end of the vicuña wool market perfectly illustrated the importance of international co-operation in the fight against the illegal wildlife trade. The legal importation of wildlife products that had been illegally exported from their country of origin potentially posed an enormous threat to the survival of endangered species. The society had been exerting pressure on the British government with regard to this issue for many years and the vicuña decision followed a string of earlier successes. Thanks to the indefatigable Colonel Boyle, a resolution from the 1960 IUCN conference had been converted into a concrete measure four years later, at least in the UK, when royal assent was granted for a bill restricting the importation of rare species. The new act gave vital protection to, among others, great apes, lemurs, rhinos and Galápagos giant tortoises. Of course, the full benefit of these restrictive measures would only be felt if all other countries adopted a similar policy. Until and unless non-compliant governments could be persuaded to fall in line and impose similar importation restrictions, the illegal traders would always find a market for their product, hence the perceived need for an all-embracing international trade agreement. It would take a whole decade of lobbying before that vision became a reality, but in 1973 the efforts of FPS and IUCN in this regard finally bore fruit.

HIGH-FLYING FRIENDS

Charles Lindbergh, American aviator, author, inventor, explorer, recipient of the Medal of Honor, social activist and, it later transpired, serial philanderer, is one of the most colourful characters in US history. His solo flight in a single-seater monoplane, *Spirit of St. Louis*, from New York to Paris in May 1927 catapulted him from virtual obscurity to instant worldwide celebrity. Among his less-vaunted claims to fame, he was a passionate conservationist, trustee of WWF International, board member of SSC and a long-term member of FPS. His largely unsung contributions to wildlife conservation included unilaterally, and on his own initiative, persuading the Peruvian authorities to stop killing blue whales. Along with Tom Harrisson, that irascible iconoclast who was so intolerant of IUCN inertia, Lindbergh was also responsible for conducting a high-level mission to save

two critically endangered species endemic to the Philippines. The monkey-eating eagle and the tamaraw were among the species featured in a comprehensive and alarming 1966 report prepared for IUCN by Lee and Martha Talbot. This highlighted the parlous state of biodiversity in a country where 'any species still surviving must be considered a threatened species'. A reputedly aggressive dwarf buffalo confined to the island of Mindoro, the tamaraw had been described by science as recently as 1888. Uncontrolled hunting for subsistence and sport had resulted in a dramatic population decline from an estimated 10,000 in 1900 to approximately 1,000 buffalo some 50 years later. By 1969, with numbers reduced to around 100 individuals, it appeared that extinction was imminent. Harrisson and Lindbergh evidently knew which buttons to press in Philippine

government circles; the dilatory officials sprang into action, deploying wardens and guards to protect the remaining tamaraw population in its principal stronghold, and prohibiting ranching within the reserve boundaries. A follow-up study conducted in 1976 found that numbers in that particular refuge had virtually quadrupled in the intervening years. The tamaraw is still critically endangered, but its continued survival owes much to the timely intervention of the dynamic duo, Lindbergh and Harrisson. ∎

Above Aviator Charles Lindbergh with his plane *Spirit of St. Louis*, in which he completed his historic solo flight from New York to Paris in May 1927.

Opposite Dr Tom Harrisson attends to a captive tamaraw during his mercy mission to the Philippines with Charles Lindbergh.

CHAPTER 5

PROFESSIONALISATION

'It wasn't being run per se; it was more of a members' club.'

John Burton, Executive Secretary 1975–87

For all its success in the 1950s and 1960s, FPS was not so much an organisation as a loose affiliation of natural history experts and enthusiasts pursuing their own personal interests. It had brought together a formidable talent pool comprising influential figures who were helping to shape the future of conservation, but this was arguably to the detriment of the society's own long-term development and collective identity. There was talk of the need for a strategic plan, but at this stage it was only talk. Even as recently as the mid 1970s, the society amounted to little more than a gentlemen's club for ageing conservationists. Professor Lee Talbot vividly recalls addressing a large auditorium of FPS members – at a time when he already thought of himself as a seasoned campaigner – and registering with some alarm that the average age in the audience was twice his own. What is more, these elderly members were starting to drop like flies. In 1975 alone, half of the society's ten vice-presidents passed away. The youngest, aged 73, had been a mere spring chicken compared to the senior citizen among them, who was 93 at the time of his death. The average age of the five officials lost to FPS was over 85. Clearly there was a crying need for an injection of new blood.

John Burton (right) concedes defeat to David Tomlinson and his eagle-eyed *Country Life* team after the 1981 Big Bird Race, a novel fundraising ruse.

Ring in the new

To his eternal credit, Richard Fitter, by then in his sixties, had the foresight to realise that such an approach was

unsustainable in the long term. He was instrumental in persuading the FPS council that a change of direction was required. With this in mind, he persuaded then vice-chairman Lord Craigton to interview a Young Turk by the name of John Burton, who had been making waves as a wildlife consultant at Friends of the Earth.

As if to emphasise the need for a revolution to overturn the established order, Burton's interview amounted to an amicable 10-minute chat over a pink gin in the Fellows' Restaurant at London Zoo, followed by lunch. He had arrived at this meeting under the misapprehension that he was there to discuss International Whaling Commission policy. He left shortly after lunch having been offered the role of assistant secretary at FPS with a brief to, in his words, 'professionalise and upgrade' the organisation. He accepted the position on condition

Opposite The Virunga Mountains, home to the critically endangered mountain gorilla, viewed from the summit of Uganda's Mount Muhabura.

that he could work part-time, which would allow him to retain his independence and leave room to pursue his writing interests in order to supplement the meagre FPS salary he was being offered.

When Burton began working for the society in late 1975, the scale of the task confronting him was immediately obvious. 'It wasn't being *run* per se; it was more of a members' club.' In addition to Richard and Maisie Fitter, there were just two other full-time staff, both of whom resigned shortly after his arrival. Burton wasted no time in appointing Vivien Gledhill as office manager, and the future Mrs Burton remained at FPS for six years – during which time her contribution was described as 'absolutely critical […] we have always been a double act' – before leaving in 1980 to work for Sir Peter Scott at the Species Survival Commission. The husband and wife team have since been reunited at the World Land Trust, which Burton went on to found after his own eventual departure from the society.

Burton's first, unofficial engagement, at his request, involved joining a delegation from FPS that flew out to attend an IUCN conference in Kinshasa. It was a valuable introduction to the international arena, and to the political machinations that were inseparable from efforts to control the illicit trade in ivory and other wildlife products. It also provided an unexpected bonus in the form of an exclusive tour around President Mobutu Sese Seko's private collection of okapis, during which Burton wisely refrained from asking whether the military dictator had a permit for his leopard-skin pillbox hat.

Birth of CITES

One of Burton's earliest contributions in his new role was to highlight the difficulties of policing the wildlife imports into Britain in the context of the recently ratified international trade convention, which was the culmination of over a decade of lobbying by FPS and other IUCN partners. At the Arusha Conference in 1961, the fledgling African governments had made it clear that their own efforts to control trade in endangered species were hamstrung by market forces outside their control, prompting Lee Talbot to suggest that an international agreement to regulate trade might offer a solution. This initial proposal had been well received and, in the wake of the 1963 IUCN General Assembly in Nairobi, agreement had eventually been reached on a convention restricting the international trade in endangered animals. The UK was one

The distinctive and ingenious CITES logo is a stylised representation of an ivory-laden elephant.

of 26 signatories out of the 88 nations represented at the so-called Washington Conference in February 1973, at which the succinctly named Convention on International Trade in Endangered Species of Wild Fauna and Flora (CITES) was born.

The convention operates through its schedules, grouping endangered species into three appendices according to the level of threat that they are facing. Appendix I comprises species that are in imminent danger of extinction and can be traded only in exceptional circumstances, while Appendix II lists those that may ultimately find themselves in the red alert category unless trade is closely monitored and controlled, or that warrant attention in order to protect species on Appendix I. Species are included in Appendix III at the request of one or more of the CITES signatories, to help prevent unsustainable or illegal exploitation by ensuring that appropriate permits are in place. Hearteningly, the convention included 'introductions from the sea' to cover marine mammals previously viewed as common property, which meant that large cetaceans would enjoy a degree of protection from exploitation by the whaling industry.

Described as a great achievement for FPS and the rest of the wildlife lobby, the embryonic agreement paradoxically posed a serious short-term threat to wildlife. There was great concern that the groundbreaking initiative might trigger a knee-jerk reaction among fur, skin, pet and leather traders, prompting them to fill their boots before the convention was ratified and legislation implemented. The aim was to secure a critical mass of signatories as soon as possible, so that those still outside the tent would find their attempts to continue trading undermined by a lack of buyers. Bearing in mind the urgency of the situation, the

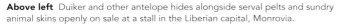

Above left Duiker and other antelope hides alongside serval pelts and sundry animal skins openly on sale at a stall in the Liberian capital, Monrovia.

Below right Dead monkey business: an enormous rug made from 38 black-and-white colobus skins takes pride of place among other animal artefacts including ivory and antelope hide.

Above right Maisie Fitter, then editor of *Oryx*, encountered this shockingly extravagant designer saddle, upholstered in jaguar skin, during a 1967 trip to the Americas.

UK government did not cover itself in glory. To the evident disgust of FPS, it fell into the trap of treating CITES as a political football and failed to sign until the following year.

CITES was finally ratified on 1 July 1975, a date described by the Solicitor General, Peter Archer, as 'a red-letter day for conservation', after the necessary ten signatories triggered the deal. This landmark agreement to limit international trade, as welcome as it was overdue, was only ever going to work if the signatories complied with the terms of CITES, with its effectiveness being largely dependent on the relative commitment of the governments of the signatory countries. With this in mind, the Survival Service Commission set up a bespoke trade study group to monitor the implementation of the convention. That organisation was TRAFFIC (Trade Records Analysis of Flora and Fauna in Commerce), another addition to the already bulging conservation glossary, and a classic example, if ever there was one, of a name being contrived in order to shoehorn it into a predetermined acronym. Many of the world's plant and animal species were moving inexorably towards extinction, but it was comforting to know that, at least where the language of global conservation was concerned, speciation was here to stay.

Green light for TRAFFIC

Unsurprisingly, given the initial paucity of financial and human resources at its disposal, TRAFFIC had come in like a lamb, and a timid one at that, but once the decision was taken to appoint Burton as chair, the organisation quickly found its roar. His experience of working on legal and illegal wildlife trade issues during his time at Friends of the Earth made Burton a logical choice for the role. It was Peter Scott, in his capacity as chairman of the Species Survival Commission, and Richard Fitter, as chairman of the steering committee for the embryonic TRAFFIC organisation, who suggested that Burton should take responsibility for developing it. The rationale was that he was already doing useful investigative work and uncovering widespread illegal activity. The FPS office in the old animal hospital at London Zoo doubled as TRAFFIC's temporary headquarters, which made logistical as well as financial sense in view of Burton's dual role. Funds were raised, primarily from FPS in the early stages, and new staff were recruited – as Burton puts it, 'we managed to cobble together enough money to hire Tim Inskipp'.

More familiar today as the co-author of numerous authoritative field guides to the birds of the Indian subcontinent, Inskipp was commissioned to investigate the illegal trade in a number of CITES-listed species. With additional funds and office space at his disposal, Burton then hired Jane Thornback for the mammoth task of compiling the next Red Data Book, this time on mammals. It wasn't long before Burton was making a nuisance of himself. The TRAFFIC team hit upon the simple expedient of demonstrating the ineffectiveness of CITES enforcement by smuggling items through customs themselves. Burton started delving further into the records of HM Customs and Excise, the government department then responsible for managing the import and export of goods into the UK. What he found was an almost impenetrable store of information on the illegal trade in furs, ivory, leathers and other wildlife products, which led to his asking some awkward, and slightly bizarre, questions. For example, was Britain importing cheetahs from Brazil?

Red rag to a panda

With Burton at the helm, TRAFFIC evolved into a self-sufficient, independent body, and moved into its own premises in Soho – inadvertently transforming a red light district into a Red List district. The organisation grew steadily both in size and capacity under his leadership,

Representative sample of illegal wildlife products confiscated at Heathrow Airport by UK customs.

and a US operation was established in 1979, the first in a series of overseas offices that have since sprung up to accommodate TRAFFIC's expanding global remit. Burton was not averse to ruffling feathers – indeed, he appears to have taken great delight in the fact that he was 'uncontrollable' – and some of his more provocative comments, articles and guerrilla tactics did not endear him to certain influential members of the conservation fraternity, including the hierarchy at WWF, which was jointly responsible with IUCN for governing TRAFFIC's activities. Sir Arthur Norman, the then chairman of WWF, demanded his resignation after a particularly embarrassing exposé relating to the illicit smuggling of panda skins out of China had unaccountably found its way onto the front page of *The Sunday Times*.

Burton emerged relatively unscathed from that particular skirmish, but the writing was on the wall. He was eventually ousted in 1981 – in his words, 'deposed by WWF in conservation's own version of the Night of the Long Knives' – but by this time TRAFFIC had already achieved critical mass and was perfectly well equipped to respond to an increasing volume of enquiries from governments and NGOs around the world. Today, TRAFFIC employs approximately 100 staff worldwide, spread across a network of 23 national offices located throughout its

The mind-bending markings of Grevy's zebra more than justify the choice of 'dazzle' as a collective noun, but they were also responsible for the species' near-demise, as poachers slaughtered the animals in unprecedented numbers to satisfy demand for their skins.

regional hubs in Africa, the Americas, Asia, Europe and Oceania. It has earned a reputation for scientifically sound and impartial analysis of wildlife trade issues, continues to promote international co-operation and local action in the context of CITES and the Convention on Biological Diversity, and is now at the forefront of efforts to change consumer behaviour.

No one doubted the need for an international convention, but CITES was no panacea. The salutary tale of Grevy's zebra served to illustrate how quickly a reasonably abundant, but unprotected, species can be brought to its knees by unbridled exploitation. Numbers in northern Kenya crashed from 10,000 to an estimated 1,000 in the space of just five years, in the face of a deadly onslaught from poachers seeking to cash in on the rocketing price of skins, coveted by the dedicated followers of high fashion. Conservationists were caught napping by the speed of the decline. Unlisted by CITES at the time, Grevy's zebra had no official protection. President Kenyatta moved quickly to announce a ban on all trade in wildlife products, but by then most of the damage had been done.

FPS co-sponsored Operation Zebra, which was launched to help fund an emergency translocation programme that would move stock from the unprotected north of Kenya to the safe havens of Samburu and Tsavo National Parks. Grevy's zebra is today listed on Appendix I of CITES, which bans all trade in the animal, but it still faces other more insidious threats to its survival, including habitat degradation and competition with livestock.

Above left Despite the restrictions imposed by CITES, the international parrot trade continues to take a heavy toll on the wild population.

Above right This young orang-utan, illegally imported into Vietnam and confined to a tiny cage, was one of numerous endangered species found languishing behind bars in a Ho Chi Minh City market.

Initially hailed as one of the most useful weapons in the conservationist's armoury, the convention has not necessarily lived up to those early expectations. With the benefit of hindsight, some level of disappointment was inevitable. As a means of preventing the extinction of a species, CITES has obvious limitations. A listing confers nominal protection, but its effectiveness at ensuring conservation on the ground is always going to be minimal, given the myriad threats faced by the wildlife it is designed to safeguard. In their eagerness to secure an agreement, conservationists at the time arguably lost sight of the bigger picture and were slow to appreciate that regulation of trade did not constitute a silver bullet.

Today, notwithstanding the technical and political difficulties inherent in securing a listing for a threatened species, the whole CITES concept is viewed in some quarters as counter-productive, particularly by those who regard sustainable use of natural resources as a vital conservation tool. Conversely, recent research has demonstrated that even controlled harvesting of some listed species is biologically – and socio-economically – unsustainable.

Zoo logic

Damaging though it was to the long-term survival prospects of endangered species, the trafficking of skins, horn and ivory was by no means the only form of trade to pose a threat to their future. The impact of zoos on the live animal trade had been a major bone of contention in conservation circles long before Burton assumed the reins at FPS. Many of the less enlightened, or less scrupulous, institutions, far from contributing to wildlife conservation, were deemed to be actually increasing the pressure on endangered species by continuing to source specimens from the wild. It was this unease that had provided the impetus for a 1964 symposium on *Zoos and Conservation*, which was held at London Zoo and chaired by The Duke of

Left to right The then FPS chairman Peter Scott was invited to chair the 1966 San Diego conference.

Major Ian Grimwood, looking dapper in suit and tie – and almost unrecognisable from the sweat-stained figure who returned triumphant from wrestling Arabian oryx in the Aden desert.

Richard Fitter, FPS secretary, speaking at the conference.

Left to right Dr William Conway, then director of New York Zoological Society and later president of the organisation in its later guise as the Wildlife Conservation Society, and a keen proponent of captive breeding programmes for endangered species.

Caroline Jarvis, editor of the *International Zoo Yearbook* from its inception in 1960 until 1968, initially with Dr Desmond Morris.

Dr Perez Olindo, who subsequently led the Kenyan delegation to CITES in Washington DC in 1972 and signed the convention on behalf of his nation.

Left to right Dr Lee Talbot, the first staff ecologist at IUCN whose seminal report was the initial catalyst for Operation Oryx.

The late Dr Eugenie Clark, affectionately known as 'The Shark Lady', was a marine biologist and ardent conservationist who pioneered scuba diving for research purposes.

The late Federico Carlos Lehmann, a Colombian conservation biologist who was instrumental in the creation of new protected areas in his country.

Edinburgh in his capacity as president of the Zoological Society of London. The society had played a leading role in the genesis of this event and was a joint sponsor. Two years later, FPS chairman Peter Scott had chaired a conference in California entitled *The Role of Zoos in the International Conservation of Wild Animals*. This was organised to coincide with the fiftieth anniversary celebrations of San Diego Zoo, renowned worldwide for its achievements in building up breeding stocks of globally threatened species and, of course, an ongoing participant in the Arabian oryx captive breeding programme. Richard Fitter and Scott himself, as usual wearing several conservation hats simultaneously, were among the speakers at this landmark conference.

Whilst there was general agreement that zoos had genuine conservation value from an educational perspective, the main message was that they had an obligation to set up and contribute to captive breeding programmes using their own stock, rather than relying on the importation of species plucked from their native habitat. Put another way, if you are dependent on nets, you are not having a net positive impact.

Good breeding

One of the undisputed pioneers in the field of captive breeding was Gerald Durrell. His vision had always been to create 'a new kind of zoo' that would provide an insurance policy against the extinction of animals in the wild, a 'reservoir for endangered species', as he put it. The Jersey Wildlife Preservation Trust that Durrell had founded was renowned for the quality of its facilities and its enviable record of captive breeding success. In 1972 Durrell and FPS joined forces to organise the first international conference that focused specifically on the captive breeding of endangered species as a means of ensuring their survival. This initiative brought together almost 300 people, many of them world leaders in their field. Hosted by Jersey Zoo and chaired by the ubiquitous Peter Scott, the conference discussed the need to improve captive breeding techniques and communicate these more widely. Alarmingly, statistics drawn from the *International Zoo Yearbook* indicated that zoos were net consumers of endangered species. There was an evident need for more zoos to participate in breeding programmes, rather than viewing endangered species as mere exhibits and box office attractions. The proceedings concluded with a declaration to the effect that captive breeding was deemed a crucial method of preventing extinctions. A second conference four years later would focus on reintroduction as the ultimate goal of captive breeding, and emphasise the importance of replenishing the captive gene pool with wild stock in order to avoid inbreeding and retain evolutionary flexibility within each species.

Symbolically, a pair of Asiatic lion cubs was formally presented to Gerald Durrell at the 1972 conference. An anonymous donation from an FPS member had enabled the society to purchase the cubs for use in a new captive breeding programme at Jersey Zoo. The Asiatic lion population had sunk ominously low in north-west India's Gir Forest, the species' last refuge. With numbers down to an estimated 150 individuals, extinction in the wild was a distinct possibility, hence the need for a contingency plan.

Giving 100 per cent

The Asiatic lion breeding programme was one of the first initiatives to benefit from the support of the 100% Fund, which by then had superseded the old Revolving Fund. For all its success, the latter scheme was terminated by mutual agreement at the end of 1970, at which point the FPS council, at the instigation of chairman Lord Craigton, put in place alternative arrangements for supporting urgent projects.

The Oryx 100% Fund, to use its full name, was launched with an appeal in the September 1971 issue of the journal. The clue was in the title; the unique selling proposition of this fund was that all donations were passed directly to conservation projects, with no deductions for administration. Typically, it costs money to raise money. No ordinary appeal could possibly undertake to pass on everything it received, but then this was no ordinary appeal. Aimed exclusively at members and friends of the society, the advertisement appeared only in *Oryx*. Prepaid envelopes donated by well-wishers were sent out with the journal mailing. In addition, the FPS council decided to match all contributions to the fund, effectively doubling the value of every donation.

The 100% Fund refreshed the parts that other funding sources could not reach. It represented the only readily available source of small grants for emergency wildlife conservation operations in any part of the world. The focus was on funding urgent small-scale projects, the idea being to leave the bigger projects to WWF, thereby avoiding duplication of effort and resources. These small grants were to prove vitally important in supporting the rapid fact-finding missions that were essential for the development of species action plans. The types of project supported included field surveys, educational

The 100% Fund was developed at the behest of then FPS chairman Lord Craigton, whom Labour MP Tam Dalyell later described in his 1993 obituary in the *Independent* as 'a curmudgeonly and irascible minister [who] metamorphosed into a genial, effective, dedicated pioneer of enlightened conservation policies'. As Dalyell pointed out, 'Long before it was fashionable, Craigton was a champion of conservation . . . No one has used his position in the House of Lords more effectively to promote the cause of ecological understanding.'

Above The 100% Fund supported initial research that led to the establishment of a captive breeding programme in Vietnam's Cuc Phuong National Park for the endangered Owston's civet, which is under threat from hunting throughout its limited range.

Right The last in a succession of leaflets issued by the society to promote the 100% Fund.

The 100% Fund

a unique way of supporting conservation world-wide

campaigns, anti-poaching activities and, as it turned out, the purchase of Asiatic lion cubs for captive breeding purposes. Applications to the 100% Fund were assessed by a committee of respected international conservationists, with projects selected on the basis of conservation importance, sound scientific principles, cost effectiveness and local involvement.

An early example of the value of the 100% Fund as an emergency response mechanism was provided by an urgent conservation intervention in Costa Rica. A £700 grant enabled the national park authorities to purchase an engine for an anti-poaching patrol boat, which was deployed to protect green turtles on their nesting beaches. As a result, poaching of turtles and their eggs in Tortuguero National Park during that particular nesting season was reduced to zero.

100% FUND – 30 YEARS OF SUPPORT

During its three decades of existence the 100% Fund supported over 700 small-scale conservation projects in almost 150 countries, enhancing the survival chances of hundreds of the world's most endangered plants and animals. It is impossible to do justice to the geographical sweep and the range of species supported, from Ader's duiker in the Arabuko-Sokoke Forest to the Zanzibar red colobus in, well, Zanzibar.

John Burton, who inherited the 100% Fund concept when he joined FPS in 1975, is keen to point out that a number of these projects have left no discernible trace today. Perhaps he had in mind his own study into the efficacy of artificial bat caves, which was supported by the fund in 1976. Speculation aside, the effectiveness – or otherwise – of these interventions in terms of their ultimate impact on a particular species is only half the story.

By way of example, a 1991 study of the conservation biology of the babirusa, the weird and wonderful 'pig-deer' confined to the Indonesian island of Sulawesi, contributed to saving the species from extinction. The recipient of this grant, Dr Lynn Clayton, has subsequently devoted her life to protecting the babirusa and its tropical forest habitat, and to ensuring the social welfare of the communities around one of its last refuges, Nantu Nature Reserve.

By providing opportunities for training, education, skill-sharing and personal development, the 100% Fund also raised community awareness, harnessed local support and inspired the conservationists of the future, thereby ensuring the long-term

sustainability of the conservation work that it was helping to fund. That is also an essential part of its legacy.

Many of today's leading lights in the global conservation community began their careers as grateful recipients of these small grants, and some have provided glowing testimonials to that effect.

'In this day and age of mega-projects and red-tape-ridden funding initiatives, it is increasingly rare to find donors willing to make those highly important, flexible funds available. The 100% Fund grants I received in the 1970s for the conservation of the scimitar-horned oryx, addax and other arid-land species made a substantial impact and they are still high on Chad's conservation agenda, something that probably would not have happened without that timely and critical support.'

John Newby, founding CEO, Sahara Conservation Fund

100% Fund support has made a vital contribution to the survival of the addax and other semi-desert antelopes.

'I was fortunate to secure two grants from the Oryx 100% Fund. Both projects resulted in valuable new data sets, published scientific papers, practical conservation recommendations and, crucially, contributed to the establishment of new protected areas (in Nepal) and new environmental legislation (in Yemen). Personally leading both these projects had a profound effect on me, enhancing my understanding of how to contribute to conservation research, policy and practice, and sparking my enthusiasm for the challenges and rewards of playing a part in international conservation efforts.'

Dr Mike Rands, Executive Director, Cambridge Conservation Initiative, former Chief Executive, BirdLife International

Portrait of a babirusa by Kitty Harvill, one of the many wildlife artists who recently lent their creative support to promote Dr Lynn Clayton's vital conservation work in Sulawesi, which began over 25 years ago with a 100% Fund grant.

'A grant from the 100% Fund back in 1979 launched my fieldwork on threatened birds in Tanzania. This initiative subsequently grew into a series of large-scale conservation projects funded to the tune of millions of dollars a year.'

Dr Simon Stuart, Chair of IUCN Species Survival Commission (retired 2016)

The full list of grantees reads like a who's who of the great and the good in conservation. Other beneficiaries have included Dr Sandy Harcourt, now Professor Emeritus at University of California, Davis, and one of the first grant recipients in 1971, as well as the primatologist Dr Dian Fossey, both of whom feature later in this chapter in the context of mountain gorilla conservation.

The society's own Dr Tony Whitten, FFI Senior Adviser, former Regional Director for Asia-Pacific and previously Senior Biodiversity Specialist at the World Bank, received funding in 1975 to study Kloss's gibbon on the remote Indonesian island of Siberut. Whitten has since parked his penchant for primates and turned troglodyte, in order to champion cave-dwelling invertebrates, particularly those confined to threatened karst limestone ecosystems, including blind cave crickets and the recently discovered Hon Chong ghost snail.

The late Dr Gerardo Budowski, IUCN's first Director-General, recipient of multiple conservation awards and an international chess master to boot, received 100% Fund support in 1977 for an analysis of endangered fauna in Costa Rica, his adopted home since 1952.

In 1988, Belinda Stewart-Cox, OBE, founder and executive director of Elephant Conservation Network, completed a bird survey in Thailand with

Karst of thousands. This recently described new species of ghost snail is one of countless neglected invertebrates – and high-profile vertebrates – whose survival is threatened by the destruction of their karst limestone habitat. Dr Tony Whitten is the driving force behind a recent FFI initiative to engage constructively with the cement manufacturers whose quarrying arguably poses the greatest threat to these ecosystems.

100% Fund support, and has devoted herself to the conservation of that country's forests and wildlife ever since.

Professor Paul Racey, whose work the fund first supported in 1979 and who served as vice-chair of FFI's council from 2006–12, is a world authority on bats and featured in 2008 as one of *BBC Wildlife* magazine's 50 conservation heroes. Among numerous other accolades, he received a lifetime achievement award from the Bat Conservation Trust, which he helped to establish in 1990.

Close-up of a female hawksbill turtle discovered nesting under a casuarina tree, photographed by Dr Jack Frazier.

Dr Jack Frazier, whose lifelong love affair with chelonids began with a sojourn among Aldabra's giant tortoises, is a legend in the sea turtle conservation community who has reputedly done more to promote global capacity to protect marine turtles than any other individual. He was a serial beneficiary of 100% Fund support from 1971 to 1994.

The late Dr Boonsong Lekagul, a physician and former hunter credited with single-handedly launching Thailand's conservation movement, had already reached retirement age by the time the 100% Fund was launched, but that didn't preclude the man known locally as 'Mr Conservation' from obtaining a grant when well into his seventies.

Professor David Macdonald, founding director of Oxford University's Wildlife Conservation Research Unit, chairman of Defra's Darwin Initiative, and placed third (one place above the legendary Sir David Attenborough) in the 2015 *BBC Wildlife* list of the UK's top 50 most influential conservation heroes, received 100% Fund support in 1986.

In 1994, Dr Peter Ng, director of Singapore's Lee Kong Chian Natural History Museum and a globally renowned freshwater crab expert, conducted a survey of Borneo's peat swamps with support from the fund.

A 100% Fund grant in 1983 enabled Dr Elizabeth Bennett, MBE, now vice-president of Species Conservation at the Wildlife Conservation Society, to conduct a pilot visit that led to the first ever detailed field study of the proboscis monkey and a 20-year association with Sarawak that saw

Dr Boonsong Lekagul (right) at the 1966 zoo conference in San Diego, a decade before he received a 100% Fund grant.

her play a lead role in developing wildlife policy and protected area planning. In recognition of her Outstanding Contribution to the People of Malaysia, she received the prestigious 2015 Merdeka Award, the country's highest civil society honour. ■

75 YEARS AND COUNTING

By 1978, the society had been contributing to wildlife conservation for three-quarters of a century. This auspicious anniversary was marked with the publication of a slim volume entitled *The Penitent Butchers*, written by honorary secretary Richard Fitter and illustrated by chairman Sir Peter Scott, which provided a brief overview of wildlife conservation and, in particular, the vital role played by the society in its evolution throughout the twentieth century. Conveniently, Sir William Collins was an FPS board member, so the task of finding a publisher did not prove particularly arduous.

Not unsurprisingly, the book received favourable reviews in *Oryx*. More revealing, however, were the references to the society's aptitude for combining with other influential individuals and organisations to great effect: 'Because of the FPS's interlocking relations with other international and national organisations, and with a host of specialists and learned bodies [...] its influence has been out of all proportion to its size.' Time and time again throughout its history, the society has succeeded in forming strategic alliances and associations that enable it to punch above its weight. ∎

The greatest ape

One of the 100% Fund's most notable characteristics, which we will revisit later, was its deliberate bias towards projects that would benefit less popular, otherwise neglected species. On the other hand, if there was a particularly pressing need, it was not averse to funding protection measures for some of the most charismatic megafauna on the planet. In its very first year, the fund awarded grants for vital work on several high-profile species that were already household names. One of these was the mountain gorilla.

Support from the 100% Fund, in the shape of a grant for a census, came at a time when the mountain gorilla population in Rwanda was at an all-time low, and it was destined to fall further as the decade wore on. The nominal protection afforded by the national park had failed to prevent agricultural encroachment, poaching for food, illegal trade and trophies, and forest degradation caused by the exploitation of natural resources for fuel and building

Above The cultivated valleys and foothills around Uganda's Mgahinga Gorilla National Park exemplify the agricultural pressure on mountain gorilla habitat.

Opposite Cover of *The Penitent Butchers*, published in early December 1978 to coincide precisely with the society's 75th birthday.

materials. Marooned on their shrinking island of forest, the gorillas were being slowly but inexorably swallowed up by the rising tide of a desperate, poverty-stricken and rapidly increasing human population. Something had to give.

Funding the mountain gorilla census in early 1972 was by no means the society's first intervention on behalf of this critically endangered primate. An editorial note appeared in the November 1956 issue of *Oryx*, expressing great concern that the Ugandan section of the mountain gorilla sanctuary in the Virunga Massif was being opened up for settlement and the collection of forest products, depriving the gorillas of crucial habitat. This article quoted a pronouncement made several decades earlier by Sir Peter Chalmers Mitchell, secretary of London Zoo from 1903–35 and a leading light in the then Society for the Preservation of the Fauna of the Empire: 'In the whole sphere of zoology there is nothing more important than that these gorillas should be preserved undisturbed.' As early as 1921, the magnificently monikered old Etonian, Edmund Gustavus Bloomfield Meade-Waldo, a globetrotting ornithologist and an active member of the society before and after the Great War, was drawing attention to the shooting of large groups of gorillas in the Virunga volcanoes region, and pointing out that 'this race of gorilla was confined to a very small area and would be easily exterminated'. Although the slaughter had taken place in Belgian territory, which was outside the society's jurisdiction, it proposed raising the issue at the forthcoming League of Nations conference. From the 1930s onwards, the society had been pressing for a national park in the area, and it had also asked for further consideration to be given to preserving the other remaining mountain gorilla stronghold in Kayonza, now known as the Bwindi Impenetrable Forest, in order to protect the great apes and their habitat from impending development.

Professor Victor Van Straelen, another giant of international nature conservation whose name is inextricably linked with mountain gorillas, was a long-term associate of the society and a vice-president of FPS until his death in 1964. It was at his instigation, with support from Belgium's King Albert, that the first 'gorilla sanctuary' was established in 1926 in Parc National Albert. After independence, his cordial relationship with the African authorities and park personnel influenced their willingness to maintain the integrity of their protected areas.

In the late 1960s mountain gorilla conservation was again uppermost in the thoughts of FPS following the revelation that the Oberbürgermeister (Lord Mayor) of Cologne, who was also president of Cologne Zoo, had been offered a pair of mountain gorillas during a VIP visit to Rwanda. This only came to light when American primatologist Dian Fossey, who was conducting a long-term study of the gorillas from her remote research camp in the Virungas, was asked to nurse back to health two sick baby gorillas that were destined for Germany. She rightly saw fit to broadcast the story, and FPS joined the chorus of protests and cabled the aforesaid mayor and the president of Rwanda, Grégoire Kayibanda. Receiving no reply from either, chairman Sir Peter Scott donned one of his many other conservationist hats and wrote to the mayor on behalf of the Species Survival Commission, berating him for this irresponsible action and pointing out that accepting an endangered species captured in a national park was not only illegal and morally reprehensible, but also set a disastrous precedent, encouraging opportunists back in Rwanda to view other baby gorillas as fair game.

Rearguard action

By 1970, according to a letter from Rwanda published in *Oryx*, the situation for mountain gorillas was already 'extremely critical'. They were, it reported, being pressurised from all sides by poachers, cattle herders and honey hunters, all of them effectively free to roam at will, with the result that it was 'not a park at all'. At this juncture, it appears that only one small area enjoyed any semblance of protection; that was the portion of the park guarded by 'a courageous American girl' who was doing everything in her power to keep the intruders at bay. This was, of course, Dian Fossey, who was fighting a valiant one-woman rearguard action to keep the gorillas in her study area relatively safe and unmolested. According to the correspondent, the future looked bleak: 'The few gorilla groups that survive are increasingly confined to the final and steepest slopes of the volcanoes. The slow process of extinction is well on its way.'

The results of the urgently needed 1972 census of the mountain gorilla population in Rwanda's Volcanoes National Park confirmed the desperate need for better protection and law enforcement to prevent the appropriation of land and reduce human interference in the Virungas. An accompanying note stressed the importance of spreading the word about the gorillas' plight, stating that: 'A proclaimed and informed interest in the gorillas by the developed world is essential to ensure their survival.'

Richard and Maisie Fitter visited Rwanda in December 1973, and their subsequent report in *Oryx* highlighted the need for positive action – including park patrols – to avert the inevitable loss of the park and its gorillas. In particular, the Fitters advocated finding a way to generate tourist income for this impoverished nation, ideally by arranging for local guides to take visitors to see gorilla groups that had been habituated to the presence of strangers. 'How long can a small, poor, densely populated country like Rwanda be expected to go on reserving large areas of cultivable land if it does not bring in a significant revenue from tourists?' they asked. The report also suggested seeking aid from the World Heritage Fund to create an international park

encompassing the forest in all three countries and policed by co-operative cross-border patrols. One thing was clear: Rwanda was going to need outside help to preserve its natural heritage.

This outside help would soon materialise, and in dramatic fashion, as a result of the intervention of a man who had been a member of the society since the 1950s and was destined to become its greatest ambassador. That man was David Attenborough.

Close encounters

First transmitted in the UK in early 1979, David Attenborough's pioneering and critically acclaimed television series, *Life on Earth: A Natural History*, not only set the gold standard for wildlife documentary film-making but also opened the eyes of the world at large to the astonishing breadth – and fragility – of global biodiversity. The most iconic scene in the series, and arguably one of the most memorable sequences in

Faces in the crowd, a snapshot of the growing sea of humanity living a mere stone's throw from Rwanda's Volcanoes National Park.

the entire history of television (in a millennium poll of Channel 4 viewers it was rated higher than the coronation of Queen Elizabeth II), was his intimate encounter with a group of mountain gorillas in Rwanda, habituated to the presence of humans thanks to the efforts of Dian Fossey and her research team. The gorillas' gentle interaction with Attenborough graphically illustrated the absurdity of their fearsome reputation and endeared them not just to viewers in England, but to a worldwide audience estimated at 500 million. Attenborough himself described the experience as 'one of the most exciting encounters of my life'.

Before he had even finished filming the *Life on Earth* series, Attenborough received the depressing news from a distraught Fossey that poachers had murdered her favourite young silverback, Digit, the poster-boy for gorillas whom she had studied for over a decade. His head and hands had been chopped off, as it later transpired for the £10 bounty

Above Wooden cross marking the burial site of Digit, the young silverback gorilla whose brutal killing provided the initial catalyst for the Mountain Gorilla Project.

Right Known as the land of a thousand hills, Rwanda has the highest population density of any country in mainland Africa, with over 12 million people attempting to eke out a living in an area not much bigger than Kruger National Park. Relieving the pressure on mountain gorillas and their habitat is contingent on enabling these impoverished communities to meet their livelihood needs without resorting to unsustainable exploitation of the forest resources on which their long-term future depends.

offered by trophy hunters. The barbaric killing was particularly significant in that it was perpetrated on a member of Fossey's study groups, which had previously appeared to be untouchable, unlike the already depleted gorilla groups elsewhere in Rwanda. 'This could be the beginning of the end', was her grim conclusion.

Attenborough felt compelled to act, and immediately contacted John Burton at FPS. The most pressing need was evidently for additional guards and equipment to combat the poachers. FPS swiftly set up the Mountain Gorilla Fund, which journalist Brian Jackman needed little persuasion to promote through an appeal in *The Sunday Times*.

Donations totalling almost £8,000 flowed in rapidly from an outraged public, including school conservation groups whose members sent in their entire savings; some of the initial proceeds were allocated to Fossey; the remainder went to the Rwandan authorities to help bolster gorilla protection in the park under the auspices of what would metamorphose into the Mountain Gorilla Project and, ultimately, the International Gorilla Conservation Programme that we know today.

Fossey herself, however, was opposed to the Mountain Gorilla Project, or indeed anything that interfered with her own relationship with the great apes. Her hostility and increasingly erratic behaviour made her many enemies, alienated even her potential allies and culminated in her (still unsolved) murder in 1985.

Massif investment

The campaign itself quickly gained momentum. An enlarged issue of *Oryx* in November 1978, commemorating the seventy-fifth anniversary of the society, included a full-page appeal on behalf of the FPS Mountain Gorilla Fund, which set an ambitious target of £50,000. Earlier in the year a small mission had been dispatched to Rwanda in order to clarify what was happening on the ground and what action needed taking. Professor Kai Curry-Lindahl, FPS vice-president and a Virunga veteran, led the trip, accompanied by Sandy Harcourt, recently appointed co-ordinator of the fledgling Mountain Gorilla Project, and Brian Jackman, the journalist who had brought the story to the wider world. They concluded that the most pressing needs were additional buildings, signage and checkpoints, training of tourist guides, publicity material both for international tourists and local inhabitants, habituation of more gorilla groups for tourism purposes, support for ongoing research and – most urgent of all – more, better-equipped and better-trained guards to combat the poachers. By the following year, deliberate gorilla killings appeared to have halted and, thanks to the generosity of donors, the mountain gorilla appeal had raised sufficient funds to kick-start two initiatives vital to long-term success: conservation education and gorilla habituation.

By 1979 fundraising was in full swing and the Mountain Gorilla Project was starting to take shape. It would evolve into a model of co-operation between FPS and other conservation groups who, despite the inherent difficulties of working as a coalition, showed themselves capable of rallying to a common cause.

Gorilla tactics

The first phase of the Mountain Gorilla Project involved four separate but mutually complementary initiatives. In partnership with the People's Trust for Endangered Species (PTES), the society took responsibility for conservation education and tourism development, including habituation of new gorilla groups. The African Wildlife Leadership Foundation (which subsequently dropped the word 'Leadership') worked with PTES and WWF respectively on ranger training and a building programme, both of which quickly became mired in bureaucracy. Although all facets of this work were vital, it was education that had the potential to exert the most far-reaching impact.

In the early stages at least, it was Bill Weber and Amy Vedder – recipients of a 100% Fund grant – who were responsible for driving this educational component. Ecology was added to the secondary school curriculum, including materials contributed by Weber and Vedder. Primatologists Conrad and Ros Aveling, fresh from an exhilarating three years working with orang-utans in Indonesia, flew in to take over the conservation education programme and, crucially, to begin habituating gorilla groups in preparation for tourist visits.

Their success in this regard relied heavily on the co-operation of the researchers who had taken over in Dian Fossey's absence. Ros Aveling recalls establishing a 'brilliant relationship' with Kelly Stewart and Sandy Harcourt, which no doubt contributed significantly to the success of the gorilla habituation process.

Above Armed rangers patrolling in the shadow of Mount Sabinyo, a dormant volcano in Uganda's Mgahinga Gorilla National Park.

Right A local craftsman in Kinigi displays handcrafted gorilla souvenirs for tourist visitors to Volcanoes National Park, Rwanda.

Opposite Rwandan banknote featuring a mountain gorilla image reproduced from a painting by wildlife artist and friend of the society Bruce Pearson.

Above The makeshift tour bus during its whistle-stop tour of Rwanda and (right) the poster that unwittingly caused offence in Kenya when it was misinterpreted by the entourage of the then president, Daniel arap Moi.

Opposite The films and slide shows screened throughout Rwanda as part of the Mountain Gorilla Project's mobile charm offensive on behalf of mountain gorillas drew large crowds wherever the travelling primate salvation show appeared.

Responsibility for the day-to-day running of the educational component of the programme was placed in the capable hands of a Peace Corps volunteer, Jim O'Keefe. An educational tour of schools and villages throughout the country was scheduled, accompanied by a Rwandan teacher in order to ensure succession planning. The tour bus – or, more accurately, Renault van – was specially equipped to show films and slide shows highlighting the exceptional nature of the country's wildlife. In a pre-digital world, it proved hugely popular with audiences throughout Rwanda. If the account in *Oryx* is to be believed, a booklet entitled *Rwandan Heritage* – outlining the importance of water, forest and gorilla conservation – was distributed to every single secondary school pupil in the country. FPS and its international partners also orchestrated a broader public awareness programme, which amounted to a global propaganda campaign on behalf of the gorillas. This wider initiative was well received in most quarters, with the possible exception of Kenya, where posters featuring a headshot of a mountain gorilla accompanied by a headline exhorting '*Protégez-Moi!*' caused consternation among supporters of the then Kenyan president who – understandably unfamiliar with French personal pronouns and affirmative imperatives – took offence at what they mistook for a deeply unflattering portrait of their great leader.

Local ownership

As with so many of the society's initiatives before and since, the secret of success for the Mountain Gorilla Project was to embed the project into the local community from the outset. It was essential to disabuse the community of the notion that the park was merely an expensive playground for rich, white visitors.

The forest regulates regional water supply, acting as a giant sponge that stores water in the rainy season and slowly releases it throughout the dry season. Chopping down their forest was tantamount to the Rwandans cutting off their own life support system. Similarly, killing the great apes themselves would deprive the community of a potentially lucrative and sustainable income stream in the form of gorilla tourism. With this in mind, a great deal of time was spent persuading the community of the wider benefits of conserving not only the gorillas themselves, but also their forest home.

Encouraging signs that the conservation message was taking root soon materialised in the shape of articles in the national press, and the composition of a pro-gorilla popular song, neither of which was a coalition initiative. In other words, the local community had already begun to take ownership of the project.

By 1981 the park was making a significant profit, helping to reinforce the arguments for conserving it. There was also evidence that the message had penetrated the decision

Ever since the original Mountain Gorilla Fund was launched with an appeal in *The Sunday Times* alongside an article penned by journalist Brian Jackman, the plight of this greatest of great apes has continued to capture the public imagination. The Mountain Gorilla Project, established in the wake of the success of that initial appeal, elicited an unprecedented level of support at home and abroad, as has its transboundary successor, the International Gorilla Conservation Programme. The poster above, which dates from the early 1980s, featured in numerous newspapers, magazines and other publications, and often formed the centrepiece of the gorilla road shows that drew large audiences wherever the society's travelling exhibition set out its stall.

published by
the Fauna and Flora Preservation Society
c/o Zoological Society of London
Regent's Park,
London NW1 4RY

Above One of the many appeal leaflets issued by the society to highlight the mountain gorilla's plight and solicit support for its conservation.

Below Numerous discussions were held among the programme partners before agreement was reached on this striking triangular design for an IGCP promotional sticker, which eventually saw the light of day in 1995.

Border remit

A 1981 survey demonstrated conclusively that the mountain gorillas in the Rwanda portion of the Virungas had benefited from the protection afforded by the Mountain Gorilla Project. The obvious next step was to expand the project's remit to encompass the other two countries where the mountain gorillas were found, in order to safeguard the subspecies throughout the rest of its range. This was, however, contingent on securing additional financial support, so a US$17,295 donation from J. Paul Getty Jr provided a timely boost to the society's fundraising efforts. With the initial firefighting activities having achieved positive results, the scene was set for the coalition to adopt a more strategic, holistic approach to mountain gorilla conservation that encompassed the entire Virungas ecosystem.

It was Ros and Conrad Aveling who, after returning to Central Africa following a brief and traumatic stint in Sudan during which the latter was kidnapped, initially set up and ran a complementary programme for the mountain gorillas on the DRC side of the shared border with Rwanda. The original idea of expanding the Mountain Gorilla Project into a transboundary initiative had its roots in a concept document written by Ros Aveling. A key figure in the discussions was Dr Samuel Mankoto ma Mbaelele, Head of Parks in DRC, without whose vision and support the proposed collaboration would have been a non-starter. The perennial problem of where the money would come from was eased somewhat, at least in the short term, when the author, screenwriter and primate enthusiast Michael Crichton, later of *Jurassic Park* fame, made a substantial donation to the cause.

makers at government level. A Rwandan banknote issued in 1982 featured a picture of mountain gorillas, taken from a Bruce Pearson painting that FPS was intending to use as its next Christmas card.

Another significant factor in the society's success, John Burton recalls, was its apparent knack of involving the right people at the right time. The project grew organically and was all the more successful for being 'permanently and seriously underfunded' because it depended entirely on the enthusiasm and commitment of the people running it. Risk-taking was actively encouraged, and 'needs must' became a powerful tool. This spirit of enterprise has been a constant thread running through the history of FFI.

The rest is history. Within a decade, the Mountain Gorilla Project had evolved into the formal coalition known today as the International Gorilla Conservation Programme. This thriving partnership is the culmination of all the earlier protection initiatives, some visionary, some little more than temporary bandages on a gaping wound. The collective determination of explorers, monarchs, scientists, governments and conservationists has helped to ensure that mountain gorillas still roam the forested slopes of the Virunga Massif to this day. All their efforts would have foundered, however, without the co-operation of the local communities and, in particular, the continued heroics of the national park staff, many of whom have lost their lives defending the gorillas.

International Gorilla Conservation Programme

The IGCP's objective is the conservation of the mountain gorilla and its natural habitat.
For further information contact : FFI, Great Eastern House, Tenison Road, Cambridge, CB1 2DT, UK.

Top Dr Annette Lanjouw visiting a mountain gorilla family with François Bigirimana, the most experienced guide in Volcanoes National Park, Rwanda. An expert in great ape conservation, Lanjouw was director of the International Gorilla Conservation Programme for 15 years until 2003. She subsequently worked for the Howard G. Buffett Foundation, during which time she was seconded to FFI as director of its Africa programme. Lanjouw currently works as executive director for the Arcus Foundation, established by US philanthropist, great ape enthusiast and FFI vice-president Jon Stryker.

Above Eugène Rutagarama, Director of the International Gorilla Conservation Programme from 2003 to 2012, was awarded the Goldman Environmental Prize – conservation's equivalent of the Nobel Prize – after risking his life to save the mountain gorilla population in his native Rwanda following the genocide, during which most of his relatives had perished. More mindful of the sacrifices of others than of his own, he used a portion of his award to set up a fund for the widows and orphans of park staff who have been killed while protecting the gorillas from poachers.

GAINS WITHOUT FRONTIERS –
A COALITION THAT TRANSCENDS BOUNDARIES

The entire world population of the mountain gorilla is confined to two small patches of Afromontane forest, the first in Uganda's aptly named Bwindi Impenetrable National Park, and the second on the slopes of the Virunga Massif, a chain of volcanic peaks that straddle the border shared by Rwanda, Uganda and the Democratic Republic of Congo (DRC). A combination of hunting and habitat destruction has driven this very rare primate to the verge of extinction.

The Mountain Gorilla Project, originally established in 1979, focused initially on Rwanda's beleaguered great apes, introducing anti-poaching measures and setting up an education programme to help change local attitudes to gorillas and forest conservation. In 1991 the project evolved naturally into the International Gorilla Conservation Programme (IGCP), which now works more widely in this impoverished and war-torn region to co-ordinate conservation action, improve park management, prevent poaching and involve the local community in gorilla conservation, particularly through ecotourism.

IGCP began as a formal coalition comprising Fauna & Flora International (FFI), the African Wildlife Foundation and the now renamed World Wide Fund for Nature (WWF). Its activities encompass the entire range of mountain gorilla habitat in Rwanda, Uganda and DRC. The partnership also incorporates the respective protected area authorities in the three countries where IGCP works. Transboundary collaboration and co-operation are vital to the overall success of the programme, not least because the gorillas themselves do not recognise international borders.

The region where mountain gorillas live has been plagued by instability for many decades, but the crisis reached a new peak in 1990, culminating in the 1994 Rwandan genocide. Since its inception, IGCP has been forced to operate against a background of violent conflict, human tragedy and economic disintegration.

The success of mountain gorilla conservation hinges above all on reconciling the potentially conflicting needs of endangered wildlife and people who are hanging on to life by their fingertips. Local communities and their basic survival strategies pose the greatest threat to the great apes, yet these same people are the ones on whom the conservation of gorillas and their habitat ultimately depend. The people are predominantly subsistence farmers, living below the poverty line and wholly dependent on agriculture. The region is one of the most densely populated in Africa, with an average of 420 people in every square kilometre. IGCP works with communities around the parks to develop enterprise compatible with conservation objectives and helps them to devise other viable and sustainable ways of earning a living. The development of income streams linked to tourism is helping to generate revenue for the community and support for forest conservation.

IGCP also works to enhance the capabilities of the park management authorities. This has involved training park staff, restructuring the institutions responsible for protected areas, developing stronger monitoring tools and improving protection activities. In keeping with its emphasis on regional collaboration, the programme has introduced a ranger-based monitoring system whereby park staff from all three countries carry out joint patrols.

Partnership and people are integral to the core values of IGCP. This spirit of co-operation is exemplified by the signing, in 2016, of the Treaty on the Greater Virunga Transboundary Collaboration on Wildlife Conservation and Tourism Development, an intergovernmental organisation for which former IGCP director Eugène Rutagarama had taken on the role of senior technical adviser in 2012.

All these efforts continue to yield positive results. The gorilla population in Virunga has virtually doubled since its nadir in 1981 and is now estimated at 480, while the latest comprehensive census in Bwindi recorded 400 individuals. The results confirm that the overall mountain gorilla population has increased by over 40 per cent since the census in 1989. This success story is all the more remarkable in that it has been achieved against a backdrop of civil war, unrest and social deprivation. ∎

Show me the money: the harsh economic realities faced by Rwanda, Uganda and the Democratic Republic of Congo dictate that conservation needs to pay its way. There is little doubt that the continued survival of mountain gorillas owes much to the success of IGCP and the respective governments in harnessing their unparalleled crowd-pulling potential for the benefit of wildlife enthusiasts, local communities and government coffers. A massive draw for tourists who might not otherwise venture into this permanently unstable and intermittently war-torn region, mountain gorillas are a significant revenue earner for all three host countries and represent one of the region's most valuable natural assets. The sustainability of this approach hinges on maintaining a delicate balance that, in essence, generates maximum revenue from, while causing minimum disturbance to, these charismatic primates, a tightrope that FFI and its partners continue to negotiate successfully. If ever there was a classic example of making conservation pay, this is it.

A CHAPTER CLOSES

Lord Willingdon, who died in 1979, was one of the towering figures in the society's pantheon. Having retired as president of FPS in 1974 after 23 years at the helm, he was elected President Emeritus and encouraged to stick around, on the basis that 'we know a good man when we see him, and we are not going to let him go as easily as that'. Despite a name and title harking back to the colonial era that spawned the society's founders, Inigo Brassey Freeman-Thomas, 2nd Marquess of Willingdon ('Nigs' to his close associates), was by all accounts a moderniser who personified the forward-thinking, adaptable approach that characterises FFI to this day. He was, wrote Richard Fitter, 'in no small part responsible for the success of Operation Noah and Operation Oryx, the two great enterprises that made the society's name in the late 50s and early 60s'. He was also one of the select band who drew up the guidelines for the British National Appeal of the World Wildlife Fund in 1961. ∎

Above 'In the FPS he will be remembered as the man who, sensitive to new thinking, changed the style of the society and steered it into the modern world.'

Left This original painting of jackass penguins, created by Sir Peter Scott specifically for the occasion, was presented to the Marquess of Willingdon following his retirement as president of the society. The choice of subject matter was a nod to his memorable 1972 helicopter flight over a vast colony of these birds in South Africa.

CHAPTER 6

DIVERSIFICATION

'At the beginning of the 20th century [...] the idea of protecting animals that people did not want to shoot, let alone plants, hardly occurred to anyone.'

Richard Fitter, *The Penitent Butchers*, 1978

Fauna & Flora International (FFI) is justifiably renowned for its success in protecting some of the most spectacular and iconic wildlife on the planet – from gorillas and rhinos in Africa to Sumatran tigers and orang-utans in Asia. Nevertheless, it is immediately evident to anyone delving into the archives that the society has an equally enviable track record with more obscure species, lavishing as much attention on tiny troglodytes as it does on popular primates and pachyderms.

Opposite This exquisite and endangered slipper orchid was photographed on Mount Samkos, the second-highest peak in Cambodia's Cardamom Mountains.

Below left The Kaikoura giant weta belongs to a genus of flightless insects from New Zealand. These 'living fossils', among the most ancient species alive today, are easy prey for invasive rodents.

Below right A diminutive tree snail, native to French Polynesia.

Guardians of the obscure

As noted in the previous chapter, one of the Oryx 100% Fund's main priorities was to help rescue species that might otherwise have fallen between the cracks. The list of beneficiaries during its 30-year history provides rich pickings for anyone seeking to compile an alternative alphabet of unfamiliar species in out-of-the-way places. The fund has supported work on, among others, Orinoco crocodiles in Venezuela, Swayne's hartebeest in Ethiopia, Anegada rock iguanas in the British Virgin Islands, the Nilgiri tahr in southern India, the Iriomote cat in Japan, the Tana River mangabey, *Partula* tree snails in Polynesia, the Hispaniolan solenodon in the Dominican Republic, the kagu in New Caledonia and the giant weta – think flightless cricket on steroids – found only in New Zealand.

Like its close relative the Arabian oryx, the scimitar-horned oryx has been rescued from the brink of extinction through a concerted captive breeding programme.

If this seems like a slightly scattergun approach to conservation, it is a reminder that urgent short-term priorities do not always fit neatly into a grand vision or cohesive long-term strategy. Then, as now, when you are struggling to hold back the tide of extinction that threatens to sweep away countless species, it is sometimes simply a question of plugging holes, particularly the holes that others do not view as a priority.

A classic example was the neglected fauna of West Africa's arid lands, where a basic lack of protection was creating a crisis for larger mammals like the addax, scimitar-horned oryx and dama gazelle. These desert, sub-desert and Sahelian specialists were not only in danger of losing their traditional dry season haunts to nomads and their cattle, but also, like the Arabian oryx, were under pressure from hunters equipped with powerful firearms and motorised vehicles. John Newby, who had begun working with these species in 1974 and received support from the 100% Fund

for his anti-poaching measures in the Sahel, had already alerted the conservation world to the dangers of digging permanent waterholes. In 1980 the society joined forces with the People's Trust for Endangered Species and launched an appeal to rescue the scimitar-horned oryx, the most endangered antelope in the semi-desert zone between the Sahara and the Sahel. Mainly confined to Chad, a country torn apart by civil war, the species might well have disappeared completely without such timely intervention.

The 100% Fund may not have had the sweep or the large-scale ambition of the more recent landscape-level programmes that, as we shall see, have since enabled FFI and its partners to protect vast swathes of habitat and entire communities of wildlife, but it fulfilled a vital

function, not least in the way it helped to kick-start embryonic conservation initiatives that evolved into grown-up projects capable of standing on their own two feet. Above all, it enabled the society to stay true to the principle of championing the underdog, putting invertebrates on an equal footing with apex predators and great apes.

Shell shock

Some of the society's successes in the dark hinterland inhabited by less familiar species have no doubt ended up buried irretrievably beneath the sands of time. Occasionally, however, the evidence resurfaces. In 2014, FFI's communications team received an email pointing out that the Zoological Society of London's long-term programme to rescue endemic Polynesian tree snails from extinction, featured in a recent edition of *Oryx*, actually originated with a 100% Fund initiative that went unacknowledged in the article. Sure enough, it transpires that in 1980 the fund awarded a grant to the then Jersey Wildlife Preservation (now Durrell Wildlife) Trust for a snailarium to house an *ex situ* captive breeding programme for critically endangered *Partula* snails. Their native island, Moorea, 17 kilometres north-west of Tahiti in the South Pacific, had been overrun

In 1985 a tip-off by the society foiled an attempt to sell a collection of rare birdwing butterflies through Sotheby's Auctioneers, including specimens of Queen Alexandra's birdwing, the largest butterfly in the world and one of the species featured at the time on the list of IUCN's Top 12 Species for Action. As a result, Sotheby's considered imposing a blanket ban on auctions of all natural history specimens.

by non-native predatory snails. Deliberately introduced into Moorea in the hope that they would eat their way through the multiplying colonies of the invasive and destructive giant African snail, the American snails evinced a marked preference for local delicacies and proceeded to hoover up the indigenous land snails. After several species were wiped out completely, colonies of five of the remaining nine species were rescued and brought to Jersey. According to John Burton, several of the sandwich boxes used to transport the snails were mixed up at some point behind the scenes at London Zoo, somewhat undermining the overall effectiveness of the programme. Calamitous cock-ups of the container kind aside, this timely intervention came during a period when the society was beginning to take an increasing interest in invertebrate conservation, as evidenced by the growing number of *Oryx* articles dedicated to insects, molluscs and marine crustaceans. It provides another reminder of FFI's global reach, and underlines its philosophy that the loss of any species, however superficially unprepossessing or apparently insignificant, impoverishes us all.

Home thoughts

One of the potential downsides of a global remit is that you lay yourself open to accusations of neglecting the wildlife on your own doorstep. Native species certainly do not feature prominently among the recipients of 100% Fund grants. Although based in the UK, FFI has always been international in outlook. Its roots, like those of our human ancestors, are in Africa, but FFI's influence has since extended throughout Eurasia, Asia-Pacific and the Americas. Nevertheless, the organisation has long recognised the hypocrisy inherent in lecturing the rest of the world on the importance of biodiversity conservation while ignoring the decline of less exotic species back home. As Richard Fitter noted wryly in *The Penitent Butchers*, published by the then FPS to mark 75 years of wildlife conservation since the society was formed, 'you can search the first six volumes of the *Journal* in vain for any reference to British mammals'.

There may be an element of poetic licence in his statement, but an exhaustive trawl through the earliest volumes unearths little beyond the occasional reference to the need to safeguard the grey seal population in the Western Isles, and a note in the 1922 minutes to the effect that owners

Limited edition print of *Badger Family*, by Robert Gillmor. All sale proceeds were donated to the society. The same artist illustrated the revised edition of the predatory mammals booklet, published in 1973, and generously permitted the society to feature several of his designs on its Christmas cards.

and tenants of Scottish deer forests were being asked to protect wild cats and pine martens.

Fitter himself deserves much of the credit for ensuring that this glaring omission was subsequently addressed. In his capacity as honorary secretary of FPS, he was the driving force behind numerous initiatives on behalf of British wildlife. Within just a few months of his appointment, he had proposed and helped organise a groundbreaking symposium devoted to British predatory mammals. Held in March 1965, this had been an unprecedented gathering of rival factions from the seemingly irreconcilable camps of conservationists, foresters, landowners and sportsmen.

One of the agreed outputs of this one-day symposium was a booklet, co-produced by FPS, which set out a code of practice for dealing with predatory mammals. Many of these species had previously been regarded as 'vermin' in certain quarters and treated accordingly by sportsmen, landowners and foresters alike. To secure such a degree of co-operation and agreement on the end product was, according to *The Times*, a remarkable achievement, 'rather as if the Federation of Pork Butchers had collaborated with the Vegetarian Society'. Put another way, this was a significant coup for the Federation of Penitent Butchers, and one that would be mirrored several decades later when FFI organised a landmark conference to promote closer co-operation between the representatives of big business and biodiversity conservation.

Deer prudence

Earlier, FPS had also played a leading role in promoting the Deer Act, enshrined in law in 1964, which introduced a close season for hunting wild deer in the UK. By May 1968 the society had two representatives on the governing body of the Council for Nature, one of whom was eligible to act as vice-chairman. This invitation to dine at UK conservation's high table was a tacit acknowledgement of the society's seniority as the second-oldest conservation society in Britain (after the RSPB), but it also constituted official recognition of the growing importance of FPS as the only society concerned with the conservation of *all* British mammals.

The society had been instrumental in securing the Seal Conservation Act, passed in June 1970, via a bill that FPS council member Lord Cranbrook had introduced into the House of Lords. It later lobbied alongside Greenpeace against the widespread culling of grey seals that was deemed to be politically motivated rather than scientifically or commercially justifiable.

FPS also intervened to tackle the apparent continuing decline of British otters in the face of the twin scourges of persecution and pollution. It politely suggested that the Mammal Society might wish to consider conducting a UK-wide survey of the otter's status, but was evidently too diplomatic to point out the need for that organisation to make slightly more proactive efforts to live up to its name. The formation of the Otter Trust, in which FPS was involved through executive secretary John Burton, ultimately led to the successful reintroduction into East Anglia of captive-bred otters that subsequently bred in the wild. When the Dorset River Board culled 50 otters, blaming them for

damage to the banks of the River Stour that subsequently proved to be the work of rats, the FPS was quick to add its voice to the howls of protest: 'It would be very remarkable if otters had developed habits unknown in otters anywhere else in Europe.' In light of the species' virtual disappearance from much of the Midlands and the south-east, the Otter Haven Project, administered by FPS, was launched in 1977 with a brief to survey England's river systems and pinpoint potentially suitable locations for otter sanctuaries.

FPS concern for Britain's native wildlife was not confined to mammals. Through Richard Fitter, the society played a crucial role on a working party set up in 1973 to advise the British National Appeal of WWF on grants intended to protect the entire spectrum of endangered UK plant and animal species. In 1981 Fitter wrote an article in *Oryx* about the most seriously threatened native plants, in which he profiled 21 species that were being pushed to the brink specifically as a result of habitat loss. Warnings from FPS about the disastrous consequences of habitat destruction for UK wildlife were a constant refrain during this period. Among them was a memorable *Oryx* feature in 1984, in which John Burton launched a scathing attack on the ecological vandalism perpetrated by Britain's farmers, encouraged by government policies and European subsidies that rewarded grubbing up hedgerows, draining ponds and chopping down trees for the sake of a few extra acres of land.

The society was instrumental in setting up several new institutions in support of UK wildlife conservation. For example, it was one of the key organisations responsible for the development of Wildlife Link, which was a much more proactive reincarnation of the moribund Council for Nature, with a larger membership and broader remit than

One of the captive-bred otters fitted with a tracking device prior to its release into the wild in East Anglia.

the somewhat ineffectual body that it replaced. This was the vehicle through which FPS and other members forcefully lobbied the UK government's Department of the Environment for complete protection of all Sites of Special Scientific Interest. 'The wildlife conservation movement is not in a mood to take no for an answer.' The society's chairman, Lord Craigton, a former government minister, used his considerable political clout to help secure the passage through parliament of numerous conservation measures including, notably, the Wildlife and Countryside Bill, which was eventually enacted in 1982.

Protecting the unloved

Many of the society's most telling, if largely unsung, contributions to UK biodiversity conservation revolved around groups of animals that tend not to win popularity contests. One notable example was singled out by John Burton as a particular success story during his tenure in the 1980s: 'We totally changed the public attitude to bats.'

Bats comprise around 20 per cent of all the world's mammal species. Their global value as pollinators, seed dispersers and industrial-scale consumers of invertebrate pests is virtually incalculable. They are characterised by slow rates of reproduction, susceptibility to disturbance and a tendency to receive a bad press due to ignorance, fear and superstition. Add to this a proclivity for roosting communally in places where a sealed entrance could destroy an entire colony in one fell swoop and it is easy to see why they are vulnerable to persecution. Putting all your bats in one exit is a behavioural trait that invites trouble.

Whilst the society did not formulate a cohesive bat conservation strategy until the 1980s, there is ample evidence that the plight of bats had been on its radar for several decades. An article on British bats by the renowned naturalist Brian Vesey-Fitzgerald had appeared in the *Journal* as early as December 1943. In the mid 1950s, FPS launched a new feature in *Oryx* enabling naturalists with a shared interest in chiroptera, as they are known in the trade, to form a 'Bat Group' whose members could correspond via the journal's pages. This paved the way for the more formal coalition of bat interests that was to follow later.

In the wake of a 1970 international conference in Amsterdam, which recommended active conservation measures for bats across the globe, a Mammal Society survey conducted at the suggestion of the FPS had confirmed that the serious decline in bat numbers in the

USA and mainland Europe was also replicated in the UK. Greater horseshoe and mouse-eared bats were revealed to be in danger of extinction, and all native bat species were clearly in dire need of a public relations makeover.

Pressure was even brought to bear at the highest political level in the United States of America. In November 1974, FPS wrote to Henry Kissinger, then US Secretary of State, to express concern about the potentially indiscriminate slaughter of bat species in Latin America that could result from attempts to prevent one particular rabies-carrying species of vampire bat from infecting cattle and humans.

In view of the drastic declines in bat populations worldwide, the IUCN's Species Survival Commission had already established a Chiroptera Specialist Group in 1975, chaired by FPS council member and bat guru, Dr Robert Stebbings. As with most IUCN initiatives, however, its work was hampered by a lamentable shortage of funding. With this in mind, the society resolved to bridge the gap by setting up its own fundraising vehicle for bat conservation projects worldwide, incorporated in the USA for tax purposes, but with offices on both sides of the pond. Texas-based Bat Conservation International, which was founded in 1982 and today employs more than 30 biologists, educators and administrators and is supported by members in 60 countries, began life as an overseas branch of FFI. Its stated aims were to prevent extinctions, protect viable populations and enhance public awareness of the importance of bats.

Bat man begins

Much of the initial funding for bat work in the UK came from the Vincent Wildlife Trust, founded by the visionary conservationist and philanthropist Vincent Weir, with whom FFI enjoyed a long and highly productive relationship right up until his death in 2014. The first official UK bat project, supported by Weir, took flight in 1984, when a full-time programme manager, Tony Hutson, was recruited from the Natural History Museum to oversee the production of educational publications intended for distribution to the media, governmental and private organisations, scientists and other interested parties. As Bat Conservation Officer, Hutson also represented the society at the meetings held regularly during the 1980s under the umbrella of the so-called 'Bat Groups of Britain', which included nature conservation bodies, county bat groups and funders. Until his appointment, the general public was largely unaware of the various legal obligations relating to bats in the UK under the Wildlife and Countryside Act 1981.

Bat Conservation Officer, Tony Hutson, and some of his bat photographs that
featured in the 1986 mobile exhibition during National Bat Year. The four species
shown here are (clockwise from top left) long-eared bat, Gambian fruit bat,
Pallas's long-tongued bat and Sundevall's leaf-nosed bat.

A subsequent TV appearance resulted in Hutson being inundated with enquiries.

In 1984, the society appointed Simon Mickleburgh as London Bat Officer to run a one-year project focusing on bats in the capital. The project was funded by the Greater London Council (GLC) and launched by its then leader, Ken Livingstone, and went on to receive support for a further 12 months from the London Residuary Body. The latter was set up after the abolition of the GLC, and its effectiveness was wickedly exposed when John Burton encouraged his colleagues to submit a tongue-in-cheek funding proposal for a spoof project entitled *'Educating minority communities in London on the importance of Caribbean bats'*. To their great surprise, the application was accepted.

The society helped co-ordinate the launch of National Bat Year in 1986 in conjunction with 60 local bat groups across the UK, and put together a mobile exhibition that toured the country. There was a perceptible upsurge in bat popularity, with thousands of letters resulting from the extensive press, radio and TV coverage, not only at home, but as far afield as Australia and Canada. Mickleburgh championed bat conservation, at both national and international levels, throughout his 20-year spell with the society, which lasted until 2005. His most valuable outputs during this time were undoubtedly the comprehensive global action plans for megachiropterans and microchiropterans (big and small bats to you and me), both co-authored with Hutson and Paul Racey, and published respectively in 1992 and 2001.

The Bat Conservation Trust, which the society established in 1990 in response to long-term funding concerns and the perceived need for a conservation organisation devoted solely to bats, exemplifies how FFI backs and nurtures nascent organisations until they are able to operate under their own steam. Under the chairmanship of Paul Racey, and with continued FFI support, the trust evolved into a thriving independent body and is today one of the leading bat conservation charities in Europe.

Champions of the neglected

If some of the world's chiropterans owe their survival to the pioneering work undertaken by FFI in its various historical guises, the same might also be said for the UK's threatened herpetofauna.

There were plenty of earlier signs of FPS concern about the fate of Britain's native amphibians and reptiles, and its recognition that they do not have the same wide appeal as birds and large

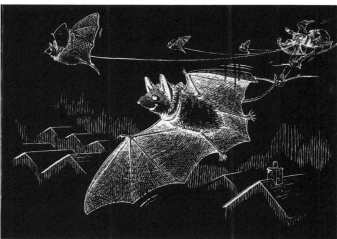

Top Appropriately enough in National Bat Year, the cover of the society's 1986 annual report featured two of its resident bat fans, Tony Hutson and Simon Mickleburgh, investigating a cave roost.

Above Wildlife illustrator Guy Troughton created this 1986 Christmas card to mark National Bat Year and donated the original drawing to the society for fundraising purposes.

Opposite Examples of the awareness literature issued by the society to promote bat conservation in the UK.

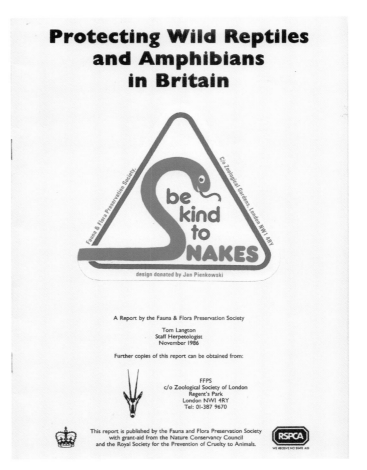

mammals. In October 1973 an *Oryx* editorial lamented the drastic declines in sand lizard, smooth snake and natterjack toad numbers and welcomed the move by the British Herpetological Society to establish a conservation committee.

Froglife, which for the past 25 years has been at the heart of efforts to conserve Britain's native amphibians and reptiles, began life as an FFI spin-off led by former staff herpetologist Tom Langton. Indeed, the charity's long-running Toads on Roads project has its origins in a campaign mounted in the early 1980s by FFI, which produced car stickers featuring a warning sign that entreated motorists to 'help a toad across the road'. Another sticker, reproduced on the *Members' diary* page in the October 1984 issue of *Oryx*, and which urged people to 'be kind to snakes', formed part of a concerted FFI campaign to improve the public image of Britain's serpents. Plans to build horse-manure heaps in order to encourage greater breeding success among dwindling grass snake populations, unveiled in that same issue of the journal, epitomise the society's unwavering commitment to the less glamorous end of the wildlife spectrum.

Drain on resources

In the early 1980s it was evident that unprecedented rates of habitat loss were precipitating a potentially catastrophic decline in the UK amphibian population. The problem was magnified in Greater London, where urban sprawl was threatening to swallow up the remaining pockets of undisturbed water bodies and uncultivated land. With the aid of a grant from the GLC, under the leadership of newt aficionado Ken Livingstone, the society undertook a detailed survey of London ponds, 90 per cent of which had been lost during the previous century. Led by Tom Langton, the survey covered approximately 1,600 water bodies, looking in particular at the status of the great crested newt and the

Above left May 1987 edition of the quarterly newsletter compiled by Tom Langton to promote the cause of neglected amphibians and reptiles.

Above right November 1986 report by Tom Langton, adorned with the iconic snake sticker designed by illustrator Jan Pieńkowski.

Opposite This exquisite painting of great crested newts by Denys Ovenden was available to buy as an open-edition print, with proceeds donated to the society.

FROM LEFT TO RIGHT

The juxtaposition of these photographs serves to illustrate one of the keys to FFI's success: its ability to transcend politics and influence decision makers across the entire political spectrum. ■

Right Tom Langton and Ken Livingstone, erstwhile leader of the Greater London Council, discussing their mutual fondness for all things amphibian and reptilian at the launch of the GLC-funded London Pond Survey.

Below left Leaflet produced to promote the launch of the society's corporate membership scheme.

Below right Tom Langton stands back and waits for Margaret Thatcher to do all the spade work at the official opening of the Lakeland Nature Reserve in her Finchley constituency. The prime minister was lending her support to the society's newly launched corporate membership scheme, whereby companies provided regular donations and sponsored conservation projects.

Lakeside
Nature Reserve

Pentland
Industries

Fauna and Flora
Preservation Society

To commemorate the
Lakeside Conservation Project
opened by
The Rt Hon Margaret Thatcher
Prime Minister
10 July 1987
on the occasion of the
launch of the
Fauna & Flora
Preservation Society's
Corporate Membership Scheme

other two native newt species. The results of the survey were incorporated into the ecological records of the GLC for the purposes of planning and used to improve environmental education in schools. A programme of pond restoration and recreation was implemented to replace much of the amphibian habitat lost to infilling, pollution and land drainage.

Tunnel vision

In 1986 the society published a report entitled *Protecting Wild Reptiles and Amphibians in Britain*, which stressed the need for improved legislation to safeguard native herpetofauna against acts of cruelty and needless slaughter. Its recommendations ultimately resulted in several amendments to the existing laws, which ensured protection for all UK amphibians and reptiles, including the more common species. Amphibian conservation received a further boost in early 1987 with the opening of the UK's first tunnel for toads, which attracted worldwide press attention, including a feature in *The New York Times* under the inspired headline: 'The Tunnel Of Love, Just For English Toads'. Its installation was fully vindicated just one month later when over 3,000 toads were recorded using it. Lord Skelmersdale, Under Secretary of State for the Environment and a former member of the society's council, praised the initiative as a prime example of 'just what can be achieved when industrialists, conservationists, government and local authorities work together as envisaged in the World Conservation Strategy'. The amphibian tunnel concept was successfully replicated later that same year on the other side of the pond, so to speak, by FFPS, Inc. and its local partners, who constructed twin tunnels that enabled spotted salamanders in Amherst, Massachusetts, to reach their breeding ponds without running the gauntlet of heavy traffic.

Ensuring that the message sticks

The mid 1980s saw the publication of a rash of stickers and decals to support awareness campaigns designed to change public perceptions and behaviour towards neglected species of mammal, reptile and amphibian, both at home and abroad. The majority of these stickers were designed specifically for the society by the prolific children's book

Warts and all: Lord Skelmersdale wearing a slightly unconventional rosette at the official opening of the UK's first toad tunnel (top) in March 1987.

illustrator Jan Pieńkowski, famous for the now classic *MEG & MOG* stories, among others.

As well as serving their primary purpose, which was to highlight the plight of these particular animals, the stickers that ended up adorning car windows and briefcases in their thousands also generated wider interest in the organisation as a whole. In July 1984, the society received favourable coverage in *The Sunday Times*: 'Having already rehabilitated the flittermouse with their *I Love Bats* promotion, they lowered the nation's squashed hedgehog tally with the *Don't Squash Me* slogan, and they were poised to launch their latest conversion campaign: *Be Kind to Snakes.*'

The snake campaign, in particular, received a welcome, if unexpected, boost when the ophiophobic Sir David Price, MP for Eastleigh, alumnus of Eton, Cambridge and Yale and general pillar of the establishment, demonstrated how out of touch he was with the zeitgeist by misguidedly demanding that the Department of the Environment introduce a campaign to exterminate adders. The regrettable proposal provoked a mini media frenzy and spawned a satirical cartoon in the *Manchester Evening News* lampooning the honourable member.

The vital importance of converting non-specialists to the conservation cause remained a constant preoccupation for John Burton. Reviewing the latest edition to the definitive conservationists' bible, the Red Data Books, he noted that the first volume dedicated to herpetofauna was inevitably focused on providing comprehensive data on the largest, most spectacular and best-known reptiles, with the result that smaller reptiles and amphibians might well be extinct before receiving coverage. Whilst acknowledging that it was impossible to accord every endangered species the same attention, Burton wondered out loud whether the information

was, in fact, too detailed and geared to the specialist, and questioned whether scientists were the best target audience. What about journalists, politicians and the general public?

In the meantime, the society was doing its best to plug the gaps, this time by turning its attention to neglected reptiles outside the UK. This included 100% Fund support for research into a Madagascar species known locally as *angonoka* and dubbed 'the rarest tortoise on Earth', which led to an *ex situ* captive breeding initiative organised by Durrell Wildlife Trust and a suite of community-led conservation measures in its native habitat.

Closer to home, a generous donation from car manufacturer Citroën enabled the society to issue three new car stickers as part of its Mediterranean Tortoise Campaign. Produced in Greek, French and Spanish, the stickers were intended to increase public awareness of the dangers posed to southern Europe's tortoises and their habitats by car collisions and scrub fires. One of the most inspired promotional ruses, which attracted favourable publicity for both Citroën and the society itself, was to convert a 2CV into a mobile giant tortoise and drive it through France, Spain and Greece. The Mediterranean initiative formed part of a worldwide programme dubbed Operation Tortoise, which helped to inform a detailed IUCN report on the conservation biology of tortoises, published in 1989.

Into flora

If the activities of FPS at the start of the 1980s were characterised by an increased focus on neglected animal species, epitomised by its sterling work with reptiles,

Above A Citroën 2CV converted into a four-wheeled tortoise draws a crowd during its European tour.

Right Children attempt to persuade a giant tortoise to sign a lucrative sponsorship deal to endorse the society's sticker campaign on behalf of its Mediterranean cousins.

Opposite Examples of the promotional stickers issued by the society.

amphibians and bats, there was also the small matter of an entire kingdom that had consistently been overlooked by the global conservation movement. Historically, plants had been even further down the pecking order than snakes and toads. The origins of Fauna & Flora International (FFI) may date back to 1903, but it is fair to say that tree and plant conservation were not uppermost in the minds of its founders. As Richard Fitter had pointed out, at the beginning of the twentieth century even the idea of protecting animals that people did *not* want to shoot was a novel concept. The importance of protecting plants would have occurred to virtually no one beyond an inner circle of botanists. Decades later, the society was still being affectionately or, more likely, pragmatically referred to as 'The Fauna'. By the time

The Penitent Butchers was published in 1978, FPS was already wholeheartedly committed to plant conservation, but the achievements celebrated in the book relate almost exclusively to the protection of animal species. You have to fast-forward virtually 80 years from its origins before the society's name gives any indication of an interest in flora.

Plants had not, of course, been completely ignored during those intervening decades. As approaches to wildlife conservation became more sophisticated and holistic, the focus was shifting from a narrow preoccupation with individual species to encompass broader habitats and even whole ecosystems. And with that shift in emphasis came a growing awareness, so to speak, that plant and tree diversity are at least as vital to the equilibrium of these ecosystems as the megafauna and mini-beasts. The symbiotic relationships between individual species of flora and fauna that co-evolve over millennia create a complicated and fragile web of mutual dependence. Zoologists and botanists alike had long conceded, however grudgingly, that animals and plants could not survive without each other.

The addition of two little words that have proved to be the stuff of nightmares for successive guardians of the society's brand.

Red plants

This tacit acknowledgement of the importance of flora had not yet galvanised the conservation community into any kind of concerted global response beyond a noble attempt to begin creating a comprehensive list of threatened plants. Once again, it was FPS stalwart Peter Scott, wearing his Species Survival Commission hat, who set the ball rolling in the late 1960s. At his invitation, a retired botanist by the name of Ronald Melville from the Royal Botanic Gardens at Kew had embarked on the compilation of a flowering plant equivalent of the Red Data Book. When it became clear that this would be a task of Herculean proportions, given the alarming number of endangered species, responsibility for the next phase of the project was shared by IUCN and Kew under the umbrella of a Threatened Plants Committee, created in 1973.

The appearance of the IUCN Plant Red Data Book in 1978, compiled by Grenville Lucas and Hugh Synge, put flora conservation firmly on the world map, but the magnitude of the conservationists' task was illustrated by the fact that this book could only skim the surface of the issue. It provided detailed status information on a mere one per cent of the estimated 25,000 threatened plant species, chosen as a representative sample. As well as stimulating many countries to produce their own Red Data books, it provided the perfect catalyst to spark the society into formal acknowledgement of its own increasing interest in plant protection.

Botanic guardians

In the absence of any other society in the world offering membership for those interested in plant conservation across the globe, FPS stepped into the breach. John Burton, who knew Lucas well, saw a window of opportunity and persuaded him to jump on board the FPS council as a prospective champion of all things botanical. At the annual general meeting in July 1980, it was agreed that the society's official remit should be amended to incorporate plant conservation.

The world's longest-established international animal conservation society could now lay claim to another historic precedent: the first international plant conservation society in the world. It marked the occasion by changing its name to the Fauna and Flora Preservation Society (FFPS), sending the unequivocal message that plant and tree conservation was on the agenda to stay.

Bearing in mind that the word 'flora' was a relatively recent addition to the society's name, there is a certain irony in the fact that it frequently enjoys unwarranted prominence when FFI features in the public domain today. If the society

DISTINGUISHED SERVICE MODELS

In 1980 the society introduced the grandly titled Roll of Honour for Distinguished Service, which provided the opportunity to pay an official tribute to the contribution of some of its most stalwart devotees.

The first recipient of this accolade, posthumously in his case, was Ian Malcolmson. A member of the society for almost half a century, Malcolmson served as honorary treasurer from 1950 to 1979. During those three decades he never missed a single council meeting.

The second person to be inducted into the hall of fame was Colonel Boyle. Secretary of FPS from 1950 to 1964, he assumed near-legendary status and remained an active supporter long after his retirement.

Two other big names were added in 1987. Lord Craigton was admitted to this illustrious club courtesy of his sterling service since 1965 in the guise of council member, vice-chairman, chairman and vice-president. The originator of the inspired Oryx 100% Fund, Craigton had also given the society considerable political clout. 'A distinguished and able political figure, he has championed the Society's conservation aims in the House of Lords.' He was joined by Major Ian Grimwood, profiled in earlier chapters, whose induction was timed to coincide with the silver jubilee of Operation Oryx, widely acknowledged as his finest hour. ■

Fauna & Flora Preservation Society
founded 1903

Roll of Honour
initiated 1980

For extraordinary services to
the Fauna & Flora Preservation Society

The name of

was placed on the Roll of Honour
at the Annual General Meeting of the Society
on

CITATION

President
Chairman

received an automatic donation every time it was mistakenly referred to as 'Flora & Fauna International', it might never need to fundraise again. Exasperating though this may be for the communications professionals who bang on about the 'brand', it does at least provide a constant reminder that plants are no longer the poor relation and are entitled to a seat at conservation's top table.

The first plant project commissioned by the renamed FFPS was a study of the trade in mahogany (a catch-all label for dark-red tropical hardwoods that actually comprised over 20 individual species), but in keeping with the prevailing ethos of the society, it was not only the household names that received attention. Before long, the FFPS was collaborating with the Royal College of Art in London to produce posters about endangered cyclamens, highlighting the decline of formerly abundant Maltese flora and investigating the unsustainable harvesting of Turkish bulbs.

Botanist Andy Byfield inspects a box of sustainably harvested Turkish bulbs.

Turkish villagers pose with a crop of premium-quality nursery-grown bulbs.

The Oryx 100% Fund supported numerous small-scale plant conservation projects, benefiting species as diverse as Mexican palms and cycads, a rare Vietnamese orchid, a CITES-listed tree fern from China and bog plants in Venezuela. It even helped to fund a Madagascar expedition in search of a close relative of the rosy periwinkle, famed for its cancer-treating properties.

Growing commitment

As the scale and breadth of the society's plant conservation ambitions increased, specialists became the order of the day. Mike Read, hired as a staff botanist in 1987, made a study of the Turkish bulb trade. At the time, Turkey was exporting 70 million bulbs annually, the vast majority sourced from wild populations, and the FFPS was pressing for stronger controls on a trade that had grown exponentially in the 1970s and 1980s to the point where it was completely unsustainable.

Turkey is one of the richest areas in the world for bulbs, including familiar garden favourites such as snowdrops, tulips, cyclamens, lilies and crocuses. Read's report exposed the large-scale trade in these bulbs and advocated the establishment of village-based nurseries where native plants could be propagated, which ultimately led to establishment of the Indigenous Propagation Project. The specific aims of this joint initiative between the FFPS and the Istanbul-based Doğal Hayatı Koruma Derneği (the Society for the Protection of Nature) were to eliminate the over-exploitation of Turkey's threatened wild bulbs, to develop a long-term economic alternative for villagers formerly involved in collection, and to

supply high-quality flower bulbs to the international market at a premium price. The work formed part of a wider campaign, however, and was one of a series of FFPS initiatives designed to help secure ratification and implementation of CITES. Under the expert eye of botanist Andrew Byfield, recruited as the locally based project manager, the scheme would go on to produce its first sustainably harvested crop in 1996 and be widely hailed as a resounding success.

It was a sign of things to come. Plants were no longer regarded as part of the scenery, but had now assumed their rightful place centre stage, at the heart of the society's conservation strategy. The enterprising spirit that originally helped to safeguard the charismatic quadrupeds of the African plains was also being brought to bear for the benefit of the world's endangered flora.

A change of name was not the only indication that the society was entering another new phase in its continuing development. In December 1980 it was confirmed that Sir Peter Scott was stepping down as chairman. At the same time, he relinquished his duties at the Species Survival Commission, to be replaced by Grenville Lucas. As already noted, Lucas had been persuaded to lend his considerable botanical expertise to the society as a newly elected council member, thereby maintaining the strong connection that existed between the two organisations. This link was strengthened further by the fact that Burton's wife, Vivien, found herself working as executive assistant to Lucas in his new role at the Species Survival Commission after he replaced Scott as chairman. After 20 years as the editor of *Oryx*, Maisie Fitter also put down her quill for the final time and departed with a warm valediction from one particularly appreciative vice-president, the former diplomat and Galápagos enthusiast Gerard Corley Smith, ringing in her ears. 'In the opinion of many of us, she made *Oryx* into the best of all wildlife journals. [She was] an inspiration to a whole generation.'

Unconventional wisdom

John Burton's tenure at the society was characterised by an opportunistic, go-getting attitude to potential new ventures and a determination to embrace change, expand and diversify. His proactive approach meant that it was not always possible to follow official protocol, as he is the first to admit. 'A lot of the time I got things off the ground and then went to the board to request approval.'

With his activist background and strong network of contacts, he enjoyed a positive relationship with the press and other media, which helped to bring the society more frequently into the public eye. In 1980 he came up with the

Above Snow drops: in August 1994 the launch of the *Good Bulb Guide* generated an extraordinary level of publicity for the society and its campaign, not only in the press, but also on television. The perennial *Gardeners' World* featured a conversation between its then co-presenter Pippa Greenwood and FFI's own Dr Abigail Entwistle, whom we will meet in a later chapter. Other TV coverage included an entire episode of *Blue Peter*, during which the unfortunate film crew found itself on the receiving end of a different kind of blanket coverage, thanks to an unseasonable snowstorm.

Left Snowdrops: clump of *Galanthus elwesii*, a species of giant snowdrop first identified in Turkey in 1874 by British botanist Henry John Elwes.

idea of challenging a team from *Country Life* magazine to a 24-hour birdwatching contest against the FFPS. Participants included the writer, comedian, future TV presenter and obsessive ornithologist, Bill Oddie. The event was so successful that it was repeated the following year and turned into a full-blown fundraiser and promotional vehicle for the society, which featured in a documentary on the recently launched Channel 4 television network. In 1984, at Burton's suggestion, the FFPS also teamed up with London's Natural History Museum and BBC *Wildlife* magazine, where he had worked as assistant editor during its earlier incarnation as *Animals*, to organise the international Wildlife Photographer of the Year competition, another opportunity to raise the society's public profile.

In response to a membership survey, *Oryx* was dragged kicking and screaming into the Kodachrome age. A number of significant design changes were incorporated into the January 1983 issue, the most obvious of which was the inclusion of a spectacular colour image on the cover. The free use of these images, which went on to grace the cover of the journal for many years, was generously granted by photographic agent Bruce Coleman, who had set up the first natural history photographic agency a decade earlier. The society subsequently benefited from Coleman's support during his various stints as council member, vice-president and company secretary, and his association with FFI endures to this day.

Youth movement

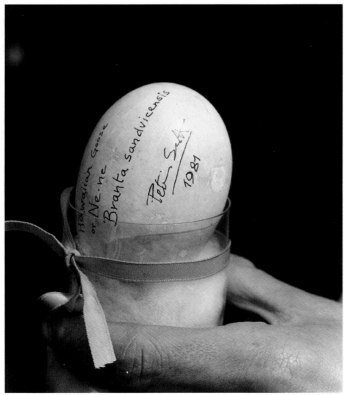

The membership survey also revealed, perhaps not surprisingly, that two-thirds of members held a university degree or equivalent qualification. More significantly, the vast majority were not exactly in the first flush of youth. The society urgently needed to redress this imbalance and therefore introduced a discounted student membership in a deliberate attempt to appeal to a younger socio-economic group. Burton was acutely aware of the need to raise additional finance for new projects. One obvious way was to increase membership, and he had secured council approval for the idea of setting the ultimate target at 10,000 members. The society needed to lose its image as some kind of elite club and provide different ways of supporting its work in future.

Above Bill Oddie cunningly attempts to lure a skulking species into the open by playing back its call during the 1981 Big Bird Race.

Left To the winners, a fitting symbol of the wild bird chase in which they had just participated: an addled ne-ne egg signed by none other than Peter Scott, saviour of that particular goose species.

Above left The first issue of *Oryx* to feature a colour image on the cover – in this case a red-eyed tree frog from Costa Rica – was published in January 1983.

Above right Initial mock-up of the new logo for the society's US operation, FFPS, Inc.

As part of this process, Burton hit upon the ruse of establishing local groups in Cambridge, Oxford, Bristol, Chester and Edinburgh, all of which proved extremely popular with wildlife enthusiasts who were unwilling or unable to travel to the metropolis. At the same time, he addressed the need to increase the society's visibility across the Atlantic by setting up a US operation, FFPS, Inc., which effectively operated as an overseas branch with its own executive director. Among the heavyweights associated with the US venture was the great Hal Coolidge, who served briefly as honorary director of FFPS, Inc. One of the pre-eminent wildlife conservationists of his time, renowned for his seminal work in separating gorilla subspecies, Coolidge was one of the founding directors of the IUCN and a long-term friend of the society. His death in 1985 prompted an affectionate tribute from Sir Peter Scott: 'He made an immense contribution largely because of his dogged energy and drive. He never took no for an answer and never seemed to rest, but was always working on about ten fronts at the same time.' If this last line reads like a description of Scott

himself, it serves to emphasise how fortunate the society was to have the support of such tireless crusaders on both sides of the Atlantic. The US operation did not last, at least not at the first attempt. It was wound up soon after Burton left the FFPS, presumably because it had been his show. Happily, however, it was subsequently resurrected to great effect, as we shall discover in a later chapter, and for many years played a pivotal role in supporting FFI's global activities.

By 1985 the society was, in John Burton's words, 'really motoring'. Unfortunately, he was beginning to appreciate that not all his fellow passengers were happy with the speed or direction of travel. Whilst he had his foot to the floor, some members of the board were busy applying the handbrake.

OLIVER'S ONE-MAN ARMY

No account of FFI's love affair with neglected species would be complete without mention of one of the greatest champions of bizarre, obscure and often visually unprepossessing wildlife. William Oliver, who worked closely with the society for almost 20 years until his untimely death in 2014, was a fanatically dedicated conservationist, talented wildlife artist and notorious curmudgeon.

Oliver's biggest passions, in no particular order, were peccaries, pigs and the Philippines. He almost single-handedly rescued the world's rarest pig,

the pygmy hog, shining the spotlight on a species previously thought extinct by Western scientists and demanding greater protection for the tiny wild population rediscovered in its native Assam. He was chairman for 32 years of the IUCN specialist group devoted to wild pig conservation. In the Philippines, his crusading efforts on behalf of vanishingly rare endemic species, such as the Negros bleeding-heart pigeon, Cebu flowerpecker and Visayan spotted deer, served to change attitudes to wildlife among a general public that had previously appeared indifferent to the fate of its unique

Clinging on by its toenails: the Negros naked-backed fruit bat was considered extinct for nearly three decades until an FFI-led team discovered a roost on the Philippine island of Cebu during a 2001 survey. The species has a precarious hold on survival and is confined to the few fragments of forest left on Cebu and nearby Negros. Other Philippine endemics on the brink include the taritic hornbill, cave wrinkled ground frog and critically endangered Visayan warty pig.

natural heritage. The Philippines Biodiversity Conservation Foundation, set up with FFI support as a direct result of Oliver's concerted pressure, was the first such institution in the country and stands as a fitting legacy

to his bloody-minded persistence. But it was his defence of all things porcine for which he will be best remembered.

In the course of a project designed to bring neglected wildlife and conservation issues to the attention of the new mobile phone generation under the banner of FFI's *wildlive!* partnership with Vodafone, of which more later, this author made the mistake of describing the Visayan warty pig as having 'a face

that only a mother could love'. Oliver was apoplectic and fired off a vitriolic email that left no doubt about the intensity of his own quasi-paternal devotion to the species and his heartfelt contempt for anyone shallow enough to trivialise such a serious issue. It was Oliver who, in 2002, engineered the first ever *ex situ* breeding of this pig, a crucial development in the conservation recovery programme of one of the Philippines' (and the world's)

Examples of William Oliver's paintings depicting (clockwise from top left) the Arabian oryx, Philippine bats, Philippine cockatoo and a series of illustrations including less familiar Asian herbivores such as the takin, serow and saola.

most endangered species. An obituary in *The Economist* dubbed him 'the world spokesman for wild pigs'. Oliver's memory is preserved in the numerous paintings of obscure and endangered wildlife that he created to promote their conservation. ■

CHAPTER 7

STAGNATION

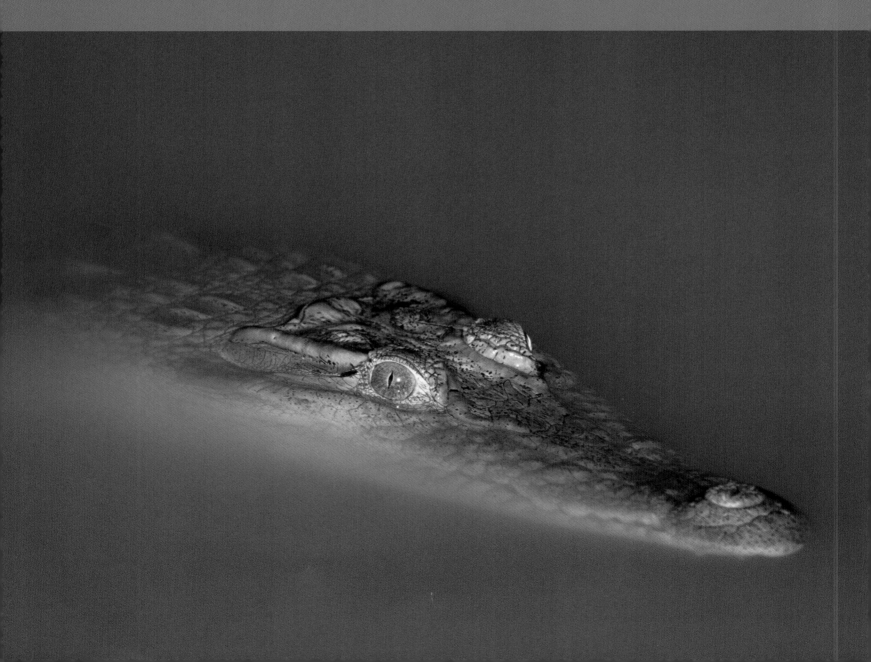

'Either we play a significant role in the coming years or we pass that role to others. I would very much like to hear from members on the subject of the future of the Society.'

David Jones, FFPS Chairman

O ne of the perils of dedicating yourself to supporting the local efforts of other individuals and organisations is that you lose sight of the importance of keeping your own house in order. All successful institutions go through times of crisis, and FFI has experienced its fair share of ups and downs. The early 1990s was a particularly turbulent period for the society, perhaps precipitated by the departure of several key figures within a relatively short timeframe.

A new chairman, David Jones, was elected in October 1987 following the resignation of the stalwart Richard Fitter, who declared himself 'confident that he is well equipped to steer the Society through the challenging years ahead'. Challenging proved to be an understatement.

Hard times

After 13 years in the saddle, John Burton announced his intention to step down as executive secretary at the end of 1987, citing the need for a full-time executive chief, a role that his other commitments precluded him from undertaking. In truth, he had become frustrated in his role. He had all the responsibility and accountability whereas the board, which comprised – as he saw it – a group of

Right Hello, goodbye. The late John Gooders in happier times, participating in a 24-hour birdwatch competition organised by his predecessor John Burton.

Opposite Funding from the Conservation Leadership Programme enabled the recipients to set up an organisation dedicated to saving the Philippine crocodile, one of the world's most threatened species.

academics with their own agenda, retained all the power. In his view, there was too much emphasis on research as a conservation solution and not enough action and activism. Whilst Burton himself advocated expansion as the recipe for success, the new chairman was adamant that consolidation was the soup of the day. It was this fundamental difference in philosophy that precipitated his departure.

Burton left to found the World Land Trust and would prove to be sorely missed. He had acquired a reputation for picking potential winners from the endless stream of worthy conservation causes that crossed his desk and recommended themselves for support. The iconic Mountain Gorilla Project is among the many that might never have seen the light of day without his instinctive grasp of where the society's meagre resources could be most productively deployed.

A new executive director, John Gooders, took over in early 1988. The next edition of *Oryx* was prefaced with a one-page *From the Director's desk* confessional, penned by Gooders, in which he styled himself a 'wildlife entrepreneur' and professed himself slightly baffled by the decision to appoint him, given his lack of practical conservation experience. Before the end of the year, he was gone.

Such was the ensuing turmoil that in early 1989 chairman David Jones felt compelled to use the editorial pages of *Oryx* to explain to members the rationale for some of the major changes. Responsibility for the successful UK bat, reptile and amphibian conservation programmes set up by the society was to be devolved to other, specialist organisations. In itself, this decision made sense; one of the distinctive hallmarks of FFI is its belief in building capacity to the point where it can leave a project in someone else's capable hands. All was not well behind the scenes, however, and there was evidently sufficient concern about cash flow and policy issues to warrant holding emergency meetings. Any attempt to put a positive spin on the overall message was undermined by the revelation that new recruit John Gooders had lasted a mere six months as executive director and would not be replaced in the foreseeable future. With the society clearly in a state of limbo, the headline *Moving forward* was a rather unfortunate choice. At best, the FFPS appeared to be treading water.

Heavy losses

When sorrows come, they come not single spies, but in battalions. In August 1989 the FFPS suffered a hammer blow

in the shape of the death of its president, Sir Peter Scott. A veritable colossus of the conservation world, he had been closely and continuously associated with the society for 28 years. Richard Fitter, who had worked hand in glove with Scott in numerous capacities both within and outside the society, paid tribute to his titanic contribution in a glowing *Oryx* obituary: 'His charisma and public relations flair made him a uniquely influential personality in both British and world conservation movements, and the Society owes him a great debt of gratitude for all the time and effort he devoted to our affairs.' Scott's passing, particularly at such a sensitive juncture, was a devastating loss for the FFPS, which recognised just how irreplaceable he was. 'Undoubtedly, we shall not look upon his like again.'

Within a year, Ian Grimwood, hero of Operation Oryx, long-standing associate of the society and another legend of the international conservation movement, had also died, followed soon after by fellow vice-president Felipe Benavides, the self-styled single-handed saviour of the vicuña.

The untimely passing of such influential figures at key stages in the society's history was nothing new. In this instance, however, the adverse effect of the losses was compounded by the regrettable timing. At the very point when the FFPS was desperately in need of a stabilising force amid the drama, a handful of its most experienced campaigners had left the stage in rapid succession.

False restart

A new logo, unveiled in 1990, was no doubt intended to refresh the society's image and demonstrate its intention to forge ahead, rather than dwelling on past glories. Unfortunately, it merely caused confusion. Many members familiar with the previous, somewhat generic, oryx design had wrongly assumed that it depicted the Arabian oryx, a species with which the society was intimately associated following its landmark rescue mission in the early 1960s. The perceived switch to a design apparently featuring a gemsbok – in their minds the 'wrong' species – left many of them mystified, if not indignant. In fact, to complicate matters further, the original logo had actually depicted a beisa oryx, virtually indistinguishable from a gemsbok to the casual observer, but nonetheless a different species. The choice dated back to 1950, well before the heroics of Operation Oryx. The new honorary secretary, Colonel Boyle, recognising the need to rename the journal in light of the society's overall change of name, had been inspired by an encounter with this species during a stroll through the

Sir Peter Scott pictured against the familiar backdrop of Slimbridge, headquarters of the Wildfowl & Wetlands Trust that he founded in 1946 as a centre for science and conservation.

gardens of the Zoological Society of London and deemed *Oryx* 'a convenient and attractive name'. On the plus side, the misunderstanding enabled the FFPS to set the record straight by publishing a clarification in the next issue of *Oryx*, but it was not the most auspicious start for the society's latest rebranding attempt.

The society announced that it was now proposing to move away from British conservation and refocus on international work, where the needs were more pressing. In particular, the intention was to capitalise on its success with mountain gorilla conservation by undertaking work on behalf of other great apes, including the eastern lowland gorilla in Africa and orang-utan in South East Asia.

By early 1990 it was widely recognised that the original aims of the Mountain Gorilla Project (already profiled in chapter 5) had been achieved. The next stage would be to increase support for gorilla and forest conservation beyond Rwanda, particularly in neighbouring Uganda and then Zaire, so the decision was made to dissolve the project and replace it with the more strategically ambitious, cohesive and all-embracing International Gorilla Conservation Programme, in which FFI continues to play a leading role. In the past, the society had largely relied on the general public to support its contribution to mountain gorilla conservation. These donations were as unpredictable as they were generous, however, making long-term planning

extremely difficult. This all changed when the Whitley Animal Protection Trust chipped in with a hefty capital grant, providing the society with a regular and predictable source of income that enabled it not only to plan ahead, but also to increase its level of activity considerably.

Hopes of broadening the society's great ape conservation remit further were also bolstered by encouraging news from the FFPS team that had returned from a fact-finding mission to the remote Itombwe forest in Eastern Zaire, as it was then known. This relatively unexplored forest had previously harboured a sizeable population of eastern lowland gorillas, but was rumoured to have been badly degraded during the political turmoil in the 1960s. FFPS staff Roger Wilson and Mike Catsis led what was the first scientific expedition to explore Itombwe in over 30 years. To their surprise and delight, they encountered a vast tract of virtually pristine montane forest, rich in biodiversity and populated by numerous, widely distributed gorilla groups. An *Oryx* editorial confirmed the society's determination to find ways of safeguarding this unprotected habitat from the development and population pressures that were affecting much of the region's forests.

Recognising the need to give greater attention to Africa's biologically rich but gravely threatened tropical forests, the FFPS launched its Forested Africa Programme in late 1990, which began to 'pull together existing forest conservation projects into a single coherent framework', in the words of that year's annual report. Among these was the recently conceived Drill Project, which evolved from an application for 100% Fund support.

Remember the drill

One of Africa's most endangered and least familiar primates, the drill has a very limited range in Cameroon, Nigeria and Bioko Island, Equatorial Guinea. Hunted ruthlessly for bushmeat and rapidly running out of habitat, it was perceived to be in urgent need of conservation action. The initial priority of this FFPS project was a comprehensive survey of the drill's distribution and status in Cameroon, which contains an estimated 80 per cent of its remaining habitat.

Whilst the primates were rarely encountered in the forest, the survey team frequently found captive drills in villages, presumably the orphans of mothers killed for bushmeat. Given the paucity of drills in existing captive breeding programmes, these infants were potentially a valuable resource. With this in mind, a handful of the orphaned drills were used as the founding population for a captive breeding initiative in Calabar, Nigeria. At the time this was the only *in situ* captive breeding programme for an endangered African ape. The Drill Rehabilitation and Breeding Centre aroused considerable international interest and attracted support from media, individuals, businesses and government, not least when it announced the birth of a healthy infant in 1994 – the first captive-born drill in Africa. By 1995, the centre boasted 30 per cent of the world's entire population of captive drills. Like the wild mountain gorillas in Central Africa, the captive drills also had considerable local educational value as a symbol of Nigeria's unique natural heritage, attracting thousands of visitors and stimulating interest in the long-term protection of their wild counterparts.

In 1996, FFPS and its local partner, Pandrillus – founded by 100% Fund grant recipient Liza Gadsby and Peter Jenkins – established a separate field site to accommodate drill groups within natural forest enclosures in the foothills of the Afi Mountain. This was an area that both organisations had been working to conserve since 1993 for the benefit of drills and other primates, including the westernmost gorilla population in the world. By 2000 these gorillas had been formally recognised as a distinct and therefore critically endangered subspecies (known colloquially as the Cross River gorilla), prompting the state government to gazette their forest habitat as the Afi Mountain Wildlife Sanctuary. According to Daniel Pouakouyou, who at that time was FFI Programme Manager for Central Africa, the greater effectiveness of local rangers and a corresponding increase in local community support virtually eliminated poaching of the gorilla and its fellow primates within the sanctuary.

Portrait of a drill. Detail from an illustration by Dr Jonathan Kingdon, council member and later vice-president of the society, whose paintings featured on several of its Christmas cards.

To this day, FFI continues to support local and international partners working to protect the Cross River gorilla and its habitat, and to raise awareness of the plight of this relatively unfamiliar subspecies. As recently as 2016, the society joined forces with other organisations and local communities to express grave concern about the proposed route of the controversial Cross River State superhighway, which would have had disastrous consequences for the gorillas and for the forest habitat that is not only a vital refuge for endangered primates but also an irreplaceable source of local livelihoods. The collective representations – including 135,000 signatories on a petition – were enough to persuade Nigeria's Cross River State government to reroute the highway.

The society's renewed concern for primates and their forest habitat was not confined to Africa. The Red Alert project, launched in 1989, was designed to promote forest conservation within the range of the orang-utan in Indonesia, focusing initially on survey work in Central Kalimantan, close to the heart of Borneo. This was by no

THE CONSERVATION WORLD'S FAVOURITE AIRLINE?

In 1992 the society benefited for the first time from the valuable support of the British Airways Assisting Nature Conservation programme. This initiative was the brainchild of one man, Rod Hall, who single-handedly set up and ran the scheme until he had garnered support from several departments that began to appreciate its PR value. An enthusiastic conservationist and wildfowl expert, Hall took advantage of the flexibility that shift work allowed him, devoting his spare time to managing the programme.

His idea was that empty cargo space could be put to constructive use for the shipment of equipment or wildlife to and from captive breeding centres and field projects in countries where BA operated. Conservation students and professionals also received free or heavily discounted tickets on flights with empty seats. The beneficiaries of this scheme included a team of conservationists flying to Nigeria as part of the Drill Project; six Livingstone's fruit bats from the Comoros Islands destined for Jersey Zoo, where they were due to form the nucleus of a captive breeding programme; and a bulky shipment of promotional leaflets heading to Athens to support Greek bat conservation.

The society was one of the many leading conservation organisations to benefit from the scheme, and was among those who nominated Hall for the MBE that he was later awarded for services to conservation.

Above left British Airways brochure with the obligatory misspelling of FFI's name.

Above right The golden-crowned flying fox was among the many endangered Philippine species to benefit from the airline's support.

Throughout the remainder of the decade the British Airways scheme continued to support the work of the society, including William Oliver's pioneering captive breeding initiatives for Philippine endemics like the Visayan warty pig, the Indigenous Propagation Project to safeguard Turkish bulbs, groundbreaking camera-trap surveys in Sumatra's Kerinci Seblat National Park and the airlifting of four Antiguan racers as part of a proposed *ex situ* breeding programme to help save this snake from extinction. ∎

A baby orang-utan manages to cling to its mother by its fingertips despite being half asleep.

means the society's first documented involvement in orang-utan conservation; throughout the 1950s the then Fauna Preservation Society had actively intervened to combat the burgeoning illegal trade in Asia's only great ape, which was in demand from the pet trade and from less-scrupulous zoos. A concerted campaign by the society had led to stringent export restrictions being imposed on Singapore in 1956. A decade later, *Oryx* had featured the findings of an orang-utan and Sumatran rhino survey conducted in northern Sumatra's Leuser (disconcertingly misspelt as 'Loser') National Park, which recommended the most stringent possible controls on the illegal trade. The late 1960s had seen FPS lobbying for the introduction of tighter controls on illegal import and export of endangered wildlife in Hong Kong and other key trading posts following revelations that Borneo was haemorrhaging live orang-utans at an alarming rate. In September 1971 an enlarged issue of *Oryx* was published specifically to accommodate the first study of orang-utan ecology and behaviour based on extensive fieldwork, conducted by zoologist John Mackinnon in the Malaysian province of Sabah. It was not until the late 1980s, however, that the society began using the orang-utan as the key species to drive its large-scale

forest conservation efforts in South East Asia. Habitat loss remains the greatest single threat to the survival of orang-utans, but these days it is the proliferation of oil palm plantations that is responsible for the devastation. The largest Bornean orang-utan population is now found in and around Gunung Palung National Park in the south-west of the island, which is where FFI and its local partners set up what was then the first community-based protection unit for orang-utans in Indonesia.

Whilst the society was actively refocusing its efforts away from native wildlife at home in the UK, it had no intention of severing its historic links with those remnants of the empire referred to collectively as the British overseas territories. In 1990 the FFPS lent its support to a forum that was set up specifically to promote conservation in the UK Dependent Territories. This had been identified as an urgent priority in a comprehensive 1987 report, *Fragments of Paradise*, compiled by former Kew botanist Sara Oldfield, who joined the organisation in 1998 and went on to play a leading role in several groundbreaking flora conservation initiatives at FFI. As Global Programmes Director, Oldfield managed and developed a suite of worldwide activities that

'The Important Plant Areas project, as it became known, was probably the first in the world to use plant diversity to pinpoint habitats worthy of conservation at a national level.'

FFPS

complemented FFI's regional portfolio, most notably the Global Trees Campaign. Brought on board to 'put the flora back into Fauna & Flora International', Oldfield was instrumental in enabling botanical conservation to blossom in a more orchestrated fashion at FFI.

There is evidence that plant-focused projects were already beginning to enjoy something of a resurgence well before Oldfield's arrival, underpinned by the support and advice of a newly established Flora Working Group. The society's research and work on the wild bulb trade had paved the way for a European Community resolution to introduce compulsory labelling for wild-collected bulbs. Following his success as Development Officer for the Indigenous Propagation Project that had helped to protect Turkish bulbs from over-exploitation, Andy Byfield set up a new FFPS project in the same country, with the aim of identifying botanically significant areas and recommending appropriate measures to conserve them. The Important Plant Areas project, as it became known, was probably the first in the world to use plant diversity to pinpoint habitats worthy of conservation at a national level.

The society provided the impetus, and the lion's share of funding, for the inaugural meeting of the Plants Committee of CITES in November 1988. Organised largely by botanical consultant Mike Read and his former boss at the FFPS, John Burton, it paved the way for a series of meetings that addressed the unsustainable trade in a broad spectrum of plants, from bromeliads, succulents and orchids to carnivorous plants, medicinal plants, cacti and tropical timber.

Saving the wood for the trees

Following up on the work commissioned by the society in the early 1980s to investigate the commercial exploitation of mahogany, the premier tropical hardwood most at risk from international trade, the FFPS launched a new forest conservation initiative. With demand for mahogany at an all-time high, the process of extracting these giant trees was causing irreparable damage to vast tracts of formerly

Mike Read (FFPS Botanical Consultant) promoting legal propagation of threatened cacti in Mexico.

pristine forest habitat. Project Mahogany was officially launched at a press conference at London's Natural History Museum, which was held to coincide with the release of the society's new booklet *Mahogany – Forests or Furniture?*, compiled by Mike Read. The project's main aims were to raise public awareness of the mahogany crisis, to ensure better protection for forests containing mahogany – particularly in West Africa – and to promote consumer use of sustainably grown tropical timber. The society subsequently drafted proposals to list two groups of African mahoganies on Appendix II of CITES.

Mahoganies were not the only tropical hardwoods suffering unsustainable levels of exploitation, and the FFPS soon turned its attention to other threatened tree species. In 1993 it launched the Ebonies and Rosewoods project, a groundbreaking collaboration with the music business designed to protect these and other threatened timber species from unsustainable exploitation by the industry. This focused exclusively on tree species that were under severe pressure due to the insatiable demand for their highly prized wood among manufacturers of musical instruments. The campaign tackled both ends of the supply

chain, encouraging manufacturers to source their materials carefully while also helping local communities to establish and run their own tree nurseries, restoring heavily exploited forests and exposing illegal logging and trade. The name of the project was soon changed to SoundWood, in order to reflect the inclusion of other vulnerable tree species adversely affected by the burgeoning demand for their wood, such as the endangered pernambuco, or *pau brasil*, a Brazilian species used for violin bows, and the African blackwood, used for clarinets and other woodwind instruments.

Restricted to a few remnants of the dwindling Atlantic Forest, *pau brasil* is Brazil's national tree, but it has been widely exploited for centuries for a dye extracted from its heartwood. Its timber is also highly prized as the raw material for stringed instrument bows. In 1997 FFI held a workshop in Brazil that brought together conservationists, local politicians and music industry representatives to produce a Conservation Action Plan for this endangered species.

The African blackwood, known locally as mpingo, had suffered a precipitous decline in its native Tanzania and Mozambique. Given that its heartwood was required to service the demand for over 100,000 clarinets every year, the only surprise was that it wasn't already *mpingone*. At a CITES conference in Fort Lauderdale in November 1994, the range states had rejected a proposal to add the African blackwood

Above left Richard Brunton (guitarist), Mike Read and David Jean Baptiste (bassoonist) at the launch of the Ebonies and Rosewoods project in December 1993.

Above right Chainsaw massacre: this image was used on the cover of an FFPS awareness booklet, *Mahogany: Forests or Furniture?*, published in 1990.

to the list of species subject to international trade restrictions. Once again, FFI seized the initiative, organising and chairing a conference in the Mozambique capital, Maputo, at which it brokered a deal to put together a sustainable trade plan as a more palatable alternative to the proposed CITES listing. This brought together all the key protagonists in the supply chain, including forestry departments, exporters, importers and manufacturers from around the world, who between them came up with a regional conservation strategy that undoubtedly helped to secure a sustainable future for mpingo. FFI's involvement did not end there, though; in 2002 the society published a seminal report, *International trade in African blackwood*, which advocated fully involving local communities in forest management to safeguard this globally important species. As we shall see, the tree subsequently became the focal species of the Mpingo Conservation & Development Initiative, the Tanzanian organisation established with support from the Conservation Leadership Programme, one of FFI's most successful and longest-running collaborations.

Above Close-up of the flowers and seed pods of pernambuco and (right) a replanting initiative to help conserve this endangered Brazilian tree.

Below The timber of the African blackwood is highly prized by the manufacturers of woodwind instruments.

Investing in the future

The Conservation Leadership Programme (informally known as CLP) was first established in 1985, in response to the need for additional scientific data on threatened species. The programme was initially conceived as a means of sponsoring UK university students to collect data on biological diversity overseas during their summer vacation.

Originally set up by the International Council for Bird Preservation as a conservation expedition award scheme to support exclusively avian projects, it was extended to cover all other life forms, including plants, when the FFPS came on board in 1988. The society joined forces with what is now BirdLife International to support the programme, which provided students and other aspiring young conservationists with expedition funding. Two years later, the scheme secured corporate backing when British Petroleum agreed to inject £125,000 of funding into its development for an initial three-year period.

The version of the programme that we know today is a partnership of three international wildlife conservation organisations – Fauna & Flora International (FFI), BirdLife International and the Wildlife Conservation Society – that benefited from the continuing support of BP plc until 2017. Over time, it has evolved into an international capacity building programme that supports conservationists in the early stages of their career, the majority of whom are working on projects in their own countries. It draws on the expertise of conservation professionals worldwide, providing project funding and training for budding leaders who are addressing the most urgent conservation priorities on their own doorstep. By investing in the professional development of young conservationists operating in difficult circumstances with minimal resources, the programme helps to hone their skills and maximise their potential.

In its original guise, the scheme supported just two projects. By 2014 it had evolved to the point where it was funding 26 projects a year to the tune of US$450,000. In the three decades since its formation, the programme has funded more than 600 projects and 80 internships in over 100 countries, and helped to kick-start the careers of over 2,500 young conservationists who now make up a formidable global conservation collective. Many past award-winners now work full time in conservation, and several are widely recognised as leading lights in their chosen field. Among their numerous claims to fame, alumni have contributed to the discovery or rediscovery of over 130 species, influenced the designation of 75 globally important conservation sites and established a string of local non-governmental

organisations, 25 of which can trace their origins to the initial support received from the programme.

Historically, CLP's geographical remit has encompassed over 100 countries from Azerbaijan to Zimbabwe. The pages of this book are not the place to try to do justice to the entire alphabetical spectrum of all the amazing amphibians, charismatic carnivores, floral phenomena, freshwater fish, marine marvels, myriad mammals, ornithological oddities and rare reptiles that have benefited from CLP support during the past three decades. Suffice to say that previous award-winners have helped to discover, rediscover, safeguard or champion an astounding array of at-risk species, from Ader's duiker, African wild dog, Antillean manatee, Amur tiger, Andean cat, Araripe manakin, Arodi bubble-nest frog and Asian elephant to the Zapata rail, Zenker's fruit bat, Zodarion spiders and the fire-tailed zogue-zogue.

The pioneering conservation initiatives supported by the programme have not been immune from difficulties, and one particular expedition ended in tragedy when a team of Cambridge graduates working in Irian Jaya was kidnapped by local self-styled 'freedom fighters' seeking independence for West Papua. Held hostage for 130 days, they were eventually freed by Indonesian crack troops, but not before two of their Indonesian counterparts had been executed by their captors. Their ordeal was the subject of a 1997 book, *The Open Cage*, written by expedition leader Daniel Start. Whilst isolated incidents such as this cannot diminish the magnitude of what CLP has achieved, they serve as a sobering reminder that conservationists take their life in their hands when they work – as FFI and its local counterparts so often do – in politically unstable conflict zones.

Opposite (clockwise from top left) Greater adjutant storks in India, blue-eyed black lemurs in Madagascar, Supatá golden frogs in Colombia, whale sharks in Indonesia, dugongs in the Comoros and horseshoe bats in Romania have all benefited from CLP funding.

'The big difference between CLP and other, more traditional, funding sources is the sense of partnership. CLP does not just provide funding to solve a particular issue. It partners with you to develop long-term conservation strategies and then helps provide the tools to achieve your goals.'

Alberto Campos, 2012 Conservation Leadership Award Winner, Brazil

RISING STARS

TREE TRADE IN TANZANIA

The Mpingo Conservation & Development Initiative aims to conserve endangered forest habitats in East Africa by promoting sustainable and socially equitable harvesting of valuable timber stocks and other forest products. As the organisation's name implies, one of its focal species is mpingo, a tree that FFI began working to conserve in 1995 as part of its SoundWood programme. FFI was the first conservation organisation to take an active interest in the species, which is not only highly prized by the makers of clarinets and oboes, but is also the medium of choice for local wood carvers. Its dark, lustrous heartwood is one of the most valuable timbers in the world, but 20 years ago the tree was under severe pressure from over-exploitation and threatened with commercial extinction. Conversely, it also had tremendous potential as a flagship species that could contribute to the wider conservation of the coastal forests and miombo woodlands of East Africa.

The initiative was established in 2004 in the wake of two CLP-funded projects in 1996 and 2004. With over US$75,000 in CLP support, these projects focused on developing sustainable community-led forestry practices for mpingo. The organisation was the first to obtain a Forest Stewardship Council certificate for community-managed natural forest in Africa. It also initiated the first commercial timber sales from a community-managed forest in Tanzania, which have generated more than US$100,000 to date, with profits ploughed back into improving local livelihoods. It was CLP support that provided the foundations on which these achievements were built.

Makala Jasper, CLP alumnus and CEO of Mpingo Conservation & Development Initiative, accepting a 2016 Whitley Award from The Princess Royal.

'Through CLP support, Mpingo Conservation & Development Initiative was transformed from a student research expedition into a practical conservation organisation in 2004. It has since supported communities to conserve more than 100,000 hectares of land.'

MADE IN MADAGASCAR

While working as a research student for a local NGO in 2004, Julie Hanta Razafimanahaka joined a CLP team on a project that focused on bats in her native Madagascar. Subsequent CLP support in the shape of a travel grant enabled her to visit the UK, exposing her to an English-speaking research environment where she grew rapidly in confidence. Less than a decade later, she became Director of Madagasikara Voakajy, the very same organisation for which she had worked in her student days. Julie now manages a team of 40 staff at this leading national NGO, which uses conservation science and community participation to protect endemic Malagasy species and their habitats.

SERENDIPITOUS IN SRI LANKA

Kanchana Weerakoon's entire life story was transformed when, in 1997, she found herself working as the local counterpart for a student expedition from Cambridge University, funded by the BP Conservation Programme (now CLP). That initial encounter helped to kick-start a career that has culminated in her setting up and running what is today one of Sri Lanka's leading conservation organisations. Along the way, bolstered by continued support from CLP, she has collected numerous accolades, including Most Outstanding Young Person of Sri Lanka and, more recently, an Eisenhower Fellowship. As a national-level leader, Kanchana is now helping Sri Lanka's next generation of aspiring conservationists to fulfil their dreams. ∎

Above Mustachioed butterfly case reopened: during a 2005 expedition funded by CLP, Dr Blanca Huertas – now senior curator of Lepidoptera at London's Natural History Museum – found a new species of butterfly on a remote mountainside in Colombia. She realised that it was undescribed when she came across additional specimens in the museum, lurking unlabelled in some Colombian collections, which dated back to 1920. The vital clue was the unusually hairy mouthparts, common to her specimen and those in the museum, confirming that the find was indeed new to science. The species was dubbed the Magdalena Valley ringlet and is now formally described.

Left Roberta Kamille Pennell, another rising star in the conservation world, is a former CLP intern who learned her trade working for Ya'axché, FFI's partner in Belize, and now acts as a CLP ambassador, supporting young professionals in her home country and throughout the globe. In 2016, Kamille embarked on a Masters in Conservation Leadership at the University of Cambridge.

Without a paddle

The society had always prided itself on the fact that its small number of core staff and severely limited financial resources did not preclude it from having a big impact. Nevertheless, it is hard to escape the impression that its sphere of influence at home and abroad was narrowing to the point of unsustainability by the start of the 1990s. There was an apparent surge in environmental awareness and green consciousness among the general public, boosted by extensive media coverage of topical issues such as tropical rainforest destruction and atmospheric pollution, yet paradoxically the FFPS seemed to be losing its way. Following the hasty departure of John Gooders, which evidently left council members so traumatised that they were in no hurry to recruit a replacement, the society was more or less rudderless for a five-year period. As John Burton observed, 'it's a miracle that it survived'. That the FFPS remained a going concern during this period he attributes to three factors: first, the fact that some projects had sufficient long-term momentum to continue virtually under their own steam; second, the individual determination of key consultants and staff like Mike Read and Roger Wilson; and third, most crucially in Burton's view, the reputation of its journal, *Oryx*, which, even in the society's darkest days, continued to be held in high regard by conservationists and the wider scientific community.

During his brief tenure, Gooders had made the decision to uproot the society from London and move its headquarters to Brighton. This decision was ostensibly driven by cost-saving considerations, although it may have had something to do with the fact that the new director lived on the south coast. Whatever the reason, it proved to be false economy, and the FFPS paid a price in other ways. Less than three years later, it relocated back to the Royal Geographical Society premises in London, shedding staff in the process, just as it had during the earlier move. According to the

annual report, the return to the capital resulted in 'an upsurge of visitors to the office' and 'a renewal of valuable contacts'. In other words, the FFPS had unnecessarily condemned itself to three years of self-imposed exile. From London down to Brighton and back again for good measure, the society was bouncing around like a pinball and badly in need of a wizard to help it get back in the game and give it a renewed sense of direction. Something needed to change.

Sink or swim

To their credit, the Executive Committee and members of council realised this, and spent the best part of a year putting together what chairman David Jones described as 'the most comprehensive development plan in the Society's history'. This process involved a thorough reappraisal of what the FFPS stood for, a redefinition of its strategic objectives and no little soul searching. A guest editorial entitled *The future of the Society*, penned by Jones for the July 1992 issue of *Oryx*, read like a cry for help from an organisation in the midst of an existential crisis. Bullish references to the society's past achievements and assertions about its continuing relevance merely served to betray an underlying insecurity about its future. At this point in time, did the FFPS have the capacity to influence the decision makers and participate fully in the range of activities that would be needed to effect real change? In a word, no.

Even the mighty *Oryx*, the society's flagship publication, was under siege from the new international conservation journals on the block. Broad appeal combined with scientific rigour had proved a successful formula until now, but keeping *Oryx* accessible and interesting to a wide readership while simultaneously retaining its academic credibility had always been a delicate balancing act. As its editor Jacqui Morris conceded, it was becoming increasingly

The general confusion that characterised this turbulent period of transition in the society's history was reflected in the use of several logos in quick succession and even, at one point, interchangeably.

difficult to walk that tightrope, and the society was faced with the very real prospect that the journal could slip from its pre-eminent position: 'We may need to make changes, to relaunch *Oryx* in a new form to ensure that we are meeting the needs of the modern conservation scientist.'

If the society had somehow contrived to paint itself into a corner, Jones felt it necessary to remind everyone that neither he nor his colleagues were the ones holding the brush. 'As the members you are ultimately responsible for the success or failure of FFPS.' These same members were left in no doubt that the fate of the FFPS was in their hands. 'The FFPS is your Society and it is support from the membership that will ultimately decide whether it grows, stagnates or dies.' Strong leadership would have helped, too, of course.

At least there was an acknowledgement that standing still was not an option, which was ironic given that John Burton's departure had been precipitated by the chairman's reluctance to countenance aggressive expansion. If the society was to grow, however, it would need to 'invest further in project co-ordination and development, so that the amount of work we ourselves are involved in increases, thus giving us a higher public profile'. Jones advocated dipping into the society's limited reserves in order to implement these expansion plans, but recognised that the FFPS would need to raise additional resources 'probably through the appointment of a chief executive with an ability to co-ordinate such activity on behalf of us all'. In other words, they needed money. Fortunately, a generous legacy had

ensured that there were now sufficient funds in the kitty to support that appointment, at least in the short term.

Early the following year, 1993, a firm of headhunters was finally commissioned to identify suitable candidates for the top job. One of the names on the shortlist was Mark Rose. A wildlife conservationist by background, Rose had lived and worked in some of the remotest and harshest environments in Africa and South East Asia. This included a baptism of fire in the Western Sahara – his first foray into the continent – and a spell in some of the least-explored regions of Papua New Guinea, where he cut his teeth as a district wildlife officer. In this latter role he was responsible for introducing an innovative, and still thriving, ranching scheme that provides income for local communities while conserving the wild crocodile population.

Rose was already familiar with the workings of the society, not only from the perspective of a long-term member and *Oryx* subscriber, but also as a former intern who, in 1979, had been lucky enough to carry out a research project for John Burton in what was the first TRAFFIC office, where he worked on a study into the trade in crocodilians.

THE NERVOUS NINETIES

The carefully choreographed birthday celebrations to mark the society's ninetieth anniversary in December 1993 were a welcome fillip for the organisation, enabling it to bounce back from an otherwise traumatic year that had been threatening to go down as one more *annus horribilis*. Months of preparation resulted in a memorable day that enabled the FFPS to showcase new projects, provide a platform for several overseas partners in conservation and celebrate its royal patronage.

On the morning of the event, the society officially launched its imaginative Ebonies and Rosewoods project, designed to protect the world's most valued and endangered trees from over-exploitation, in close co-operation with the music industry.

A series of anniversary lectures introduced by chairman David Jones were the highlight of the afternoon session. These featured speakers from Uganda, Indonesia and Turkey, where the FFPS had recently been working with local partners to help tackle their most salient conservation problems.

The event culminated in an evening reception at which Her Majesty The Queen, the society's patron, was guest of honour. Accompanied by His Royal Highness The Duke of Edinburgh, the Queen was introduced to a panoply of society members, sponsors, supporters and staff, including recently appointed director Mark Rose. ∎

Above Guest speakers Widodo Ramono, Professor Frederick Kayanja and Nergis Yazgan are introduced to Her Majesty The Queen.

Right Her Majesty The Queen, patron since 1952, addresses the guests at the society's ninetieth birthday celebrations, held at London's Royal Geographical Society.

Below Indonesia's Widodo Ramono delivering one of the anniversary lectures.

Below right His Royal Highness The Duke of Edinburgh in conversation with FFPS council member Dr David Chivers.

He had subsequently carved out a successful career working for several prominent UK conservation organisations, including The Wildlife Trusts, where he had achieved notable success in transforming their fortunes and gained a reputation as something of a turnaround specialist.

In short, his credentials seemed impeccable. Naturally, the job was offered to someone else on the shortlist. Fortunately for Rose and, as it turned out, for the future of the society, the first-choice candidate declined. After he was re-approached, Rose was magnanimous enough to accept the offer, no doubt determined to demonstrate to council how misguided they had been not to appoint him in the first place. Rose was by no means a popular choice with the few staff still working at the society. To his credit, Jones stuck his neck out as chairman and disregarded their concerns, which largely revolved around the fact that they were about to be dragged out of their comfort zone.

The minutes of an FFPS council meeting held during this turbulent period also reveal a collective unease about proposed expenditure on the new post, which was destined to take the cash flow deficit to what some regarded as an unacceptably high level. The then treasurer, Edward Wright, reminded those present that the decision to appoint a new director 'had been taken following receipt of a valuable legacy from the late Miss Wood' and that whilst the appointment would inevitably be a drain on the reserve in the first instance, he was confident that Rose 'would prove more than equal to redressing the deficit'. Wright also had the perspicacity to suggest that the projected overspend 'should be regarded as an investment for the Society's future'. Rose was finally installed as director in October 1993 and immediately set about overhauling the organisation.

Prior to his appointment as the new director of the society, Mark Rose had gained ample exposure to the wild side of conservation, not least during his sojourn in Papua New Guinea, where his role as a district wildlife officer brought him face to face with some of the less scrupulous protagonists in the lucrative crocodile skin trade.

CHAPTER 8

VINDICATION

'The Society has a fine record and I am sure that it will make an even more significant contribution in the critical years ahead.'

Her Majesty Queen Elizabeth II, Patron, 15 December 1993

In late 1993 the baton for the society passed to Mark Rose. Or, more accurately, he picked it up from where it had been lying forgotten for several years after being so unceremoniously discarded by his predecessor. As John Burton recalls, it wasn't so much a baton as a 'poisoned chalice'.

By the time Rose took over, the prolonged interregnum had seen the society's activities diminish to a mere handful of active projects, managed by a skeleton staff of five people. His number one priority was obviously to grow a work programme and a larger team, in order to achieve some kind of critical mass. All very well in theory, but in practice, how was he going to set about that task? Well, I wouldn't start from here, as the old joke goes.

Fast-forward to 2017 where, against all the odds, we find that Rose is still very much in charge. He has held the reins for almost a quarter of a century, first as director and subsequently as chief executive, and is now among the longest-serving leaders in the society's history. During that time he has been instrumental in transforming FFI into a multifaceted global conservation charity with a work programme comprising more than 140 projects in over 40 countries, spanning five continents. It is a far cry from the almost moribund organisation that he inherited. We need to rewind to late 1993 in order to understand how that transformation unfolded.

Once on board, Rose wasted no time in developing and implementing a business plan that advocated a 'full speed ahead' expansionist approach. It was a calculated risk, but the

alternative was to fade away. How much appetite there was among the old guard for this new gung-ho approach is a moot point. Rose recalls inviting Richard and Maisie Fitter to provide feedback on his proposed business plan and receiving a non-committal response that left him wondering whether they were too polite to disagree with it, or just didn't understand it. Universally welcomed or otherwise, the changes came thick and fast and prompted the departure of several council members.

Although he had supported Rose's appointment, David Jones himself stepped down as chairman in 1994. He was replaced by Lindsay Bury, a venture capitalist and entrepreneur whose financial skills were to prove vital in helping the society to negotiate the delicate business of managing a shoestring budget in those early stages of the rebuilding process. Bury also put his own money behind the society, providing generous annual support for its core operations. Other new recruits to the council fold included geographer Dr Bill Adams, a Cambridge academic and enthusiastic conservationist with whom Rose had worked closely during his time with The Wildlife Trusts.

In order to accommodate the anticipated growth and development, the society moved its headquarters from London to Cambridge. This was an astute and deliberate choice of location; not only did it offer cheaper, more spacious premises, but it also made strategic sense, bringing the society into close proximity with the cluster of internationally focused wildlife conservation organisations already based in and around the city. A decade later, FFI would be one of the driving forces behind moves to harness this critical mass of expertise by establishing a formal coalition familiar today as the Cambridge Conservation Initiative, which we will revisit later.

Opposite Herd of Cape buffalo in Mozambique's Niassa National Reserve, one of Africa's most important wildlife havens.

A society by any other name . . .

Rose also felt that the society was saddled with an old-fashioned, slightly parochial name that did not exactly conjure an image of a forward-thinking organisation with global aspirations. He was conscious of the need to reflect its international outlook and worldwide remit, so in 1995 he persuaded the powers-that-be to approve the latest and possibly final name change in the charity's history. Fauna & Flora International (FFI) had arrived.

As early as 1994, there was a renewed sense of momentum, with membership increasing for the first time in six years. By the following year, the level of conservation activity had expanded considerably, bolstered by increased support from corporate sponsors and donors, many of them newly recruited to the FFI cause by Rose.

The inaugural issue of *Fauna and Flora News*, the society's first official newsletter, was distributed to members in April 1994. Until this juncture, updates on the society's own activities had been confined to a postscript at the back of the quarterly *Oryx* journal. This marked the end of an era for *Oryx*, which had begun life as the society's mouthpiece but had long since transcended that narrow role and was well on the way to establishing its reputation as the world's go-to publication for conservation practitioners.

The introduction of a newsletter was symptomatic of a renewed determination to raise the society's profile, but it was also a question of pragmatism. The range of projects was expected to increase dramatically in light of Rose's ambitious expansion plans, and the journal simply would not have been able to accommodate the volume of additional news without neglecting its broader purpose.

Removing all the society-specific subject matter from *Oryx* also gave it a new lease of life as a peer-reviewed journal.

By the turn of the century, the newsletter itself had doubled in length and gleaned an award as the best environmental charity publication of its kind, but despite appearing twice a year it was struggling to convey the sheer breadth of FFI's activities. The first issue of a new, enlarged magazine, *Fauna & Flora*, appeared in October 2001. Some 16 years later, this publication continues to be extremely well received by members and supporters.

One of the magazine's defining characteristics was – and remains – the high quality of images used to illustrate project updates and topical features. This is thanks in large part to the extensive portfolio compiled by FFI's then in-house photographer Juan Pablo Moreiras (many of whose images grace the pages of this book) and additional contributions from, among others, freelance photographer Jeremy Holden, whose work also features prominently here.

In light of the imminent increase in the scale and sweep of the society's work, activities were rationalised, grouped more logically by topic or region, and incorporated into existing or newly created programmes defined as Africa and the Indian Ocean, South East Asia, UK Dependent Territories and Species in Trade. Wildlife management specialist Chris Huxley, who was retained as a consultant during this period, helped Rose to expand FFI's Africa portfolio beyond its work with gorillas and branch out into countries such as Guinea and Mozambique. Huxley proved to be, in Rose's words, 'a tremendous fount of knowledge and vital

The first issue of *Fauna and Flora News*, which acquired an ampersand later in life, was published in April 1994. Thereafter the newsletter appeared twice a year until 2001, when it was superseded by a new magazine.

confidant'. Being outside the system, he always provided a different perspective and helped Rose through a crucial and difficult period of expansion. Another area where Huxley's expertise proved valuable – due in no small part to the experience he had amassed in his former role as the deputy secretary of CITES – was the Species in Trade programme. This consolidated and enabled closer co-ordination of the many plant protection initiatives that the society had pioneered through its close association with CITES, including the Ebonies and Rosewoods project that metamorphosed into the more ambitious SoundWood programme.

Today, you will search the FFI website in vain for any mention of SoundWood. As the scope and ambition of the society's tree conservation work continued to broaden, the programme was eventually subsumed under the all-embracing umbrella that we now know as the Global Trees Campaign. Originally developed in conjunction with the UNEP World Conservation Monitoring Centre, the campaign is a joint initiative between FFI and Botanic Gardens Conservation International. Officially launched in 1999, it

Above FFI's members' magazine, *Fauna & Flora*, was first published in October 2001, and has been saddled with the same editor ever since.

Below This UK consumer guide to choosing and using timber wisely – produced in collaboration with Friends of the Earth – was written by FFI's Dr Georgina Magin.

SOUND SCIENCE

SoundWood was set up to safeguard the future of trees that are used to make musical instruments. The campaign did not advocate blanket bans, boycotts or the exclusive use of synthetic substitutes, but focused on encouraging wise use of forest resources that would enable trade to continue, albeit at a sustainable level. Specifically, SoundWood promoted local partnerships that would ensure sustainable management of timber, implemented educational programmes in schools across the globe, fostered co-operation within the music business and created a certification scheme that enabled manufacturers to procure their timber from well-managed sources.

The campaign secured endorsements from a broad spectrum of renowned classical and contemporary musicians on both sides of the Atlantic, which included Jamiroquai and Jules Holland, classical, blues, folk and rock guitar legends John Williams, Bonnie Raitt, Richard Thompson and Mark Knopfler, and Eagles drummer Don Henley. The programme also received a huge boost when the distinguished violinist and conductor Yehudi Menuhin agreed to become SoundWood's first patron. ∎

Left A display of guitars made from sustainably managed timber.

Below right The *SoundWood Guide to the Guitar*, published in 1999, featured 19 guitar companies and their efforts to reduce pressure on threatened tree species.

Below left One of the many SoundWood leaflets issued to safeguard against the unsustainable exploitation of timber used to make musical instruments, alongside a clarinet manufactured from African blackwood.

Above A flowering emergent tree towers above the rainforest canopy in Panama's Parque Internacional La Amistad.

was the first, and is still the only, international programme dedicated to safeguarding all the world's 9,600 threatened tree species, of which over 1,850 are at imminent risk of extinction unless urgent action is taken to save them.

The campaign focuses specifically on the protection of tree species on their own merit, recognising that landscape-level conservation measures will not necessarily do that job, and that individual tree species may require very specific conservation attention that they would not receive as part of broader forest protection initiatives. This intervention includes encouraging and empowering local communities to develop appropriate *in situ* protection measures. In 2000 the Global Trees Campaign received an Arbor Day Foundation award in recognition of its work.

Whilst FFI's project portfolio was becoming more geographically widespread and biologically diverse, it remained true to the spirit of the society, continuing to focus largely on plant and animal groups that were not on the

radar of other conservation organisations. This underlying insistence that there was more to conservation than saving cute and cuddly mammals was already implicit in FFI's everyday activities, but that distinguishing characteristic was brought firmly into the public domain when, in 1997, it organised the provocatively named conference, *Has the Panda had its Day?* This thoroughly entertaining two-day symposium provided the perfect showcase for many of FFI's

Left Published by Cambridge University Press in July 2000, this mischievously subtitled book brought together a variety of perspectives on modern approaches to mammal conservation.

TREE MUSKETEERS

Under the auspices of the Global Trees Campaign, FFI has continued to devise imaginative solutions to the problem of safeguarding threatened tree species across the globe, supporting tree conservation in more than 25 countries, including magnificent magnolias in China (see opposite), Madagascar's mystifying baobabs, enigmatic conifers in Vietnam, Kyrgyzstan's wild fruit trees and the majestic monkey puzzles of Brazil's beleaguered Atlantic Forest.

Below right This diminutive nursery-grown coffin tree seedling may eventually grow into a giant conifer, attaining a height of 50 metres.

Bottom right An avenue of Grandidier's baobabs, another target species of the Global Trees Campaign.

Below left Selection of leaflets illustrating the variety of FFI's tree conservation initiatives.

In 2005, FFI's Global Trees Campaign intervened to rescue a critically endangered but hitherto overlooked species of Chinese magnolia. Despite its popularity as an ornamental tree, *Magnolia sinica* was sliding inexorably and virtually unnoticed towards extinction in the wild. Confined to a remote tract of karst rainforest in southern Yunnan, it enjoyed nominal protection within a reserve, but this had not prevented its population from dwindling virtually to the point of no return. Working with protected area staff, local partners and the surrounding communities in order to address the main threats to the magnolia's survival, FFI succeeded in reinvigorating what was, to all intents and purposes, a reserve in name only.

It soon became apparent that this 'paper park' problem was not confined to one particular protected area. Once it realised that the plight of *M. sinica* was symptomatic of a wider problem with other magnolia species across China's reserves, FFI used its convening power to bring together botanical experts and government representatives. In a classic case of capacity building, it supported the development of a coherent plan to resurrect protected area management in a form that would tangibly improve the survival prospects of China's threatened magnolias and wider biodiversity.

Gratifyingly, the Global Trees Campaign is now largely surplus to requirements where *M. sinica* is concerned, and this iconic species is now enjoying the conservation attention it so desperately needed a decade ago. ∎

A Global Trees Campaign survey conducted in December 2005 confirmed that the wild population of *Magnolia sinica* (far left) was down to single figures, prompting emergency action to save this critically endangered species from extinction. Other Chinese magnolias to have benefited subsequently from the intervention of FFI and its partners include the critically endangered *Magnolia omeiensis*, the exquisite *Magnolia insignis* (left) and *Manglieta nucifera* (above left).

classic conservation interventions, which were profiled in the form of rolling news on the BBC's newly launched 24-hour television channel, BBC News 24. Published some three years later by Cambridge University Press, the accompanying volume that grew out of the proceedings featured contributions from over 40 authors, including some of the world's most eminent conservation scientists and conservation biologists, and remains one of the all-time best sellers in the renowned *Conservation Biology* series.

Indeed, it was during this fertile period, with new projects proliferating at an unprecedented rate, that some of FFI's most iconic campaigns on behalf of previously neglected species first saw the light of day. There seems little doubt that this emphasis on the underdog was influenced by the council members at the time, and the overlap with their individual interests is surely no coincidence. As was the case a decade earlier, bats, reptiles and amphibians featured prominently.

Realising its vision of a bespoke, self-sufficient bat conservation organisation on home soil did not preclude FFI from keeping its own finger on the UK pulse, but it meant that more time and resources were available to focus on bats found further afield. In the early 1990s a grant application alerted the society to the fact that a large species of fruit bat endemic to a remote offshore island was threatened with imminent extinction. The Pemba flying fox, named after the Tanzanian island to which it is confined, had always been hunted by the islanders as a source of food, but the balance of power shifted when the Pembaris discovered that shotguns were a more efficient weapon than traps affixed to long poles. Too efficient, as it turned out. The besieged fruit bat's crisis was compounded by the loss of many of its traditional tree roosting sites due to widespread deforestation. By the time the international conservation community was alerted to the problem,

numbers were reportedly down to just a few hundred, which led to the species being formally categorised by IUCN as Critically Endangered.

In 1995, FFI made up for lost time by supporting efforts to rescue the Pemba flying fox, initially via that old faithful, an Oryx 100% Fund grant. Subsequent support from, among others, the Disney Wildlife [now Worldwide] Conservation Fund enabled FFI to assist Pemba's forestry department in implementing a broad spectrum of conservation measures. As it turned out, the communities on Pemba were shocked to learn that a species unique to their island was in such dire straits. They took little persuading to mobilise themselves into actively protecting the bats, and put in place their own local and island-wide by-laws. The use of shotguns to kill bats is now largely prohibited and, as a result, many of the most important roosts are now secure and the Pemba flying fox population has recovered dramatically to over 22,000 individuals at the last count.

The recipient of that initial 100% Fund grant was Abigail Entwistle, who had recently completed her PhD on British bats at Aberdeen University under the supervision of Professor Paul Racey. A prominent FFI council member, Racey himself had also benefited from 100% Fund support in his formative years and subsequently repaid the favour many times over, not least through his sterling work in mentoring a succession of budding conservationists like Entwistle, whose work so impressed FFI that it recruited her. Twenty years later, and a raw recruit no longer, Dr Entwistle is still with the organisation.

Below left Pemba flying fox, living up to its name.

Below right Cluster of Pemba flying foxes at a traditional roosting site. The species is now off the critical list.

ABI'S ROAD

Dr Abigail Entwistle was the first person to walk through FFI's door looking for a job after the society had relocated to Cambridge in 1995. She had just completed her PhD before undertaking a survey of Pemba's fruit bats, courtesy of a 100% Fund grant. FFI had very little money at the time, and although Entwistle herself was equally short of cash, she accepted a volunteer position. That quickly changed to a staff role and the ensuing two decades have seen her involved in a broad spectrum of initiatives relating to the Indigenous Propagation Project, the 100% Fund, Halcyon Land & Sea, the Marine Programme and the Eurasia Programme, of which she was director. She was also responsible for the comprehensive report that led ultimately to the formation of the Cambridge Conservation Initiative referred to earlier in this chapter. At the time of writing, Entwistle holds the position of Director, Conservation Science and Design, but not as tightly, perhaps, as she clutches the

Hiding in the back row, Dr Abigail Entwistle attempts to blend in with the crowd during a break from her work with the Pemba Island community.

long-service medal that was presented to her by Sir David Attenborough after FFI's annual general meeting in 2016, not to mention the two *Blue Peter* badges that she acquired through her involvement in promoting the *Good Bulb Guide*. ∎

If the spectacular resurgence of an obscure fruit bat was a notable feather in FFI's cap, its last-ditch heroics on behalf of a harmless, unspectacular Caribbean serpent must rate as the equivalent of a headdress stacked with bird of paradise plumes. In 1995, when FFI first intervened, the recently rediscovered Antiguan racer was probably the world's rarest snake, with a total population numbering just 50 individuals on one tiny offshore islet.

A little over two decades later, thanks to a recovery programme that included eradication of invasive alien predators, a nationwide public education campaign and

reintroduction to rat-free islands, snake numbers have increased twentyfold. The racer has become a tremendous source of national pride and a diminutive, scaly standard-bearer for Antigua's biodiversity as a whole.

Some conservationists had advised against intervention on the basis that the snake was too rare and too unpopular. As usual, FFI was undeterred by the seemingly insurmountable obstacles, a source of evident satisfaction for the project leader, Dr Jenny Daltry: 'I am so glad we have proved the doubters wrong, and helped turn around the fortunes of this unique and lovely animal.'

THE RACE AGAINST TIME

The Antiguan Racer Conservation Project is one of the longest-running and most successful conservation initiatives in the Caribbean, and bears many of the hallmarks of FFI's most effective interventions: focus on a neglected species; pooling of multidisciplinary resources to capitalise on local knowledge, international experience and specialist skills; and the appliance of science.

The Antiguan racer disappeared from the Antiguan mainland and most offshore islands well over a century ago, the inevitable result of deforestation, agricultural encroachment, persecution and the unwelcome attentions of invasive alien predators – chiefly black rats inadvertently brought ashore by European settlers and the Asian mongooses that were deliberately introduced in an ill-advised attempt to control the rodent plague.

Top Panoramic view from the high point of Great Bird Island, last refuge of the Antiguan racer at the time of this critically endangered snake's rediscovery.

Above right Fifty shades of racer: mature Antiguan racers are highly variable in colour and pattern, ranging from extremely pale morphs to this striking reddish form.

Above left Kevel Lindsay (left) and Mark Day, the dynamic duo who rediscovered the Antiguan racer on Great Bird Island.

Clockwise from top Many of the snakes captured during the first survey were disfigured as a result of rat bites; the willing team of ratbusters, ready to perform a removal service; a block of rat bait covered in telltale bite marks; a black rat investigating a recently laid block of bait; bait had to be laid throughout even the least accessible parts of the island, including the steep cliffs.

A few snakes survived the onslaught, pinned into a corner on a tiny mongoose-free island not much bigger than a superstore car park. Forgotten by the outside world and harassed by rats, the last remaining population clung on, its future hanging by a single thread.

By the time the species was rediscovered on Great Bird Island in the early 1990s by a local naturalist, Kevel Lindsay, and an FFI herpetologist, Mark Day, the snake was close to extinction – although nobody knew just how close. FFI's Jenny Daltry, the project leader, conducted a three-month survey which confirmed black rats as the main threat to the racer's survival. A military-style eradication campaign was carried out, mainly by staff from the local Environmental Awareness Group and the Antiguan Forestry Unit, who laid blocks of rat poison across the entire island, including ledges on the precipitous sea cliffs.

Just two years after the rat removal, the Antiguan racer population had doubled, but by 1999 the project had become a victim of its own success, as the snakes ran out of lizards to eat on their microdot in the ocean. Other offshore islands suitable for the reintroduction of racers were quickly identified, and several new colonies established there.

The project partners launched a nationwide snake charm offensive in Antigua to change local and tourist attitudes towards the harmless, docile racer, emphasising what a rare privilege it is to have a species on your doorstep

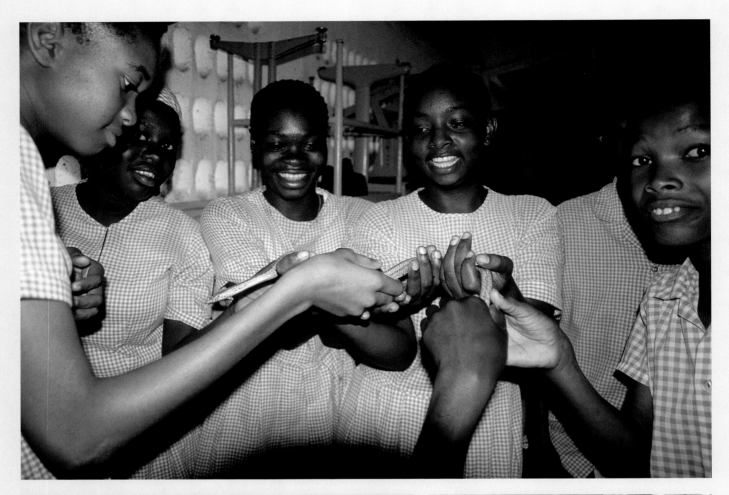

Clockwise from top Schoolchildren are encouraged to handle the harmless, docile racer; Dr Jenny Daltry marks a snake under the watchful gaze of young admirers; McRonnie Henry, head of the Antiguan Forestry Unit, radio-tracking the snakes, which were fitted with miniature transmitters to help follow their movements.

Opposite (clockwise from top left) Durrell Wildlife Conservation Trust successfully bred the Antiguan racer in captivity at Jersey Zoo, but the snakes later succumbed to a parasite; this website aimed to show younger audiences how a model conservation project unfolds; the brown pelican and the Antiguan ground lizard, two of the many endangered species to have benefited from rat eradication.

that is found nowhere else on the planet. A documentary, *Race Against Time*, appeared on national and regional television. The project was featured on BBC World Service, Antiguan radio and television, in national newspapers and the in-flight magazine of the regional airline, as well as in several UK national newspapers. An educational website covering the battle to save the Antiguan racer was set up in collaboration with Wildscreen, providing an insight into how the jigsaw pieces of a complex conservation project fit together. Today the Antiguan racer figures prominently in the national curriculum.

Harnessing the new enthusiasm for this reptilian national treasure, the project provided the necessary training, equipment and resources to develop the skill sets of students, tour operators, volunteers and budding scientists to enable them to participate fully in the long-term conservation of Antigua's unique snake and the wider island ecosystem. Trained local volunteers now monitor the microchipped racers and keep their islands rat-free.

Retaining the snake as its symbol, the project evolved into the locally managed Offshore Islands Conservation Programme, which was instrumental in the creation of a new protected area covering over 3,000 hectares of Antigua's coastline. Other endangered species on the offshore islands, including a rare endemic lizard, brown pelicans, West Indian whistling ducks, white-crowned pigeons and nesting marine turtles, have benefited significantly from activities such as rat eradication and ecological restoration. Some bird colonies have increased more than thirtyfold.

In 1999, the project leader won the Iris Darnton Award for International Wildlife Conservation, presented by HRH Princess Anne, but Daltry prefers to emphasise the vital contribution of the Antiguans themselves: 'Special credit must go to the local volunteers. This success is a testament to their dedication.' And, it should be said, to hers. Jenny Island, a tiny islet named in Daltry's honour by her colleagues from the Antiguan Forestry Unit, stands as a permanent local tribute to her efforts. FFI paid its own tribute to her in 2016, in the shape of a medal commemorating 20 years of unbroken service.

The Antiguan Racer Conservation Project now serves as the exemplar for *in situ* conservation of other endangered reptiles on islands throughout the Caribbean. ∎

One of the five Antiguan racers hatched at Jersey Zoo. Their births increased the world population of the snake by 10 per cent

First births in captivity of world's rarest snake

By Nick Nuttall

THE world's rarest snake, the Antiguan racer, has been successfully bred for the first time in captivity, raising hopes that the species can be saved in the wild.

Five eggs have hatched into young, weighing just three grams, to the delight of staff at Jersey Zoo. They are the offspring of four adult snakes flown from the Caribbean last year as part of a British-led rescue plan.

The births take the estimated population of *Alsophis antiguae*, which is clinging on at Great Bird Island in Antigua, to 55 specimens. Mark Day, of Fauna and Flora International in Cambridge, which is orchestrating the rescue programme with funding from the Foreign Office, said yesterday that it was hoped to introduce the species to uninhabited islands in the area. He said that the team of conservationists was considering several Caribbean islands, including York and Redhead, where there were plans to clear non-native plants and animals such as rats.

Many of the snakes on Great Bird Island had been killed in the mistaken belief that they were venomous, he added. The team had also found that more than half the snakes had been injured by rats biting the tails that house their reproductive organs.

This website has been developed by Wildscreen, ARKive and Fauna & Flora International, to show how a real conservation project works.

The knock-on effects of the Antiguan Racer Conservation Project still reverberate around the region to this day. In early 2015, grateful staff at the Bahamas National Trust contacted FFI to explain what a vital contribution its timely rat eradication work had made on the 15-hectare White Cay.

A 1997 survey had revealed that the population of the White Cay iguana, a subspecies of one of the world's most critically endangered lizards, was down to a mere 150 individuals, including just ten adult females. Under the guidance of Mark Day, erstwhile manager of FFI's Caribbean Programme, a pair of British volunteers who had proved their mettle removing invasive rodents from Antigua's offshore islands were persuaded to work their Pied Piper magic on White Cay.

For less than US$10,000, the island was restored to its former rat-free glory. The most recent survey counted well over 2,000 iguanas on White Cay, enabling local conservationists to establish a satellite population on a nearby island in 2014. At five dollars per lizard, that must surely rank as outstanding value for money, particularly when compared to the cool US$35 million expended on Californian condor conservation.

FFI vice-president Sir David Attenborough introduces Miss Petra Dorling, chief executive of Cabouchon, to Her Royal Highness The Duchess of Kent at a Royal Gala Dinner, held at London's Banqueting House in 1995 to celebrate the twenty-fifth anniversary of the society's Oryx 100% Fund.

Fowl taste

In the wake of the 1995 volcanic eruption on the island of Montserrat, which destroyed the capital and forced two-thirds of the population to flee, FFI carried out sterling emergency work on behalf of another endangered Caribbean species, this time an amphibian.

Once found on at least five major islands in the Lesser Antilles, the giant frog – ominously known as the mountain chicken – is now confined to Dominica, where it has the misfortune to feature as the national dish (hence its local nickname), and to a small area on Montserrat covering less than 20 square kilometres. The initial survey and subsequent monitoring work focused outside attention on this declining species for the first time.

The devastating fungal disease chytridiomycosis reached Montserrat in 2008, prompting the decision to evacuate as many healthy mountain chickens as possible and conserve them through *ex situ* captive breeding programmes. There is little doubt that the entire population would have succumbed, out of sight and out of mind, had the species not already been in the international spotlight as a result of FFI's earlier intervention in 1995.

Any period of rapid growth will inevitably see the occasional setback. Some of the best-laid plans for amphibians went badly awry, with FFI learning the hard way that you have to take the warty with the smooth. The Global Amphibian Campaign, conceived as a three-way coalition with IUCN and Conservation International, was, in the words of Simon Stuart, the former long-time chair of IUCN's Species Survival Commission, 'an ill-fated collaboration that never got off the ground'. By all accounts, the experience left a bitter taste in Mark Rose's mouth, no doubt more akin to licking a toad than a mountain chicken, for years afterwards. Encouragingly, it has not deterred FFI from becoming a formal partner in the latest umbrella group, the Amphibian Survival Alliance, which aims to co-ordinate and streamline global efforts to halt the continuing decline in amphibian populations worldwide.

The Oryx 100% Fund was still justifiably renowned as an effective rapid-response vehicle that enabled the speedy allocation of resources wherever they were most urgently required, but there was a perceived need for the society to gravitate from a fire-fighting mentality and focus instead on forward planning. With this in mind, FFI began collaborating with IUCN/SSC on a series of so-called Action

Above left Detail from the cover of an early Arcadia Fund brochure, designed by Juan Pablo Moreiras and featuring his own photographs of some of the landscapes that the fund was created to help safeguard.

Above right Dr Lisbet Rausing, philanthropist and now FFI vice-president, whose initial and ongoing support for the society has done so much to turn FFI's ambitious landscape-level conservation plans into reality.

Right Zorkul Nature Reserve in Tajikistan, home to endangered snow leopards and a rich diversity of other threatened species, is one of the many landscapes to have benefited from Halcyon Land & Sea support.

Plans that would anticipate the needs of certain vulnerable groups of species. Under the umbrella category of Endangered Species Policy and Support, plans were drawn up for groups as diverse as insectivorous bats, freshwater fish and carnivorous plants.

Whilst FFI could still appreciate the importance of supporting small-scale species-specific work via the 100% Fund, there was a growing recognition of the limitations of this piecemeal approach to conservation. With regard to long-term strategy, the smart money was on landscape-level conservation that protected entire ecosystems.

One obvious way to protect vast swathes of threatened habitat was to purchase the land. For an organisation with the limited financial resources of FFI this might have remained something of a pipe dream, but a major donation from Dr Lisbet Rausing in 1998 changed all that, after a meeting with Mark Rose at London City Airport paved the way for the launch of the Arcadia Fund, which was subsequently renamed Halcyon Land & Sea to avoid confusion with Rausing's similarly titled personal charity.

'In making donations, I don't respond to unsolicited approaches.
I define my goal and do research to find the organisation that
can help me achieve it most cost-efficiently. My goal was to help
protect our natural world; my research led me to FFI.'

Dr Lisbet Rausing, FFI vice-president and benefactor

Sunlight breaks through the tangle of riparian vegetation in the biologically rich
Golden Stream Corridor Preserve. This irreplaceable haven of biodiversity and
crucial source of local livelihoods was the first to be rescued from destruction
with the support of Halcyon Land & Sea.

Halcyon years

Halcyon Land & Sea was conceived as a land purchase mechanism designed for the specific purpose of safeguarding biologically rich areas of habitat that were in imminent danger of destruction. A key criterion of such purchases was that the land rights would not be retained in the long term by FFI itself, but would be entrusted at the earliest opportunity to local ownership, while ensuring that those local partner organisations had been equipped with the necessary skills and capacity not only to manage these sites, but also to prosper as independent organisations in the long term. As part of this process, FFI would provide ongoing support to its local partners and help to develop appropriate legal safeguards to ensure that the land was protected in perpetuity.

To date, the fund has enabled FFI to secure some 9.5 million hectares of vital habitat that would otherwise have been irretrievably lost, and contributed directly to the conservation of nearly 56 million hectares, an area almost the size of Kenya. Some interventions now take the form of straightforward site management support rather than outright land purchase, but the principle of ensuring local management or ownership is universally applied. The fund also stimulates local livelihood and enterprise initiatives which generate direct income for the surrounding communities.

As with the Oryx 100% Fund, one of the most valuable aspects of Halcyon Land & Sea is that it allows rapid response to emergency situations where intervention is urgently required to avert ecological disaster. With one crucial difference: the scale of its impact.

The first emergency purchase supported by the fund safeguarded almost 4,000 hectares of lowland tropical forest in Belize from logging and wholesale conversion to citrus plantations or prawn farms. This was a relatively small piece of land, but it formed an integral part of a wider landscape corridor. The Golden Stream Corridor Preserve harbours a rich diversity of plant and animal life, including all five wild cat species native to Central America, and forms a vital dry forest corridor between the Maya Mountains and the mangrove forests and coral reefs of Belize's southern coast. Further purchases have since increased the protected area to more than 6,000 hectares, thereby securing the entire Golden Stream watershed, mitigating the adverse effects of land-use changes on the marine reserve that forms part of a UNESCO World Heritage site, and helping local partner Ya'axché influence the conservation management of a much wider area which, at the latest estimate, exceeds one million hectares.

The support of Arcadia, a charitable fund of Lisbet Rausing and Peter Baldwin, has provided a level of purchasing power unprecedented in FFI's history. More recently, that purchasing power was further enhanced when another benefactor came on board. The highly successful London-based hedge fund manager and committed conservationist Hugh Sloane was sufficiently impressed with FFI's work to pledge his own additional – and substantial – support for Halcyon Land & Sea, thereby enabling the society to invest in some particularly ambitious large-scale projects and intervene in operationally complex places like Mozambique and South Sudan.

In the intervening years the fund has been deployed repeatedly to safeguard areas of high conservation value throughout the world, rescuing irreplaceable habitats from threats as disparate as viticulture, shrimp farming, logging, citrus cultivation and soya plantations. Halcyon Land & Sea has now supported over 40 projects, the scope of which typically extends well beyond basic land purchase, and this holistic approach is perfectly illustrated by one particular model project in South Africa.

Flower power

The Cape Floral Kingdom is one of the most biologically rich regions on the planet, and one of the most threatened. Covering 90,000 square kilometres at the southernmost tip of Africa, it is by far the smallest of the world's six floral kingdoms and the only one confined to a single country, yet it harbours more species of native plant, relative to its size, than even the richest tropical rainforest. It is home to around 8,500 plant species, of which a staggering 5,800 are found nowhere else in the world. The dominant vegetation, known locally as *fynbos*, includes medicinal plants and a super-abundance of spectacular flower types familiar to gardeners and flower arrangers, such as gladioli, freesias, proteas and lobelias. This entire landscape is threatened by invasive alien tree species, urban expansion, agricultural encroachment and unsustainable exploitation of wild flowers.

In 1998, FFI was informed that Flower Valley, a 550-hectare botanical treasure house operating as a wild-flower harvesting business, was in imminent danger of being sold, ploughed up and converted into vineyards. Seeing the potential to influence biodiversity conservation across the region, FFI purchased the land with help from Halcyon Land & Sea, and set up a local partner, Flower Valley Conservation Trust, to manage the farm as a going concern. Flower Valley had traditionally purchased wild flowers from

neighbouring farms, turning them into bouquets for export to the European market. By conducting research that has helped to underpin the first sustainable harvesting guidelines and by sharing these findings, FFI has been able to influence the conservation and management of *fynbos* over a much wider area. Crucially, the project has created sorely needed economic and educational opportunities for the impoverished local rural communities, thereby reinforcing the message that conservation of natural resources pays dividends. Thanks to a programme of diversification, Flower Valley now offers year-round employment to the local workforce, and profits from the flower export business have been ploughed back into the local economy. An Early Learning Centre was established on the farm at the first opportunity, providing preschool childcare and educational facilities for the young families of the flower pickers.

A code of practice has been developed in conjunction with the government and the flower industry to prevent over-harvesting, with the result that 56,000 hectares of *fynbos* now benefit from greater protection. Local employment stands at a record

high, and the market for these flower products has increased sixfold, with substantial volumes of ethically sourced *fynbos* bouquets sold in the UK and South Africa itself.

It is hoped that the success of this financial model is helping to convince landowners, private businesses and local communities that sustainable use of South Africa's natural heritage offers significantly better long-term economic prospects than alternative agricultural land uses. FFI's approach at Flower Valley has been so effective in demonstrating that social, economic and environmental concerns can be addressed simultaneously that it now serves as a blueprint for wider conservation and poverty relief initiatives in the Cape.

Unsurprisingly, given FFI's reputation for championing the underdog, Halcyon Land & Sea funds are frequently deployed in locations that, from a conservation perspective, are off the beaten track. This enables FFI to intervene on behalf of the biodiversity found in neglected landscapes and inhospitable regions where others are reluctant to tread. Nowhere is this more evident than in Eurasia.

Clockwise from top left *Fynbos* landscape at Flower Valley; close-up of a floral bouquet; a solitary silver-edge pincushion stands out against a backdrop of purple blooms; children playing at the Early Learning Centre; local workers demonstrating that sisters are doin' it for themselves at Flower Valley; clearing invasive acacias, one of the alien plants posing a constant threat to *fynbos*; Cape sugarbird feeding on a limestone sugarbush.

Opposite Flower Valley worker carrying a freshly harvested bunch of proteas. The farm provides year-round employment for the younger and older generation alike, but the provision of an Early Learning Centre has ensured that young women, in particular, are able to secure permanent, full-time work and, with it, greater financial independence.

NEGLECTED LANDSCAPES

The Eurasia region covers a quarter of the global land area, but it's a pretty safe bet that it doesn't receive a proportionate amount of conservation attention. Too often viewed as somewhere that you need to fly over en route to the real biodiversity hotspots, countries like Kazakhstan and Kyrgyzstan are the geographical equivalent of a neglected species, which might go some way to explaining why FFI is bucking the trend and working there.

As we have already seen, FFI has had a continuous presence in Eurasia for decades, through, for example, long-term projects to protect important plant areas and wild bulbs in Turkey, awareness campaigns aimed at safeguarding tortoises throughout the Mediterranean, and numerous small-scale activities supported by its 100% Fund. In the years following the collapse of the Soviet Union, however, FFI became increasingly active behind the former Iron Curtain and, since the turn of the century, has made Eurasia a strategic priority, addressed through a bespoke regional programme.

ATYPICALLY UNTROPICAL

At a time when international NGOs were converging in their hordes on the world's tropical hotspots, FFI chose not to run with the pack. Instead, it had its eyes firmly fixed on other, largely unappreciated, natural jewels, like the Eurasian steppe, the Portuguese *montado*, and the Tien Shan and Pamir mountain ranges of Central Asia. Ignoring the feeding frenzy that was taking place in the tropical rainforests, FFI chose instead to shine the spotlight on the sumptuous spread of biodiversity offered by a region that stretches from the Azores in western Europe to the Kamchatka Peninsula in north-east Russia.

Towards the end of the 1990s, the society succeeded in cornering the market in the development of BSAPs (pronounced 'BeeSap' by those in the know). Biodiversity Strategy and Action

Plans, to give them their full name, were a phenomenon linked to the implementation of the Convention on Biological Diversity. In the period of transition – a euphemism for what was effectively social, political and economic turmoil – following the fall of the Berlin Wall, each of the former Soviet countries was suddenly confronted with the need to formulate a coherent national conservation strategy. That problem was accentuated by the serious lack of resources at the disposal of the respective governments.

A MULTITUDE OF 'STANS

FFI was ideally positioned to help, adapting the trademark capacity building techniques that it had applied successfully in other regions to a Eurasian context, and the initial testing ground was Kyrgyzstan. Since no one had any idea how to write a BSAP, FFI took on the task of writing a manual. The United Nations Development Programme was so impressed with the results that it subsequently posted the BSAP support materials – produced from scratch by FFI – on its website as a model of good practice. Virtually overnight, FFI became the de facto expert in this niche market and, as word spread throughout the region that it was helping to make a new plan for the 'stans, demand for its specialist services quickly grew. With the Kyrgyzstan plan in the bag, FFI went on to work with a succession of governments on a whole series of BSAPs covering Kazakhstan, Turkmenistan, Armenia, Azerbaijan, Georgia, the Caspian and Macedonia, with Bermuda thrown in for good measure, presumably to keep everyone on their toes.

The society was also involved in implementing many of the projects that had been highlighted as priorities in these plans. The Eurasia pages of the annual report for the year 2000 included the news that 'Azerbaijan, Tajikistan and Turkmenistan are

Opposite These dramatic landscapes are typical of the imposing mountain scenery for which Kyrgyzstan is renowned.

Above left By supporting the development of co-operatives that led to a resurgence in traditional crafts, FFI has helped to promote better working conditions for women in countries such as Kyrgyzstan.

Above right Hunting with golden eagles is a well-established Kyrgyz tradition.

beginning work under Enabling Activity Phase I of the CBD, while Armenia and Kazakhstan have reached Phase II.' This was undoubtedly more interesting than it sounds, and the dry statutory reporting style fails to do justice to the real progress that was being made on the ground. Other reports from that period give a better flavour of the practical conservation measures that were being put in place. In Kyrgyzstan, for example, FFI helped initiate the first national discussion on sustainable tourism. It also provided a platform for dialogue and information exchange between community NGOs and the businesses that were deemed to have been riding roughshod over local livelihoods and well-being. Today the focus is primarily on three core areas,

namely Central Asia, the Caucasus, and Central-Eastern Europe and the Balkans, but according to its website FFI does not rule out emergency interventions in countries outside these core areas. This is not the place to question the recent addition of São Tomé and Príncipe and Cape Verde to the Eurasia portfolio, but it could be either a throwback to the society's colonial days when these islands were considered part of Portugal, or an indication that the regional staff were having tropical island withdrawal symptoms after spending too long in the mountains. It certainly makes sense from a socio-cultural perspective, but it also demonstrates that FFI's regional teams do not operate in silos, and have the flexibility to apply their skills in an unfamiliar geographical context.

The region's breathtaking landscapes support globally important populations of endangered wildlife including the saiga antelope, wolves and brown bears, and charismatic cats like the Eurasian lynx and its vanishingly rare Iberian counterpart, as well as the more familiar but no less elusive snow leopard.

If the fall of the Soviet Union was dramatic, it precipitated an even more spectacular, almost catastrophic, collapse in the saiga population. For the uninitiated, the saiga is a wondrous antelope – perfectly adapted to the harsh conditions of the Central Asian steppe – with a proclivity for mass migration that rivals the wildebeests of the Serengeti, a nose that resembles a crumple zone, and an alarming tendency to crash and burn at random intervals in the kind of mass die-offs that leave even seasoned experts scratching their heads. In May 2015, however, around 200,000 antelope – 70 per cent of the world's total complement of saiga – died within a fortnight. Even for a species whose populations have a habit of fluctuating dramatically, this latest episode – probably caused by climate change – could not be dismissed as 'business as usual', particularly in the context of other pressures.

Saiga once roamed the Eurasian steppe in their millions, but vast numbers are no guarantee of long-term survival, as the salutary lesson of the passenger pigeon has taught us. When your population has a natural tendency to collapse, you need additional, unnatural, pressure like a

hole in the head, which is precisely how tens of thousands of them succumbed when the demise of the Soviet Union opened the floodgates to rampant poaching for their horn and meat.

One of the prime motivators for the original intervention of FFI's founders was the story of the near-total wipeout suffered by the bison on the North American plains in the face of an industrial-scale free-for-all. The brewing magnate and founder member of the society Samuel Whitbread was among those expressing grave concern that a similar fate could befall the formerly vast herds of plains game in Africa. A century later, the once plentiful saiga population was in even greater danger. This was one of the catalysts for FFI to scale up its presence in the region, and to this date the society continues to work for the protection of this critically endangered antelope, focusing on the Ustyurt Plateau, a temperate desert that extends for 200,000 square kilometres across Kazakhstan and Uzbekistan.

Among Central Asia's most valuable ecosystems – in a cultural and economic, as well as an ecological, sense

– are its ancient fruit-and-nut forests. They comprise a rich tapestry of wild apple, pear, plum, cherry, pistachio, almond and walnut trees that not only support local community livelihoods, but also harbour extraordinary biodiversity. Many of these tree species are the wild ancestors of more familiar domesticated varieties, and several of them are seriously threatened with extinction as a result of over-harvesting, uncontrolled grazing and timber

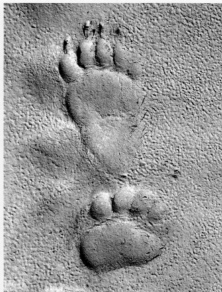

Opposite (clockwise from top left) Local hunter with captive grey wolf; horseback is often the default mode of travel in the mountains; saiga painting by William Oliver.

Above left An estimated 90 per cent of Central Asia's fruit-and-nut forests have been destroyed in the past 50 years.

Above right Telltale signs of the presence of European brown bears. Pawprints are encountered far more frequently than the large carnivores themselves.

extraction. FFI is working with in-country partners in Tajikistan and Kyrgyzstan to support the sustainable use and effective protection of these priceless natural resources.

Georgia straddles the border between the vast continents of Europe and Asia. In this remote hinterland where east meets west, climatic conditions range from semi-arid to montane to subtropical. The resulting assemblage of species is an intriguing combination of familiar European wildlife and animals that would normally be associated with Asia or Africa. Nowhere is this phenomenon more readily observable than in the Vashlovani region, where brown bears, badgers and otters find themselves in a biological melting pot with jungle cats, jackals and striped hyenas.

'14th September 1910. Heard a stag roar, a roebuck bark, a chamois whistle, a turr squeak within half an hour of camp, one after the other.' This is an extract from the diary kept by Major Anthony Buxton, DSO, youngest son of the society's founder, during one of his two trips to the Caucasus before the outbreak of the Great War. As he later remarked in the *Journal*, 'it gives an indication of what may be found in the great virgin forest which clothes the steep southern slopes'. That same account goes on to refer to the plethora of other species encountered or discussed with his guides, including 'a fluffy leopard, but yellow, not grey like a snow leopard'.

A century later, in a 2014 issue of *Fauna & Flora* magazine devoted to the society's work with 'neglected nature', Paul Hotham, director of FFI's Eurasia programme, was extolling the virtues of that very same region in similar terms. 'Vashlovani is remarkably rich in biodiversity with an assemblage of species that would be difficult to find elsewhere.' The stunning array of carnivores still found there today may possibly still include that same, sporadically sighted and endangered, Persian leopard.

Unsustainable hunting of endangered species, weak legislation and capacity and an explosion in livestock numbers have all taken their toll on the Georgian landscape and its biodiversity. The latest threat to emerge in the Caucasus is the illegal trade in wildlife. After conducting their own assessment of the issue, Hotham's team is now working with its local partners to address the problem, focusing in particular on migratory raptors, and several species of wild sturgeon that are riding uncomfortably high on Georgia's endangered list.

There are no prizes for guessing that FFI's original involvement with Georgia came about at the height of its BSAP spree, which is when it began to work closely not just with the government, but also with NACRES, then an embryonic local NGO. In the following years FFI supported NACRES on issues such as human–wildlife conflict mitigation, addressed through a joint Georgian Carnivore Conservation Project. Now one of the leading conservation organisations in Georgia, NACRES is another example of the many local partners that FFI has helped to nurture through to independence. ∎

In the Pamir Mountains of Central Asia, which connect the Himalayas with the vast steppes of Kazakhstan and Uzbekistan, support from the fund has enabled FFI to provide the equipment and training that were a prerequisite for establishing regular patrols in Tajikistan's Zorkul Nature Reserve, home to snow leopards and an array of wildlife rich enough for it to qualify as a global biodiversity hotspot.

Further west, the purchase of an area of 'high nature value' farmland and associated investments to promote cost-effective land management and preserve local customs has helped to encourage the continuation of traditional farming practices in Romania's Transylvania region, without which the area's floral diversity would be greatly diminished. This farmland is characterised by small, rounded hills – known locally as *movile* – and boasts what are, for Europe, remarkable botanical riches.

Halcyon Land & Sea funding also underpins another FFI initiative in Romania, this time to protect the so-called Zarand Landscape Corridor, an area in the Carpathian Mountains. Over half of this entire mountain range lies within Romania, making this country one of the last natural havens in Europe for species like the Eurasian wolf, brown bear and lynx, which depend on vast areas of forested habitat.

The Prince of Wales in conversation with Mark Rose during a visit to Romania's *movile*, led by Nat Page (right), director of local partner Fundația ADEPT.

Situated at the ecologically crucial nexus between the southern and western Carpathians, Zarand is a heavily forested landscape with a rich cultural heritage of traditional land use. But the forest corridor is narrowing year on year, creating what is known in the trade as a 'pinch point'. Without careful management of this remaining habitat, the bottleneck could eventually narrow to the point where it seriously inhibits – or even completely prevents – the free movement of large carnivores. Through a series of strategic land purchases, combined with community initiatives that uphold local traditions and maintain the landscape mosaic, FFI is safeguarding and strengthening this vital corridor. With its gaze firmly fixed on the long-term future, FFI is helping to support the recently formed Zarand Association, a local NGO that will ultimately take the initiative forward. This entire work programme and, in particular, the early support for FFI's local partner, was kick-started with invaluable – and still ongoing – funding from The Marcela Trust.

In 2003, FFI and its local Portuguese partner, Liga para a Protecção da Natureza, began negotiating a series of land

Above left A red-band fritillary, one of the wealth of invertebrates that benefit from traditional management of Transylvania's ancient flower-rich grasslands.

Above right Nodding sage, one of the many rare flower species found on the small, rounded hills known locally as *movile*.

Left Helping to ensure that we never have to say goodbye to the weakest lynx.

management agreements with local landowners to establish an 18,500-hectare wildlife corridor of cork oak forest and native scrub for the Iberian lynx, arguably the world's rarest cat. In 2010, a lynx was sighted in the project area for the first time in nearly a decade. More recently, FFI has also prepared the ground for the reintroduction of captive-bred lynx by ensuring that the habitat is ready to accommodate them.

Even on FFI's more familiar stomping ground in Africa, a key facet of Halcyon's role has been to refresh the parks that others cannot reach. In the fledgling South Sudan, a country in transition if ever there was one, Halcyon has provided crucial support for the resuscitation of active patrols in Southern National Park, of which more later. In Mozambique, another country recovering from the ravages of civil war, a US$1 million donation from the fund enabled FFI and its local partner, Sociedade para Gestão e Desenvolvimento da Reserva do Niassa (a name often left unspoken, or abbreviated to SGDRN), to re-establish management of the Niassa National Reserve, initially at the behest of the visionary conservationist, Halvor Astrup.

Large-scale ambition

Niassa National Reserve, a 4.2-million-hectare mosaic of miombo woodland, meandering rivers and majestic inselbergs, is a remote haven of biodiversity in northern Mozambique. From the ground, it is difficult to comprehend the magnitude of this virtually pristine wilderness. Viewed from above, the bigger picture emerges; it takes one and a half hours to cross the reserve in a light aircraft. Niassa harbours 40 per cent of Mozambique's entire elephant population, not to mention impressive numbers of sable antelope, Cape buffalo, Crawshay's zebra and numerous other species characteristic of this landscape. Spectacular herds of herbivores are just one feature of a tapestry that is rich in wildlife. The reserve is also one of the most important refuges on the entire continent for two of Africa's most charismatic – and increasingly threatened – carnivores, the lion and wild dog.

Ironically, it is the very scale of this landscape that poses one of the greatest threats to the long-term survival of the wildlife it supports. The effective conservation management of an area the size of Denmark presents enormous logistical difficulties. The recent resurgence in the demand for ivory and consequent explosion in poaching activity has exacerbated that problem.

FFI has been supporting Niassa – and working with the impoverished communities whose livelihoods depend on the reserve's natural resources – for almost 15 years. Working with local partner SGDRN, headed by the dynamic and determined Annabella Rodriguez, it made tremendous strides in halting the decline in the reserve's wildlife populations after years of conservation neglect. As part of this painstaking and sometimes painful rehabilitation process, FFI and SGDRN took the radical step of restructuring Niassa into 16 separate concessions, breaking down the overall reserve into discrete and more manageable enterprises. This approach created unprecedented opportunities for innovative public–private partnerships and heralded a new dawn for conservation in Niassa.

State of emergency

Regrettably, the end of SGDRN's management tenure at Niassa in 2012 coincided with an exponential rise in ivory poaching and a surge in illegal mining and logging activity. Management capacity across the separate concessions had not yet achieved critical mass, meaning that they were struggling – individually and collectively – to resist the onslaught. A decade of conservation achievement was in danger of unravelling.

Swift intervention was required to safeguard the future of Niassa's elephants and the reserve's other remarkable biodiversity. Recognising the urgency of the situation, but aware of the futility of trying to protect the entire expanse of Niassa with resources that were stretched to breaking point, FFI took the strategic decision to secure a key area of the reserve situated at the coalface of the poaching threat and home to the most significant concentrations of wildlife. Chuilexi Conservancy was the result.

Opposite The vast wilderness of Niassa, pockmarked with these distinctive inselbergs, is crucial to the survival of Mozambique's elephant population.

Below left Bull African elephant slaughtered for its ivory in early November 2011 by poachers equipped with AK-47 assault rifles..

Below right Chuilexi is a vital refuge for the severely threatened African wild dog.

Above In 2016 alone, nearly 700 snares were removed from Chuilexi Conservancy.

Left Year-round patrols throughout Chuilexi are a significant deterrent to poachers.

Grand vision

Formed from three adjoining tourism concessions, Chuilexi Conservancy is the beating heart of Niassa. This 'reserve within a reserve' is a vast area in its own right, covering well over half a million hectares. It was carefully chosen to ensure maximum conservation impact by protecting the highest densities of wildlife within the most severely threatened part of Niassa as a whole.

But Chuilexi was not conceived purely as the last bastion for Niassa's elephants and other besieged wildlife. It was also intended to serve as a model of conservation best practice. Here was an opportunity to safeguard one of Mozambique's most valuable natural assets while at the same time testing the effectiveness of Niassa's pioneering public–private approach to conservation management. Chuilexi was envisaged as a financially self-sufficient conservancy where high-end tourism supports effective wildlife protection and simultaneously addresses the everyday livelihood and development needs of some of the remotest and most impoverished people in Africa.

Thanks to an ambitious programme of anti-poaching measures and community outreach, supported by intensive investment in critical infrastructure that provides access to

the furthest reaches of the conservancy, FFI's vision is being realised. Chuilexi Conservancy is taking shape as a model of excellence that could serve as a blueprint for effective conservation management throughout the rest of Niassa and beyond. More recently, it has teamed up with adjoining conservancies to form the Niassa Conservation Alliance.

High impact

Establishing Chuilexi Conservancy has been a labour of love, but the decision to invest in this innovative conservation model shows every indication of being fully vindicated. Communities that were previously hanging on by their fingertips are now reaping the benefits of a genuine partnership that has the potential to transform their lives.

The effect on biodiversity has been equally dramatic, particularly when compared to the carnage outside the protective cloak of the conservancy. Some of the surrounding concessions where active management is lacking are relatively devoid of animals, a stark reminder of how Chuilexi would have fared without FFI's intervention. The number of elephant carcasses recorded inside and

outside the conservancy since it was established provides a graphic, if distressing, example of the contrasting fortunes of Chuilexi and unprotected areas of the wider reserve. One neighbouring concession without active management has an elephant carcass density almost 15 times higher than in the conservancy. At the time of writing, Chuilexi continues to witness a significant year-on-year decrease in elephant mortality.

With intensive investment, Chuilexi has blossomed into a well-established and functional conservancy – one of the largest private concessions in Africa. Financial support has come not only from Halcyon, but also from other conservation partners who share FFI's long-term vision for the wider Niassa landscape. They include the aforementioned Mr Sloane, the American billionaire businessman David Bonderman, and Dr Claudio Segré, founder of Fondation Segré, which has realigned its strategic priorities in recent years to concentrate specifically on the protection of species and their habitats, a remit that ties in perfectly with the many FFI projects that it has helped to fund.

Land purchase does not, in itself, solve the problem of how to rescue habitats from destruction. FFI operates on the basis that the long-term success of these interventions hinges on equipping local organisations to assume responsibility for their future protection. The Golden Stream Corridor Preserve, for example, is owned and managed by Ya'axché, FFI's

Friends in high office: Lisel Alamilla's rise to prominence gave conservation a voice at government level in Belize. In May 2012 she received a Whitley Fund for Nature Award, presented by The Princess Royal at a ceremony in London.

partner in Belize, which began as a handful of committed individuals and evolved into a nascent grassroots group of environmentally conscious people. Today, it is a flourishing and nationally recognised leader in conservation and sustainable development. In 2008 the Belize government selected Ya'axché as the co-manager of the 40,000-hectare Bladen reserve, one of the most biologically rich areas within the whole of Central America. The increasing independence of its local partner epitomises how FFI's approach is helping local communities to become effective custodians of their own natural heritage.

If the institution has blossomed under the supportive gaze of FFI, so have its staff. In March 2012, the prime minister of Belize appointed Ya'axché's Executive Director, Lisel Alamilla, as Minister of Fisheries, Forestry and Sustainable Development, sending an unequivocal message that the government of the day intended to keep nature conservation at the heart of the country's development plans. Alamilla cut her conservation teeth as Country Director of FFI's Belize programme before assuming the reins at Ya'axché in 2008. Her elevation to such a position of influence demonstrates what FFI hopes to achieve by nurturing talent and vindicates an approach that values capacity building above empire building.

CHAPTER 9

TRANSFORMATION

*'I have the privilege of working with some of the brightest,
bravest and most committed people on the face of the planet.'*

Mark Rose, FFI Chief Executive

FFI had always worked on the premise that solutions to conservation problems lay in local hands, but it was in the mid 1990s that this philosophy was given formal expression. When FFI first actively began to promote the idea of empowering local conservation partners, capacity building was a narrow concept. In those days, furnishing a struggling NGO with the means to operate more effectively tended to mean donating a few spare chairs and a desk. The more holistic interpretation of capacity building that FFI helped pioneer proved so successful that it was widely adopted by others in the conservation business. These days, it is considered standard practice.

According to Mark Rose, much of the credit must go to Martin Hollands, who came on board in 1995 and carried out a rough-and-ready gap analysis to identify new areas of focus for FFI, as a result of which the pair hit upon the idea of setting up the so-called Conservation Development Unit. This new unit was responsible for strengthening the capacity of local organisations and government departments in developing countries with high species diversity but limited resources.

In recent years that initial vision has been turned into an all-encompassing, cross-cutting programme that permeates every facet of FFI's conservation activities, due in no small part to the efforts of Marianne Carter and a dedicated capacity team. Operating beneath the radar, they are the invisible giants on whose shoulders others stand, oiling the wheels, building networks and running training workshops that are rarely newsworthy but which are no less integral to the complete conservation package than headline-grabbing new discoveries, the designation of new protected areas or the successful resurrection of a species on the brink of extinction.

Above Mike Appleton (back right) hitches a ride through the forest during his days as director of FFI's Asia Pacific programme.

Opposite Areng waterfall in Cambodia's Cardamom Mountains.

Another key figure in the early stages of developing this initiative was Mike Appleton, who specialised in building tailor-made solutions to the conservation needs of local partners across the globe, particularly those working in protected area management. Appleton was by no means a one-trick pony, however; his first appearance in FFI colours was as a Middle East project officer, and his decade-long tenure included stints in Jordan, the Philippines and Cambodia, ultimately as director of FFI's Asia Pacific programme, by some distance the largest and most unwieldy of its regional programmes.

Putting its own house in order

If Rose and Hollands were responsible for articulating the need to expand and formalise FFI's capacity building efforts, it seems clear with the benefit of hindsight that they would have struggled to sustain that ambitious growth trajectory – not least where FFI's own internal capacity was concerned – without the support of a certain Ros Aveling, whom we encountered earlier in a mountain gorilla context. After helping to turn the International Gorilla Conservation Programme into a reality, Aveling had remained in Kenya with one of the programme's founding partners, the Nairobi-based Africa Wildlife Foundation. This work brought her into regular contact with Rose, and she was aware of his ambitions for FFI and his dogged determination to grow the organisation irrespective of whether there was money available to do so.

FFI was grasping opportunities and adding them to its expanding portfolio, without necessarily focusing on how they would all fit together into a coherent, manageable whole. By the turn of the century, large cracks had started to appear in the organisational edifice. There was an obvious need for a stabilising influence to tie it all together and help move the organisation forward in a cohesive fashion, and Aveling provided that stability. Although adamant that she is not a systems and processes person, she nevertheless succeeded in putting in place a solid institutional framework to support growth plans that might otherwise have foundered on the rocks of ambition. As part of this process, Aveling set up a Project Management Unit that somehow ran without a budget, and devised ways to support and encourage staff who found themselves holding down unaccustomed – and multiple – roles. Her *pièce de résistance* was the cross-cutting Conservation Partnerships Programme. This had to be constructed like a three-dimensional jigsaw that would only function when all the pieces – in this case the right people with the right

Strictly Samburu: Dr Rosalind Aveling working – and dancing – with community groups in Kenya's northern rangelands.

skills, the appropriate funding and the relevant support structures – had fallen into place. In 2008, Aveling was asked to combine her responsibilities as FFI's Director of Conservation Partnerships with the role of Deputy Chief Executive. Rose has described that position as one of the hardest in any organisation, presumably alluding to the difficulties inherent in all deputy roles, rather than this particular one. Referring to the award presented to Aveling in 2016 by Sir David Attenborough in recognition of her unique contribution to the society, Rose paid this touching tribute to his friend and colleague: 'Ros has been the heart and soul of the organisation, as well as the provider of fine wisdom over the years. To say that she has been integral and central to the success of FFI, having a hand in everything we have achieved, would be a gross understatement.'

Local routes

Today, FFI works with roughly 300 partner organisations around the world and provides direct assistance to around 200 of these, helping them to improve their conservation knowledge, achieve greater independence and run their own conservation programmes. The Conservation Capacity Programme acts as a focal point and support function for all FFI's capacity building activities across the globe.

Some of these partnerships with local organisations are still in their infancy, while others are decades old, but they all represent a long-term commitment typified by FFI's close association since the 1970s with the Kenya-based East African Wild Life Society (EAWLS), one of the oldest conservation organisations in Africa.

Above The hirola, or Hunter's antelope, in its natural range on the Kenyan-Somali border.

Below (clockwise from top left) Rangers from the Kenya Wildlife Service restrain a blindfolded hirola while it is inspected by a vet; a captured antelope is loaded onto a Cessna plane bound for Tsavo East National Park; the herd of translocated hirola awaiting release from their holding pen at Tsavo; the first antelopes are released into their new home.

Endangered antelopes are a recurring theme. A quick trawl through the archives reveals that FFI has supported conservation measures for the semi-aquatic sitatunga at Saiwa Swamp, an ultimately unsuccessful translocation of a threatened population of roan antelope from western Kenya to Shimba Hills National Reserve and, in the mid 1990s, an experimental translocation project for the hirola, Africa's most critically endangered antelope species. In the late 1990s, when EAWLS was, in Rose's words, 'on its knees', FFI was instrumental in resuscitating the organisation at the behest of its then chairman, the well-known surgeon and environmentalist Dr Imre Loefler. FFI provided crucial financial support and assistance with fundraising, wrote a new conservation policy and helped to hire new staff, including chief executive Ali Kaka. At a recent meeting, recalls Rose, he was asked when the current contract with EAWLS was due to end. His answer was simple: 'This isn't a contract; it's a relationship.' Sure enough, the partnership continues to this day and, at the time of writing, FFI and EAWLS are still collaborating.

LONG-TERM SUPPORT

OLD FRIENDS

Jordan was the site of FFI's first formal capacity building initiative. In fact, Mark Rose was already working on this project when he took over as director in 1993. While still in charge at The Wildlife Trusts, he had set up his own environmental consultancy, Cambridge Ecological, and the most valuable job in its portfolio was a World Bank project in support of the Royal Society for Nature Conservation in Jordan. Rose's World Bank counterpart in those early days was John Fraser Stewart, a natural resource specialist who was himself seconded to FFI a decade later, spending two years as head of its Asia Pacific programme. When Rose joined FFI, he brought the Jordan project with him and the financial leverage it provided enabled him to call on the capacity building expertise of Martin Hollands. Thanks largely to the efforts of the Royal Society for the Conservation of Nature, which FFI helped at a crucial stage in its existence, Jordan now boasts a large and diverse network of natural reserves and parks, including the world famous Dana Biosphere Reserve, which comprises four different biogeographical zones. The biggest reserve in Jordan, the 300-square-kilometre Dana is now financially self-sufficient through ecotourism and craft-based enterprise. These protected areas are helping to safeguard a rich diversity of wildlife, including rare migratory birds, threatened mammals such as the Arabian oryx, Nubian ibex, Blandford's fox and the elusive sand cat, and many of Jordan's 2,500 plant species, 100 of which occur nowhere else.

'FFI's organisational development support allowed us to reach our potential and was the catalyst for the growth of the Royal Society for the Conservation of Nature into its current regional conservation role. FFI's support and commitment over the past decade has enabled us both to learn from each other and share our expertise.'

His Excellency Khaled Irani, former Director General, the Royal Society for the Conservation of Nature, Jordan, and Minister of the Environment, Minister of Energy and Mineral Resources.

BLAZING TRAILS

Liberia's forests harbour many species found nowhere else in the world and others that are virtually extinct outside the country, such as pygmy hippo, Jentink's and zebra duikers and Liberian mongoose. In 1996, as Liberia was beginning to emerge from seven years of brutal civil conflict, FFI was invited by the Society for the Conservation of Nature in Liberia (SCNL), the country's oldest environmental conservation group, to help restart nature conservation. No one was more influential in this respect than Jamison Suter after he joined FFI at the end of 1997. Moving from the World Bank, where he had worked on grant making for the recently created Global Environment Facility, Suter drew on his cultural anthropology and environmental science background as manager, and then director, of FFI's extensive African project portfolio. He focused in particular on West Africa, where nature conservation was characterised by the need to operate amid civil unrest and post-war reconstruction. Working closely with Alex Peal, his counterpart at SCNL, Suter battled to keep Liberia's

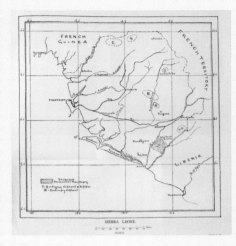

Liberia's wildlife was already on the society's radar in its colonial days, as this map of a proposed sanctuary for the pygmy hippo and forest elephant on the border with Sierra Leone illustrates.

commercially valuable but biologically priceless forests intact against a backdrop of political turmoil largely instigated by the then president, Charles Taylor, now serving a 50-year sentence for his part in what the presiding judge Richard Lussick described as 'some of the most heinous and brutal crimes recorded in human history'. Throughout and since that turbulent period, FFI has worked with its partners to establish national parks, increase forest protection and ensure that Liberia's threatened forests receive the attention they deserve. Through its co-operation with SCNL and other partners in Liberia, FFI has become a trusted adviser to the government and has since worked closely with ministers, advising on legal reforms to amend legislation that had promoted logging, and negotiating a trailblazing carbon credits deal that could see the country reap financial rewards for keeping its forests standing.

CORRIDORS OF EMPOWERMENT

Extending from Panama, through Colombia and down to northern Ecuador, the Chocó is one of the last coastal tropical rainforests in the world. The wettest habitat on Earth, Chocó forest is a global conservation priority, due to the tremendous diversity of the wildlife that it harbours, including thousands of plant species, 800 kinds of bird, nearly 150 mammal species and over 250 different reptiles and amphibians. Many Chocó species are found nowhere else in the world.

The last remaining Chocó forest in Ecuador's north-west is under severe pressure from logging and oil palm enterprises, which are indiscriminately clear-felling vast swathes of this irreplaceable landscape. In 1998, with help from Halcyon Land & Sea, FFI made the first of what eventually became 56 separate land purchases – cumulatively amounting to thousands of hectares – from under the noses of the loggers. It has since made a series of further strategic purchases that, together, make up the Awacachi Corridor, a vital ribbon of

rainforest linking the region's two most important reserves. When FFI transferred responsibility for managing this land to a local partner, Fundación Sirua, it was raw, inexperienced and, to all intents and purposes, San Lorenzo's first truly committed conservation organisation.

With FFI's support, Fundación Sirua took its first tentative steps towards self-sufficiency. It earned the respect of the local communities and helped them to generate sustainable income from cacao and bamboo production. In turn, this has engendered a greater degree of respect for the integrity of a priceless watershed that not only protects spectacular wildlife like the endangered great green macaw, but also provides essential ecosystem services such as clean water to San Lorenzo's 40,000 inhabitants. Significantly, it has also established credibility with demanding international donors and now submits grant proposals independently.

REBUILDING A NATION

Anyone seeking an example of a country lacking the wherewithal to conserve its

Panoramic view of the Cardamom Mountains, which harbour a spectacular array of species, many of them only recently discovered.

exceptionally rich natural heritage need look no further than the traumatised nation that was Cambodia after the downfall of the tyrannical Pol Pot regime. The intellectual vacuum created by the murderous Khmer Rouge, who destroyed books and slaughtered or enslaved the literate, the educated and even the bespectacled, left Cambodia ill-equipped to make informed decisions about the conservation and environmental management of its stunning biodiversity. The eventual restoration of the monarchy in 1993, following a period of further turbulence that culminated in Vietnamese forces occupying the country, initially restored some semblance of order, but this relative stability was shattered once more by a *coup d'état* in 1997. At the start of the new millennium, FFI decided that the time was ripe for venturing into this political fallout zone.

In early 2000, FFI-led expeditions to Cambodia's vast and remote Cardamom

Mountains unearthed some spectacular biological discoveries, including 400 unidentified species and globally significant populations of highly endangered animals such as the tiger, Asian elephant, gaur, pileated gibbon and Asian wild dog. One of the most momentous finds was the rediscovery – by a team led by FFI's senior conservation biologist Dr Jenny Daltry – of several viable populations of the Siamese crocodile, which had been presumed extinct in the wild.

Paradoxically, it was the long-term conflict, and in particular the presence of Khmer Rouge soldiers and their deadly land mines, that had protected much of this wildlife, by effectively turning the entire forest into a no-go zone. The return of political stability and increased security brought with it new threats in the shape of uncontrolled logging, poaching and other forms of encroachment. It was

immediately obvious that urgent action was needed to safeguard the future of this virtually undisturbed forest wilderness. It was equally clear that Cambodia lacked the necessary resources to tackle the emerging threats to this jewel in the crown of its remarkable natural heritage.

Some 15 years later, the support that FFI has provided to groups as disparate as local communities, government officers, park rangers, educators and science students is bearing fruit across its entire Cambodian project portfolio. Its intervention in Cambodia is characterised by an awareness of the bigger picture and a noticeable emphasis on catering for the longer-term social, economic and environmental needs of the country.

Working with impoverished ethnic minority communities to develop organic farming methods that improved

Above left Neang Thy (left) conducting a herpetological survey in the Cardamom Mountains.

Above right Following the rediscovery of the critically endangered Siamese crocodile, FFI established the Cambodian Crocodile Conservation Programme. This partnership with the Cambodian Forestry Association is helping to monitor and protect the species, as well as reinforcing the wild population by breeding crocodiles in captivity and releasing the juveniles once they are large enough to fend for themselves.

Below left The green-blooded turquoise-boned Samkos bush frog was arguably the most extraordinary of several new amphibian discoveries.

Below centre The future of the Cardamom banded gecko, a lizard new to science, is threatened more by logging and development than by natural predators.

Below right A wolf in krait's clothing: among the most thrilling discoveries during the first biological survey of the Cardamom Mountains in 2000 was a black-and-white banded snake bearing a superficial resemblance to the highly venomous Malayan krait. Picking up a potentially deadly serpent that no scientist has seen before is not for the faint-hearted, but the expedition leader noticed differences in scale structure, which told her this was a new species, and had no hesitation in collecting the first specimen of what is now known as the Cardamom wolf snake.

rice yields threefold, for instance, FFI has watched them go on to produce sufficient and even surplus food, thereby removing one of the main drivers of poaching and other forest crime.

At the other end of the capacity building spectrum, FFI joined forces with the Royal University of Phnom Penh in 2005 to launch an MSc course in biodiversity conservation, thereby equipping a new generation of Cambodian scientists with the knowledge base required to ensure a sustainable future for their country in the twenty-first century.

It was as much for her all-round, long-term contribution to the rebuilding process as for the rediscovery of the Siamese crocodile that the Royal Government of Cambodia saw fit, in 2010, to bestow on Daltry the title of Officer of the Order of Sahametrei, the highest honour accorded to a non-national, for her 'distinguished services to the King and to the Nation'.

Above left Close-up of the parasitic flower *Sapria poilanei* – a relative of the more familiar *Rafflesia* – blooming on Phnom Samkos, the second-highest peak in Cambodia.

Above right Livingstonia palms growing on the summit ridge of Phnom Khmoch, which translates as 'ghost mountain'.

Below right As part of FFI's ongoing efforts to help Cambodia's rebuilding process, it worked with the Royal University of Phnom Penh to launch the country's first peer-reviewed scientific journal, *Cambodian Journal of Natural History*.

Below left Dr Jenny Daltry (centre), holding her distinguished service medal, poses for a group photograph with FFI colleagues, conservation partners and Cambodian ministry staff following the award ceremony in January 2010.

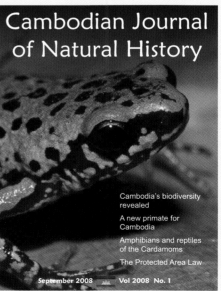

LASTING LEGACY IN VIETNAM

The Hanoi-based Education for Nature – Vietnam (ENV) is the country's first non-governmental organisation dedicated specifically to wildlife and nature conservation. ENV sprang from a seed planted by FFI back in 1996.

Vietnam is witnessing exponential population growth, economic development and modernisation, placing intense pressure on the nation's natural resources. Cuc Phuong, Vietnam's first national park, is one of the last remaining fragments of protected forest in northern Vietnam and a vital refuge for the region's threatened wildlife.

The park comprises 22,000 hectares of rich tropical forest, which forms what is effectively an island of biodiversity in the midst of an area of intensely farmed lowland. Almost 30 per cent of all Vietnam's plant species are found in Cuc Phuong. It is also home to a rich variety of endangered and threatened wildlife, including Delacour's langur, clouded leopard, Owston's palm civet and a number of species found only in Vietnam.

Thousands of people, mostly of the Muong ethnic minority, live in or around Cuc Phuong. Many of them depend on the park's natural resources for their livelihood; they hunt, cut timber, collect firewood and other forest products and clear land for agriculture.

In 1996, at the instigation of its then vice-chairman Dr David Chivers, FFI established the Cuc Phuong Conservation Project with a grant from the BP Statoil Alliance, with the aim of addressing the threats to the park and its wildlife posed by human encroachment.

The Conservation Awareness Programme was a key component of the project. It addressed the issue of resource use by local communities through a series of education and awareness campaigns.

A youthful Miss Vu Thi Quyen (right) in her early days as FFI's education officer, pictured here with her colleague Claire Beastall and local schoolteachers.

From humble beginnings as a conservation club set up at one local school in 1996, the programme expanded rapidly. Within a couple of years there were thousands of active club members in dozens of schools. Children responded extremely positively, even to the extent of attempting to influence the behaviour of their parents, a significant breakthrough in a society where unswerving respect for the values of the older generation is so deeply ingrained.

This successful model provided the template for a series of similar environmental education and conservation campaigns in and around other protected areas. More significantly, it led ultimately to the formation of an autonomous, locally managed wildlife conservation organisation, the first of its kind in Vietnam.

The original co-ordinator of FFI's Cuc Phuong Conservation Project was Vu Thi Quyen. The driving force behind the hugely successful awareness campaign, she identified the need for a local conservation group that could make the nation more self-reliant: 'We can't expect foreigners to come and save our country. The work should be done by Vietnamese.'

Quyen founded ENV in 2000, with initial support from FFI in the form of a vital kick-starter grant. Shortly after, in recognition of her achievements, she received the prestigious Whitley Award.

Like the organisation that spawned it, ENV has a creative and innovative approach to conservation. In the 15 years since its formation, it has made tremendous strides in training environmental educators, fostering greater public understanding about the need to protect Vietnam's rich natural heritage and combating the illegal wildlife trade, arguably the greatest threat to the country's remarkable biodiversity.

'Thanks to the encouragement and support of Fauna & Flora International, ENV was established as a pioneer in civil society development within the environmental sector of Vietnam.'

The success, and longevity, of organisations like ENV is a perfect illustration of how FFI's influence, discreet but inexorable, continues to pervade the conservation world. It is not about flags on maps, but once you start mapping the genome of the myriad conservation bodies around the globe, it is evident that many of today's champions of biodiversity have traces of FFI in their DNA. ∎

Business plan

If this instinctive awareness of the value of empowering local partners to help themselves had been the driving force behind much of the capacity building initiated during Rose's first few years in charge, by the late 1990s it was the perceived benefits of a very different, and potentially controversial, form of partnership that commanded FFI's attention. Corporate partnerships were by no means an alien concept at that stage, as the society had already enjoyed mutually beneficial collaborations with the likes of Pentland Industries, British Petroleum and British Airways, but these had principally been in the shape of straightforward sponsorship arrangements, whereby money changed hands, projects received a welcome injection of funds or pro bono assistance and companies gained a few more brownie points, or more accurately greenie points, before the two sides patted each other on the back and went their separate ways until the next time. The nature of this relationship changed when FFI concluded that both parties were missing a trick and decided to set about making the business case for conservation.

As early as 1996, Rose was robustly defending FFI's policy of working in partnership with industry, a policy increasingly called into question by members in light of a series of unfortunate events involving multinationals with which the society was associated: 'FFI has always chosen to work with industry to effect change, and believes that this is more constructive than setting up barriers.' The extent to which FFI's approach diverged from prevailing attitudes was laid bare in a debate on the issue published in the July 2004 edition of *The Ecologist*, in which Rose locked horns with Marcus Colchester, director of Forest Peoples Programme.

Rose's rationale was simple, as his guest editorial in the April 2000 issue of *Oryx* made clear. 'Businesses affect biodiversity in many ways, the most obvious being activities such as mining, timber extraction or oil exploration. Only by working with companies can we promote sustainable use, help them to establish environmental controls that minimise the ecological impact of their activities and demonstrate the value of consulting local stakeholders. It is the responsibility of conservation to promote greater understanding of the relationship between biodiversity and business.'

At a time when many conservation organisations were reluctant even to dip a toe into the shark-infested waters of big business, for fear of being embroiled in a greenwash scandal, FFI dived in head first. While the more militant environmental campaigners were busy condemning all forms of fraternisation with the business community as tantamount to sleeping with the enemy, FFI began openly

FFI's chief executive Mark Rose and Cynthia Carroll – the first woman CEO of a mining company – putting pen to paper at the start of a productive and ongoing long-term partnership between FFI and Anglo American.

cultivating closer relationships with multinationals, particularly those operating in the sectors that posed the greatest potential threats to biodiversity. The idea was to persuade these companies that their bottom line would benefit if their corporate policy and practice took account of biodiversity issues.

Adding fuel to the fire

Sensibly enough, FFI's primary targets were businesses that aspired to be market leaders in their sector and were demonstrably committed to reducing their environmental impact. The most obvious candidate was BP, given the strong links that already existed with the energy giant via its support for the Conservation Leadership Programme that, in those days, bore its name. A conversation between Rose and BP's then chief executive Sir John Browne (which boiled down to answering three questions – why, how and how much?) was the spark that lit the flame. The Global Business Partnership was conceived in 1998, with BP and mining conglomerate Rio Tinto as founder members. It was formally launched two years later at a groundbreaking business and biodiversity conference, the first such international event, held at London's Chatham House. The business partnership concept is now accepted practice among many conservation organisations; indeed, at the time of writing, former staff members who were involved in developing and managing this FFI initiative are heading up the respective business and biodiversity teams at two other Cambridge-based conservation organisations, BirdLife International and UNEP World Conservation Monitoring Centre.

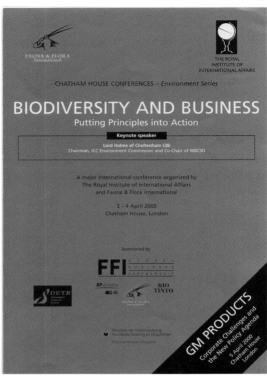

Above Mark Rose congratulates then Sir John Browne (left) on his 1999 Earth Day award, watched by Jan Hartke of EarthVoice (centre).

Right FFI's Global Business Partnership was formally launched in April 2000 at this groundbreaking business and biodiversity conference.

In 2000, a third conglomerate joined the party when a consortium of international conservation organisations led by FFI signed a memorandum of understanding with British American Tobacco, possibly the most controversial choice of business partner in the society's recent history, but a pragmatic one in that it offered an unprecedented opportunity to exert a significant influence on biodiversity policy in another of the most environmentally damaging sectors of industry. The members committed to undertake a programme of conservation activities within the agricultural landscapes and wider ecosystems affected by the global operations of this international tobacco group. The following year, the Global Trees Campaign was selected as the company's centenary charitable project, a significant milestone in FFI's history of working with the corporate sector. But this wasn't simply about the money. The British American Tobacco Biodiversity Partnership provided a mechanism for collaboration on an extensive programme of activities for over 15 years.

FFI has gone on to form mutually beneficial partnerships with a broad spectrum of companies – well over 30 at the last count – in the extractive, mining and agribusiness sectors, developing strategic alliances, collaborations and interventions that take an innovative, science-based approach to biodiversity protection and management.

Top of its class

In 2001, FFI played a leading role in establishing the Energy & Biodiversity Initiative, one of the earliest examples of the constructive partnerships with the oil and gas sector that unfolded during this period to promote the integration of biodiversity conservation into development activities. Although not originally involved in this initiative, Italian oil and gas company Eni recognised the need to engage with biodiversity in a more strategic and structured manner and, in 2003, formed a partnership with FFI through its upstream business unit. The company is now one of the top rated in its sector for biodiversity management. In 2011, Eni was ranked second among leading oil and gas companies according to the Natural Value Initiative – the first benchmarking tool to enable investors to assess the sustainability of businesses from a biodiversity perspective. Eni's achievements and leadership on biodiversity issues have also gained peer recognition. From 2010–15, Paola Maria Pedroni, Senior Environmental Advisor for Eni's upstream business unit, chaired the joint IPIECA-IOGP Biodiversity and Ecosystem Services Working Group. FFI's constructive engagement with Eni has taken the company above and beyond its original biodiversity goals. At the time of writing, this productive partnership is continuing to ensure that the company's operations and environmental management system take full account of biodiversity.

'The partnership with FFI has been invaluable in helping Eni to recognise, assess and manage biodiversity issues in relation to our global operations.'

Paola Maria Pedroni, Senior Environmental Advisor, Eni Upstream

Arguably the most creative of FFI's corporate partnerships had its origins in newspaper headlines in 2001, blaming the decimation of eastern lowland (Grauer's) gorilla populations in war-torn Democratic Republic of Congo on the explosion in mobile phone use and, more specifically, the illegal mining of coltan. This raw material contains tantalum, a rare metal highly prized for its conductivity and resistance to corrosion, making it a vital material for capacitors in electronic gadgets. A surge in demand for mobile phones and a perceived shortage of tantalum had led to market prices rocketing and precipitated a veritable 'coltan rush' in Central Africa's national parks, where the mineral is easily surface-mined with nothing more complicated than a shovel and a sieve. Among the parks affected by the invasion was Kahuzi-Biega, a UNESCO World Heritage site and vital refuge for the endangered Grauer's gorilla. The only source of food for the remote, overcrowded coltan mining camps was the local wildlife. As a result, elephants, buffaloes, antelopes, chimpanzees and gorillas were being slaughtered indiscriminately and on an industrial scale.

Vodafone was recruited into the partnership fold by Karen Hayes, the then director of what was FFI's Corporate Affairs

department, whom colleagues described as 'multi-talented and super-sharp'. Like other mobile phone companies, Vodafone was reluctant to acknowledge its share of responsibility for the crisis, but magnanimously agreed to support FFI proactively in helping avert a humanitarian and wildlife disaster. A blanket ban on the purchase of so-called blood coltan was deemed unrealistic, and even counter-productive, given that sanctions might exacerbate the economic problems of this poverty-stricken region. Instead, the partners took on the challenge of doing business in a war zone. The idea was to openly negotiate a long-term deal whereby an approved coltan collective would be paid a sensible price for an ethically sourced product. Hayes and

Right Letter of thanks from the then Secretary-General of the United Nations, Kofi Annan, in the wake of the World Summit on Sustainable Development.

Below A handful of coltan dust.

25 September 2002

Dear Mr. Rose,

I write to thank you for your valuable contribution to the Global Compact event in Johannesburg on 2 September 2002, held in connection with the World Summit on Sustainable Development.

This meeting brought together a unique coalition of government officials, business leaders and representatives from labour and civil society. It helped us to identify new ways to promote sustainable business in least developed countries by building coalitions of like-minded stakeholders.

The challenge before us now is to translate political goodwill and resources into country-level efforts that will help make markets work for the poor. The Global Compact and the relevant United Nations entities -- the United Nations Development Programme, the United Nations Conference on Trade and Development and the United Nations Environment Programme-- stand ready to work with you in that endeavour.

I hope I can count on your continued support in helping us carry this initiative forward.

Yours sincerely,

Kofi A. Annan

Mr. Mark Rose
Executive Director
Fauna & Flora International
Cambridge

Rose presented this proposal to world leaders, including UK Prime Minister Tony Blair, French President Jacques Chirac and several African heads of state, at the World Summit on Sustainable Development in August 2002. FFI was one of only two conservation organisations invited to attend the UN Global Compact Heads of State Round Table hosted by Secretary-General Kofi Annan at this summit. A subsequent meeting in Kinshasa between FFI staff and government ministers led to them securing a groundbreaking agreement, literally and metaphorically, whereby environmental and social factors would be given priority when granting coltan mining concessions.

Given the political instability in the region, this initiative was never going to achieve success overnight, but the timely intervention of FFI and Vodafone focused international attention on the coltan issue and secured government and industry commitment to address the problem. It also paved the way for other joint ventures with the telecommunications giant, including a scheme to encourage environmentally responsible disposal of the end product, whereby funds generated through the Fonebak phone recycling initiative were used to support FFI's work with Asian elephants, mountain gorillas and Vietnamese primates. There was more to come from the partnership, in the shape of an inspired idea to promote an active interest in wildlife and its conservation among the new mobile phone generation. For reasons that will become clear in the next chapter, this would prove to be one of the most productive, but ultimately most frustrating, ventures in FFI's recent history.

Flagship enterprise

As the Global Business Partnership continued to evolve, FFI was able to capitalise on its blossoming relationship with founder members BP and Rio Tinto by securing their support for another new scheme. The 100% Fund, which for 30 years had been considered an essential ingredient in FFI's overall recipe for conservation success, was deemed to be past its sell-by date. Whilst the society had not exactly lost its appetite for the bite-sized projects that the fund had traditionally championed, there was a new hunger for the kind of wider impact on entire ecosystems that land purchase had enabled FFI to achieve.

Launched in late 2001, the Flagship Species Fund was a joint initiative with the UK government's Department for Environment, Food & Rural Affairs (Defra). It originated in FFI's engagement at the – deep breath – Fifth Ordinary Meeting of the Conference of the Parties to the Convention

Above One of the earliest schemes to encourage recycling of mobile phones, the Fonebak initiative helped to support FFI's work with flagship species such as the mountain gorilla.

Left Brochure promoting the Flagship Species Fund, a joint initiative between FFI and Defra.

on Biological Diversity, which was held in Nairobi in May 2000, and reflected Defra's interest in channelling private sector investment into conservation. It was felt that business support could best be harnessed by focusing on popular, high-profile species belonging to certain key taxonomic groups, and given that FFI was already actively working to conserve primates, marine turtles and threatened trees, it seemed sensible to start there. One of the fund's earliest contributions was to support activities that led to the creation of an official protected area for *pau brasil*, the endangered national tree that is confined to Brazil's dwindling Atlantic Forest. It also, among other notable milestones, funded the development of conservation strategies for Mexico's oak species, over 30 of which are threatened with extinction. These so-called flagship species serve as symbols for the wider conservation cause, eliciting public support in their own right as well as stimulating broader measures to protect crucial habitats and the other, less charismatic, species that also depend on them.

The UK's then Minister of the Environment, Michael Meacher, revealed that Defra would be supporting the fund to the tune of £300,000 over three years, with FFI securing

THE ELEPHANT MAN

By all accounts, the late Mark Shand lived life to the full before his untimely death in 2014. His obituary in *The Times* summed him up as 'Adventurer, conservationist, travel writer and one-time playboy who dodged hurricanes and cannibals and rode across India by elephant'. The bookends to that evocative encapsulation are the most relevant to Shand's relationship with FFI, which began in earnest when he met Mark Rose for drinks at London's Royal Geographical Society where, beneath the watchful gaze of several famous explorers' portraits, they hatched a plot to establish the Asian Elephant Conservation Programme.

Shand devoted the latter half of his life to highlighting the plight of Asia's elephant and was a tireless early ambassador for FFI's own work in this regard. Thanks to his charisma and influence, FFI was able to secure a higher public profile for its activities through the endorsement and support of celebrities including Goldie Hawn, Bianca Jagger and Julia Roberts. Joe Walston, now at the Wildlife Conservation Society, and whom Shand mentored when they worked together two decades earlier on FFI's Asian elephant programme in Vietnam, paid him this tribute: 'It is only through 20 years of conservation in Asia and Africa that one realises just how important people like Mark have

FFI's Asian elephant appeal received a welcome boost when actress Goldie Hawn – arriving on a spectacular, life-sized model elephant – gave her time to open the 1997 January Sale at Harrods, at which she was presented with a cheque for $25,000 by owner Mohamed Al Fayed.

been, and are, and will be. Mark not only put Asian elephants back on the map when the world's attention was on their African cousins, but created whole new constituencies for conservation that people like me could never hope to capture.' The relationship was a two-way street, and Shand readily conceded that FFI was the organisation that had taught him about conservation. ∎

matching funding, primarily from corporate coffers. In recognition of the value of maintaining support for small-scale projects, a proportion of the money was ring-fenced to ensure that the original ethos of the 100% Fund would be upheld in future.

The flagship species concept was nothing new for FFI, even if the terminology employed might occasionally vary, as witnessed by this extract from a 1990 *Oryx* article: 'Although we use the gorilla as the *focal* [my italics] species in this part of Africa, the forests are home to many other species, some of them also threatened, and all will benefit from conservation activities.' The fund that evolved a decade later was simply the formal mechanism that supported an approach already favoured by FFI and which had been clearly articulated back in 1997 at the *Has the Panda had its Day?* symposium that focused on mammals as flagship species.

Mountain gorillas and other examples of so-called charismatic megafauna were on FFI's radar long before the Flagship Species Fund materialised. At first glance, this might appear to conflict with a stated preference for riding to the rescue of less popular species. In fact, closer scrutiny of the wildlife in question reveals a familiar pattern and reflects FFI's awareness of the fact that different species matter in different ways to different audiences. Compared to their closest kin, the species or subspecies singled out for special treatment by FFI are very much the poor relations. African elephants are rarely out of the spotlight, but it is their neglected Asian cousins, threatened by forest clearance, illegal logging and poaching, that are in even greater need of conservation attention. Similarly, while the fate of India's tigers has long been headline news, the world appeared relatively indifferent to the fate of the critically endangered Sumatran tiger before FFI began fighting its corner.

Lest we forget

FFI's association with the Asian elephant dates back many decades. In the 1970s, for example, the then Fauna Preservation Society sponsored a project that yielded a comprehensive survey of the species' distribution and status from India to Indonesia. At the time of the survey it was estimated that 'only' 30–40,000 Asian elephants remained in the wild. Today those numbers would be welcomed as the fulfilment of some utopian ideal. Many of the 13 countries where the Asian elephant occurs hold wild populations of just a few hundred, often in small, fragmented groups. Space is at a premium in these densely populated areas, and large numbers of people live within national parks or close

Two examples of the appeal literature produced on behalf of Asian elephants.

to their boundaries. As their natural habitat diminishes and traditional migration routes are severed, the elephants are forced onto agricultural land or into urban areas. The subsequent confrontations can result in death or injury to both animals and humans.

Since 1995, FFI has been at the forefront of elephant conservation in South East Asia, focusing predominantly on Indonesia, Vietnam and Cambodia. In partnership with governments, NGOs and local communities, the Asian Elephant Conservation Programme worked to increase understanding of their needs, safeguard their habitat and reduce conflict between elephants and people.

The effectiveness of using flagship species to protect the wider ecosystem and its rich biodiversity is exemplified by FFI's Conservation of Elephant Landscapes initiative in Aceh, Indonesia's troubled westernmost province and an acknowledged global biodiversity hotspot on the island of Sumatra. In the face of severe economic and political difficulties, this integrated programme went on to secure a US$750,000 grant from the World Bank's Global Environment Facility, the first such award for the country. The Indonesian government subsequently invited FFI to assist with the development of a national elephant conservation strategy. Other notable firsts in Indonesia achieved by the programme included a moratorium on logging in Aceh announced by the governor of the province, and the introduction of local legislation on nature conservation.

In Indochina, where FFI's formal involvement in Asian elephant conservation began in 1996, the species has enjoyed mixed

A sedated Asian elephant is examined by a vet during the emergency relocation exercise that saw six animals successfully rescued from a shrinking fragment of forest and moved to a protected area.

fortunes. In Vietnam, widespread habitat loss and fragmentation has left the dwindling population on a collision course with its human neighbours. Nationwide surveys led by FFI at the turn of the century established conclusively that the number of Asian elephants permanently resident in Vietnam was almost certainly down to double figures. Survey data were incorporated into a comprehensive National Elephant Conservation Status Review, itself of elephantine proportions. Gratifyingly, from a capacity building perspective, the majority of lead authors in the report were local specialists rather than international experts. Less hearteningly, its conclusions made sobering reading: 'To all intents and purposes, elephants in Vietnam are already ecologically extinct.' The best way forward was deemed to be to focus conservation efforts on the source populations in Laos and Cambodia, while simultaneously persevering with an awareness programme that could change Vietnamese attitudes to elephants and pave the way for their dispersal back into the country in future.

In 2001, with the support of – among others – the recently established charitable foundation of jewellery designer, philanthropist and former fashion model Elsa Peretti, FFI

engineered the ambitious and hazardous, but ultimately successful, emergency relocation of one of Vietnam's last surviving wild Asian elephant herds. Fragmentation of their forest habitat due to illegal logging had forced the elephants to migrate into a populated rural area, where increasing conflict with villagers was threatening to end in tragedy. Regrettably, two elephants died from injuries sustained during the difficult translocation process, but the remaining six elephants were successfully relocated to the relative safety of Vietnam's Yok Don National Park on the Cambodian border.

The remote and biologically rich forests of Cambodia's Mondulkiri province, which borders Yok Don, are noted for harbouring significant numbers of elephants. It was this knowledge that induced FFI to host an historic bilateral conference between the governments of Vietnam and Cambodia, the first ever on elephant conservation. The respective delegations who attended the 2001

THE SHORT MAN OF SUMATRA

Persistent rumours of the presence in Sumatra's rainforests of a mysterious, hairy bipedal primate, dubbed *orang pendek*, or short man, by Dutch settlers, led FFI to secure commercial sponsorship for a concerted and sustained attempt to track down this putative new species of great ape. Given the alarming rates of deforestation caused by commercial logging and slash-and-burn agriculture, there was a real fear that habitat loss would precipitate the extinction of this and other species before its existence could even be validated.

It was the intrepid Deborah Martyr, a London journalist and primate enthusiast, who set the ball rolling, following an initial visit to Sumatra in the 1980s during which she first heard about *orang pendek*. Her relentless pursuit of what would have been a sensational newspaper story eventually attracted the attention of Dr David Chivers, a Cambridge primatologist who also

happened to be FFI's vice-chairman. In 1995, a team including Martyr, zoologist and wildlife photographer Jeremy Holden and primatologist Achmad Yanuar, a Sumatran doctoral student at Cambridge, was sent to investigate. Its mission was to document systematically all eyewitness accounts of the primate and to obtain photographic evidence of its existence using camera traps.

The project generated considerable media attention, including a documentary filmed by the BBC's Natural History Unit, but failed to obtain conclusive proof other than several footprint casts that appear not to match any known primate species. The actual camera traps, which had been improvised out of plywood, were not fit for purpose. Keith Scholey, a producer at the Natural History Unit, who would go on to be appointed as its new chief in 1998, conceded that whilst he did not find the story of *orang pendek* convincing, he nevertheless found it 'compelling'. All subsequent

attempts to validate its existence have proved fruitless. Tantalisingly, additional casts and hair samples have since been collected and analysed, but the truth about *orang pendek* appears destined to remain a riddle wrapped in a mystery inside an enigma. ∎

Below left Press cutting from an article in *The Sunday Times* published on 12 October 1997.

Bottom left Cast of the mysterious footprint ostensibly belonging to *orang pendek*.

Below right The *orang pendek* expedition may have failed to achieve its primary goal, but some of its other discoveries were noteworthy in their own right. This parasitic flower, *Rafflesia hasseltii*, had been found at only three other sites since 1900, and never before at Kerinci. The project recorded species never previously photographed in the wild – such as Salvadori's pheasant and a rare melanistic form of the golden cat – and others that no scientist had set eyes on since the nineteenth century, including the giant pitta, which is rather less appetising than it sounds, unless you specialise in eating shy, ground-feeding rainforest birds.

conference in Danang signed up to unprecedented transboundary co-operation in the shape of joint conservation initiatives to protect Asian elephants and one of Indochina's most important ecosystems, the dry deciduous forest shared by Vietnam's Dak Lak province and Mondulkiri in Cambodia.

The latter province is not the only elephant stronghold in Cambodia, as the FFI-led biological surveys of the Cardamom Mountains confirmed, and in 2002 it began spearheading an initiative to protect and manage the populations that range widely throughout the 1.4 million hectares of forest in that relatively pristine landscape. Key to the success of the Cambodian Elephant Conservation Group, which was formally launched in 2005, was the contribution of Tuy Sereivathana. This government officer from the Ministry of the Environment joined FFI on secondment in 2003 to work on elephant conservation, before leaving his government position in 2006 to become manager of the project. The person who hired him, FFI's Joe Heffernan, recognised a man who was 'made for the job'. Vathana, as he is known, instinctively understood the importance of working closely with local communities, who referred to him affectionately as 'Uncle Elephant', and he even succeeded in converting former hunters of wild elephants into champions of their conservation. In 2010 he was awarded the Goldman Environmental Prize for his work in developing innovative, low-cost solutions to mitigate human–wildlife conflict in his native Cambodia.

Tuy Sereivathana, winner of the 2010 Goldman Environmental Prize and a 2011 National Geographic Emerging Explorer award for his groundbreaking work with FFI's Cambodian Elephant Conservation Group, made history by becoming the first Cambodian other than diplomatic staff to meet President Obama, when he was among the prizewinners invited to the White House. Vathana even had the presence of mind to pass on his business card as he parted company with the then leader of the free world at the end of their brief encounter in the Oval Office.

The stripe protectors

Kerinci Seblat National Park is the nexus of FFI's efforts to conserve the Sumatran tiger. This vast protected area is under tremendous pressure from the surrounding human population; almost two million people, and rising, live around its borders. The smallest and most secretive of all the surviving subspecies, the Sumatran tiger is critically endangered, with an estimated wild population of no more than 400 individuals.

FFI's original involvement with tiger conservation in Kerinci Seblat came about in slightly unconventional fashion. Initial forays into the park were intended to confirm the existence of *orang pendek*, the Sumatran equivalent of North America's Bigfoot and the Abominable Snowman of the Himalayas. The jungle yeti remained dispiritingly elusive, but the original team had the dubious consolation of witnessing something genuinely abominable: the appalling slaughter of Sumatra's tigers to satisfy the burgeoning trade in tiger skins and body parts. This discovery was the catalyst

MARTYR TO THE CAUSE

Originally a London-based journalist, Debbie Martyr never planned to work in conservation, but a speculative visit to Sumatra in search of a storyline about a legendary bipedal ape known as *orang pendek* changed all that. The following year she was introduced to FFI, the beginning of an association that has lasted over two decades.

As manager of FFI's Kerinci Tiger Project and overall leader of the tiger protection teams, Debbie works to ensure the survival of the Sumatran tiger and its forest habitat in Kerinci Seblat National Park. Her dedication to tiger conservation was acknowledged in the New Year Honours List for 2015 when she was awarded an MBE,

a decision hailed by FFI's deputy chief executive Ros Aveling as 'well-deserved recognition for a true conservation hero'.

Almost as camera-shy as the tigers that she has dedicated much of her life to saving, Martyr shuns the limelight and prefers her local colleagues to receive the plaudits, but she grudgingly acknowledges the vital role that she has played. 'Protected areas need long-term friends. Career people move onwards and upwards, park personnel are rotated to new positions, challenges change over time. In the end what remains is this incredible forest and its wildlife. Someone has to commit and say "I want future generations to see what I have seen". In this case, it turned out to be me.' ∎

for a reassessment of FFI priorities in Kerinci Seblat, which ultimately led to the formation of the now legendary Tiger Protection and Conservation Units (TPCU).

The Sumatran Tiger Project was launched in 1998, with the initial emphasis on survey and monitoring work to amass data on tigers and other species in the park, but it quickly became evident that anti-poaching measures were an urgent priority in light of the renewed onslaught brought on by the prevailing economic crisis. Attempts had previously been made to set up anti-poaching units. Although these were defunct at the time, their potential effectiveness, given the appropriate financial support, was not in doubt. FFI joined forces with the national park authorities to create the Tiger Protection Project, which supported the work of hard-hitting, semi-autonomous anti-poaching teams. The units are purposely dynamic and light on their feet, meaning that they can react to any situation, whether it be a tiger threatening a farmer's livestock or a poacher offering a tiger skin for sale.

The original idea for resurrecting the TPCUs came from Debbie Martyr, who had assumed the mantle of project leader soon after joining FFI's ranks, but the concept actually took shape over months of informal, sometimes heated, discussions with friends from the national park, and that is why it has stood the test of time. 'In retrospect, it was a classic FFI approach – drawing on each other's strengths and skill sets to build something that worked from all our perspectives – a team embedded within the national park but outside the hierarchy, able to take the kind of executive field decisions that are beyond the legal capacity of an NGO, with the freedom of manoeuvre that so many protected area personnel don't have, unburdened by bureaucracy, but with FFI in Jakarta and the UK backing us up when we needed advice or strategic support.'

Despite operating on a shoestring budget, the first TPCU had an immediate impact; the arrest, prosecution and subsequent imprisonment of a tiger poacher sent shock waves through the network of illegal traders who had previously operated with impunity. Dealers were recorded refusing to buy tiger pelts, citing fear of prosecution as a result of TPCU undercover operations. Regular patrols, intelligence gathering and lobbying by the tightly knit team of rangers proved so successful in reducing poaching

activity that a decision was made to establish additional units, of which there are now four. In 2003, the team achieved a remarkable coup, engineering the first ever arrest of an elected member of parliament for tiger trafficking. This high-ranking politician was the local head of a national political party, and the resulting media frenzy helped to spread the word that no one was above the law.

Thanks to the heroics of the four TPCUs, the first decade of FFI's Tiger Protection and Conservation Programme was a resounding success. Kerinci Seblat was one of the few protected areas in Asia where tiger encounter records had stabilised and even perceptibly increased.

There was growing confidence that Sumatran tiger conservation had turned a corner, with threats to tigers and tiger prey having fallen for five successive years. By 2012, that assumption had been turned on its head. Active poaching, and black market prices, started to go through the roof. In 2013 FFI teams recorded a 400 per cent increase

Clockwise from top left View of Gunung Kerinci, domain of the Sumatran tiger, seen here entangled in a poacher's snare; snares do not discriminate between predator and prey – this is the first ever photograph of a Sumatran muntjac, taken by Debbie Martyr before she freed the hapless deer; tigers are not the only endangered felines to benefit from the vigilance of the Kerinci enforcement teams. This flat-headed cat had a lucky escape when it was confiscated from a local market trader and re-released into the forest.

in the number of snares detected and destroyed in the national park. Suddenly, the TPCUs were running to stand still. Tellingly, the dam did not burst. In the face of the most serious, concentrated poaching ever recorded at Kerinci, tiger densities held steady, thanks largely to the indefatigable efforts of Martyr and her national park colleagues. Camera-trap monitoring indicates that tiger numbers are unchanged since 2011, even though the threats have escalated to an unprecedented level of intensity. Kerinci Seblat National Park has become synonymous with tigers and tiger conservation, and continues to be held up by the Ministry of Environment and Forestry as a model for other national parks to emulate.

REMEMBRANCE OF THINGS PAST

In March 1999, Lieutenant-Colonel Charles Leofric Boyle OBE, secretary of the then Fauna Preservation Society from 1950 to 1963, died at the grand old age of 100. With his passing, the last surviving link between FFI and its original incarnation was effectively severed. Born in 1899, several years before the Society for the Preservation of the Wild Fauna of the Empire first saw the light of day, Colonel Boyle came within nine months of achieving the scarcely fathomable feat of experiencing life in three consecutive centuries. The changes that he witnessed must have been truly astounding, but he was no mere spectator. After retiring from a 30-year military career that took him to Ireland, Jamaica and India, he was quick to stamp his mark as secretary, embracing his new role with renewed gusto and, in the words of his *Oryx* obituary, 'bringing a zest to conservation in general and, more precisely, to the society'.

Finding himself under-employed during his early days at the helm, the good colonel occupied his time constructively by paying regular visits to London's Heathrow airport to monitor the quantity and variety of imported wild animals – a practice that effectively sowed the seeds for the idea of forming CITES, the Convention on International Trade in Endangered Species of Wild Fauna and Flora. It was he who renamed the society, rebranded its journal and adopted the oryx logo that is now synonymous with the organisation. He moved quickly to help orchestrate Operation Noah, having already witnessed the construction of the Kariba Dam during his 1957 visit to Africa and anticipated the disastrous impact on wildlife in the flooded gorge. Colonel Boyle's handwritten card index system for documenting endangered species, rudimentary though it may

Man out of time. Colonel Boyle with his personal copy of the *RSPCA Book of British Mammals*, which he edited.

seem today, was a revolutionary idea born out of the perceived need for a comprehensive database, and it provided some of the inspiration for the Red Data Books later compiled by Peter Scott. One of his final, and most enduring, contributions was as a prime mover in the Operation Oryx rescue mission, which was already underway by the time he retired in 1963. Quite an impressive legacy, by any measure.

By all accounts, Colonel Boyle was a gentle, modest man with an evident talent for self-deprecation. Apparently, he took particular delight in regaling his grandchildren with the story of the occasion when – finding himself locked in the grounds of London Zoo after working inordinately late at the office one night – he had attempted to climb out and suffered the indignity of ending up suspended by just one shoe, hanging bat-like from the top of the railings. How he extricated himself from this predicament, we can only guess.

Even in his dotage, if such a term is not an insult to someone who 'steadfastly refused to let mere old age get in the way of living', Colonel Boyle was a frequent visitor to the old FPS offices adjacent to the parrot house at London Zoo. John Burton, one of the colonel's more recent successors as secretary, recalls seeing him regularly. 'He was still cycling into London Zoo in his nineties.' It must surely have been a source of some satisfaction to Colonel Boyle that he not only reached his centenary, but also beat FFI to this auspicious landmark and elicited a congratulatory note from its patron, Her Majesty The Queen, whose long-standing association with the society was, at that time, narrowly eclipsed by his own. ∎

Lieutenant-Colonel Charles Leofric Boyle OBE (1899–1999)

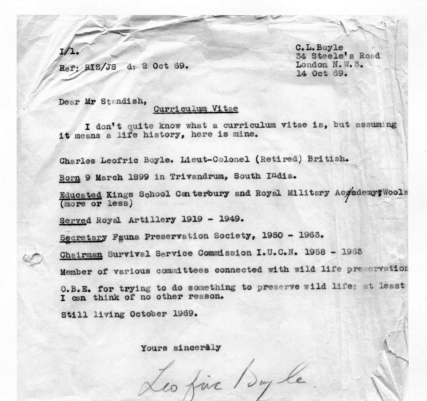

I/1.

Ref: RIS/JS d: 2 Oct 69.

C.L.Boyle
34 Steele's Road
London N.W.3.
14 Oct 69.

Dear Mr Standish,

Curriculum Vitae

I don't quite know what a curriculum vitae is, but assuming it means a life history, here is mine.

Charles Leofric Boyle. Lieut-Colonel (Retired) British.

Born 9 March 1899 in Trivandrum, South India.

Educated Kings School Canterbury and Royal Military Academy Woolw (more or less)

Served Royal Artillery 1919 - 1949.

Secretary Fauna Preservation Society, 1950 - 1963.

Chairman Survival Service Commission I.U.C.N. 1958 - 1963

Member of various committees connected with wild life preservation

O.B.E. for trying to do something to preserve wild life; at least I can think of no other reason.

Still living October 1969.

Yours sincerely

Leofric Boyle

10 DOWNING STREET

9th November 1978

Dear Ritchie,

As President of ACOPS, I am writing to say how very sorry I am to hear that Colonel Boyle is retiring from the Committee.

He was one of the founder members of the Committee when it was first set up in 1952 and has represented the Fauna Preservation Society on it every since. He has attended all our conferences, national and international, and we have benefited much from his wide experience and wise counsel on conservation and natural history matters.

We shall all miss him very much, and send our thanks and good wishes to him and to Mrs. Boyle.

Yours ever
Jim Callaghan

Lord Ritchie-Calder, C.B.E.
Chairman, Advisory Committee on Oil
Pollution of the Sea

Above left Still seeking gainful employment at the ripe old age of 70, and evidently a firm believer in the maxim that brevity is the soul of wit, Colonel Boyle provides a delightfully succinct response to a request for a copy of his CV.

Below left In recognition of his 'outstanding service in the cause of nature conservation', Colonel Boyle is appointed as Ridder in the Most Excellent Order of the Golden Ark by His Royal Highness Prince Bernhard of the Netherlands at a ceremony in Soestdijk Palace in May 1973.

Above right Correspondence from the then Prime Minister James Callaghan reveals the sterling contribution made by Colonel Boyle – for over a quarter of a century – to the Advisory Committee on Oil Pollution at Sea, of which he was a founder member.

Below right After retiring as secretary, Colonel Boyle continued to serve as a council member and then vice-president of the society. His extraordinary contribution was recognised in September 1982 when he was admitted to the society's prestigious roll of honour.

Fauna & Flora Preservation Society
founded 1903

Roll of Honour
initiated 1980

For extraordinary services to
the Fauna & Flora Preservation Society

The name of
LIEUT-COL C.L. BOYLE

was placed on the Roll of Honour
at the Annual General Meeting of the Society
on

8th September 1982

CITATION

Over the past 40 years he has supported and served the Society in a variety of posts. In 1950 he took over as Hon. Secretary and was the first Hon. Editor of Oryx. He held both these posts until 1963 and under his guidance the Society and its journal flourished, and the membership more than doubled. Among numerous conservation achievements he was largely responsible for the success of Operation Oryx. Since retiring he has continued to serve the Society as a Council Member (1965-71) and a Vice-President (1972-)

President Peter Scott
Chairman Croughton

CHAPTER 10

CELEBRATION

'This is a special milestone not just in the history of FFI, but in the history of conservation. Some of the finest minds and greatest figures ever to work in conservation have been part of FFI. Institutions and standards that we now take for granted were started by FFI. Some of the Earth's most famous protected areas exist because of [its] efforts.'

Sir Neil Chalmers, then Director of the Natural History Museum, London, 2003

On 11 December 1903, a group of like-minded establishment figures with a penchant for shooting large African mammals sat down in London's Natural History Museum and created the Society for the Preservation of the Wild Fauna of the Empire. Precisely one hundred years and several name changes later, in the very same venue where that historic meeting took place, Fauna & Flora International (FFI) held a birthday party to celebrate a century of conservation achievement.

One hundred years of solicitude

This was no ordinary birthday party. Dwarfed by the museum's iconic diplodocus skeleton and surrounded by other powerful reminders that a century is just an evolutionary blink of an eye, the great and the good from the worlds of commerce, natural history broadcasting, entertainment and politics were not there just to watch FFI blow out the candles on its cake. The event was as much about moving forward as it was about looking back, and the assembled guests were left in no doubt that fundraising for future conservation work was the primary focus. Even before they had picked up their cutlery, the museum's long-standing director, Sir Neil Chalmers, had this unequivocal message for them: 'Tonight, ladies and gentlemen, you are sitting surrounded by the history of the Earth, pledging your commitment to the future of the Earth.'

Top The hottest ticket in town.

Opposite Guests at FFI's centenary dinner begin to wonder whether the caterers are operating with a skeleton staff.

Above Table settings at the dinner included a birthday card designed by long-time FFI supporter Sir Quentin Blake.

Opposite More literati than glitterati: snapshots of the great and the good, including stalwarts of the society, long-term FFI associates, familiar faces and new acquaintances. Top row: (left to right) television and radio presenter, Anneka Rice; Sarah Papineau Marshall, former acting chair of FFI Inc., and brother David; the legendary Richard Fitter, former honorary secretary, chairman and vice-president of the society, with grandson Oliver. Second row: wildlife conservationist and television presenter, Saba Douglas-Hamilton, with Kule Chitepo, executive director of ResourceAfrica; art historian, curator, writer and broadcaster, Sir Roy Strong; Edward Hoare, FFI vice-president and former treasurer, with Adeline Nolan. Third row: Dr Lisbet Rausing, FFI vice-president and benefactor, flanked by Anne Jenkin, who helped organise the event; Joanna Lumley reinforces FFI's message by brandishing a copy of Bill Adams' recently published *Against Extinction*; Lindsay Bury, former FFI chairman, with Saba Douglas-Hamilton. Fourth row: Paul Green, founder of Halcyon Gallery; Richard Buxton, cousin several times removed of FFI's founding father, Edward North Buxton, with Suzie Hoare; Jacob, Lord Rothschild, sharing a joke with actress Lara Cazalet. Bottom row: Sigrid Rausing, philanthropist, anthropologist and publisher, with stepchildren Alexis Abraham and Natalia Conroy (née Abraham); Professor Bill Adams, former FFI council member, and his fellow guests, enjoying Joanna Lumley's speech; Sir Tim Rice, multi-award-winning lyricist, with television writer Lise Mayer.

Above Sir Neil Chalmers (left), then director of the Natural History Museum, addresses the assembled dinner guests; Joanna Lumley (right) bewitches members of the audience into spending their children's inheritance on biodiversity conservation.

The evening marked the official launch of the Centenary Appeal, which aimed to raise £34 million over five years. The ten-year strategy and five-year business plan were based around a series of ambitious conservation targets, and achieving these would be contingent on generating sufficient funds. It was clear that FFI would not have time to sit back and await the congratulatory telegram.

The campaign had already hit the ground running, thanks to what Mark Rose described as the 'incredible generosity and untiring chairmanship' of Dr Lisbet Rausing. As head of the Centenary Development Committee, she not only pledged the lead gift of £3 million to kick-start proceedings, but also persuaded others to dig deep for the conservation cause. By early 2004, the appeal was already one-third of the way to its five-year target. Among the other big guns mobilised by FFI to raise the profile of its fundraising drive, Sir David Attenborough was the most prominent; he not only narrated the Centenary Appeal film that was first screened

at the dinner, but also voiced the special BBC Lifeline charity appeal, broadcast on national television in aid of FFI.

The star-studded guest list at this centenary dinner included Princess Laurentien of the Netherlands (destined to become FFI's next president), composer Sir Tim Rice, Theresa May MP (whose subsequent meteoric rise to power was no doubt inspired by a burning desire – ignited that very evening, but carefully concealed thus far – to put biodiversity conservation, climate change and other environmental issues at the top of the UK government agenda), actress Joanna Lumley and wildlife documentary presenters Charlotte Uhlenbroek, Saba Douglas-Hamilton, Bill Oddie and Chris Packham. The pulling power of the Rothschilds and the Rausings helped to ensure the presence of other major philanthropists. Sir David Attenborough and John Cleese joined in the celebrations via satellite link from Los Angeles, where they were guests of honour at a fundraising luncheon held simultaneously on the other side of the Atlantic.

Back in the USA

The LA event served a dual purpose: as well as generating financial support stateside for the Centenary Appeal, it also provided the perfect backdrop to the official unveiling of FFI's shiny new US operation, which was seen as a vital support vehicle for its growing global conservation portfolio.

This was by no means FFI's first foray into the United States, but there had been several false starts prior to this. The original attempts to establish an American presence dated back to the late 1970s, when the society recognised that the work of a British charity with a global remit would benefit from financial and technical access to the US market. The first US office opened in 1981 in Ayer, Massachusetts, headed up by Gerard Bertrand, then president of the Massachusetts Audubon Society, and FFPS, Inc. was formally registered and granted charitable status. Reorganised two years later to enable it to help increase membership and play a more active role in the work of Bat Conservation International and the Mountain Gorilla Project, it seems to have fallen off the radar once John Burton left FFPS in 1987. To all intents and purposes the US operation was dormant for the next few years, which coincided with the society's period in the doldrums.

Thereafter, notwithstanding its ongoing commitment to the transatlantic activities of SoundWood, FFI did not have any formal representation in the US until the end of the 1990s. It did, however, benefit from a fruitful collaboration with Earthvoice International in Washington and, more specifically, the services of Adriana Dinu. Variously referred to in annual reports as Programme Coordinator of the FFI Earthvoice Partnership and, later, the equally nebulous title of Director for Programme Development, Dinu was by all accounts a fanatically dedicated addition to the team who, during her five-year sojourn, made a key contribution to the society's forward motion. According to Mark Rose, Dinu was instrumental in designing, developing and managing several significant and successful projects in countries such as Belize, Mozambique and South Africa. In 1999 an attempt was made to re-establish an official FFI presence in the US, this time in sunny California. An office was formally established in San Francisco the following year, and Mark Rose persuaded Daphne Astor, daughter of the noted philanthropist Mary Warburg, to become president of the US board. A trio of consultants was commissioned to raise FFI's US profile and implement a fundraising strategy for, in particular, SoundWood, the Global Trees Campaign and South Africa's Flower Valley project. Robert Garner, a professional musician with experience of the non-profit world, was appointed as the new director of SoundWood's

US programme. Several additional, proactive board members were recruited, including Melissa Shackleton Dann, Clea Newman (daughter of the actor, entrepreneur and philanthropist Paul Newman) and Dielle Fleischmann, who remains a vice-president of FFI to this day. Almost US$1 million was raised during the year from foundations and individual donors. This early success augured well for the future of fundraising in the United States, and by 2003 Rose felt ready to hire a US executive director, another first for FFI.

He contacted Katie Frohardt, who had previously worked for FFI during the 1990s in post-genocide Rwanda under the auspices of the International Gorilla Conservation Programme. A coffee-shop reunion with Rose in Washington DC was all that it took to persuade both parties that she was the right person to drive through FFI's ambitious growth plans on her side of the Atlantic. Their gut instinct proved correct, at least initially, and Frohardt ran Fauna & Flora International, Inc. until 2016. At this point, as is frequently the case with transatlantic relationships, diverging priorities led to a mutual parting of the ways.

Call of the wild

If the centenary event was a timely reminder of FFI's longevity and illustrious past, it also provided the ideal launch pad for a corporate-backed initiative that exemplified its innate ability to move with the times, in this case through a cutting-edge telecommunications project. A joint venture with Vodafone, the *wildlive!* concept – complete with obligatory exclamation mark – tuned into the zeitgeist by harnessing the potential of the very latest in fixed and mobile communications technologies, in order to promote an active interest in wildlife and conservation among a mass audience, namely the new generation of Internet and mobile phone users. It worked as a conservation information and activity service available on mobile phone handsets through *Vodafone live!* and online as a bespoke and dynamic community website. Users were able to download wildlife wallpapers, animal ringtones and educational games, receive conservation news, participate in a community forum, read field diary extracts and enter competitions.

Developed over a ten-month period and officially launched at FFI's centenary dinner, *wildlive!* quickly made its mark as a novel way to keep in touch with, and support, FFI's global conservation effort. The first phase proved such a roaring success that plans were made to roll out the service on a global basis. The project's development was funded by the Vodafone Group Foundation, and Vodafone UK passed on

EVER-INCREASING CIRCLES

As a follow-up to the centenary celebrations, FFI launched the Founders' Circle in the United Kingdom and the Conservation Circle in the United States. The former was designed to encourage descendants of the society's original founder members to become actively involved with the organisation and support the conservation work begun a century earlier by their forebears. Reading between the lines, it was a thinly disguised attempt to attract additional high-net-worth individuals to the fold. Its US counterpart, having no such colonial hook on which to hang its hat, was more transparent about its fundraising ambitions and openly targeted wildlife enthusiasts with deep pockets. The two were ultimately rationalised into a single concept. Co-ordinated by Diana van de Kamp, the Conservation Circle comprises an inner sanctum of supporters and advisers from the UK, US, Australia and Singapore, who are making a crucial long-term investment in FFI. One of the most valuable facets of this elite club is that its members make a vital annual commitment towards unrestricted funds. In other words, these people put food in the nosebag of the white charger, but leave FFI in control of the reins, allowing the conservationists in shining armour to ride to the rescue of whatever cause is deemed most pressing. ■

Ahead of its time: the first conservation-based mobile phone fundraising and awareness-raising portal when it appeared in early 2004, *wildlive!* harnessed the huge potential of what was just becoming a massively popular consumer device. The mountain gorilla image (left) was among the high-quality wildlife wallpaper images – all taken by Juan Pablo Moreiras – sold on the *wildlive!* service. Home page of the *wildlive!* website (middle), which was also accessible from mobile devices via the *Vodafone live!* network. The mobile phone games developed for the *wildlive!* project included *Silverback* (right), which simulated the threats facing mountain gorillas in the wild and received glowing reviews in the specialist press.

A LIFE LESS ORDINARY

'Being a naturalist is an emotional as well as
an intellectual activity.'

Dame Miriam Rothschild CBE, FRS: 1908–2005

FFI's centenary celebrations provided the perfect opportunity to honour two of its most distinguished vice-presidents and long-standing supporters, Dame Miriam Rothschild and Sir David Attenborough, who were presented with awards for their 'lifetime contribution to conservation' in the shape of specially commissioned oryx sculptures by Judy Boyt.

Clockwise from top right Dame Miriam Rothschild in her later years, relaxing at home with one of her constant companions; Jacob, Lord Rothschild, flanked by Joanna Lumley, delivers a short tribute to his aunt Miriam; close-up of Judy Boyt's stunning oryx sculpture.

Sir David Attenborough was presented with his award by John Cleese, his fellow guest of honour at the Los Angeles gathering, which took the form of a luncheon to ensure transatlantic synchronicity. The nonagenarian Dame Miriam was too frail to attend the London event in person, but her nephew Jacob, Lord Rothschild accepted the award on her behalf. She died in 2005 at the age of 96, by which time she had left an indelible and highly individual stamp on natural history, conservation and the work of the society. ∎

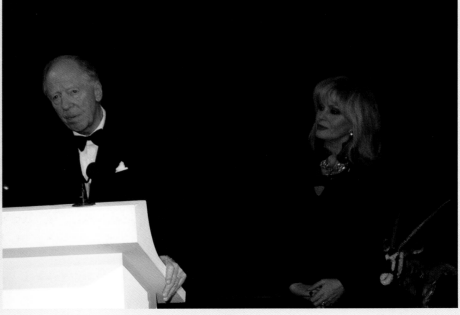

100 per cent of the income generated directly to FFI. In its first year of operation, *wildlive!* raised approximately £100,000 for conservation. Much to the chagrin of project manager Karen Hayes and her tightly knit team, *wildlive!* was put on the back burner when funding dried up just as the venture appeared poised to go global. It was eventually shelved indefinitely, one of the numerous casualties of an across-the-board cost-cutting exercise conducted by a money man. Brought in to help improve FFI's bottom line, he set about his appointed task with such gusto that many conservation activities were slimmed down to the point where they were positively skeletal.

The relationship with Vodafone was a prime example of how FFI used corporate expertise to encourage the conservation community to embrace new technology. In 2004 the two organisations held a joint symposium that brought together interested parties from the worlds of conservation, business, education and government to share their experiences of projects that were benefiting from technological innovation. Among the most creative of these was *t4cd* (Technologies for Conservation and Development), a research project conducted by FFI and Resource Africa to examine ways in which governments, society, corporates and conservationists could put technologies to work for the combined benefit of disadvantaged communities and conservation. One of the first projects of its kind, *t4cd* produced the first comprehensive electronic library of tech-related information for the conservation practitioner, in the form of a website and an interactive CD.

Centenaries at FFI come in convenient double packs. The society's scientific journal, *Oryx*, was also poised to celebrate a century of dispensing conservation wisdom in printed form. In truth, it jumped the gun slightly in publishing a centenary issue in April 2003, but it seems churlish to quibble over a few months. The society had changed beyond all recognition as the twentieth century unfolded, and nothing embodied that transformation better than the journal itself, which had undergone a complete metamorphosis from an in-house pamphlet to the conservationist's vade mecum, widely acknowledged as one of the pre-eminent international publications in its field.

The society and its journal had come a long way, but a guest editorial from chief executive Mark Rose to introduce that very centenary issue of *Oryx* left no one in any doubt that, in his view, the song remained the same: 'Not much has changed. We are still fighting the same battles, still facing the same problems.' In this same piece Rose reiterated the importance of two key planks of FFI's approach, the first of which demands a focus on sustainable livelihoods: 'Unless we can

Above left The centenary issue of *Oryx* put in a slightly premature appearance in April 2003.

Above right Commemorative issue of *FIRST* magazine, devoted entirely to FFI's centenary celebrations. It included case studies of key success stories and words of congratulation from the society's patron, Her Majesty The Queen, and the then Prime Minister, Tony Blair.

develop mechanisms that help people realize value from their environment then we are destined to fail. Crudely, this means putting bread on the table.' Secondly, he emphasised the need to 'take a holistic approach to capacity building, not only assisting local people to achieve their own goals, but helping them to construct good governmental, non-governmental and community organizations and systems'. Rose could not resist a sideswipe at the methods of some players on the international conservation stage, likening them to 'behemoths, planting their scaled-down national level organizations like Victorian missionary societies [...] It is not sustainable or efficient to deliver conservation globally using teams of expatriate experts, rappelling down into areas of species richness.' He neglected to specify whom he had in mind, but no doubt his readers had a pretty good idea.

In his concluding comments, Rose touched on the perennial problem of persuading decision makers throughout the global community to acknowledge that biodiversity, more than money, makes the world go round: 'We have to formulate strategies that bring all interested parties together – to support the realization that biodiversity is not just a bolt-on extra, but is at the centre of both the development agenda and of life itself.' This observation turned out to be particularly apposite in the context of the devastating tsunami that swept away lives, livelihoods, infrastructure and wildlife across much of South East Asia just a year later. This catastrophic event put all day-to-day concerns into perspective and conservation was put on temporary hold as resources were devoted to the relief effort in the areas where FFI and its partners operated.

Wave of destruction

In the devastating earthquake that shook South East Asia on Boxing Day 2004, one of the hardest-hit locations was Aceh, the westernmost province on the Indonesian island of Sumatra, just 250 kilometres from the quake's epicentre. Aceh has over three million hectares of forest cover, more than half of its total area. This highly diverse forest system is home to many endangered species, such as Sumatran tiger, elephant, orang-utan and rhino, and provides essential ecosystem services – chiefly water regulation and carbon sequestration. As is often the case, this biological richness contrasts starkly with the social and economic deprivation endured by the local communities. Aceh is one of Indonesia's poorest provinces, with over a quarter of the population living below the poverty line. It had also only recently emerged from civil war, but – in typical FFI fashion – the society had already been working there well before the end of hostilities.

An estimated 150,000 people were killed and upwards of one million people displaced when the tsunami hit Aceh. A husband and wife working with FFI's Sumatran elephant conservation programme were among the many who perished, and local partner the Provincial Nature Conservation Agency lost 14 staff.

As one of the few charitable organisations already working in Sumatra when disaster struck, FFI was better placed than most to help both with emergency relief operations and, subsequently, the painful rehabilitation process. A constant presence in the province since 1998, when it first embarked on a wide-ranging programme to conserve Aceh's globally important forest ecosystem using the Asian elephant as a flagship species, FFI already had close links with the Acehnese authorities and local communities dating back to the early 1990s. The strength of this well-established relationship not only made it a trusted and valued partner, but also gave it a voice in the long-term

FFI DELIVERS VITAL AID TO SUMATRA

Also inside: Turtle Appeal update

Above left Frank Momberg, seated left, during a visit to Myanmar.

Above right The first issue of *Update*, FFI's redesigned newsletter, included a report on the society's post-tsunami emergency relief operation.

Opposite A boat washed inland by the 2004 tsunami provides a surreal backdrop to a family's temporary shelter.

planning process. Crucially, this enabled FFI to influence decisions that would have huge repercussions for the future of biodiversity conservation in the region. Faced with the mammoth task of rebuilding infrastructure and shattered lives, it was vital that the Acehnese, and indeed the humanitarian aid agencies, did not take short cuts that would jeopardise livelihoods in the longer term. FFI used its local clout to ensure that environmental and biodiversity considerations were factored into the recovery and reconstruction plans. In particular, FFI stressed the importance of using the forest sustainably, rather than plundering it in the desperate rush for timber and other urgently needed resources.

Given the collective effort that went into helping Aceh to recover from this cataclysmic event, it may seem insensitive to single out individual contributions to the rescue and rehabilitation process, but from a narrow FFI perspective, one man in particular stood out. That man was Frank Momberg. A maverick figure whose unorthodox approach treads a path perilously close to the line that separates effective from infuriating, Momberg has a happy knack of getting things done. He originally came on board in 1999 as programme manager for Indochina and at the time of writing is director of FFI's Myanmar programme, but in 2004 his focus was Indonesia.

Virtually overnight, Momberg transformed FFI's local operation into a relief organisation and proceeded to run it for the next 18 months until some semblance of normal service could be resumed in Aceh. His first move was to commandeer a boat and start delivering supplies to some of the stranded communities. This short-term humanitarian intervention probably saved many individual lives, but it pales into insignificance alongside a more monumental achievement: with a persuasiveness and persistence that is part diplomat, part Rottweiler, he urged everyone who would listen – and many who wouldn't – to import the timber required for rebuilding rather than lay waste to the protected forests that are the lifeblood of the region. In certain quarters that message fell on deaf ears, but it was embraced by enough decision makers to ensure that the Acehnese didn't compound their own misery by resorting to wholesale ecosystem destruction in the name of reconstruction.

If Momberg's heroics helped to prevent the haemorrhaging of Aceh's forest resources in the immediate aftermath of the tsunami, it was a local hero who took centre stage in the ensuing efforts to protect the province's magnificent rainforests. That Irwandi Yusuf was still alive after the floods receded was nothing short of miraculous. A veterinarian by training, he had worked for FFI in Aceh since returning home following a US scholarship that saw him complete his masters degree. As a prominent long-time activist with *Gerakan Aceh Merdeka* (the Free Aceh Movement), he had repeatedly incurred the displeasure of the Indonesian authorities, and in 2003 he was arrested and incarcerated. He was still being held as a political prisoner when the tsunami struck, and as the waters rose he narrowly escaped drowning by punching a hole through the ceiling of the second-floor prayer room and scrambling onto the roof. The peace settlement negotiated in the wake of the disaster ultimately saw him elected as governor in the first democratic election for nearly three decades. Dubbed 'the man with the green plan' by his international allies, Governor Irwandi put rainforest protection at the top of his reform agenda, declared a moratorium on all logging in the province, and – as we shall see later in this chapter – embraced the concept of carbon trading in order to reinvigorate the economy while keeping the forests standing.

Ensuring that short-term development goals are not achieved at the long-term expense of the environment was nothing new for FFI. As early as 1979, one of the society's vice-presidents, Kai Curry-Lindahl, was lamenting the myopia of multilateral and bilateral aid providers that were obsessively focused on economic growth at all costs. He estimated that around US$27 billion in technical assistance was being spent on projects that actively contributed to long-term environmental degradation and loss of renewable natural resources. In a visionary address to the then Fauna Preservation Society, Curry-Lindahl lambasted the United Nations Development Programme, FAO and World Bank for their collective refusal to confront ecological realities in their planning and implementation of development programmes: 'Through the projects they initiated, encouraged or financed, as well as by their philosophy, the UNDP and the World Bank constitute the two most serious obstacles to conservation organisations trying to influence the decision-making of governments in developing countries.' Such accusations have a familiar ring to them even four decades later, particularly in the context of post-trauma recovery.

Promotional leaflet for a fundraising event on the theme of post-conflict intervention to relieve pressure on wildlife and natural resources.

Troubleshooters

FFI's unswerving commitment to improving the livelihood prospects of Aceh's shell-shocked communities in the wake of the 2004 tsunami was an extreme example of a familiar concept. Like the conservation equivalent of a storm chaser, the society appears to be magnetically drawn to the world's conflict and disaster zones. This intrepid willingness to go boldly where few have gone before, and where most are disinclined to venture in future, is motivated by the knowledge that biodiversity is at its most vulnerable in such situations. There is an apocryphal account of a conversation between the head of another leading global conservation organisation and one of its corporate partners, during

which the former confided that FFI was making it possible to gain access to problematic areas and providing a platform for others to build programmes in places that might otherwise be out of bounds.

In the society's 1999 annual report, Rose had already alluded to the fact that a significant proportion of its work had been undertaken in countries where the integration of nature conservation with post-crisis recovery was a critical success factor, stating that, 'Post-crisis conditions create a special set of circumstances that represent both a threat and a significant opportunity for nature conservation. FFI

Above left Experience has taught FFI that the immediate aftermath of a period of prolonged conflict tends to present a brief window of opportunity for driving through the conservation agenda. In post-conflict Liberia, Jamison Suter, then director of the Africa Programme and a veteran operator in the country, suggested that FFI hire a local lawyer, Anyaa Vohiri. Born and raised in Liberia, but educated in the USA, Vohiri had studied environmental law before returning home in 2000. She completely rewrote the country's forest protection laws and helped to ensure their smooth passage through the new parliament that replaced the transitional legislative assembly put in place following the resignation of Charles Taylor.

Above right Indiscriminate and illegal logging represents one of the greatest threats to Liberia's rich biodiversity, but in recent years the spectre of legal and illegal mining has also loomed large, even in protected areas like Sapo National Park.

is working hard to develop a co-ordinated strategy for this increasingly prevalent phenomenon.' As we have already seen, conducting biological surveys in a former Khmer Rouge stronghold liberally strewn with land mines, defending mountain gorillas against armed poachers in war-torn Central Africa and gathering data on endangered Caribbean amphibians in the shadow of an active volcano are viewed merely as occupational hazards. Not infrequently, there is a high price to pay for such bravery. Several rangers loyal to the International Gorilla Conservation Programme were killed after they stayed behind to defend the great apes and their forest habitat rather than fleeing the 1994 Rwandan genocide. One of FFI's Cambodian counterparts succumbed to a deadly strain of drug-resistant malaria during the first expedition to the remote Cardamom Mountains in early 2000.

It is no coincidence that some of the world's most notorious trouble spots overlap with biodiversity hotspots. Liberia – already mentioned in the context of the society's capacity building activities – has been the cornerstone of FFI's West African programmes for almost two decades. Throughout its turbulent recent history, dedicated local and international staff repeatedly put their lives on the line in order to safeguard the country's threatened biodiversity. One of the main causes of conflict in Liberia, as elsewhere, was the urge to lay claim to valuable natural resources, particularly timber.

The signatures on the peace agreement were barely dry when FFI first arrived in Liberia in 1997 to help restart forest conservation in Sapo National Park at the end of a brutal six-year civil war that had killed 10 per cent of the population, displaced half of it and left the economy in tatters. The respite was brief; within three years, a civil war in neighbouring Sierra Leone had spread into Liberia, but FFI staff doggedly pursued their conservation goals until early 2003, when they were forced to suspend field activities in light of the country's descent into total anarchy. Within months of discredited president Charles Taylor stepping down, however, FFI was back in Monrovia to resurrect its programme, following closely on the heels of the UN peacekeeping force that was deployed to help the new transitional government maintain order. The efforts of FFI and its local partner culminated in the drafting of new legislation to protect Liberia's forests from the looming spectre of industrial-scale logging.

Interestingly, there was a fleeting moment in the society's evolution when it appeared that FFI might focus exclusively on post-conflict areas. This idea was floated by council members in the context of a discussion about FFI's need for a coherent strategy and a perceived need to differentiate itself from the crowd in what was becoming quite a congested marketplace for conservation organisations. The proposal was rapidly shelved, however, after Mark Rose pointed out that it would send FFI's insurance premiums through the roof.

Quick thinking

The Rapid Response Facility (RRF) is a logical extension of FFI's particular interest in supporting protected areas whose integrity is in danger of being undermined by conflict or natural disaster. Established in 2006, and now operated jointly with UNESCO World Heritage Centre and the Swiss-based Franz Weber Foundation, this emergency small grants programme was designed to safeguard natural World Heritage sites from sudden threats or crises and, as its name implies, to do so in double-quick time.

Anyone delving into the archives could not fail to be struck by the obvious parallels between the RRF and the so-called Revolving Fund, the emergency response vehicle devised by the society some 40 years earlier. In truth, the latter had been mothballed indefinitely after just five years of operation, so strictly speaking they were not so much reinventing the wheel as retrieving the prototype from the attic, dusting it down and modifying it to suit a new era. Certainly, the original 1965 model did not purport to 'catalyse innovative financing mechanisms as part of long-term support programmes', but perhaps that was no bad thing.

One of the unique selling points of the RRF is that decisions on applications for funding are typically made within just eight days. There is no compromise on the thoroughness of the review process, which is as rigorous as it is rapid. Rather, an extensive network of contacts means that the necessary due diligence can always be completed at short notice without cutting corners. Such a quick turnaround helps to ensure swift intervention, which is often the key criterion in preventing a soluble crisis from snowballing into an ecological horror show. Since inception, the fund has awarded grants totalling close to one million dollars, thereby helping to avert disaster at dozens of the most valuable biodiversity hotspots on the planet, from Colombia to Côte d'Ivoire. Perhaps unsurprisingly, almost a quarter of the grants awarded in the first decade supported emergency intervention in the

Democratic Republic of Congo (DRC), a country that embodies the difficulties of conservation in a conflict zone. And if ever there was a microcosm of that turbulent African region where fragile biodiversity is under constant siege, it has to be Garamba National Park in north-eastern DRC.

In 1996, an alarming spike in poaching activity led UNESCO to add Garamba to its so-called World Heritage in Danger list. One of 46 sites enjoying that dubious privilege, the beleaguered national park has benefited from RRF support on more than one occasion in recent years, but it has been on the society's radar for considerably longer – since the days of the Revolving Fund, in fact. One animal whose fortunes seem to have been inextricably linked with those of the park itself is the northern white rhinoceros.

As long ago as the 1960s, *Oryx* was reporting the disastrous consequences of Garamba's occupation by armed soldiers and rebels at the time of the notorious 'Congo Crisis', during which the park's rhino population plummeted from around 1,200 to a mere 100 individuals. A decade of relative calm ensued, during which numbers recovered temporarily. Aerial surveys conducted in 1976 by a Kenyan team that included Operation Oryx expedition vet Michael Woodford revealed that the population exceeded 400, including significant numbers of calves.

The long-term survival prospects of the subspecies were a different matter, however. The ever-present threat of further conflict was the pachyderm in the room, and sure enough, by 1986 numbers had fallen off a cliff. A maximum of 50 animals were estimated to survive in the wild, including fewer than 20 in Garamba and only 13 were known in captivity, the majority of them in a Czech zoo, Dvůr Králové. Conservationists were already talking about the 'last chance' to save the northern white rhino.

Once an FFI-led proposal to round up Garamba National Park's remaining individuals for captive breeding purposes had fallen foul of the interim government's intransigence – with hindsight a huge missed opportunity – their fate was effectively sealed. An *Oryx* contributor expressed frustration at the general inertia: 'It is five years since northern white rhinos were accorded higher conservation priority than any other rhinos in Africa, yet very little concrete has been achieved for them.' A further two decades elapsed, during which the nearest thing to a concrete achievement was an extension to the enclosure floor of the last captive rhinos at Dvůr Králové Zoo, a belated attempt to create an environment more conducive to breeding. With extinction beckoning, FFI hatched an ambitious and controversial last-ditch rescue plan to save the northern white rhino.

Top When conservationists talk about firefighting, they sometimes mean it literally. Emergency fire protection work in Chapada dos Veadeiros and Emas National Parks in the Brazilian central plateau helped to safeguard the *cerrado* biome, a rare savannah ecosystem widely regarded as one of South America's most important sites for large mammal conservation. In the context of climate uncertainty, these protected areas are becoming an increasingly important refuge for rare and endemic plants and animals, and will be vital in maintaining hydrological stability.

Above Garamba National Park is situated in a transition zone between the tropical forests of the Congo Basin and the Guinea-Sudano savannahs, hence its unique biodiversity. It is home to African forest elephants and bush elephants, as well as hybrids of the two species. In 2014 Garamba witnessed a military-style poaching onslaught, with helicopters and advanced weaponry used to target entire herds. At the height of the crisis, 78 elephants were killed in less than three months. Following the introduction of new anti-poaching measures supported by the RRF, elephant mortality was dramatically reduced.

Rhinos will fly

In December 2009, the last known breeding individuals in the world – just four animals – were translocated from their Czech zoo to the lush savannah grasslands and wide-open spaces where their ancestors, and indeed one of the captive rhinos, Sudan, had once thrived. The initiative provoked heated debate. Northern white rhinos had not been spotted in Garamba National Park, their last known natural refuge, for several years. The logical conclusion was that the subspecies was extinct in the wild and, therefore, doomed unless FFI intervened.

Leading rhino specialists concurred that translocation offered the best, if not the only, hope of resurrecting the population. Nevertheless, the risks to the rhinos and the overall costs of the venture were not inconsiderable. Given that the alternative was to let the subspecies slip quietly into oblivion, FFI felt morally compelled to act. To everyone's relief, the rhinos arrived safely and, gratifyingly, soon began exhibiting natural behaviour once they had acclimatised to their new home. Breeding prospects remain remote, but the secure, stress-free environment has

maximised their chances of defying the odds. In 2014 a contingency plan was put in place whereby southern white rhinos were introduced to their northern counterparts, with a view to encouraging carefully choreographed breeding combinations. Whilst any offspring would not be genetically pure, they could ultimately be bred back with pure northern whites and may therefore offer the most realistic chance of saving a dying lineage. According to Dr Rob Brett, FFI's Senior Technical Specialist and a member of the IUCN/SSC African Rhino Specialist Group since 1993, 'There are options available in the future, such as assisted reproduction. This could potentially see the generation of pure northern white rhino offspring using sperm and eggs collected from living animals, and from those that have died. However, these methods may take time to yield results.'

The last-chance saloon in which the world's remaining northern white rhinos have taken up permanent residence is Kenya's Ol Pejeta Conservancy. One of FFI's greatest and most fascinating African success stories, this 36,000-hectare sanctuary at the foot of Mount Kenya forms an integral part of the wider Laikipia ecosystem in northern Kenya, helping to safeguard essential migration corridors and an

Founder members of the new conservancy, Mark Rose, Jon Stryker of Arcus Foundation (second left) and Ian Craig of Lewa Wildlife Conservancy (right), pictured with Ali Kaka of EAWLS.

Above left Dr Peter Morkel, the Zimbabwean vet who accompanied the northern white rhinos on their voyage from the Czech Republic to Kenya, dehorning one of his charges before it is released (below) into the unfamiliar natural surroundings of Ol Pejeta Conservancy to experience the novelty of a concrete-free landscape.

Above right FFI vice-president and ambassador Stephen Fry bottle-feeds a black rhino calf at Ol Pejeta watched by the late Alastair Lucas, who funded the dramatic northern white rhino translocation from the Czech Republic to Kenya. Fry narrated *Return of the Rhino: A Last Chance to See Special*, a BBC documentary broadcast in October 2010.

ELOQUENCE PERSONIFIED

*'In the big sweet shop of conservation charities
and NGOs, you're just drawn to the one
that makes your saliva juices go, and FFI
was the one for me.'*

Stephen Fry

Actor, writer and polymath Stephen Fry has been a roving ambassador for FFI since 2009 and came on board as a vice-president that same year. Arguably best known for his comedy roles, Fry also takes an active interest in conservation issues and was persuaded to lend his name to FFI's global campaigning after gaining an insight into the society's distinctive methodology. Described by Mark Rose as 'a national treasure', Fry uses his prominent public profile to help promote FFI's work. His value in helping to spread the conservation message to a wider audience was immediately evident when a casual reference to his new ambassadorial role on his Twitter account sent a substantial proportion of his one million followers scurrying for the FFI home page and brought the website to its virtual knees. The multi-talented, globetrotting Fry has proved to be a big draw and an eloquent mouthpiece for FFI at events such as the inaugural meeting of Australia's version of the Conservation Circle and the launch of the Conservation Business Club. ∎

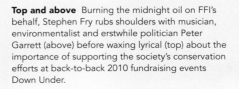

Top and above Burning the midnight oil on FFI's behalf, Stephen Fry rubs shoulders with musician, environmentalist and erstwhile politician Peter Garrett (above) before waxing lyrical (top) about the importance of supporting the society's conservation efforts at back-to-back 2010 fundraising events Down Under.

Above right The internationally acclaimed Australian actress Cate Blanchett and the then British High Commissioner to Australia, Baroness Valerie Amos, FFI vice-president since 2010, were among the many high-profile guests in attendance at the luncheon and dinner.

impressive array of East African wildlife that includes rarities such as Grevy's zebra, Jackson's hartebeest, black rhino and the rest of the obligatory 'Big Five'.

Ol Pejeta has what can only be described as a colourful history. It first came to prominence as the luxury safari getaway of the ostentatious Saudi Arabian billionaire arms dealer Adnan Khashoggi. Once labelled the world's richest man, Khashoggi fell from grace when he was implicated in the Iran-Contra arms-for-hostages affair that exposed uncomfortable truths about the political machinations of the Reagan administration. Using Ol Pejeta as collateral, Khashoggi had borrowed a jaw-droppingly large sum of money from the business magnate Tiny Rowland, himself no stranger to controversy. When the deal collapsed, Rowland laid claim to Ol Pejeta and it was absorbed into his African hotel empire along with his other safari interests.

In its current form, the conservancy owes its existence to the foresight and generosity of US philanthropist Jon Stryker, whose donation through the Arcus Foundation enabled FFI to purchase the property in 2004 'for the wildlife and people of Kenya'. In keeping with FFI's policy

of placing conservation in local hands, ownership was transferred to a Kenyan not-for-profit organisation the following year.

Of communities, cattle and canines

Ol Pejeta has hit upon an ingenious business model that combines wildlife conservation, livestock grazing, ecotourism, wheat production and community outreach. Originally a sophisticated and highly productive cattle ranch that was hostile to any form of wildlife intrusion, by the 1970s it was struggling to keep out the elephant herds that demolished fences as they sought refuge from poaching in the north. Eventually, the management team bowed to the inevitable, set up a game reserve and refocused on the more lucrative wildlife tourism business. A bizarre role reversal ensued, whereby the cattle were now perceived as unwelcome intruders, at least initially. Perceptions have since changed, however.

Counter-intuitive though it may sound, herds of livestock are not only generating income in their own right, but also, thanks to carefully controlled grazing, are accommodating an increase in wildlife numbers, which is leading to higher prey densities that in turn attract more crowd-pulling predators. This mix-and-match approach between wildlife tourism and controlled agriculture and livestock grazing makes the most economic sense, primarily because the tourism benefits more than offset any reduction in profit due to lower livestock numbers. The cattle themselves are quite charismatic and photogenic in their own right; alongside the world's largest herd of pure Boran are other rare breeds, including the spectacular Ankole longhorn, which more than lives up to its name.

This trailblazing approach to maximising biodiversity is gaining credence throughout East Africa, and other private conservancies and state parks are beginning to follow suit. Profits are ploughed back into wildlife conservation and into a wide-ranging community development programme that has already benefited from investment to the tune of almost US$5 million in areas such as health, education and water supply.

Above left A marabou stork stands sentinel on the lawn in front of Ol Pejeta House.

Left Black rhinos and other species are thriving at Ol Pejeta under the capable leadership of Richard Vigne, who has been at the helm for 20 years.

Ol Pejeta holds burgeoning numbers and a growing diversity of plains game that support some of the highest predator densities in Kenya. It also provides a lifelong refuge for rehabilitated and orphaned chimpanzees from West and Central Africa. Most significantly, it boasts the largest population of the eastern black rhino in Africa. This valuable breeding nucleus now exceeds 100 individuals and has consequently been ranked in the top 'Key 1' category in terms of continental importance and priority for conservation by the IUCN/SSC African Rhino Specialist Group. The conservancy is demonstrating that high standards of protection and management can boost population growth to a level that counteracts the adverse effects of poaching, a potential game changer for rhino conservation.

Poaching is a perennial problem, but in recent years the dramatic surge in demand for rhino horn in consumer countries like Vietnam and China has led to an alarming escalation in well-planned assaults on Ol Pejeta's rhinos. The need for increasing vigilance has led the conservancy to experiment with novel anti-poaching initiatives. Since 2013,

As well as providing sanctuary for large herbivores, Ol Pejeta is also a crucial haven for Africa's dwindling and increasingly endangered lion population.

highly trained and well-armed rangers who put their life on the line have been able to call on technological and canine support in the shape of unmanned aerial vehicles – drones to you and me – and a versatile dog squad. The drones allow remote monitoring of potential threats to wildlife, while each member of the canine defence force can do the work of a 70-person search team, day or night. Thanks to the expertise of professional trainers, Ol Pejeta's multi-talented dogs have been programmed to seek out crime scenes and track, confront and disarm poachers.

The initial success of the canine experiment looked to have paved the way for a centre of excellence at Ol Pejeta as part of a ten-year plan to provide dogs and handlers for all the poaching hotspots of northern Kenya, but that plan was shelved after it met with resistance in some quarters. Some dogs have since been deployed in other conservancies, however, and the proven training techniques have been rolled out across the continent.

Ol Pejeta's detractors point to the fact that the conservancy, surrounded as it is by an electrified fence, is not a natural area in the strictest sense, but this elephant-proof perimeter has proved vital in preventing human–wildlife conflict and helped to strengthen relations with surrounding communities. The Ol Pejeta model has garnered numerous awards. It was named 'Private Conservancy of the Year' at the 2012 Eco-Warrior Awards run by Ecotourism Kenya, in recognition of its 'responsible, respectful and sustainable' approach. This vindication of its unorthodox methods came hot on the heels of a TripAdvisor Certificate of Excellence Award that honours hospitality excellence.

More gratifying still, from a pure conservation perspective, Ol Pejeta and nearby Lewa Wildlife Conservancy were the only two protected areas in Africa to be included on the inaugural IUCN Green List, the gold standard of best practice launched at the 2014 World Parks Congress in Australia to recognise and promote the successful management of some of the most valuable natural landscapes on the planet.

FFI is also closely linked with Lewa Wildlife Conservancy, and in particular with its co-founder Ian Craig. It was Craig who introduced FFI to Jon Stryker, setting in train the purchase and rehabilitation of Ol Pejeta. As the community conservancy concept grew in popularity in northern Kenya, there was an obvious need for an umbrella organisation capable of supporting such initiatives. Craig conceived the idea together with the then Speaker of the National Assembly of Kenya, Francis ole Kaparo, and they approached FFI to help fund it.

The Northern Rangelands Trust (NRT) was established in 2004 to represent the interests of the pastoralist communities in what was previously regarded as a no-go region torn apart by tribal conflict. As one of its founder members, FFI has been involved with NRT since its inception, helping to fund a variety of activities that benefit both people and wildlife by recreating a wildlife-rich landscape. NRT's first chief operating officer was FFI's own Matt Rice, who joined the newly formed organisation on secondment. With FFI support, NRT is helping the conservancies to transform lives, keep the peace and use natural resources sustainably. Over 500 permanent jobs have been created, and NRT now works with more than 30 community conservancies across a total area covering close to two million hectares of land, which harbours increasing densities of wildlife and which, in 2011, generated revenue in excess of US$1.2 million.

Community conservancies in northern Kenya supported by FFI are vital refuges for species such as the critically endangered hirola.

ABSENT FRIENDS

Any discussion about the efficacy of combining wildlife and tourism interests for the benefit of the African people must include mention of Paul van Vlissingen, the FFI vice-president and philanthropist who died in 2006 after a long battle with cancer. For many years the head of a Dutch food and energy conglomerate from which he derived his personal fortune, van Vlissingen devoted his retirement years to the task of rehabilitating failing game reserves and was, in the words of FFI chief executive Mark Rose, 'a tireless champion of conservation throughout Africa'. His African Parks Foundation, which he launched in 2003, continues to carry out pioneering work to safeguard the continent's wildlife tourist attractions, using the income generated to help improve the lives of some of Africa's most impoverished communities. ∎

What price biodiversity?

Short-term profiteering that results in the loss of forest cover has serious long-term environmental and economic consequences.

The secret of success for a community conservancy such as Ol Pejeta or Lewa, and indeed the NRT enterprise as a whole, is to demonstrate that habitat conservation can reap economic rewards comparable to, and more sustainable than, the financial returns generated by habitat conversion for agricultural or industrial ends. This principle is just as valid for the world's rainforests as it is for Africa's wide-open savannah grasslands. Taken in isolation, timber extraction is a highly profitable business, but it comes at a high price. Once the associated costs are taken into consideration – soil erosion, nutrient loss, flooding, lower water quality, reduced carbon storage, temperature changes and rainfall patterns, not to mention wildlife habitat destruction – it quickly becomes apparent that forests are worth more standing than lying horizontal on the back of a logging truck.

By 2008, FFI was talking openly of the need to put a price on biodiversity and, indeed, saw fit to devote an entire issue of its annual magazine to the subject. The terminology was a potential turn-off, of course. Diving into the murky depths of the conservationist's lexicon, it resurfaced with another pearl: *valuing ecosystem goods and services*. Whilst this did not have

quite the same ring as saving Sumatran tigers or protecting a pristine primate paradise, the underlying message was nevertheless a valid one. As the introductory article pointed out, beneath the regrettably dull terminology lay an issue fundamental to the long-term survival of humankind and all the other species with which we share this planet. FFI's project portfolio is crammed with examples of how 'avoided destruction' – keeping ecosystems intact – can add value.

As early as 2006, FFI had listened with interest to the first mutterings about the use of so-called carbon credits as a novel mechanism to protect forest ecosystems. At first, the idea of rewarding countries and local communities for keeping their carbon-capturing forests standing was greeted with scepticism at best. Attitudes changed in light of the findings of the Stern report, which confirmed that 20–25 per cent of global carbon dioxide emissions were the result of deforestation, but who would be bold enough to accept the challenge of converting a wacky academic theory into a practical conservation tool? With characteristic bravado, FFI took up the gauntlet.

Right Sumatran tigers are occasionally recorded by judiciously placed camera traps, but are otherwise very rarely caught on camera. This photograph of a male tiger in Ulu Masen was captured in broad daylight in 2016 by Teuku Boyhaqi, one of FFI's intrepid team of rangers, who was concealed just 30 metres away when he pressed the shutter, no doubt with trembling fingers.

Below Asian elephants on Sumatra are among the so-called charismatic megafauna whose long-term survival will depend on the continued existence of large tracts of undisturbed wilderness such as the Ulu Masen rainforest complex.

The biologically rich Ulu Masen forest complex in the Indonesian province of Aceh is a crucial last refuge for endangered Sumatran tigers, elephants, rhinos and orangutans. It also guarantees water supplies to five million people and prevents an estimated 3.3 million tonnes of carbon dioxide emissions every year. It was here that FFI began to promote the concept of avoided deforestation in an effort to ensure that post-tsunami reconstruction in Sumatra did not wreak further environmental devastation.

As the key government partner in Aceh, spearheading the biggest NGO-led conservation project in Asia at the time, FFI was in an influential position, not least because the then governor of the province – and de facto decision maker on forest management – was a former member of its field staff, openly committed to a green, sustainable policy for Aceh. If ever there was a perfect opportunity to test the water, this was it. Once the provincial government had registered the fact that there was a potential profit to be made from *not* subjecting its forests to the archetypal chainsaw massacre, its response was overwhelmingly positive.

FFI teamed up with Carbon Conservation, a small Australian company and self-proclaimed 'global leader in Avoided Deforestation voluntary carbon credit creation and financing', and set about developing a model that would illustrate the value of an intact forest when compared to an anticipated future scenario in which logging, oil palm plantations, urban expansion and road development were the order of the day. The relevant paperwork was completed in time for the invitingly named *13th Conference of the Parties of the United Nations Framework Convention on Climate Change*, held in Bali in December 2007.

This latest attempt to secure agreement on the shape of a new set of dentures for the largely toothless Kyoto Protocol provided FFI with a timely opportunity to showcase how an avoided deforestation project might work in practice. The inconvenient truth, according to no less a figure than former US vice-president Al Gore, was that there were too many obstacles to success. Undeterred by the hopelessness of the uphill struggle, FFI accepted its Sisyphean task and was rewarded when its Aceh project became the darling of the avoided deforestation movement at the conference. It was here that *Reduced Emissions from Deforestation & Degradation* (REDD) was rescued from the ruins of climate change policy negotiations, reinvigorating the international process.

The vast Ulu Masen rainforest ecosystem in northern Sumatra, which harbours some of Asia's most iconic wildlife and acts as a vital watershed for the human population, became a testing ground for the REDD concept, whereby biologically rich but economically challenged countries are rewarded for keeping their forests standing.

REDD is the new green

By venturing into the REDD zone, FFI was effectively committing itself to developing a new financial product. Joe Heffernan, the driving force behind the project at that time, readily acknowledged that they were out of their depth. 'Little of what we were doing seemed to have ever been done before. This was truly groundbreaking stuff and we were on a steeper learning curve than we had believed possible.' In need of a hard-nosed, innovative commercial partner, FFI signed a three-year agreement, the first of its kind, with Australian bank Macquarie Group. The mission of this joint task force was to develop a suite of projects aimed at generating sustainable revenues from the sale of carbon credits, in order to reward local communities and authorities for protecting their forests.

This was merely the first step on what has proved to be a long, arduous and frequently frustrating journey. Detractors would argue that the only tangible plus point since REDD was launched has been the mathematical symbol that now adorns the latest iteration of the concept. The addition of a 'plus' sign indicates that this new, improved version of REDD+ includes 'forest conservation, sustainable management of forests and enhancement of forest carbon stocks'.

REDD+ is described on FFI's website as 'an evolving mechanism', the long-term effectiveness of which will depend on combining a top-down policy-led approach with grassroots project-based initiatives in forest areas under threat. FFI has invested heavily in developing a portfolio of REDD+ projects designed to test the practicality of the concept across six countries. Progress at government level has been painfully slow, however; in 2012, Frank Momberg, FFI's Regional Project Development Director for Asia-Pacific at that time, was lamenting the fact that REDD+ is severely constrained, particularly in certain countries, by the need to negotiate an endless bureaucratic minefield: 'In relation to the huge amounts of donor funding available in Indonesia, the outputs are very limited.' With its uncompromising commitment to zero corruption and super-clean governance, FFI has inevitably found itself at the back of the queue. In the meantime, FFI continues to promote the REDD+ concept through field-based demonstration activities and policy work and is a regional leader in the development of what it calls community forestry REDD+. In Indonesia, where REDD+ is just one of many components in a broad, sustainable forest agenda, FFI can claim to be delivering on the principles of REDD+ even though a financial mechanism that obviates the need for donor funding remains elusive. It is clearly a complicated

business, but FFI deserves a great deal of credit – of the non-carbon variety – for persevering in the face of seemingly insurmountable odds. And that perseverance is starting to reap tangible rewards. In West Kalimantan, analyses of peat depth conducted by FFI led to the re-designation of approximately 20,000 hectares of peat swamp forest, affording it legal protection from conversion to oil palm plantation. Across the Indonesian archipelago, efforts to support communities in securing legal rights to their traditional forest areas have contributed significantly to national social forestry targets, bringing more than 70,000 hectares under community management in one project area alone and simultaneously safeguarding vital Sumatran tiger habitat.

Pilot project

In Liberia – where, as we have seen, the society has had an enduring presence since the mid 1990s – FFI is pioneering the development of the country's first REDD+ project in close collaboration with a government whose enlightened attitude to forest conservation is a refreshing contrast with the wholesale plundering that characterised Charles Taylor's tenure. The site of this project is the Wonegizi Proposed Protected Area, which forms part of a massive transboundary forest complex. The Wonegizi Community REDD+ pilot, as it is known, will establish a new kind of rural economy in Liberia, combining sustainable agricultural practices that reduce deforestation with income generation from the sale of carbon credits to create financial incentives for the communities that are directly linked to the continued protection of the forest. The project has the potential to serve as a model of best practice not only in bottom-up REDD+ development but also for collaborative, community-led management of protected areas within and outside Liberia.

As FFI began to delve more deeply into the complexities of the latest financial instruments, it was apposite that this coincided with the election of a new chairman with impeccable financial services credentials. A former director of Schroders plc, with responsibility for private banking and alternative investments, Andrew Sykes had already served an apprenticeship as treasurer – and worked closely with FFI's chief executive Mark Rose – for three years prior to his appointment as chairman in 2007. In conjunction with his successor as treasurer, Philip Prettejohn, Sykes has helped the organisation to navigate its way relatively smoothly through the potentially choppy waters of an ambitious expansion programme.

COSTING THE EARTH

FFI's work on REDD+ forms an integral part of its Conservation Finance & Enterprise programme, originally launched in 2007 as the Environmental Markets programme to combat the inexorable erosion of what it calls 'natural capital'. It aims to ensure that the true value of ecosystem goods and services is fully appreciated by the individuals, businesses and governments that benefit from them. In particular, it has developed and tested a range of innovative – yes, that word again – market-based instruments that promote the protection of threatened habitats and help secure tangible benefits for the local communities who depend on them. One such example was the FFI-led Natural Value Initiative, which 'helps financial institutions to understand and address the biodiversity impacts and associated risks of the financial services they provide', so that they can build these considerations into the decisions that they make regarding their investments. Established in 2007, and focusing particularly on the food, beverage and tobacco industries, the initiative provided a benchmarking tool that would enable institutional investors to understand whether, and to what degree, companies were managing their impacts on biodiversity and so-called ecosystem services such as water, clean

The Natural Value Initiative was the brainchild of Annalisa Grigg who, as the then Director of Corporate Affairs and Environmental Markets for FFI, spearheaded the development of a number of tools and methodologies for evaluating corporate biodiversity performance that have since been widely embraced.

air and healthy soil. The benchmarking tool was created in conjunction with investors from Europe, Brazil, USA and Australia that collectively manage around £400 billion in assets. The companies that fail to pass muster in the eyes of increasingly sophisticated and eco-savvy investors risk losing out in future. ∎

*'Having seen what they do first-hand all over the globe,
I can wholeheartedly endorse what FFI stands for.'*

Rove McManus

New frontiers

It was no accident that FFI's REDD brigade teamed up with an Australian bank in 2008. By that stage moves were afoot to establish a permanent presence in the country, partly as a focal point for the society's existing programme of work in the Asia-Pacific region, but also in response to Australia's perceived determination to play a more significant role in supporting global conservation. FFI Australia was formally launched in August 2008, with a remit to support local conservation infrastructure, consolidate existing relationships with several of the country's key zoos and secure additional support from foundations, philanthropists and business leaders with a shared commitment to protecting the natural world.

With FFI's traditional supporter base on both sides of the Atlantic in the grip of a global recession, this proved to be an opportune moment to tap into Antipodean beneficence. And a dynamic marketing professional by the name of Rachel Etherington proved to be the ideal choice as director of development to help open doors Down Under. Among the new recruits to the ranks of FFI's major donors was Alastair Lucas, then vice-chairman of Goldman Sachs in Australia. It was Lucas who helped finance the translocation of the four northern white rhinos to Ol Pejeta. The laconic Aussie declined to reveal the details of his donation, and inquisitive journalists had to be content with a deadpan response: 'Shipping rhinos across the world is not cheap. They don't fit in economy seats.'

Three years later, FFI Australia launched its own version of the Conservation Circle, described on the website as 'an exclusive group of forward-thinking philanthropists, scientists and business executives who are concerned about conservation and have the power to make a big difference'. Founder members included Oliver Yates, formerly an investment banker at Macquarie Group, who had earlier recommended Etherington as a star fundraiser in the making.

The Australia programme also began supporting conservation initiatives in several local areas, including the recently designated Great Sandy Biosphere in south-east Queensland,

Top Rove McManus, former stand-up comedian and now Australia's most successful talk-show host, has been a vice-president of FFI since 2008 and, as a roving ambassador for the society, can also lay claim to being a living, breathing example of nominative determinism.

Above The late Alastair Lucas, seen here addressing fellow guests at a luncheon event to promote FFI, funded the northern white rhino translocation.

where FFI and the Burnett Mary Regional Group joined forces to promote the idea that conservation is not incompatible with social, economic and cultural development.

Indawgyi Lake, one of FFI's flagship project sites in Myanmar, was designated as
a UNESCO Biosphere Reserve in 2017, thereby ensuring that this vital wetland is
sustainably managed for local communities and biodiversity. The lake and its
watershed support the livelihoods of some 50,000 people and also harbour a
multitude of mammals, birds, fish and reptiles, including the lesser whistling duck
(top left) and freshwater needlefish (top right).

Burmese days

Australia was not the only new frontier that beckoned for FFI at the end of the decade. Improvements in the political situation in Myanmar, which culminated in the release from house arrest of Aung San Suu Kyi in November 2010, opened up the country to an unprecedented degree. Frank Momberg, still FFI's man in Indonesia at the time, took advantage of this new climate of opportunity to satisfy his curiosity about the status of Myanmar's fauna and flora. Ostensibly wearing a tourist hat, but inevitably viewing the experience through a biologist's eyes, he was struck by the enormous potential to influence conservation policy at a crucial juncture in Myanmar's metamorphosis. At his behest, FFI wasted no time in trying to establish links with the emerging grass-roots organisations that were keen to secure a voice for local communities.

Although the country's natural capital, particularly its timber, has already been heavily exploited by overseas interests working in tandem with the military regime, Myanmar still harbours biological riches that most countries can only dream of. Its remaining tracts of forest are home to some of the most spectacular wildlife in mainland South East Asia. With two-thirds of the country's population living below the poverty line, local communities depend heavily on natural resources for survival, yet have been largely excluded from decisions about how to safeguard Myanmar's protected areas.

To rectify this situation, FFI joined forces with a local partner, Biodiversity and Nature Conservation Association (BANCA), to help nascent environmental organisations in northern Myanmar overcome the teething problems that would inevitably arise as they began working alongside the state authorities to tackle threats such as illegal logging,

First ever artist's impression, by Martin Aveling, of the Myanmar snub-nosed monkey, *Rhinopithecus strykeri*, named in honour of Jon Stryker, who has made a valuable contribution to the conservation of this and other primate species.

hunting and agricultural encroachment. Funding was secured from, among others, the European Union to help support an ambitious long-term partnership programme focusing on collaborative protected area management and community forestry.

If evidence was needed that Myanmar's biodiversity was one of Asia's best-kept secrets, the first joint surveys undertaken in early 2010 by FFI and local conservationists certainly provided it. The biggest revelation was a primate species that proved to be new to science. Descriptions furnished by local hunters of a monkey with unusual facial features had already aroused considerable interest among the scientific community, and a dead specimen collected during an expedition to the remote state of Kachin confirmed the presence of a new species, the Myanmar snub-nosed monkey. The first recorded images of a live specimen were captured the following year by camera traps set judiciously in suitable montane forest habitat close to the border with China. In 2014, a member of the FFI field survey team became the first biologist in the world to encounter the new species in the wild and, despite his hands shaking wildly with excitement, succeeded in filming a large group of this elusive primate leaping across a gap in the forest canopy. Euphoria at the discovery of a new species was quickly tempered by the knowledge that its situation was precarious. With a total population estimated at around 300 individuals, confined to an area of north-east Myanmar where hydropower development and logging are having a seriously detrimental impact, it was no surprise when the Myanmar snub-nosed

monkey was classified by IUCN as Critically Endangered. Mercifully, at the time of writing the area seems destined to be gazetted as a new national park, a designation that should help to encourage dialogue with the Chinese authorities and discourage illegal transboundary logging. Whilst Myanmar amounted to new territory for FFI from a

Above In 2011, camera traps set by an FFI-led survey team recorded the first ever images of the recently described Myanmar snub-nosed monkey.

Opposite Saw Soe Aung (left) and That Nhei Aung (centre) celebrate capturing the Myanmar snub-nosed monkey on film.

CAUGHT ON CAMERA

The camera-trap images of the Myanmar snub-nosed monkey were a classic example of how this valuable tool of the trade has contributed to the discovery of new and vanishingly rare – or just secretive, cryptic and maddeningly elusive – species at potential and current FFI project sites. Undeterred by the disappointment of failing to capture footage of the mythical *orang pendek*, freelance photographer Jeremy Holden has enthusiastically embraced camera trapping as an indispensable weapon in his armoury, and was responsible for securing many of the intriguing images featured here. ■

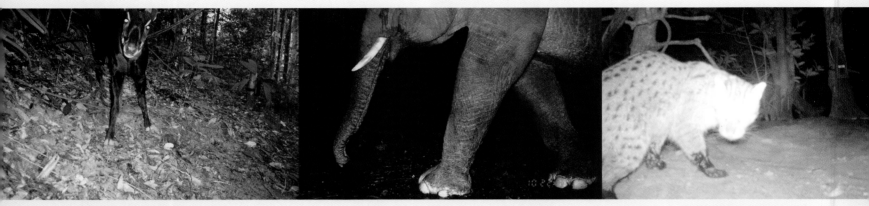

SAOLA, VIETNAM   ASIAN ELEPHANT, SUMATRA   FISHING CAT, CAMBODIA

CHIMPANZEE, LIBERIA   BONGO, SOUTH SUDAN   BANTENG, CAMBODIA

OWSTON'S PALM CIVET, VIETNAM   MALAYAN TAPIR, SUMATRA   TAKIN, MYANMAR

SUN BEAR, SUMATRA   CLOUDED LEOPARD, SUMATRA   RED PANDA, MYANMAR

SUMATRAN TIGER, SUMATRA   HAIRY-NOSED OTTER, VIETNAM   GIANT PANGOLIN, SOUTH SUDAN

SIAMESE CROCODILE, CAMBODIA   SUMATRAN RABBIT, SUMATRA   ASIAN WILD DOG, SUMATRA

PYGMY HIPPOPOTAMUS, LIBERIA   FOREST ELEPHANT, SOUTH SUDAN   ZEBRA DUIKER, LIBERIA

THE DISCOVERY CHANNEL

Discovering new species or new populations of a species is not an end in itself for FFI, but discovery is one of a number of channels through which it communicates its broader conservation message to the global community. As we have seen, the rediscovery of the Antiguan racer, for example, provided the catalyst for a broader and hugely successful conservation programme that has benefited other endangered Caribbean wildlife. The first images of a snub-nosed monkey, photo-trapped in a remote corner of Myanmar, ignited national interest and pride in the country's unique natural heritage and focused global attention on the importance of conserving its forests.

In a world where we are in danger of losing species more quickly than they can be described, new discoveries provide vital ammunition in the battle for hearts and minds that is central to the fight against biodiversity loss. The list of finds in which FFI and its partners have historically had a hand is a long one, and any attempt to do justice to them here would have made this book – to quote Laurie Anderson – thick enough to stun an ox.

Grazing on the smorgasbord of examples scattered throughout the previous chapters certainly whets the appetite, but the veritable feast of recent discoveries relating to Vietnamese primates warrants special mention here. The twenty-first century has already witnessed a steady stream of morale-boosting ape and monkey revelations with which FFI is intimately linked, including the 2002 rediscovery of the cao vit gibbon in north-east Vietnam. Potentially game-changing new populations of

Vietnam boasts one of the most diverse and spectacular arrays of primate species on the planet, including the critically endangered Tonkin snub-nosed monkey (above left), and FFI continues to find innovative ways to highlight their plight, both locally and internationally. In 2017, a spontaneous collaboration between FFI staff and a dynamic Facebook group, operating collectively as Artists & Biologists Unite for Nature (ABUN), led to the production of this series of artworks (above right) to promote the society's conservation efforts on behalf of the critically endangered Delacour's langur.

other critically endangered primates – the Tonkin snub-nosed monkey, Francois' langur and, most recently, Delacour's langur – have also come to light during the course of other FFI-led surveys in Vietnam. The situation for all three of these monkeys remains perilous, of course, but every new population represents another potential lifeline for the species and a small beacon of hope. ∎

This treetop camera trap in Myanmar captured images of the arboreal, elusive and endangered red panda.

geographical perspective – at least since the heady days when Burma formed part of the old empire – the forest protection issues that it needed to address were really just a variation on a familiar theme. As usual, the critical success factor would be to devise locally driven solutions, in this case a community-based conservation programme that aims to create alternative livelihood opportunities for a forest-dependent indigenous population. Given its long association with the conservation of terrestrial ecosystems such as tropical rainforests, combating deforestation amounted to just another day at the office for FFI. But the threats to Myanmar's biodiversity and local livelihoods were not confined to the destruction of its forest landscapes; its coastline, coral reefs and marine diversity were also under pressure, and their plight was symptomatic of a far wider problem.

During a 2003 interview with the society, FFI's vice-president and benefactor Dr Lisbet Rausing lamented the destructive, wasteful and unsustainable exploitation of the world's marine resources, encapsulated in this graphic image: 'Imagine huge aerial fishing fleets floating over the African savannah, their giant nets scooping up all life – all elephants, all wildebeest, all zebras, all lions – uprooting trees and bushes, grass and flowers, and then grinding that squirming mass into animal feed. This is what is happening at sea.'

This growing crisis for marine life across the globe was already on FFI's radar, and it had been unobtrusively but actively committed to coastal marine conservation for many years – from mangrove protection in Indonesia to the creation of sea turtle sanctuaries in East Africa and Nicaragua. But there was a sense that it could be doing more. In that same interview, Rausing had given voice to the wish that the society might one day be in a position to become more actively and widely involved in this relatively neglected area of conservation: 'I hope that as FFI grows, it will focus also on marine conservation, especially in coastal areas.' Some eight years later, that hope would be realised.

CHAPTER 11

FULL CIRCLE

'FFI has been tireless in its efforts to protect terrestrial habitats and wildlife in the last century; it intends to put the same energy and commitment into securing the future for ocean life in the next hundred years.'

Professor Callum Roberts, Marine Conservation Biologist, 2011

In worldwide conservation terms, the crisis in our oceans has long been the blue whale in the bathroom, but as the third millennium unfolded it was becoming increasingly hard to ignore. Among those adding their voice to the growing clamour for action was Callum Roberts, Professor of Marine Conservation at the University of York and a key protagonist, both before and after his appointment to council, in FFI's decision to take up the gauntlet and make a more strategic commitment to marine conservation.

Sea change

Back in 2003, Dr Lisbet Rausing had urged FFI to put marine conservation on its map, expressing the view that saving marine life was the most urgent global challenge. Rausing had also made it clear that the Arcadia Fund would not be averse to providing significant financial support for such an initiative. Serendipitously, it transpired that behind the scenes FFI had already been quietly but methodically putting together its very own marine conservation strategy, ably assisted by Professor Callum Roberts, whose role as a member of council was pivotal in enabling the society to develop its marine programme. FFI was renowned for being willing and able to operate outside its comfort zone, and, driven by a genuine angst about the unremittingly depressing reports of precipitous species declines, coral reef devastation, ocean plastics pollution and the unsustainable

Opposite Shoal of juvenile fish in Koh Rong Archipelago, the site of Cambodia's first large-scale marine protected area.

hoovering of marine resources, it had already resolved to champion what was the ecosystem equivalent of a neglected species. By the time Rausing had reiterated her interest in supporting marine conservation – and, with Peter Baldwin, had provided an initial US$1 million injection of funds to enable FFI to put together a programme – the society's strategy was already set fair. Buoyed by the support of a further US$5 million grant from Arcadia, FFI formally launched its ambitious marine programme in 2011.

There is no evidence that the unsustainable exploitation of fish and marine mammals was on the agenda of the society's founders, whose primary concern was the dramatic decline in terrestrial wildlife. Nevertheless, a trawl through the early decades of its *Journal* reveals an increasing interest in marine conservation issues and, in particular, a preoccupation with the unbridled short-term profiteering of the whaling industry. As early as 1913, contributors were bemoaning the lack of effective legislation to halt the mindless slaughter of Antarctic whales and pointing out the inevitable long-term consequences of over-harvesting. At a meeting in the House of Commons that year, Edmund Meade-Waldo, whom we previously encountered as an early champion of mountain gorillas, condemned the destruction of whales, elephant seals (which he referred to as 'sea elephants'), penguins and albatrosses by Norwegian whaling stations in the Falkland Islands and proposed to write to *The Times* in order to publicise the problem and pressurise the Colonial Office into greater vigilance. In 1929, lamenting humankind's inability to resist 'killing the goose that lays the golden eggs', the society predicted that the last whale would disappear before the law-makers had got their act together.

Toothless whale watchers

Nearly half a century later, in the early 1970s, we find honorary secretary Richard Fitter and Ian Grimwood, of Operation Oryx fame, pressing the whaling nations to reduce quotas in order to protect Antarctic whales from unsustainable hunting levels.

The society had repeatedly found itself at loggerheads with the International Whaling Commission (IWC) from the moment this was set up in 1948, ostensibly to regulate the catching of the great whales. Throughout the following decades, a procession of the society's representatives took their seats at a succession of IWC meetings. One after another, they lobbied for the introduction of scientifically recommended quotas, and even moratoria, that would allow global whale stocks the chance to recover, but to little effect. Isolated minor victories were overshadowed by the overall sense of an inexorable descent to the point of no return. Rather than reflecting badly on the society's powers of persuasion, the lack of progress is testament to the blind intransigence of the whaling nations and the toothlessness of the commission itself at this time.

At the IWC meeting in London in 1973, for example, the society pushed in vain for a ten-year global moratorium on whaling, with Fitter condemning the 'tunnel vision' of the so-called specialists who denied the biological case for a temporary respite from the slaughter. Two years later, it was déjà vu all over again, as the honorary secretary was to be heard lambasting the IWC for taking on a full-time secretary and moving to new offices in Cambridge just as the industry it represented was on the brink of self-destruction. So great was the society's frustration that the cover of the December 1977 issue of *Oryx* was emblazoned with the dramatic headline: *Whaling Industry Commits Suicide*. The following year, another disastrous decision –

9

THREATS TO ARCTIC ANIMALS

INTERNATIONAL MEASURES NEEDED FOR PRESERVATION

From a Special Correspondent

The Arctic is being thrown open to man; meteorological stations, air fields, and defence bases are spreading northwards. We ought to consider carefully the animals whose territory we are thus invading, if we are to avoid a repetition of the tragic effects of man's impact on the fauna of other new countries.

The musk ox inhabits arctic and near-arctic regions from Greenland to Alaska, including most of the larger islands except Baffin Island. It is well able to defend itself against its natural enemy, the wolf, for the musk oxen stand their ground in a solid phalanx, guarding their calves. But these tactics, so successful against the wolf, have been its undoing against men armed with firearms, and 50 years ago it became in danger of extinction.

That the northern climate also may bear hardly on the musk ox, as on other arctic animals, has been shown by Professor Spärck of Denmark. He tells how in east Greenland last winter a heavy snowfall formed a layer of snow two or three metres thick. Hundreds, perhaps thousands, of musk oxen died of starvation, probably including all the one- and two-year-old calves.

In Canada the musk ox is now carefully protected, notably in the Thelon

game reserve in the North-West Territories, ... during the nineteenth century, but was reintroduced in 1930, when 34 young musk oxen were brought from Greenland and placed on Nunivak island. These have increased, but in the spring some of them seem to have a tendency to go out on to the sea ice, and when the break-up comes they are drowned.

The continued existence of the caribou is necessary not only for its own sake but because it forms an important part of Eskimo diet. Its only important enemy apart from man is the wolf, and so efforts have been made to protect the caribou from the wolf. But nature is seldom as simple as that, and recent investigations have shown that however good the summer grazing the critical time for the caribou is the winter. Its food is then lichen, without which it cannot survive. Lichen can easily be destroyed by over-grazing, and as it grows slowly cannot then re-establish itself in time to save the caribou from starvation. So survival of the caribou depends upon limitation of its own numbers and this, in the interior of the far north, can be carried out only by the wolf. The wolf, therefore, not only preys on the caribou but helps to preserve it.

No arctic animal is harder to investigate than the polar bear, for in winter climatic conditions preclude observation and the females are in winter quarters beneath the snow. In summer the bears are out on the ice floes where any estimate of their numbers is extremely difficult, and where they are usually outside territorial waters and thus not within reach of ordinary legal protection.

HUNTING POLAR BEARS

In Canada varying degrees of protection are afforded to the polar bear. Manitoba does not allow sportsmen to hunt it. The Federal Government levies a royalty of $5 on each skin exported from the North-West Territories: for the year 1952-53 the total was 433. The area is vast and this may not be considered a great number. But besides this the United States has a fortnightly meteorological air service to the Pole, and a necessary survival service in Alaska.

It has been alleged that the depredations of this service on the polar bear population, and also on the great Alaskan brown bear, are heavy; in fact that " you cannot come back from the Arctic without having shot a polar bear." The effects of this must still be local and comparatively small, but the number of these meteorological stations will increase. Furthermore, in Canada

hunting of polar bears by Eskimos. This is understandable and could not have been questioned in the days before Eskimos acquired firearms. Perhaps the time has come for a reconsideration of this policy, in some areas at least.

Since about 1930 there has been a heavy decline in the stock of polar bears on the shores of Greenland. This may be judged by the number of polar bears shot, which has been falling everywhere each year, especially on the east coast. Protection is certainly necessary and the Danish Government has established a close season for the polar bear on the northern part of the east coast of Greenland from June 1 to the end of October.

NORWEGIAN SANCTUARY

There are many polar bears in the Spitsbergen archipelago, where the Norwegian Government has made a complete sanctuary of the island of King Karl's Land, thought to be an important breeding-place. On the other hand, fortnightly shooting trips are made by one vessel during the summer to Spitsbergen, at a time when the polar bear skin is almost useless. One such trip resulted in 14 polar bears being shot. The bears are also killed by sealers, chiefly to obtain live cubs, which fetch high prices.

The walrus is an essential animal to the Eskimo. It provides meat for man and dog, blubber for heating, leather for harness, and tusks for trade. The Eskimos of the Thule district of north-west Greenland depend almost entirely on it throughout the winter. Yet the walrus is steadily decreasing. In the seventeenth century it was said to breed on Sable Island, off Nova Scotia, and within the past 200 years was commonly hunted in the Gulf of St. Lawrence. Now it seldom appears south of Hudson Strait. And whereas the walrus used to appear in large herds on the west coast of Egedesminde, just within the Arctic Circle, it is now rarely seen south of Melville Bay, 600 miles to the north. This contraction northward has been caused not so much by changes of climate as by man.

The food of the walrus consists mainly of bivalves, which it must seek in comparatively shallow waters, and this makes it vulnerable on its known foraging grounds. There is a resident population of walrus at Foxe Basin, west of Baffin Island; but the walrus is also a migrant, though its movements are not yet fully understood. Some walruses, after breeding in the ice-floes of the Davis Strait, move up the coast of Greenland past Melville Bay and there join in wintering stock in the Thule district. Migration continues so far north as Inglefield Land, and perhaps even to Washington Land, at latitude 80deg. N. Later there are southward movements along the Thule peninsula and the east coast of Ellesmere Island. In fact the migration more or less encircles Baffin Bay, but it does not seem to be annual; walruses possibly spend several winters on the way.

NEED FOR PROTECTION

The Danish Government is aware of the importance of walrus conservation. Protected areas and close seasons have been established and walruses may be killed only by Greenlanders and in limited numbers at that. Although in the Thule district there is no limitation on the rights of the polar Eskimos to hunt walrus, there is a valuable rule which in most cases forbids the use of the rifle until the walrus has been harpooned. This prevents the waste and cruelty involved in the escape of wounded animals.

It would be good if a similar regulation could be made in Canada, where the possession of rifles by Eskimos, combined with Government relief and family allowances, has reduced the importance of careful stalking and economical killing. There are reports of much reckless shooting, pregnant females being killed and wounded animals escaping. The Canadian Government is, of course, aware of this situation and steps to remedy it are being considered.

Animals of the Arctic, because of their habits and distribution, need consideration on an international level. In order that necessary action may not be taken too late the International Union for the Protection of Nature has set up a committee under Professor Spärck, of Denmark, to consider the status as ...

---

sanctioning a ninefold increase in the north Pacific sperm whale quota on the basis of questionable data from a single Japanese scientist – was greeted with near apoplexy. A statement from the then Fauna Preservation Society, read out at the end of the 1978 IWC meetings, amounted to a searing indictment of the commission: 'The Society believes in the use of wildlife resources for the benefit of the human population of the world. All the IWC has succeeded in doing in the past 30 years is to deprive the world of an extremely valuable natural resource.' The normally mild-mannered Fitter was moved in *The Penitent Butchers* to accuse IWC of doing little more than to 'preside over a slight slowing down of the process of extinction'.

It wasn't all doom and gloom for Antarctic wildlife. In May 1967 the erstwhile FPS president Lord Willingdon spoke in the House of Lords debate in support of the bill that spawned the Antarctic Treaty Act, aimed at conserving that pristine continent's fragile flora and fauna, including pelagic mammals. In stark contrast to the head-in-the-sand approach of the whaling fraternity, here was a treaty being drawn up in good time, before irreparable damage had been done, rather than after the event.

Another example of a pre-emptive strike for marine conservation came in 1972 when the Antarctic Treaty nations signed a convention to protect all Antarctic seals on the sea ice in the Southern Ocean – an area covering one-fifth of the surface of the globe. This was the first time that governments had acted to protect animal populations *before* commercial exploitation had actually begun. The six species to benefit from these measures were the crabeater, leopard, Ross, southern elephant, southern fur and Weddell seals.

Decades earlier, the plight of their northern counterparts and other Arctic fauna had become the focus of conservation attention at the IUCN conference in Copenhagen, after the society led a successful protest against the proposed slaughter of walruses by a 1954 hunting expedition in Norwegian waters.

On the home front, the FPS was successful in securing a ban on the import of baleen whale products, and no sooner had it received government assent in 1973 than it pressed for a similar ban on sperm whale products. It was also quick to

Writing anonymously in *The Times* in 1955, the society's then secretary Colonel Boyle commended the Danish government's enlightened walrus conservation policy and politely suggested that Canada might wish to follow their example.

SEAL APPEAL

The Mediterranean monk seal is one of the world's most endangered marine mammals, with a highly fragmented global population thought to number no more than 500 individuals. Persecution by fishermen, who view the seals as direct competitors for their catch, has contributed to the species' decline.

In 1981 the society launched its Mediterranean monk seal appeal, designed to raise funds that would enable Greek fishermen in the northern Aegean Sea to be paid compensation for loss of income. A *Sunday Times* article by the journalist Brian Jackman, who had already put his penmanship to good use to help mountain gorillas, elicited a generous response from readers to the tune of £8,000. The society's intervention on behalf of the endangered seal led directly to the establishment of what is now the National Marine Park of Alonnisos Northern Sporades, currently the largest marine protected area in Europe. As John Burton – secretary of the society at that time – was quick to point out, this is yet another example of a very successful but little-known FFI initiative.

Over three decades later, by a quirk of fate, the same species is once again playing a central role in FFI's marine conservation efforts in the Mediterranean, this time in Turkey. With its remote cliffs, caverns and secluded coves, Gökova Bay is one of the last remaining sanctuaries for the Mediterranean monk seal. As Turkey's first community-managed marine protected area, it is also an acknowledged global biodiversity hotspot that supports important seagrass beds and harbours endangered fish species including angel sharks, giant devil rays and dusky groupers. FFI and its partners are encouraging local communities here to take an active role in protecting the marine environment, as well as creating opportunities for fishermen to supplement their income by venturing into the realms of sustainable tourism. ∎

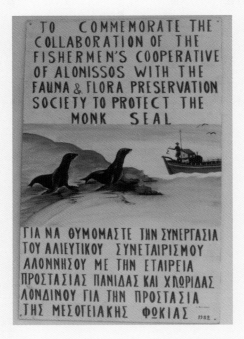

Bilingual poster from the society's 1981 campaign on behalf of the Mediterranean monk seal in Greece and (below) an intimate encounter with a semi-tame Mediterranean monk seal that frequents Turkey's Gökova Bay.

The society was urging the protection of grey seals 50 years before they featured on this 1979 FPS Christmas card courtesy of artist Bruce Pearson.

savage the perceived incompetence of the Natural Environment Research Council, an umbrella body comprising several previously autonomous environmental research organisations, for a 'lamentably timid' report on marine wildlife conservation produced by its own working party, which was reluctant to recommend establishing coastal nature reserves and marine parks.

The society was advocating conservation action for marine reptiles as early as the 1960s. Writing in *Oryx* in September 1969, the firebrand Tom Harrisson, that familiar scourge of IUCN bureaucracy, warned of an impending marine turtle tragedy and outlined a scenario in which extinction by the end of the twentieth century was a real possibility for several species. The society helped Harrisson to promote the work of the Species Survival Commission's specialist turtle group, calling for immediate action to halt the decline of marine chelonids. The proposed conservation measures included incubation and hatching schemes, research into global patterns of exploitation, a wide-ranging public information campaign and the establishment of scientifically managed sanctuaries.

Once more onto the beach

A seven-year study of the marine turtles on islands scattered over more than one million square miles of the western Indian Ocean, assisted by FPS, revealed that the number of nesting green turtles was down to around 5,000 females. This figure was disconcertingly low in its own right, but when juxtaposed with the fact that 80 years earlier 12,000 turtles were recorded on a single island, it was indicative of a catastrophic decline driven by overexploitation and habitat destruction.

FFI has long recognised that one of the keys to success in marine turtle conservation is to focus on the protection of the most globally significant nesting beaches, where it can directly safeguard a new generation of hatchlings and thereby bolster repopulation efforts. One of those vital hotspots is Chacocente, a wildlife refuge on the coast of Nicaragua where five species of endangered sea turtle haul themselves out of the Pacific to run the gauntlet of hunters and illegal egg harvesters. Among them is the leatherback turtle, whose critically endangered Pacific population

Above Close-up of a nesting female leatherback turtle, an increasingly rare sight on the world's beaches, particularly on the Pacific coast.

Left Painting by the late William Oliver of a leatherback pursuing its favourite prey. Many marine turtles die from suffocation or starvation after consuming plastic bags they have mistaken for jellyfish.

declined by 90 per cent in the last decade of the twentieth century. Older members of the local community vividly recall a time when it was common to see 100 leatherbacks nesting in a single night; by the end of the 1990s they were lucky to find that number of nests in an entire season. Poachers would collect virtually every egg laid, as a clutch of leatherback eggs was worth more than six times the average daily wage in the area.

In 2001 FFI began working with local partners to protect key nesting beaches, raise public awareness and develop sustainable livelihoods for coastal communities. As part of the wider programme, it hit upon the idea of paying local community

members, including many former poachers, to patrol nearly 30 kilometres of vitally important nesting beaches at Chacocente and the nearby Isla Juan Venado. It also launched an inspired awareness campaign dubbed *Yo no como huevos de tortugas* (I don't eat turtle eggs), in an attempt to dissuade Nicaraguans from eating leatherback eggs, which many believed to be an aphrodisiac.

Using billboards, T-shirts, public bus banners and other media, FFI set about transforming attitudes to turtle egg consumption across a significant area of the country. Today, over 90 per cent of leatherback nests in Nicaragua are protected and poaching levels have fallen dramatically. In 2012 alone, the team helped an estimated 1.4 million hatchlings of leatherbacks and other endangered sea turtles to reach the sea.

Clockwise from top left When FFI first began working in Nicaragua, marine turtle eggs were frequently sold illegally at local markets; the message on these T-shirts reads 'Do it for me. Don't eat turtle eggs'; using national celebrities to endorse its campaign, FFI succeeded in reducing demand; two of the millions of marine turtle hatchlings that FFI's work has helped to safeguard.

Right FFI's work with the Local Ocean Trust in Kenya led to the partners mobilising an entire community in response to the accidental dumping at sea of a large load of plastic bags.

What lies beneath

Turtles and pinnipeds need to come ashore to breed and whales have to surface in order to breathe, so it was a relatively straightforward process to identify reptile and marine mammal hotspots and implement protection measures. For the diminishing fish stocks beneath the ocean surface, however, it has all too often been a case of 'out of sight, out of mind'. As recently as July 1986, the society felt compelled to point out in an *Oryx* editorial that not a single species of marine fish was listed at that time by CITES, despite all the warning signs.

Decades before *Finding Nemo* smashed box office records with the story of a cute clownfish and inadvertently exacerbated the very problem that the film had served to highlight, the then FFPS was using its 100% Fund to help finance a study into the exploitation of coral reef fishes for the aquarium trade, carried out on behalf of the Marine Conservation Society.

In 1990, the FFPS local group in Bristol raised funds specifically earmarked for the great white shark, a species that was desperately in need of conservation attention and had recently been listed as Insufficiently Known in the IUCN Red List of Threatened Animals. Determined to improve the public image of this much-maligned denizen of the deep, the society funded the compilation of an up-to-date report into all known aspects of the great white's biology and launched a media campaign. An article published in *The Sunday Times* on 19 August 1990 under the headline 'Have mercy on the shark' reminded readers that 'In the last few years, man has done far more harm to this rare predator than the shark has done to man.'

Long before the formal launch of its marine programme, therefore, FFI had been on the case, but 2011 marked the official start of a concerted campaign to address the widening disparity between marine conservation efforts and the growing threats to our oceans. A review of operations revealed that marine and coastal biodiversity were under-represented in the FFI portfolio. With a mere 10 per cent of projects focusing on these neglected ecosystems, there was clearly a pressing need for the society to prove that it wasn't taking the definition of fieldwork too literally. Building on FFI's existing areas of expertise, and using the Arcadia grant as a springboard, the programme's stated aims were 'to safeguard species, habitats and livelihoods

Published in *The Times*, this 1990 article stemmed from the society's work to change attitudes to the great white and other sharks.

Have mercy on the shark

The much-feared great white is in danger of being wiped out, warns JOHN HILL

A NEW saga of the deep unfolds: the great white shark, malevolent snatcher of swimmers in Peter Benchley's novel Jaws and succeeding clear-the-beach cinema horrors, is in reality a sorely tried creature that may die out before its life cycle is known to science.

As a conservative feeder best pleased by seals or sea lions, the enormous fish, up to 17ft long, sometimes mistakes people for the real thing, but quickly rejects them with distaste.

The new outline script comes from the offices in Brighton, Sussex, of the Flora and Fauna Preservation Society (FFPS), champion of harassed species.

There Jaws is given the dignity of a definitive name, *Carcharodon carcharias*, and the same respect as the mountain gorilla and Arabian oryx, beneficiaries of earlier campaigns. The FFPS is funding a study that pulls together what is known about the great white shark. So far, it makes brief, melancholy reading.

Seas may be shark-infested, but not by the great white, which seems never to have been plentiful and may now be down to between 1,500 and 2,000 individuals scattered in coastal regions. "In the last few years, man has done more harm to this rare predator than the shark has done to man," the FFPS says.

Dr Keith Banister, a fish and fisheries consultant and a member of the society's council, is the author of The Book of the Shark. "Four were killed in the Farallon islands off California about six years ago: none has been seen there since," he says. "They are top-level predators and in their absence sea lions have multiplied, affecting fishermen's catches and damaging nets.

"Great whites have become very scarce off the Queensland coast, where 12 to 15 used to be caught in a year. Now the figure is four. They were almost certainly found in the Mediterranean." Thomas Pennant drew Britain's only recorded great white, which he called the beaumaris shark, found in the Bristol Channel in 1776. Other areas in which it is — or was — found include the eastern seaboard of the United States, the Bay of Biscay and the Atlantic coast of North Africa.

Banister is concerned for the entire, persecuted shark family — "they are, after all, sentient beings" — and fish in general, which, he feels, receive derisory attention from conservationists. "Over half of all the vertebrate animals are fish, yet protection for them is virtually nil. There may be fewer than 2,000 great white sharks left in the world, but there has been no public outcry of the kind that grew over the admittedly awful

● *Jaws: Hollywood's view*

trade in ivory, though elephants are still numbered in tens of thousands."

A file kept by the United States Navy shows a worldwide average of 28 shark attacks a year since 1940, of which fewer than 35% were fatal.

As lone wanderers, too large to be kept satisfactorily in oceanaria, and the only species in the *carcharodon* genus, the great white withholds many secrets from biologists, including its longevity, reproductive cycle, maximum size — the average seems to be about 1,700lb for 15-footers — and breeding grounds.

The FFPS, convinced a worldwide agreement to end hunting of great whites is needed, has yet to decide on tactics. One course would be to press for its inclusion among animals protected under Cites, the Convention on International Trade in Endangered Species.

through effective protection and management of marine ecosystems, to encourage more enlightened policy and practice, and to ensure the long-term sustainability of conservation measures by strengthening the ability of local partners to effect lasting change'.

Whilst marine conservation presents its own unique set of challenges, not least the sheer scale of the problems faced, FFI's tried-and-tested formula is equally valid in this context, whether it is working on marine protected areas in Kenya, policy engagement in Costa Rica, or support for local institutions in Indonesia. Special emphasis has been placed, in the words of FFI's Robert Bensted-Smith, on 'empowering coastal communities to be the custodians of the marine resources on which they depend.'

Deep and meaningful: wildlife imagery is a vital weapon in the battle to conserve biodiversity, but securing footage of marine species can be particularly problematic. Many of the spectacular images in this chapter, and the time taken to secure them, were generously donated to FFI by marine photographers including underwater cameraman Phil McIntyre and the award-winning Paul Colley, whose work in Koh Rong Archipelago has been instrumental in raising awareness of the importance of Cambodia's previously neglected marine resources.

Marine blueprint

FFI's marine conservation blueprint for the vast Indonesian archipelago had humble beginnings in a post-tsunami project on Pulau Weh, a small but biologically rich island off the northern tip of Sumatra. The aim was to put in place a model strategy designed to ensure that the Acehnese coastal communities affected by the devastating 2004 tsunami received equitable treatment in the subsequent scramble for control of the fisheries sector. The three-point plan involved establishing a community-led conflict resolution system, boosting the local economy through community-run nature tourism and, crucially, making marine conservation an integral part of government policy in Aceh.

As part of this process, a task force co-ordinated by FFI's local marine manager set about identifying suitable locations for a network of 'Locally Managed Marine Areas' – considered to be global best practice for community-based fisheries management – using a technique known in the trade as spatially explicit priority-setting analysis (mercifully, SEPSIS appears to have been deemed an acronym too far). The initiative has helped to reinvigorate pre-tsunami management systems that date back 400 years and are based on the Islamic model of village authority, enabling coastal communities to overcome many of the most serious threats to their long-term livelihood by putting in place customary limits on fishing to ensure sustainability.

On the other side of the globe, thanks to Halcyon Land & Sea support, a project that began with funding from the Darwin Initiative has evolved to address fundamental issues affecting the integrity of Galera-San Francisco Marine Reserve and other protected areas on the Ecuadorian coast. FFI and its partners are helping coastal communities to exercise their right to participate in the management of the natural resources on which they depend, removing obstacles to the establishment of so-called No Take Zones (areas closed to fishing) that enable fish stocks to recover, and exploring ways to ensure preferential access for local users rather than a free-for-all system that helps perpetuate unsustainable activities.

Cambodia's territorial waters are no less worthy of conservation attention than its biologically rich terrestrial landscapes. They comprise an abundance of vital marine habitats including coral reefs, seagrass meadows and mangrove forests, all of which face serious threats. FFI and

By embedding marine conservation in government policy in Sumatra, FFI aims to help safeguard Aceh's spectacular coastal riches.

Clockwise from top left Planting mangroves to restore fish nursery habitat on the Cambodian coast; fish congregating around a barrel sponge; clownfish sheltering in the tentacles of a sea anemone; fisherman in Koh Rong Archipelago.

Licensed to save: Myanmar's first ever PADI-certified divers reporting for duty. Three weeks of FFI-led training equipped these young scientists with the skills and knowledge to undertake some of the first coral reef surveys ever conducted in the country.

its local partners have worked closely with the government's Fisheries Administration since 2011 to support the design of the country's first large marine protected area (referred to locally as a marine fisheries management area, but let's not quibble about terminology) with a view to ensuring a sustainable level of resource use that is compatible with tourism development, poverty reduction and biodiversity conservation. In June 2016, five years of tireless effort culminated in the landmark official government proclamation of Cambodia's first large-scale marine protected area, encompassing some 400 square kilometres of the Koh Rong Archipelago.

FFI has similar ambitions for Myanmar's extensive but poorly known Myeik Archipelago, and is helping to lay the foundations for long-term conservation of this unique marine environment. Myanmar's coastline boasts a rich diversity of vital wetland and marine habitats, including mangroves, mudflats, sandy beaches, seagrass beds and coral reefs. Four species of globally threatened marine turtles and 58 shark species – many of which are also endangered – have been recorded in Myanmar waters. The country's marine and wetland habitats are a vital refuge for other charismatic wildlife, including the dugong, the Irrawaddy river dolphin and the critically endangered spoon-billed sandpiper.

FFI was the first marine conservation organisation to establish a programme of work in Myanmar after the military regime began to loosen its grip on the reins of environmental management, and is at the forefront of numerous initiatives to help the government and local communities protect the country's valuable marine and coastal resources.

When FFI first became involved, very few biodiversity assessments had been undertaken, meaning that there were yawning gaps in knowledge regarding the relative importance of different areas from a conservation perspective. The paucity of data was partly due to a historical lack of capacity and resources within university and government institutions, an issue that FFI is helping to address.

FFI Myanmar's national marine science team has already gained several years of relevant field experience through its marine and coastal conservation programme in the south of the country, where at least 250 sites have been surveyed throughout the Myeik Archipelago. In parallel, FFI has worked with offshore fishing communities, including the once entirely nomadic – and historically marginalised – Moken people, and piloted Locally Managed Marine Areas at various sites within the archipelago.

Oil be damned

Concern about the effects of pollution on the marine environment was also evident from an early stage in the society's evolution. In March 1933, for example, it passed a resolution urging the government to convene an international conference to tackle 'the continued and increasing destruction of Sea-birds, Fish, Marine plants and animalculae (*sic*) wrought by oil pollution'. If you use an obscure scientific term for microscopic organisms without understanding how a neuter plural is formed in Latin, you could end up with ovum on your face, but nit-picking aside, this extract from the society's *Journal* reveals an early awareness of a problem that has now become impossible to ignore. A 1956 *Oryx* editorial revisited the issue of dumping waste oil at sea, expressing the holier-than-thou view that the USA, Panama and Liberia, who controlled 14 million tonnes of shipping between them, would do well to follow

Jackass penguins lit by the last rays of the evening sun waddle ashore at Cape Agulhas in South Africa's Western Cape.

the fine example set, apparently, by British ships. There is evidence of a steely determination on the part of the society at that time to continue making waves until it is illegal for any ship to dump oil.

In 1972, the dire consequences of a cavalier attitude to waste disposal were brought home sharply to the society's own president. By way of a thank you to the then FPS for its support of the Southern African Foundation for the Conservation of Coastal Birds, Lord Willingdon had been treated to a helicopter flight over the vast jackass penguin colony on South Africa's Dassen Island, and had marvelled at the sight of an estimated 50,000 birds on their breeding grounds. Three weeks later, an unidentified tanker released bilge oil and contaminated 5,000 of these birds, which are particularly vulnerable to oil spills as they spend so much time on the surface of the sea. Galvanised no doubt by this horrific spectacle, the society helped to organise a conference in London later that same year, at which 57 countries ratified an international agreement to control waste dumping at sea, and to ban specific highly toxic substances.

Plastics surgery

In 1984, an *Oryx* editorial lamented the fact that a Chilean biologist had made the depressing first discovery of plastic debris on the continent of Antarctica. Three decades later, with global plastic production estimated to exceed 280 million tonnes each year, it is no surprise that the world's oceans are awash with a disposable product initially famed – and now notorious – for its indestructibility. This plastic flotsam and jetsam poses severe, well-publicised problems for marine fauna and tends to be the main focus of attention for consumers, businesses and governments, not least because it is such an obvious and ubiquitous blot on the marine and coastal landscape.

True to form, FFI spotted a gap in the market and resolved to tackle a more insidious form of marine plastic pollution in the shape of microplastics. These minuscule particles pervade our oceans and shorelines like so many toxin-laden miniature time bombs, working their way inexorably up the marine food chain to the point where they could potentially have a deleterious effect on global ecosystems,

fisheries and – in due course – even human health. In a bid to stem the flow of microplastic pollution into the world's oceans, FFI began working with both producers and consumers of the offending items. As part of this work, it has spearheaded global efforts to stop the use of microplastic ingredients in cosmetics and toiletries such as face scrubs. At the supply end, FFI and its partners have succeeded in persuading market leaders such as PZ Cussons and Procter & Gamble to phase out the use of microbeads in their products. Consumers have also been encouraged to vote with their wallets and send an unequivocal message to manufacturers and high-street retailers that there is no demand for these unnecessary pollutants. The *Good Scrub Guide*, which FFI produced in partnership with the Marine Conservation Society (and which was modelled on the seminal *Good Bulb Guide* issued by the society two decades earlier), helps the wider public to make informed choices when purchasing exfoliators. In 2013 FFI joined forces with two Dutch NGOs to promote a new smartphone app that allowed shoppers to scan the barcode of personal care products in order to verify whether they contain plastic microbeads. As the campaign gained momentum,

No skin off our nose? Promoting fish-friendly facial scrubs.

FFI and other organisations that had also been sounding the alarm about the deleterious effects of microbeads on the marine environment came together to form an informal coalition. Playing to their respective institutional strengths, the individual partners combined in a pincer movement that owed something to the good cop, bad cop routine, with pressure groups Greenpeace UK and the Environmental Investigation Agency campaigning vociferously for a ban, while behind the scenes FFI and the Marine Conservation Society continued to compile the scientific evidence that confirmed how ubiquitous solid microplastics were in household products and which companies were dragging their feet in addressing the issue. With pressure building, the UK government ordered an inquiry led by the cross-party Environmental Audit Committee, during which FFI's Marine Plastics Programme Manager, Dan Steadman, was called to give evidence as an expert witness.

Given that the society began life as the aristocratic equivalent of a pressure group, whose success in lobbying the British government hinged on establishing its credibility as an independent source of expert advice, there was a delicious irony in the fact that, an entire century later, FFI had come full circle, propelled back into those same corridors of power thanks to its intimate knowledge of the matter in hand, and once again in a position to put its case directly to political decision makers.

By 2016, the campaign had captured the public imagination to such an extent that over 300,000 people had signed a petition calling for a ban on microbeads. Mindful of the adverse publicity that could result from a perceived reluctance to take appropriate action – and no doubt concerned that the *Daily Mail* had picked up the story – the UK government issued a formal announcement in September 2016 that it planned to ban the sale and manufacture of cosmetics and personal care products containing plastic microbeads.

Dr Abigail Entwistle, whom we first encountered as the youthful saviour of the Pemba flying fox but whose numerous claims to fame during her subsequent 20 years with the organisation include launching the initiative that has since established FFI as a world leader on tackling marine microplastic pollution, was understandably delighted with the news: 'Microplastic pollution is a ubiquitous problem in all of the world's seas and oceans, but a comprehensive ban will put the UK at the top of the leader board on this issue. We are confident that, by consulting with the right experts, the UK government can set the gold standard for other nations to work towards and ultimately make our blue planet much healthier, both now and for generations to come.'

Coast to coast

One notable aspect of FFI's marine programme is that it has provided an opportunity for the society to reacquaint itself with conservation at home in the UK. The Firth of Forth, on Scotland's east coast, harbours a wealth of marine life, but this diversity is under pressure as a result of increased industrialisation. In particular, the area is plagued by the proliferation of so-called nurdles. Vast quantities of these small, pre-production plastic pellets, spilled during manufacture and transportation, inevitably end up in our rivers and seas, where they are frequently mistaken for food and enter the food chain. FFI has undertaken significant research behind the scenes to understand this issue and had begun to forge links with the plastics industry with a view to developing potential solutions. The lessons learnt have subsequently proved extremely useful as part of a collaboration with Fidra, a local environmental group in Scotland. The Forth estuary is a notorious hotspot for this form of plastics pollution, and in 2013 Fidra launched The Great Nurdle Hunt, using the powerful tool of citizen science to help raise awareness of the problem and pressurise companies involved in the industry to address it constructively.

Of course, the most effective way to reduce this pollution, as with microbeads, is to prevent these noxious pieces of plastic from entering the marine food chain in the first place, a point emphasised by Dan Steadman during his discussions with the UK Environmental Audit Committee: 'There are many ways that small plastic particles can reach the sea, and once there they can be eaten by marine life. Some of these sources are more difficult to prevent than others but the use of microplastics in down-the-drain consumer products and poor handling of pre-production pellets are two direct sources that can be easily prevented.'

Scotland boasts over 16,000 kilometres of coastline, including 800 islands, and its productive seas have supported a once-thriving fishing industry for centuries. Widespread concern about recent steep declines in fishing stocks has been the catalyst for a number of community conservation initiatives in Scotland, and FFI is supporting efforts to ensure the sustainable management of the country's marine resources.

Any conservation initiative worth its salt comes complete with its own clever acronym, and they don't come any more apposite than COAST, shorthand for the Community of Arran Seabed Trust. This island community off the west coast of Scotland has been campaigning for greater protection of the seas around Arran since 1995, when two

local divers, Howard Wood and Don McNeish, shocked by the decline in the surrounding marine habitats caused largely by destructive bottom trawling, resolved to take things into their own hands. In 2008, as a direct consequence of COAST's persistence, Scotland's first No Take Zone was established at the north end of Arran's Lamlash Bay, in order to protect the maerl seaweed beds that serve as vital breeding grounds and nurseries for adult and juvenile fish respectively. Some five years later, surveys supported by FFI revealed that the unmolested seabed was 40 per cent more complex and healthy than the surrounding area. In 2014 the waters off south Arran were designated as an official marine protected area, along with 32 other such sites around the coast of Scotland. Meanwhile, FFI continues to provide ongoing support to COAST, helping it to develop and deliver an effective marine conservation strategy.

Building on this relationship, FFI has established a scheme to provide co-ordinated technical and practical support and best practice guidance to other communities around the Scottish coast who are seeking to fulfil their own marine

Clockwise from left Kelp beds play an integral role in a highly productive marine ecosystem around the coast of Arran in western Scotland; recent FFI-funded surveys revealed that lobster weight and catch rates are substantially higher within the isle of Arran's No Take Zone than in neighbouring fishing grounds, demonstrating that marine reserves can act as a safe haven for lobsters, allowing them to reach sexual maturity, greater fecundity, abundance and sizes; the abundance of spiny starfish, sunstars and brittlestars is a notable feature of Arran's coastal waters.

management aspirations. The ultimate aim is to create a network of like-minded groups that can share experiences and collaborate to ensure that Scotland's seas are managed sustainably.

As part of its work in the Firth of Clyde, FFI is also supporting the Scottish Inshore Fisheries Trust, which promotes more progressive fisheries management that will allow Scotland to have its fish and eat it, so to speak, yielding increased economic returns whilst ensuring that fishing practices are more sustainable, in order to improve the future productivity of these once-bountiful seas.

Back to the future

If the recent success in influencing government policy on microplastics harked back to the glory days when the society's well-connected founders were able to fraternise freely with ministerial men of means, there is also a pleasing symmetry in the fact that FFI is now supporting the development of conservation in the world's newest country, the Republic of South Sudan.

It was concern for the fate of Sudan's game that induced Edward North Buxton, verderer of Hatfield Forest, to recruit his own exclusive band of merry gentlemen and champion the cause of the White Nile Reserve under the auspices of the newly founded Society for the Preservation of the Wild Fauna of the Empire back in 1903. When FFI began working in the region again in early 2011, this time in the newly independent Republic of South Sudan, there was a sense that the society was returning to its roots. Intervening in a country with so many problems might seem adventurous, to put it mildly, but FFI has ample experience of operating in this kind of environment and was never likely to decline what then programme manager Matt Rice described as 'an unprecedented opportunity to embed conservation within the government development agenda in the formative years of this new nation state'.

One of only two international conservation organisations operating in South Sudan, FFI was well aware of the magnitude of the task ahead, and its strategy was to start small, concentrating principally on one protected area – Southern National Park – within the state of Western Equatoria.

Rangers on a training exercise in South Sudan's Southern National Park take time out for a photo call.

After decades of neglect, the most pressing priorities were training, provision of equipment and the development of basic infrastructure, in order to boost morale and inspire confidence in the wildlife service. In the long run, success will hinge on addressing community needs.

In one sense, FFI is starting with a blank sheet of paper in South Sudan, which does not have the baggage of unpopular conservation policies that have alienated local communities and authorities in other parts of Africa. The challenge for FFI will be to harness community and government goodwill. In this respect, it has made a promising start. The current biodiversity monitoring and protected area management programme involves the development of a unique, albeit small-scale, peace-building model between government representatives and community members, and has elicited an impressive level of commitment from all parties.

It remains to be seen whether the political context in which FFI is operating will be conducive to progress. At the time of writing, the world's newest country has descended once more into the kind of civil conflict that plagued Sudan for the five decades prior to independence. Until further notice, short-term survival is the only game in town. Conservation initiatives, and indeed any form of development activity, may not be high on the government's agenda for the foreseeable future, but FFI remains on standby, ready to help resurrect the rebuilding process at the earliest opportunity. In the meantime, the programme continues to inch forward until it can pick up speed again, playing a vital role in creating havens of peace for what would otherwise be rival groups. In the short term, it is developing

Reminders of the society's original links with Sudan continue to punctuate its history. In 1974, a 100% Fund grant provided essential vehicle support for a survey of Sudan's wildlife-rich Southern Darfur province. Some 30 years later, FFI's Matt Rice is pictured contemplating embarking on a new programme of work on the redrawn map in South Sudan.

community forestry activities alongside biodiversity protection; its long-term goal is the demarcation of two protected areas and their associated community forests, which could be managed as cohesive units to promote greater diversification of livelihoods and help combat the poaching crisis.

One of the most exciting components of FFI's plan to restart conservation in South Sudan was the tantalising prospect of finding a wild northern white rhino. Throughout the past decade there have been sporadic, unconfirmed reports of sightings of this vanishingly rare subspecies. With no realistic prospect of discovering a remnant population in war-torn Garamba National Park in the Democratic Republic of Congo, South Sudan is almost certainly the last throw of the dice. Locating even a single northern white rhino there could be a game changer for the captive breeding initiative at Ol Pejeta, though this now seems increasingly unlikely.

Only time will tell whether FFI's recent intervention in South Sudan has come too late to save the northern white rhino, but there is no doubting the renewed resolve of the international community to tackle the alarming escalation in poaching that is threatening to overwhelm not only the world's last remaining rhinoceros populations, but also myriad other species that fall victim to the illegal wildlife trade.

MEET THE ANCESTORS

Anyone interested in playing the generation game at FFI will discover rich pickings without needing to dig too deep. A number of FFI supporters and staff have ancestral links with the very first members of the society, and it is relatively easy to stumble across family ties and serendipitous connections spanning the entire history of the organisation.

FAMILY AFFAIR

Samuel Howard Whitbread, heir to the brewing dynasty established by his great-grandfather, was a member of the society from the outset, and a signatory to the original petition that was the catalyst for its formation. As a long-serving MP, he was instrumental in bringing the society's concerns to the attention of the British political establishment.

His own great-grandson, Charles Whitbread, was elected to the FFI council in 2005 and became vice-chair in 2012. Paradoxically, he had been a long-standing member and ardent supporter of FFI for many years before he became aware of his ancestral links with the original society.

LIKE GRANDFATHER, LIKE GRANDSON

Sir Rhys Rhys-Williams was a founder member of the society. He attended the very first meeting at London's Natural History Museum and went on to serve as honorary secretary for a decade. He was also the original editor of the journal subsequently known as *Oryx*. A century later, his grandson, Sir Gareth Rhys Williams, has re-established the family connection with the society.

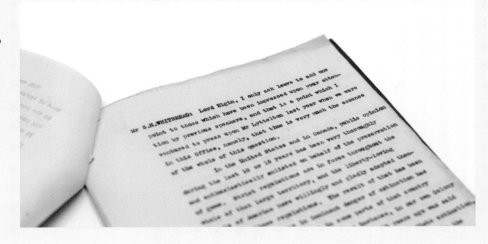

Extract from the society's own minutes of its 1906 meeting with Lord Elgin at the House of Commons, recording Samuel Whitbread's forceful contribution to proceedings.

Elected to the FFI council in 2012, he also actively supports FFI through membership of the Conservation Circle, and has added considerably to the pictorial interest of the early chapters in this book by providing access to his grandfather's personal archive, which dates from a period in the society's history that was otherwise largely bereft of material.

RECRUITING OFFICERS PAST AND PRESENT

The Lady Emma Kitchener LVO, lady-in-waiting to HRH Princess Michael of Kent, is the great-grandniece of the 1st Earl Kitchener of Khartoum. One of the society's first honorary members, Lord Kitchener was a powerful ally and valuable early ambassador for the conservation cause. An FFI vice-president since 2013, Lady Emma was previously instrumental in the launch of its Founders Circle initiative in 2005, which recruited a group of supporters from descendants of the society's original members and subsequently evolved into the Conservation Circle.

CURZON LINE

Matt Rice (pictured on page 287) worked for many years as FFI's programme manager for north-east Africa. Beyond his involvement in Sudan, he has also played an integral role in the establishment of some of Africa's most successful community-based conservation programmes in Namibia, northern Kenya and, most recently, Chuilexi Conservancy. It is apposite that the portrait looks like a throwback to the colonial era that spawned the original society. He has a direct link with a prominent statesman from that time, one of several who were astutely roped in by FFI's co-founders in order to curry political favour. Rice's great-grandmother was the second wife of Lord Curzon, who was Viceroy of India at the time of the society's formation, in which capacity he was invited to be one of its very first vice-presidents. Curzon was largely responsible for bringing up Rice's grandmother and her brothers, a duty that he combined with his day job as Foreign Secretary in Lloyd George's post-war cabinet. It's comforting to imagine this vociferous opponent of women's rights and former head of the Anti-Suffrage League grappling with the glorious irony that his stepdaughter might one day exercise her hard-won right to vote by helping to unseat him.

Rice's links with the society's past do not end with the Curzon connection. His grandfather's second cousin was Denys Finch Hatton, who – as recounted in the first chapter of this book – had guided founder member Colonel Patterson's photographic trip to the Serengeti in 1929. Like the society with which he was closely associated throughout this period, Finch Hatton was a vocal advocate for the establishment of protected areas in East Africa.

Charcoal portrait of Sir Rhys Rhys-Williams, founder member and first honorary secretary of the society.

BRAND RUSSELL

Lord Robin Russell, a dedicated conservationist who served as a council member from 1998 to 2003 and gave sterling support to FFI's Asian elephant conservation work in particular, was simply following in the footsteps of his illustrious forebears. One hundred years earlier, Herbrand Russell, 11th Duke of Bedford, and his wife Mary du Caurroy Tribe, the aviator and ornithologist, had both played a pivotal role in the society's foundation, and cemented their reputation as ardent conservationists by giving sanctuary to the last of the world's Père David's deer and helping to safeguard the future of the European bison, which was hunted to extinction in the wild during the early twentieth century. Their son, Hastings Russell, 12th Duke of Bedford, who had opened his Woburn Abbey estate to the public during the 1951 Festival of Britain specifically to help promote the society's conservation work, was a keen naturalist with a particular penchant for parrots. Not to be outdone by the sterling captive breeding efforts of his parents, Hastings Russell successfully reared a number of exotic species in captivity, including the Tahiti blue lorikeet and ultramarine lorikeet, both believed to be world firsts. He reputedly fed them chocolate, which might possibly explain the origins of the phrase 'sick as a parrot'.

GRANDE DAME

Dame Miriam Rothschild was a staunch long-term supporter of FFI and served as a vice-president of the society for over a decade from 1994 until her death in 2005. A self-taught zoologist and naturalist, and world authority on parasites and their hosts, Dame Miriam witnessed many of the seminal moments in the evolution of conservation, including the inaugural meeting of the IUCN, the first

Portrait of a young lady: Miriam Rothschild in her youth, photographed by Hugh Cecil.

conference where conservation was the primary focus. It was here that she was greatly inspired by the words of Julian Huxley, another heavyweight associate of FFI. Miriam Rothschild was brought up in a household where natural history was a way of life. She was the daughter of the banker and entomologist Nathaniel Charles Rothschild, himself a founder member of the society. Her father was one of the first people to appreciate the importance of preserving habitats as well as species, and an ardent campaigner for a national network of nature reserves. Rothschild was the founder and first chairman of the Society for the Promotion of Nature Reserves. This organisation ultimately metamorphosed into The Wildlife Trusts, which – by a strange quirk of fate – was where current chief executive Mark Rose made his mark before assuming the reins at FFI in 1993. Interestingly, Rothschild was a fervent believer in basing conservation policy on sound science, a view that underpins the work of FFI to this very day. ■

United front

FFI has always adopted a pragmatic approach to wildlife conservation, recognising that many communities with which it works may well be actively involved in exploiting wildlife and other natural resources. As we have seen, the Convention on International Trade in Endangered Species of Wild Fauna and Flora (CITES) and TRAFFIC, the wildlife trade monitoring network, both owe their existence to FFI-led initiatives. Nevertheless, the society is acutely aware that tacit acceptance of sustainable forms of wildlife use, provided that this does not involve illegal exploitation of endangered species, may ultimately have a net positive effect, not necessarily in strict biodiversity terms, but in the sense that it recognises the rights of local communities to feed themselves, pursue their traditional way of life and retain their connections with the natural world.

In some cases, however, current levels of exploitation are patently unsustainable, and this problem is exacerbated by the rampant illegal wildlife trade. The cumulative effect of inadequate law enforcement, inconsistent policy across

range states, corrupt officialdom, increasing sophistication among organised crime networks and slow reproductive rates among target species has had a profoundly damaging impact. Globalisation, ease of international travel, the proliferation of weapons and increased access to forest areas have accentuated the problem. Above all, the exponential rise in demand for wildlife products among the expanding and increasingly affluent consumer base in China and other parts of Asia is having a devastating effect.

In light of the escalating problem, FFI recognised that it needed to adapt its traditional approach and explore new ways of addressing the issue through innovative alliances. One such initiative is the United for Wildlife partnership, announced in 2013, which was set up specifically to tackle major conservation crises. Evidently deeply affected by his experiences in Kenya's Lewa Conservancy, The Duke of Cambridge was keen to lend his personal support to the fight against the illegal wildlife trade. A subsequent conversation instigated by Dr Jonathan Baillie, then Director of Conservation Programmes at the Zoological Society of London, was one of the catalysts for the Royal

Foundation of The Duke and Duchess of Cambridge and Prince Harry to announce a collaboration with seven of the world's most influential conservation organisations, including FFI.

This ten-year alliance is intended to bring together conservation's finest minds from around the world, drawing on that vast pool of talent to tackle issues such as illegal wildlife trafficking in a more coherent fashion, and on a previously unprecedented scale. The skills and expertise of global leaders in business, communications, technology and the creative industries are also being harnessed in order to maximise the effectiveness of the response to the crisis. Aligning with the Royal Family on this issue to give it additional clout is also a tactically astute move.

Above United for Wildlife collaborators (from left to right): John Robinson, Wildlife Conservation Society; Glyn Davies, World Wide Fund for Nature; Simon Stuart, IUCN; Rosalind Aveling, FFI; HRH The Duke of Cambridge; Jonathan Baillie, Zoological Society of London; Peter Wheeler, The Nature Conservancy; Stephen Blakey, United for Wildlife.

Clockwise from top left Bull elephant killed for its ivory in Mozambique's Niassa National Reserve; the impressive double horn of this white rhinoceros makes it a prime target for poachers; the gruesome reality: a slaughtered and dehorned black rhino in Lewa Wildlife Conservancy, Kenya.

Opposite African elephant browsing on foliage in Lewa Wildlife Conservancy.

In February 2014 the United for Wildlife president, HRH The Duke of Cambridge, lent his weight to a two-day symposium at which conservationists on the front line, policy experts, donors and government representatives shared their collective wisdom. The event was timed to coincide with the London Conference on Illegal Wildlife Trade, organised by the office of the then UK Foreign Secretary, William Hague.

With echoes of the original London Conference of 1900 that presaged a new era of international co-operation in wildlife conservation, this international gathering brought together representatives from 46 countries. It also served as a timely reminder of the importance of royal connections throughout the long and distinguished history of FFI, with Prince William the latest in a long line of supporters from the House of Windsor that stretches back beyond the reign of his great-grandfather, King George VI. With Prince William himself at the helm, the subsequent campaign could not fail to focus global attention on the urgent need for action, and its impact was confirmed when, in late 2016, state media in China reported that it would ban all domestic ivory trade by the end of 2017.

Collective vision

As a global conservation organisation with partnerships in over 40 countries, FFI has always understood the need to work together towards a common goal. The formal launch of the Cambridge Conservation Initiative campus in 2013 was the culmination of a vision – to create the world's first science-based conservation hub – that had begun to take shape almost two decades earlier. Shortly after his arrival at the society, Mark Rose had proposed relocating to Cambridge. A major part of his rationale had been that it would make strategic sense to join the growing network of wildlife conservation organisations that were starting to accumulate there. The suggestion did not meet with universal approval among the trustees, and there was apparently plenty of blood on the walls by the end of the acrimonious meeting in 1995 at which the resolution was carried.

The net result was that the society moved into the Forestry Commission offices at Great Eastern House, a mere colugo glide away from Cambridge railway station. Collaboration followed hard on the heels of relocation, with FFI, BirdLife International, TRAFFIC and the World Conservation Monitoring Centre (WCMC) as principal partners, and Mark Collins of WCMC in the driving seat. This informal coalition had envisioned a kind of campus that would be constructed around the existing WCMC premises. When the subsequent proposal for Lottery funding was rejected, however, the project was shelved indefinitely.

Nevertheless, the seed of an idea had been sown and within a decade it was successfully resuscitated by FFI, who had worked quietly behind the scenes with, among others, Dr Jon Hutton – former director of its Africa programme and director-in-waiting at WCMC – to keep it alive. The re-engineered project was given much greater kudos and momentum thanks to the involvement of Professor Dame Alison Richard, the then Vice-Chancellor of the University of Cambridge and herself a renowned anthropologist and conservationist, without whom the project might never have come to fruition.

Following a meeting between Rose, Richard and Lisbet Rausing, it was agreed that FFI would undertake a Cambridge-wide consultation exercise and follow up with a report that would incorporate the views and establish the priorities of all the relevant players in the Cambridge

HRH The Duke of Cambridge, president of United for Wildlife, launches the Whose Side Are You On? social networking campaign.

conservation conglomerate, including the Cambridge Conservation Forum and the Tropical Biology Association. Among the academic heavyweights who contributed to the discussions from a university perspective were the triumvirate of Bill Adams, now Moran Professor of Conservation and Development in the Department of Geography; Andy Balmford, Professor of Conservation Science in the Department of Zoology; and Bill Sutherland, Miriam Rothschild Professor of Conservation Biology – a position named, fittingly, in honour of one of FFI's staunchest long-term supporters.

The resulting wish list included two of the above biodiversity professorships, a collaborative fund, a new master's degree in Conservation Leadership and, last but not least, a campus. Opinion was divided regarding the need for a physical campus, as some felt that a virtual campus would suffice. In the event, the two were developed in parallel.

The Cambridge Conservation Initiative (CCI) was formally launched in 2007 with a mission to stimulate joined-up thinking across conservation practice, research and policy. Dr Mike Rands, former head of BirdLife International, was brought on board to drive it forward, and he succeeded in

balancing the disparate needs of the many different interest groups in order to see the project through to fruition. With generous support from Arcadia, a Collaborative Fund for Conservation was established to encourage innovative, collaborative conservation projects undertaken by CCI partners, thereby creating a programme of work that is greater than the sum of its parts. As part of its commitment to provide world-class learning and leadership opportunities, CCI is also helping to train future conservation professionals via a bespoke master's degree, established with the support of MAVA Foundation. To date, FFI has provided the lion's share of professional placement opportunities for graduates on the programme.

The plan for the CCI Conservation Campus itself was officially launched in April 2013 at a ceremony attended by, among others, Sir David Attenborough and HRH The Duke of Edinburgh. It would be a further three years before the architect's vision was realised, but the result – a unique global campus at the intellectual heart of Cambridge – would prove to be an inspiring symbol of a new and exciting phase in the evolution of worldwide conservation.

Masters in Conservation Leadership students meet Sir David Attenborough in their new teaching room.

CHAPTER 12

NEW BEGINNINGS

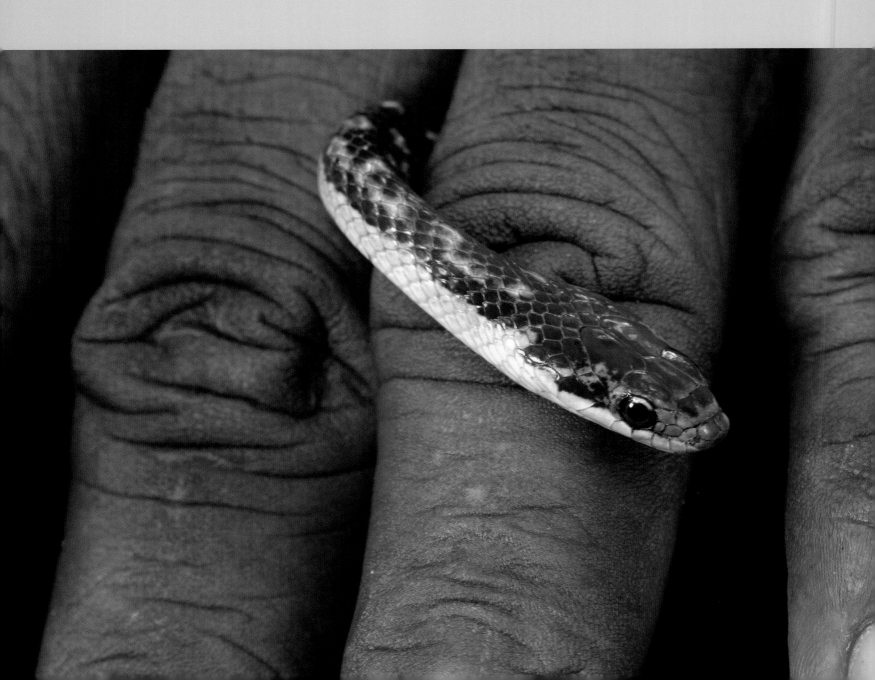

'FFI is ideally positioned to capitalise on this momentum shift, this new sense of urgency. But in doing so, we never walk alone. In fact, partnering with others is central to all our work across the globe. It is only with our existing supporters and partners and those new to our work that we can seize this opportunity. There is no time to waste.'

HRH Princess Laurentien of the Netherlands, FFI President

Constructed as part of the now redeveloped New Museums Site in Cambridge, the CCI Conservation Campus opened its doors for business in December 2015, although it was not officially opened until the following April. The building's impressive atrium, complete with its living wall of plants, displays the name of André Hoffmann, entrepreneur and chair of MAVA, a philanthropic foundation exclusively focused on biodiversity conservation, in recognition of his generous support for the site's facelift.

The new campus in which FFI and other CCI partners are based sits at the academic epicentre of the city and is expected to stimulate innovative collaborations that will shape the future of conservation. It was named the David Attenborough Building, a fitting tribute to the naturalist, broadcaster and FFI vice-president who has done so much to popularise the conservation cause and promote the work of the society.

Opposite New hope for arguably the world's rarest snake in the shape of a baby Saint Lucia racer.

Above President of FFI since 2012, HRH Princess Laurentien is a passionate believer in giving the next generation a voice in deciding the planet's future.

LET ME COUNT THE WAYS

The veteran broadcaster and naturalist Sir David Attenborough has been a member of FFI since the 1950s and a vice-president since 1979. His long association with the society may not feature anywhere among the myriad responsibilities, achievements and other biographical information enumerated in his Wikipedia profile, but from FFI's perspective that relationship has been hugely significant.

In normal circumstances, describing someone as a great ambassador for an organisation might reasonably be considered a fitting accolade. In this case, it doesn't begin to do justice to how FFI has benefited – not least in terms of scientific credibility and popular appeal – from its close ties with this conservation legend.

Despite a schedule of commitments that would leave ordinary mortals reaching for the smelling salts, Sir David has consistently made time to endorse FFI's work, provide moral support and help promote its campaigns and activities. He is also a source of inspiration to everyone associated with the society. It is interesting to note that FFI staff – past and present – frequently cite him as the main catalyst for their choice of career. ∎

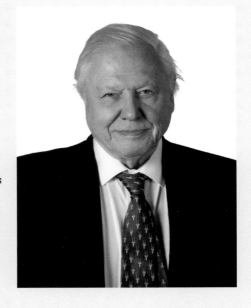

Sir David Attenborough sporting the latest in a series of oryx ties many of which have mysteriously vanished from his wardrobe.

At the grand old age of 90, Sir David could have been excused for wanting to retire to a quiet corner and live out his remaining years watching reruns of *Life on Earth* from the comfort of his armchair. Far from putting his feet up, however, he declared his intention to abseil down the living wall of evergreen plants inside the CCI building at its official opening.

The insistence of this remarkable nonagenarian on moving with the times rather than resting on his laurels echoes the forward-thinking attitude of the 114-year-old charity with which he is intimately associated. Ensconced in new premises in the heart of Cambridge, FFI shows no inclination to play the conservation dinosaur and rest its weary bones amid the prehistoric skeletons, fossils and other monuments to extinction in the Sedgwick Museum next door. In fact, one of the secrets of the society's longevity is its adaptability and willingness to evolve, and that tendency is very much in evidence both in its recent initiatives and in some of the ambitious plans that are still at an embryonic stage.

Central to these plans is the work of FFI's Conservation Partnerships team, led by environmental economist Joanna Elliott, which focuses on the various interventions that can make conservation effective and sustainable.

Capacity for conservation

Capacity development is not a concept to fire the public imagination in the same way as mountain gorilla conservation or a dramatic airlift to save the last northern white rhinos on the planet, but building a worldwide network of strong conservation organisations is fundamental to all that FFI has achieved and will achieve in future.

FFI has invested in sharing practical conservation lessons since the publication of the society's very first journal, and for many years has led the way in supporting organisational and personal development in the conservation arena. Success in this area is not always easy to measure – it can be hard to demonstrate how support for an individual or institution has resulted in direct conservation impact. In FFI's case, it can point to flourishing careers, new sites designated for conservation, new laws enacted and scientific discoveries made, not to mention an impressive list of awards and award nominations, at home and abroad, for the local conservationists it has supported. As the complexity of conservation issues has increased, FFI has recognised the need for closer collaboration between global leaders in this field so that their experiences and lessons learned can be shared more effectively.

Traditionally, every one of FFI's local partners has benefited from one-to-one support tailored to its own specific needs. In reality, however, many of these organisations encounter the same generic problems time after time. With this in mind, FFI is now encouraging its local partners around the world to develop peer support networks for themselves. As part of this process, the society joined forces with other members of the Cambridge Conservation Initiative to develop and launch a website: *capacityforconservation.org.*

This site enables organisations to assess and plan their own development while simultaneously benefiting from FFI's one-to-one bespoke partner input. Resources and case studies are shared among partner organisations to create a community that can learn from the experiences and mistakes of those who have already trodden a similar development path.

Right Portrait of a lady: an elderly member of the Hmong community, with which FFI has worked closely for more than a decade as part of a long-term gibbon conservation programme in northern Vietnam.

Opposite Sir David Attenborough descends from the concrete jungle equivalent of the rainforest canopy at the official opening of the building named in his honour.

Human rights

FFI has a long history of empowering local communities to act as effective custodians of the threatened natural resources on which they depend, and there is growing recognition that biodiversity conservation and sustainable resource use are inseparable from the issue of people's rights to a secure livelihood. Accordingly, FFI policy has progressed from a 'do no harm' position to a more proactive engagement with governance and human rights issues, whereby socio-economic goals are integrated seamlessly into the project-planning process.

As a conduit for this work, FFI set up its Conservation, Livelihoods and Governance programme. This cross-cutting initiative provides direct support and a plethora of tools, case studies and other documents designed, as the FFI website puts it, 'to help conservationists facilitate participatory processes with local stakeholders'. The kind of jargon that plagues this sphere of activity is unlikely ever to win a plain English award, but the notoriously impenetrable language should not be allowed to detract from the crucial importance of the work itself. In short, it starts from the premise that rural livelihoods are a way of life, not merely a means of earning a living, and gives communities a voice in decisions that have implications for their emotional and cultural well-being as well as their environmental and economic security. It addresses issues such as land and resource use rights, gender equality, minority rights and the multifaceted value of nature. If the methodology is sometimes lost in translation, there is no doubting its importance, or its effectiveness on the ground.

Small is beautiful

This brings us neatly to the latest developments in another area infested with acronyms and technical terminology, namely Reduced Emissions from Deforestation and avoided Degradation (REDD+), a concept first encountered and explained in an earlier chapter. Among the salutary lessons taken away from its bruising encounters with the commercial and political minefield surrounding REDD+ in its various guises, FFI has learned the hard way that investor, political and conservation timeframes are sometimes irreconcilable. This has led to a fundamental shift in strategy from big landscape goals to local, community-based solutions. By securing tenure and rights over land for local communities, FFI is effectively taking out an insurance policy against deforestation, at least in the short term, so that people and wildlife will ultimately benefit regardless of whether REDD+ turns out to have been more red herring than panacea.

Success in Indonesia, where FFI is helping communities to access tangible, immediate, traditional sources of income linked to sustainable forest management, is the culmination of years of hard graft whereby FFI was able to extend its sphere of influence by building a solid network of support including passionate local conservationists, community leaders, journalists and government

REDD+

Community Carbon Pools Programme

The Community Carbon Pools programme aims to overcome some of the core challenges associated with REDD+ by bringing together neighbouring community forests under a common management and benefit-sharing system.

representatives. By FFI's own admission, its project approach was a traditional one, with the notable difference that the deal was packaged and financed in an original way.

Once again, the society has demonstrated its happy knack of identifying a gap in the market and occupying the space that others are neglecting. Recognising that someone has to nail down the unglamorous, small-scale projects that achieve incremental gains and refine blueprints for future expansion, FFI is increasingly working with small- and medium-sized investors, rather than with the global Goliaths who have vast amounts of cash to burn, but demand correspondingly (and unrealistically) spectacular returns on their investment.

Recent experience has confirmed what FFI, instinctively, seems always to have known: that conservation is a local, low-returns business. Leaving others to work at the global level in this arena, FFI has focused on developing innovative finance mechanisms that link small businesses to conservation activities, providing access to finance that helps to build rural economies linked to, for example, sustainable forest management. This kind of grass-roots empowerment creates what is commonly referred to in the trade as a win-win situation for conservation and local livelihoods. It's a cliché, but no less powerful for that.

At a time of increasing global volatility, where macro-level decision making is hampered by the instability of the world's political landscape and markets, FFI's modus operandi enables it to cut through the uncertainty. Small, mission-focused, responsive and working through local partners, it appears well equipped to carry on regardless in the face of shifting global trends.

This is equally true of FFI's approach to tackling climate change. Sooner or later, one imagines, if we are to avert the impending cataclysm, this threat to the planet's future needs to be addressed via a collaborative, orchestrated response from global heads of government beyond the perennial wailing and gnashing of teeth. The 2015 Paris climate change conference (known to its close friends as the twenty-first session of the Conference of the Parties) was a step in the right direction, but as long as a climate change denier has the keys to the Oval Office, all bets are off. Let's have the audacity to hope that the Trump presidency will not turn out to have been the disaster for the planet that some forecast, and that other, more enlightened leaders will choose not to follow him down the cul-de-sac to coal-fired catastrophe. In the meantime, FFI has bypassed the high-table negotiators fiddling while the forest burns, choosing instead to look for practical solutions at a local level.

Fieldwork with a difference

The head of Upsala Glacier in Argentina's Los Glaciares National Park, renowned for the rapidity of its retreat.

In 2015, FFI began working at five pilot sites in agricultural landscapes to identify ways in which climate change will affect people, biodiversity and ecosystem services, and to plan accordingly. The aim was to combine big predictions and scientific data with grass-roots information gleaned from local communities. To quote just one example, farmers on the freshwater island of Ometepe, a UNESCO Biosphere Reserve in Lake Nicaragua where FFI has worked for over a decade, are being encouraged to harvest rainwater and experiment with crop diversification as a form of climate adaptation. The idea in each case is to adopt a 'no regrets' approach and take action that will be beneficial irrespective of what happens next. FFI's ultimate objective is to build resilience to climate change at *all* its project sites worldwide.

This is one of the numerous manifestations of FFI's wider commitment to biodiversity conservation within agricultural landscapes, which is where the society anticipates that some of the critical pressure points will occur in the wake of increased demands on land. Played out against a backdrop of human population growth, changing diets, degradation of land, water, nutrients and climate change, making food production sustainable is one of the greatest conservation challenges of this century.

There seems little doubt that we stand at a pivotal moment in human history, where long-term survival will depend on shifting to sustainable agricultural systems that can support both people and the planet into the future.

FFI recognises that agricultural landscapes are important for the world's biodiversity, much of which occurs in developing countries where large-scale plantations and smallholder farmers provide agricultural products for local and global markets. If well managed and well planned, agricultural practices have the potential to help conserve biodiversity, use natural resources sustainably and bring people out of poverty.

Regrettably, agriculture all too often has the opposite effect, and the sector is more responsible than any other for land conversion that threatens species with extinction. It also undermines the very ecosystem services on which agricultural production and rural populations depend, leading to decreased water quality, increased vulnerability to pests, diseases, floods and droughts and adverse effects on soil formation and nutrient cycling. Rather than bemoaning this fact, FFI has identified it as an opportunity to harvest some low-hanging fruit. Viewed from an alternative perspective, agriculture offers enormous potential to produce gains for biodiversity, ecosystem services and rural livelihoods. By establishing a discrete agricultural landscapes programme, FFI is influencing the choices over land conversion, to help protect and restore areas of high biodiversity or ecosystem value, and to champion sustainable intensification methods that increase food production while minimising pressure on the environment.

The good, the bad and the ugly

Working with the big beasts of industry does, however, have its problems and pitfalls. Historically, these relationships were founded on shared objectives that served both FFI's mission and the strategic aims of the respective companies, but the nature of corporate partnerships is changing. Preoccupied as they are with fluctuating commodity prices and short-term economic considerations, companies tend to lose sight of the bigger picture. Biodiversity is constantly vying for attention alongside other sustainability concerns (such as water and climate change) that companies wrongly perceive as separate, and more pressing, issues. Even the Sustainable Development Goals – a universal call to action to end poverty and protect the planet – are not yet fully understood by companies, let alone integrated into mainstream practice. Unless a partnership continues to deliver benefits for biodiversity conservation, the relationship has outlived its usefulness, and FFI has already demonstrated that it is prepared to walk away.

In early 2016, FFI finally delivered the *coup de grâce* to one particular long-term corporate partnership that had been inexorably disintegrating for many years. Contemplating the massive environmental footprint left behind by an intransigent industrial behemoth that had flagrantly ignored the lending requirements stipulated by its financial backers and had openly reneged on its original commitments to achieving a net positive impact for biodiversity, FFI was forced to call time on the relationship. The last straw was a monster mine at which the company studiously ignored all recommendations and failed to implement the suite of proposed mitigation measures, leading to what Pippa Howard, director of FFI's Business & Biodiversity Programme, described as a 'catastrophic decline in biodiversity'. When individuals in a company openly laugh at the business case for biodiversity, claiming that it has no impact on the bottom line, the writing is on the wall. As civil society finds its voice, however, even the least environmentally enlightened companies are starting to sit up and take notice. As FFI has repeatedly pointed out, when companies alienate local communities by competing for or destroying the natural resources on which the latter depend, a backlash is inevitable.

FFI remains committed to elevating biodiversity higher up the corporate agenda. Time will tell whether the relevant companies are, for their part, genuinely committed to achieving no net loss, or even – stop all the clocks – a net gain in biodiversity. In the meantime, FFI's overriding concern is to avoid impact – and ensure stringent application of appropriate minimisation and mitigation measures – in situations where development is inevitable. In a nutshell, damage limitation.

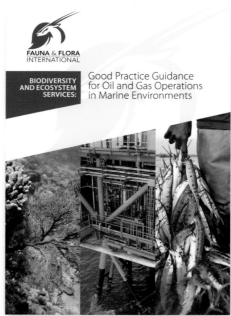

Above FFI's latest Business & Biodiversity brochure, alongside the recently launched guidance document aimed specifically at oil and gas companies operating in a marine context.

Opposite Calling card of the **WILD**LABS.NET partnership, an online platform where the worlds of conservation and technology collide constructively.

As one boardroom door slams shut, another opens invitingly. In 2016, FFI established a formal partnership for coastal biodiversity conservation in Myanmar with Australian company Woodside Energy. The initial aim was twofold: firstly, to carry out a comprehensive baseline assessment of coastal and marine biodiversity along the portion of Myanmar's west coast that falls within Woodside's exploration area; secondly, to equip the marine science departments of local universities with the requisite skills to enable them to participate fully in future biodiversity surveys, environmental impact assessments and monitoring.

This is the first partnership agreement between a conservation organisation and an oil and gas company operating on the Myanmar coast. As well as being significant in its own right, the pilot project has the potential to serve as a blueprint for an environmentally sensitive approach to wider oil and gas exploration activities along Myanmar's entire coastline. For energy companies seeking to minimise their environmental footprint, the acquisition of robust scientific data for the purposes of impact assessment and decision making is a crucial component in the design, construction and operational phases of their activities. The intention is that this project will become a model of best practice for other operators with oil and gas concessions in Myanmar.

FFI has also spotted a gap in the market relating to offshore oil and gas developments and their effects on marine biodiversity and ecosystem services. Guidelines on applying, monitoring and enforcing industry standards in this area have been conspicuously lacking, leaving companies all at sea, so to speak. With this in mind, its Business & Biodiversity team has put together a comprehensive document to help oil and gas sector operators minimise their impact on the marine environment. Officially launched in June 2017, *Good Practice Guidance for Oil and Gas Operations in Marine Environments* is the first of its kind, and this digital equivalent of a weighty tome should go a long way to ensuring that the industry no longer has any excuse for operating in an environmentally irresponsible manner.

FFI's partnerships with the business sector take many forms. A groundbreaking collaboration with ARM that began in 2013 resulted in FFI and its United for Wildlife partners joining forces with Google.org in 2015 to launch **WILD**LABS. NET, which, to judge by its curious quasi-logo of a name, is intending to half-boldly go where no tech initiative has gone before. This online platform enables conservationists and technologists to share ideas, information, tools and resources that can help address some of the most pressing conservation challenges with which we are now confronted,

including the fight against the illegal wildlife trade. Members of this open community are encouraged to join online discussion groups which address topics such as camera-trapping techniques, wildlife crime and acoustic monitoring systems that can be deployed, for example, to thwart crop-raiding elephants, pinpoint illegal logging activity and promote citizen science. Such collaborations hold the key to developing new solutions to biodiversity loss.

Watch this white space

Institutionally hard-wired to embrace new opportunities, FFI is already alive to the potential of new technologies that can be harnessed for conservation purposes such as combating the burgeoning illegal wildlife trade. So-called 'white-space' technology, which employs unused frequencies on the broadcast spectrum as pathways for wireless Internet signals, offers a means of providing wireless service in areas lacking coverage. Mobile broadband penetration is estimated at 32 per cent globally, but only 23 per cent and 19 per cent in Asia-Pacific and Africa respectively. According to the tech gurus, white-space technology has the potential to extend Wi-Fi coverage to new places by exploiting vacant portions of the radio-and-TV broadcast spectrum. Improving this technology could eventually allow FFI and its partners to deploy more affordable, more extensive wireless access to some of the countries where its researchers do fieldwork. For example, using white spaces could bolster and expand early-warning systems for anti-poaching efforts in protected areas like Ol Pejeta Conservancy. In such a rapidly evolving ecosystem – a word that the tech community seems to have commandeered and repurposed – progress reports risk being redundant before they are written, so it is not beyond the realms of possibility that white space will have been superseded by another technological new kid in town by the time this book sees the light of day.

Turning the page

In 2015, FFI and Defra announced the decision to discontinue their Flagship Species Fund partnership. Launched in 2001, this joint initiative garnered many plaudits and made a vital contribution to species-focused conservation. The official record shows that it awarded a total of £1.78 million in support of 132 projects that contributed directly to the conservation of 110 threatened species in 54 countries. Of course, these bald statistics don't tell the whole story; innumerable other species that shared their habitat have also benefited directly from this work.

Even as it announced that it was closing the book on this particular partnership, FFI was already working on the sequel. A new chapter in species-focused conservation is now unfolding under the auspices of a new Species Fund. This large-scale support mechanism has been designed to help safeguard critical populations of seriously threatened plants and animals, particularly in times of crisis.

Another hallmark of FFI's success is its ability to maintain long-term relationships with its donors as well as its corporate and local partners. Having set itself the ambitious task of raising US$20 million for the Species Fund, FFI almost immediately found itself one-third of the way to this target courtesy of a single pledge. This was no unexpected windfall following a chance encounter with a benevolent philanthropist, but rather the culmination of a decade of scrutiny. Before pledging US$7 million to the fund, Michel and Charlene de Carvalho-Heineken had been interested observers of FFI's work for over ten years. Their decision was made on the basis of a hard-nosed assessment of ecological value for money.

Building on FFI's successful history of species conservation and its contribution to species recovery, the Species Fund aims to restore key populations of threatened species to viable levels over the next quarter of a century. A parallel fund provides flexible funding for emergency action, where timely interventions in species management can reduce the long-term extinction risk for species that FFI considers an absolute priority. Currently the Species Fund is supporting some of FFI's most critical species interventions, including its work with Siamese crocodiles and hawksbill turtles. It has already helped to support urgent conservation measures on behalf of the saiga antelope and Saint Lucia racer (of which more in a moment) with more time-sensitive funding through its Emergency Response Fund.

With support from the Species Fund, FFI is establishing additional sanctuaries in Cambodia, the last stronghold of the critically endangered Siamese crocodile.

History repeating

At the time of writing, the dubious honour of being 'the rarest snake in the world . . . probably' has island-hopped through the Lesser Antilles, like some malign virus, from one beleaguered Caribbean reptile to another. The unwelcome mantle has passed from the Antiguan racer to the Saint Lucia racer (global population possibly as few as 20 individuals; worldwide range 12 hectares), whose fate now lies in the lap of the conservation gods. Or in this case, goddesses. Fortunately for the conservation world, another phenomenon appears to have gone viral; an epidemic of female herpetologists is following in the footsteps of people like Dr Jenny Daltry and embracing snake conservation. In yet another example of the capacity building for which FFI is justly renowned, the baton has been passed to local conservationists such as Antigua's Andrea Otto, and Saint Lucia's own Saphira Hunt has also recently joined the race against racer extinction. The lessons learned during the hugely successful Antiguan project may hold the key to success in Saint Lucia.

This Caribbean jewel of an island also provides the setting for a wider species and habitat protection programme, including a characteristically unconventional snake-saving scheme that epitomises FFI's knack of devising off-the-wall but highly effective solutions to particularly thorny conservation problems. If persuading Caribbean islanders and tourist visitors to cherish a harmless, docile, but nevertheless scaly species seemed like quite a challenge, imagine trying to persuade them to feel the love for a highly venomous six-feet-long serpent. The Saint Lucia fer de lance is a viper on steroids, described by Professor David Worrell, a hard-bitten expert not prone to hyperbole, as 'the most dangerous snake in the world'. You could be forgiven for thinking this was a bridge too far, but defeatism is not in the FFI dictionary. The proposed solution in this case involves bringing the local community up close and personal with this non-aggressive Saint Lucia endemic, to demonstrate that they can co-exist safely with the snake, and persuade them that it should be viewed as a national treasure rather than public enemy number one.

Go wilder

Ecological restoration and reintroduction has long been seen as a vital weapon in FFI's armoury. Eradicating invasive ship rats from a tiny Caribbean islet was the initial catalyst in bringing back the Antiguan racer from the brink of extinction, but the long-term survival of the species has hinged on a back-to-the-future-style reversal of the process whereby the snake's range shrank to a single island refuge too small to support a viable population.

Arguably the most radical form of ecological restoration, rewilding takes the concept of reintroduction to its logical

Above FFI is encouraging the community on the Caribbean island of Saint Lucia to recognise the cultural, ecological and biomedical value of the much-feared and seriously threatened Saint Lucia fer de lance.

Right Saphira Hunt holding what is possibly one of the last 20 Saint Lucia racer snakes on the planet.

Opposite Andrea Otto, who now leads the annual Antiguan racer census, showing local children and a camera crew how to measure a snake.

extreme by reversing centuries of ecological damage and returning species and habitats that have been absent from the landscape for some considerable time. At the time of writing, FFI is beginning to grapple with its own official stance on rewilding, although it has yet to step into the fiery furnace of the debate and, like its CCI partners, is studiously avoiding using the term and steering clear of the heated public exchanges. There is talk of creating a so-called 'Fund for Europe' with the help of major donors who are sympathetic to the concept of establishing connected core wilderness areas capable of supporting reintroduced keystone species, but the next act of this restoration drama is still to unfold.

'Things are getting tougher out there, ecosystem and species resilience is being tested to – and in many places beyond – its limits, but we're determined to harness the energy and capabilities of the great and growing network of FFI projects and partners to deliver real conservation gains at local level across a vast array of land and seascapes.'

Joanna Elliott, Senior Director, Conservation Partnerships at FFI

Beyond protected areas

Maintaining ecological connectivity across landscapes where people and wildlife co-exist – such as this mosaic of forest, meadows and farmland in Romania – is vital for the future of our planet's biodiversity.

Whatever its views on the wisdom or otherwise of returning to a world where apex predators roam the countryside unchecked, there is no doubt where FFI stands on the importance of weaving conservation into the fabric of the wider landscape and, indeed, of everyday life.

There is no denying that protected areas – the concept which the society's founders strained every sinew to promote – continue to play a vital role in species and habitat conservation, but as FFI's approach tacitly acknowledges they cannot unilaterally hold the line against the loss, fragmentation and degradation of the world's wild spaces. Unless we can retain, or in many cases reinstate, the ecological connectivity between protected areas, they become little more than glorified large-scale zoos or, put another way, wildlife oases in an ecological desert.

The only way forward, as Mark Rose continues to remind us, is to make conservation relevant – not only to communities, but also in government and corporate circles – to the point where it comes to be seen as fundamental to people's daily lives, rather than an optional extra. At the official opening of the new David Attenborough Building, Rose made a point of referring to conservation as 'a social process underpinned by science', an expression first coined by FFI's current co-chair Professor Nigel Leader-Williams in the 2010 book, *Trade-offs in Conservation: Deciding What to Save*. As early as his October 2008 editorial for *Fauna & Flora* magazine, Rose was pointing out that times have changed, and with them the scope and complexity of the issues that conservationists need to address: 'We need to start from the premise that *all* natural environments are valuable and not confine our conservation efforts to particular hotspots of biodiversity. We have to value the planet as a whole rather than singling out tiny fragments for special attention.'

CHANGING TIMES

Above left The high-flying Kathie Alban, enjoying a rare break from her desk, sits in a Cessna 206 alongside FFI's then programme manager and regional representative in East Africa, Dr Arthur Mugisha, while Mark Rose takes a back seat.

Above right The long-serving Ken Richard pictured in 2004 surrounded by the trappings of office. Richard swapped his former life as a field biologist with the British Antarctic Survey for a 20-year stint as FFI's membership and donor secretary.

The historical and continuing success of Fauna & Flora International has hinged on the collective efforts of a rich cast of characters encompassing conservation professionals, local community members, technical experts and enthusiastic amateurs, government officials, business executives, philanthropists, celebrity supporters, volunteers and, of course, generations of unsung backroom heroes who have brought vital stability to an organisation where living on the edge has sometimes appeared to be an occupational hazard. Mark Rose recently remarked that FFI's ability to attract and retain high-quality staff and trustees has been pivotal to the society's success during his 20-year tenure, and he was keen to emphasise that he was referring to those behind the scenes as well as to staff on the front

line. Rose singled out current chairman Andrew Sykes for particular praise, describing his 'invaluable' contribution as 'an exemplar for others'. No doubt he also had in mind people like recently retired Ken Richard and Kathie Alban, who began her FFI life as Rose's long-suffering (his words) executive assistant back in 1997 and is now head of human resources.

Rose is also acutely aware that women have played an increasingly prominent role in the society's success, a phenomenon that he recalls discussing with Her Majesty Queen Noor of Jordan in April 2000, when she was guest of honour at an awards ceremony to mark the tenth anniversary of what was then the BP Conservation Programme. FFI has come a long way since the days when it was an

exclusively male preserve, dominated by toffs in tailcoats. When the society was founded in 1903, women were still, incredibly, 15 years away from being permitted to vote, or 25 years in the case of those under the age of 30. The Duchess of Bedford was elected as a vice-president of the society as early as 1928, but a further 60 years had elapsed before it condescended to admit another lady, former *Oryx* editor Maisie Fitter, to its inner circle. The society's first female council member from outside the nobility, a Mrs Diana Spearman, was elected in 1962, sandwiched between The Lady Tweedmuir and The Lady Medway. At the time of writing, 41 per cent of FFI staff, 36 per cent of members and 43 per cent of supporters are female. If that upward trend continues, FFI may soon be fortunate enough to have a female president. Oh, wait . . . ■

Never-ending story

As the twenty-first century unfolds, it is clear that the challenges facing conservation will only accelerate and intensify. Further habitat destruction and a rash of extinctions appear to be inevitable given the trends in consumption patterns, unsustainable production, human population growth, poor spatial planning and climate change. It remains to be seen whether a growing awareness of the adverse impacts of biodiversity loss on human well-being will translate into collective action on an appropriate scale. Our effectiveness in turning back the tide will depend on building the necessary institutions, governance, policy and enforcement systems, and on replicating more widely the efforts of FFI and other like-minded conservation organisations, a point emphasised by Sir David Attenborough when he declared open the building named in his honour: 'Our natural world is threatened as never before. The threats are both numerous and interrelated, and no single institution, however effective, can hope to address them all alone. It is for this reason that the work of the Cambridge Conservation Initiative is so exceptional. By bringing together leaders in research, practice, policy and teaching, we stand the greatest chance of developing the solutions required to save our planet.'

FFI continues to play an integral role in that collaborative initiative, while simultaneously ploughing its own furrow and sowing the seeds of sustainable conservation using techniques that have been gradually honed and refined since 1903, but which still bear its unique hallmark. FFI has never aspired to save the planet single-handedly and has made no secret of its historical reliance on cultivating relationships with affluent, powerful and influential friends, just as it sets great store by working hand in hand with local organisations that are equally influential in their own way, but that hasn't stopped it from blazing a trail for others to follow throughout the previous century. Here's hoping that FFI's swashbuckling attitude will continue undiminished for the foreseeable future, if not for another one hundred years.

The next time you refer to Fauna & Flora International by its initials for the sake of brevity, and someone asks you what FFI stands for – which they will, believe me, given the society's propensity for flying beneath the radar – you will find yourself spoilt for choice. You could rattle off the full name in all its unwieldy glory and run the risk of eliciting another blank look. You could play the brand awareness card and answer: 'Innovative conservation since 1903.' Best of all, and even more succinctly, you could save your breath and simply hand over a copy of this book.

Chairman Andrew Sykes (front left) with the FFI family (see overleaf for details) in front of the David Attenborough Building, September 2016.

Acknowledgements

Firstly, we would like to thank Sir David Attenborough for not only enthusiastically agreeing to write the foreword to the book, but for the support and leadership he has given over the life of his membership and, in particular, the last 20 years. Supported by his daughter Susan, no organisation could wish for a better vice-president.

A thank you to individuals who have taken part in the consultation process, and reviewed draft manuscripts including: John Burton, Greg Alexander, Professor Bill Adams, Professor Lee Talbot, Ros Aveling and Abigail Entwistle.

As well as words, images and documentation have been essential to illustrate the society's history. Thanks go to Ken Richard, Cella Carr, Jo Carlill and Lizzie Duthie for their picture-sourcing skills and additional thanks go to our communications team including Sarah Rakowski and Olivia Bailey for their general support. Many of the most iconic images have been made freely available by key figures in FFI's history; in this respect we are indebted to Veronica Denby, Lord Robin Russell, Siria Harthoorn and Sir Gareth Rhys Williams.

When sourcing a publishers we looked no further than HarperCollins, not only because of their pedigree in publishing conservation books but also because the late Sir William Collins, a pioneer of conservation himself, was a former Trustee of the Fauna Preservation Society. Thankfully Myles Archibald agreed to publish the book and provide assistance in the form of Liz Woabank, our thanks extends also to designer Jon Allan and photographer Ida Riveros.

It is at this point that words seem inadequate however, and we give a heartfelt thank you to all the dedicated supporters, volunteers and staff who have been instrumental in ensuring that FFI is an effective force in the field of conservation, with the hope that we continue to make this world a better place.

Cambridge
August 2017

THE FFI FAMILY

As shown in the photograph on pp.308–9:

Steps left of barrier (descending, left to right):
David Gill, Alice Bucker, Jonathan Knox, Dan Steadman, Andy Cameron, Vanessa Evans, Shanna Challenger, Alison Gunn, Philine von Guretzky, Zoe Quiroz-Cullen, Jeannie Ambrose, Dr Dorothea Pio, Dilyana Mihaylova, Laura Fox, Lydia Murphy, Dr Georgina Magin, Ann Ferry, Svetlana Ignatieva

Steps right of barrier (ascending, left to right):
Marianne Carter, Dr Stephen Browne, Carl Wahl, Gavin Shelton, Pippa Howard, Dr Jenny Daltry, Alison Mortlock, Josh Kempinski, Liesje Birchenough, Paul White, Nick Bubb, Michael Pearson, Liz Eaton, Kathie Alban, Camilla Iturra, Alison Cowan, Joanna Cary-Elwes, Rebecca Costello, Tim Knight, Suzanne Tom

Balcony (left to right):
Diana van de Kamp, Charles Whitbread, Professor Nigel Leader-Williams, Charlotte Grezo, Professor E.J. Milner-Gulland, Dr Bhaskar Vira, Andrew Joy, John Wotton, Philip Prettejohn, Rebecca Plant, Olivia Bailey, Sophie Benbow, Dr Tony Whitten, Julio Bernal, Jessica Haskell, Cella Carr, Sarah Rakowski, Sara Calçada, Mary Rider, Aditi Jha, Laurence White, Mike Appleton

Below balcony (back row, left to right):
Dr Kathryn Phillips, Rob Harris, Eleanor Bell, Luke Hodgkinson, Paul Hotham, Dr Rob Bensted-Smith, Stuart Paterson, Katie Weeks, Matthew Shale, Jack Rhodes

Below balcony (middle row, left to right):
Jessica Farish, Lizzie Duthie, Katie Lee-Brooks, Adel Laszlo, Thalia Liokatis, Hannah Becker, Fiona Warder, Anna Lyons, Stephanie O'Donnell, Kerstin Brauneder, Merodie Rose, Laura Owens

Below balcony (front row, left to right):
Dr Martin Fisher, Alison Mollon, Dr Abigail Entwistle, Guy Smith, Dr Thomas Maddox, Kimberley Handley, Joanna Elliott, Annie Cooper, Gail Thacker

Foreground (left to right):
Andrew Sykes, Ros Aveling, Sir David Attenborough, Mark Rose

Picture credits

Endpapers: courtesy of Gareth Rhys Williams; p.2: © Denys Ovenden; p.6: © Jonathan Kingdon. Courtesy of David Dickie; p.8: courtesy of Sir David Attenborough

Chapter 1 FOUNDATION

p.10: © The Trustees of the Natural History Museum, London; p.12: courtesy of Forum Auctions; p.13 T: courtesy of Gareth Rhys Williams; p.14: from the Woburn Abbey Collection; p.15 TL: © National Portrait Gallery, London; p.15 TR: © The Trustees of the Natural History Museum, London; p.15 CL: © ZSL; p.16: © The Trustees of the Natural History Museum, London; p.17: Library of Congress, Prints & Photographs Division (LC-USZC4-3858); p.19 TL: Ernst Mayr Library of the Museum of Comparative Zoology, Harvard University; p.19 TR, BR: courtesy of Gareth Rhys Williams; p.21 (both): courtesy of Gareth Rhys Williams; p.22 T: courtesy of Gareth Rhys Williams; p.22 B: Roosevelt 560.61-185. Houghton Library, Harvard University; p.24 B: © ZSL; p.26: © Wildlife Conservation Society. Reproduced by permission of the WCS Archives; p.27 TL: © Dr Graham Renshaw; p.27 TC: courtesy of Professor Henri Auguste Ménégaux; p.27 BL: © York & Sons; p.30: © Anthony Hall-Martin; p.31: © SANParks

Chapter 2 PROTECTION

p.34: © Nicky Jenner; p.38 TC, BL, BR: © Juan Pablo Moreiras/FFI; p.38 TR: © Tim Knight; p.39 T: © Jeremy Holden/FFI; p.39 CL, BR: © Juan Pablo Moreiras/FFI; p.39 BR: © Tim Knight; p.41: © Captain R.J.D. Salmon. Reproduced by kind permission of the Royal Collection Trust; p.42 TL, TR: courtesy of the family of Theodore Hubback; p.42 B: © Edward Pritchard Gee; p.43 and p.44 (all): courtesy of the family of Theodore Hubback; p.46 T: © Eric Hosking; p.48: © IUCN; p.49: © Thurston Hopkins/Getty Images; p.51 T, BR: courtesy of the family of Colonel C.L. Boyle

Chapter 3 MUTATION

p.52: © Christian Randrianantoandro; p.57 TL: © Barbara Prescott; p.57 TR: © The Times/News Syndication; p.59 B: courtesy of Sarah Rakowski; p.60: © Juan Pablo Moreiras/FFI; p.61 T: © Lee Talbot; p.65: permission of The Linnean Society of London; p.68 (all), p.69, p.70: © Dr Toni Harthoorn; p.72 and p.73 (all): Edward Pritchard Gee

Chapter 4 INNOVATION

p.74: © Sir Peter Scott; pp.76–7: © William Collins; p.78: © John Hillaby; p.80: © Michael Woodford; p.81 TL: © Peter Whitehead; p.81 TR, B and p.82 TL, B: © Michael Woodford; p.82 TR: © Anthony Shepherd; p.83: courtesy of HRH The Duke of Edinburgh; p.84: © Anthony Shepherd 1965; p.85 TL, TR, CL, CR: © Phoenix Zoo; p.85 B and p.86: © Larry Mishler; p.87 T: courtesy of HH Sheikh Qassim bin Hamad al Thani; p.88 (all): © Anthony Shepherd; p.89: © Los Angeles Zoo; p.91 T: © John Clarke/WWF; p.91 B: © Dr H. Jungius; p.92: © Gary Hodges; p.96 (all) and p.97 TL, TC: © IUCN; p.97 TR: © IUCN and UNEP; p.98: © A. Bannikov; p.99: © Barry Driscoll/IUCN; p.100 (both): © David Shepherd; p.102

TL, TR, BR: © Denys Ovenden; p.102 TC: © Keith Shackleton; p.102 CL: © Maurice Wilson; p.102 CC: © Charles Tunnicliffe; p.102 CR: © Jim Channell; p.102 BL: © Bruce Pearson; p.102 BC: © Freda Webster Green; p.103 TL, TC: © Robert Gillmor; p.103 TR: © Miss Robin Tomkinson; p.103, second row, L to R: 1, 2 and 3 – © Ralph Thompson, 4 – Maurice Wilson; p.103, third row, L to R: 1 – © William Oliver, 2 – © Guy Troughton, 3 – © Miss E.D. Tinne, 4 – © Maurice Wilson; p.103, bottom row, L to R: 1 – © Bruce Lattig, 2 – courtesy of M. Thorburn, The Glenbow Foundation and the Tryon Gallery Ltd, 3 – © Jonathan Kingdon, 4 – © William Oliver, 5 – © Bruce Pearson; p.105 TR: © Mrs Robin Wrangham; p.105 BR: courtesy of Parco Nazionale d'Abruzzo; p.106 (both): © Pete Oxford/naturepl.com; p.108: © Library of Congress, Prints & Photographs Division (LC-USZ62-68852); p.109: © Timothy Green

Chapter 5 PROFESSIONALISATION

p.100: © Juan Pablo Moreiras/FFI; p.112: © CITES; p.113 TL: © Sonia Jeffrey; p.113 TR: © Maisie Fitter; p.113 BR: © Russell A. Mittelmeier; p.115: © Hans Klingel; p.116 TL: © Bruce Coleman; p.116 TR: © Tim Knight; p.117 (all): © Ron Garrison/ San Diego Zoo; p.119 T: © Shelagh Rosenthal/FFI; p.121: © Kitty Harvill; p.122: © Jaap Vermeulen; p.123 T: © Dr Jack Frazier; p.123 B: © Ron Garrison/San Diego Zoo; p.125, p.127, p.128, p.129 and p.130 (both): © Juan Pablo Moreiras/FFI; p.132 L: © Conrad & Ros Aveling; p.132 R: © Dr Sandy Harcourt; p.133: © Jean-Pierre von der Becke; p.136 (both) and p.138: © Juan Pablo Moreiras/FFI; p.139 B: © Sir Peter Scott

Chapter 6 DIVERSIFICATION

p.140: © Jeremy Holden/FFI; p.141 L: © Mike Meads; p.143 (both): © The Trustees of the Natural History Museum, London; p.144: © Robert Gillmor; p.145: © Philip Wayre; p.147 TL: © Eric Roberts/Westminster Press Ltd; p.147 R, CL, BL: © Tony Hutson; p.149 T: © Frank Greenaway; p.149 B: © Guy Troughton; p.151: © Denys Ovenden; p.154 BL, BC: courtesy of Jan PieÐkowski; p.155 (both): © ZSL; p.157 B and p.158: © Mike Read/FFI; p.159 B: © Andy Byfield/FFI; p.160 T: © B.R. Ivison; p.161 L: © M.P.L. Fogden/Bruce Coleman Ltd; p.162 TL: © Juan Pablo Moreiras/ FFI; p.162 TR, BL, BR: © Jeremy Holden/FFI; p.163 TL, BL, BC, BR: © William Oliver. Courtesy of World Land Trust; p.163 TC: © William Oliver. Courtesy of Simon Mickleburgh; p.163 TR: © William Oliver

Chapter 7 STAGNATION

p.164: © Juan Pablo Moreiras/FFI; p.167: © WWT; p.168: © Jonathan Kingdon; p.169 L: © British Airways; p.169 R: © Juan Pablo Moreiras/FFI; p.170: © Juan Pablo Moreiras/FFI; p.171: © Mike Read; p.172 L: © Findlay Kember; p.173 TL, TR, C: © Global Trees Campaign; p.175 TL: © Purnima Devi Barman; p.175 TR: © Sylviane Volampeno; p.175 CL: © Szilárd Bücs; p.175 CR: © Giovanni A. Chaves Portilla; p.175 BL: © Laura Dinraths; p.175 BR: © Mahardika Rizqi Himawan; p.176: © Whitley Fund for Nature; p.177 T: © Blanca Huertas; p.177 B: © Maximilliano Caal; p.179 L: © RGS-IBG; p.180 (all): © Findlay Kember; p.181: © Melvin Bolton

Chapter 8 VINDICATION

p.182: © Mauro Pinto/FFI; p.183: quotation © Her Majesty Queen Elizabeth II, 2017; p.186 C: © Mike Read; p.187 T: © Juan Pablo Moreiras/FFI; p.188 TC: courtesy of BBC Worldwide; p.188 TR: © Center for Plant Conservation, Vietnam; p.188

BR: © Richard Jenkins/Madagasikara Voakajy; p.189 (all): © Jackson Xu/FFI; p.190 (both): © Evan Bowen-Jones/FFI; p.191: © Nadia Corp; p.192 T, BR: © Jeremy Holden/FFI; p.192 BL: © Mark Day/FFI; p.193 T, CR: © Jenny Daltry/FFI; p.193 CL: © Antiguan Racer Conservation Project; p.193 BL, BR: © Mark Day/FFI; p.194 T: © Antiguan Racer Conservation Project; p.194 BL: © Jenny Daltry/FFI; p.194 BR: © John Cancalosi/FFI; p.195 TL: © The Times/News Syndication; p.195 TR: courtesy of Wildscreen/ARKive/Adam Warrick Design; p.195 BL: © Jenny Daltry/FFI; p.195 BR: © Jeremy Holden/FFI; p.196: © Findlay Kember; p.197 TR: courtesy of Dr Lisbet Rausing; p.197 BR: © Alex Diment/FFI; p.198: © Juan Pablo Moreiras/FFI; p.200: © Flower Valley Conservation Trust/Kobus Tollig Photography; pp.201, 202, 203 (all), 204 TL: © Juan Pablo Moreiras/FFI; p.204 TR: © Chris Loades/FFI; p.204 B: © William Oliver; p.205 L: © Chris Loades/FFI; pp.206, 207 TL, TR: © Fundatia ADEPT; pp.208, 209 L: © JABRUSON; p.209 R: © Thomas Prin; p.210 (both): © Mauro Pinto/FFI; p.211: © Whitley Fund for Nature

Chapter 9   TRANSFORMATION

p.212: © Jeremy Holden/FFI; p.213: © Findlay Kember; p.214: © Ros Aveling; p.215 (all): © EAWLS; p.217 and p.218 TL, TR, BL: © Jeremy Holden/FFI; p.218 BC, BR: © Jenny Daltry/FFI; p.219 TL, TR, BL: © Jeremy Holden/FFI; p.221: © Daniel Lewis; p.222 L: © Mark Peterson/ Redux/Eyevine; p.223 L: © Juan Pablo Moreiras/FFI; p.225 L, TR: © Findlay Kember; p.225 BR: © Paul Massey/FSP Gamma; p.227 and p.228 BR: © Jeremy Holden/FFI; p.228 BL: © Dr David Chivers; p.229: © Pete Souza/ Goldman Environmental Foundation; p.230 and p.231 TL, BL: © Jeremy Holden/ FFI; p.231 TR, BR: © Debbie Martyr/FFI; p.232 and p.233 (all): courtesy of the family of Colonel C.L. Boyle

Chapter 10   CELEBRATION

p.234, p.235 B, p.236 (all) and p.237 (both): © Gill Shaw; p.239 BL, BC, BR: courtesy of Ken Banks; p.240 T: © Clive Boursnell; p.240 BL, BR: © Gill Shaw; p.241 R: courtesy of FIRST magazine; p.242: © Juan Pablo Moreiras/FFI; p.243L: © Jeremy Holden/FFI; p.245 (both): © Jeremy Holden/FFI; p.247 T: © Marcelo Scaranari; p.247 B: © Nuria Ortega; p.248: © Juan Pablo Moreiras/FFI; p.249 (all): © Ol Pejeta Conservancy; p.250 (all): © Belinda Mason; p.251 (both) and p.252: © Juan Pablo Moreiras/FFI; p.253: © EAWLS; p.254: © Jeremy Holden/FFI; p.255 T: © Teuku Boyhaqi; p.255 B: © Jeremy Holden/FFI; p.257: © Juan Pablo Moreiras/FFI; p.260 T: courtesy of Rove McManus; p.260 B: © Belinda Mason; p.261 (all): © Jeremy Holden/FFI; p.262 T: © Martin Aveling; p.262 B: © Jeremy Holden/FFI; p.263 (all): © FFI/BANCA/PRCF; p.264 TL: © EC SFNC; p.264 TC, BL, BC, BR: © Jeremy Holden/ FFI; p.264 TR: © FFI/RUPP; p.264 CC: © FFI & Bucknell University; p.264 CR: © Caleb Jones/Integrated Solutions Asia Cooperation/FFI; p.265, top row, L, C: © Jeremy Holden/FFI; p.265, top row, R: © FFI/BANCA/PRCF; p.256, second row, L, C: © Jeremy Holden/FFI; p.256, second row, R: © FFI & Bucknell University; p.265, third row, L, C, R: © Jeremy Holden/FFI; p.256, bottom row, C: © FFI & Bucknell University; p.266 L: © Le Khat Quyet/FFI; p.266 R: courtesy of Artists & Biologists Unite for Nature (ABUN); p.267: © Jeremy Holden/FFI

Chapter 11   FULL CIRCLE

p.268: © Paul Colley; p.270: © Karl W. Kenyon; p.271: © The Times/News Syndication; p. 272 B: © Zafer Kizilkaya; p.273: © Bruce Pearson; p.274 T: © Jeremy Holden/FFI; p.274 B: © William Oliver; p.275 TL: © Juan Pablo Moreiras/ FFI; p.275 CL: © Ally Catterick/FFI; p.275 B: © JABRUSON; p.276: © The Times/

News Syndication; p.277: © Phil McIntyre; p.279: © Rakhmet Dirgantara/FFI; p.280 T: © Jeremy Holden/FFI; p.280 CL, BR, BL: © Paul Colley; p.281: © Sophie Benbow/FFI; p.282: © Juan Pablo Moreiras/FFI; p.283 L, C: © Roger Ingle/FFI; p.285 (all): © COAST; p.286: © Rob Harris/FFI; p.288: courtesy of Sir Gareth Rhys Williams; p.289 T: reproduced with the permission of The Trustees of The Rothschild Archive Trust Limited; p.289 B: courtesy of Sir Gareth Rhys Williams; p.290: © Juan Pablo Moreiras/FFI; p.291 TL: © JABRUSON; p.291 TR, BR: © The Royal Foundation; p.291 CR: © Juan Pablo Moreiras/FFI; p.292: © The Royal Foundation; p.293: © Sir Cam/CCI

Chapter 12   NEW BEGINNINGS

p.294: © Jeremy Holden/FFI; p.295: © Chris Loades/FFI; p.296 T: Gary Morrisroe; p.296 B: © Sir Cam/CCI; p.297: © Jeremy Holden/FFI; p.299: © Juan Pablo Moreiras/ FFI; p.301: © WILDLABS.NET; p.303: © Jeremy Holden/FFI; p.304: © Tom Aveling; p.305 T: © Jeremy Holden/FFI; p.305 B: © St Lucia Racer Project; p.306: © Lizzie Duthie/FFI; p.307 (both): © Juan Pablo Moreiras/FFI; p.309: © Gary Morrisroe

Index